ECCLESIASTICAL LATIN

ECCLESIASTICAL LATIN

A Primer on the Language of the Church

ಆನಿ

Charles G. Kim, Jr.

Catholic Education Press
Washington, D.C.

Copyright © 2025

Catholic Education Press

The Catholic University of America, Washington, D.C.

All rights reserved

The paper used in this publication meets the minimum requirements of
American National Standards for Information Science—
Permanence of Paper for Printed Library Materials, ANSI Z39.48-1992.

∞

Cataloging-in-Publication Data is available from the Library of Congress

ISBN: 978-1-949822-48-9 (paper)

ISBN: 978-1-949822-49-6 (ebook)

CONTENTS

෪

Acknowledgments	xvii
Preface	xix
Chapter Layout	xxii
Note About Using This Textbook	xxiii
Introduction: On Pronunciation and the *Orationes Hebdomadae*	xxiv
A Review of Basic Grammar Concepts Related to Latin	xxviii

Chapter 1

§ 1.	Nouns: Singular and Plural in Masculine, Feminine, and Neuter as Subjects	1
§ 2.	Nouns: Direct Objects and Accusative	4
§ 3.	Verbs: Third Person Singular and Plural in the Four Main Patterns (Conjugations)	6
§ 4.	Verbs: Introduction to *esse*, the "to be" Verb	7
§ 5.	Syntax: Articles	8
	Sententiae Summāriae (Summary Sentences)	8
	Cavēte et Mementōte (Be Aware and Remember)	9
	Vocābula Memoranda (Vocabulary to Be Memorized)	9
	Fābula Parva (Latīna Ficta) (Small Story, Made-up Latin)	11
	Sententiae Interpretandae (Sentences to Be Translated)	11
	Sententiae Fictae Interpretandae (Made-up Sentences to Be Translated)	12

Chapter 2

§ 6.	Nouns: Possessive Nouns, Singular and Plural in Masculine, Feminine, and Neuter	13
§ 7.	Relative Pronouns: Nominative and Genitive	15
§ 8.	Adjectives: An Introduction	16

Sententiae Summāriae	. . . .	17
Cavēte et Mementōte	. . . .	17
Vocābula Memoranda	. . . .	18
Fābula Parva (Latīna Ficta)	. . . .	20
Sententiae Interpretandae	. . . .	20
Sententiae Fictae	. . . .	21

Chapter 3

§ 9.	Prepositions: The Ablative and Accusative	. . . .	22
§ 10.	Demonstrative Pronouns: An Introduction	. . . .	24
§ 11.	Relative Pronouns: Direct Objects and Accusative and Interrogative Pronouns	. . . .	26
§ 12.	Conjunctions: *quia, quod,* and *quoniam*	. . . .	27
Sententiae Summāriae		. . . .	28
Cavēte et Mementōte		. . . .	28
Vocābula Memoranda		. . . .	28
Fābula Parva (Latīna Ficta)		. . . .	30
Sententiae Interpretandae		. . . .	31
Sententiae Fictae		. . . .	32

Chapter 4

§ 13. Nouns: Vocative	. . . .	33
§ 14. Verbs: Indicative and Imperative Mood	. . . .	33
§ 15. Special Uses of Interrogative and Relative Pronouns	. . . . .	35
Sententiae Summāriae	. . . .	36
Cavēte et Mementōte	. . . .	37
Vocābula Memoranda	. . . .	37
Fābula Parva (Latīna Ficta)	. . . .	38
Sententiae Interpretandae	. . . .	39
Sententiae Fictae	. . . .	40

Chapter 5

§ 16. Nouns: Dative and Indirect Objects	. . . .	41
§ 17. Demonstrative Pronouns: *ille, illa, illud* and *hic, haec, hoc*	. . . .	44
§ 18. Syntax: Dative with *Esse* and without *Esse*	. . . .	47
Sententiae Summāriae	. . . .	48
Cavēte et Mementōte	. . . .	48

Vocābula Memoranda 48
Fābula Parva (Latīna Ficta) 50
Sententiae Interpretandae 50
Sententiae Fictae 51

Chapter 6

§ 19. Nouns: Ablatives of Means 52
§ 20. Verbs: Passive Voice 53
§ 21. Verbs: Passive Voice with an Agent 54
§ 22. Question Words: *nonne* and *numquid* 55
Sententiae Summāriae 55
Cavēte et Mementōte 55
Vocābula Memoranda 55
Fābula Parva (Latīna Ficta) 57
Sententiae Interpretandae 57
Sententiae Fictae 59

Chapter 7

§ 23. Verbs: Full Paradigm for Present Active Indicative 60
§ 24. Pronouns: First and Second Person 64
§ 25. Pronouns: Reflexive 65
§ 26. Syntax: *et ... et/ neque ... neque/ non solum ... sed etiam* . . 65
Sententiae Summāriae 66
Cavēte et Mementōte 67
Vocābula Memoranda 67
Fābulae Parvae 68
Sententiae Interpretandae 70
Sententiae Fictae 71

Chapter 8

§ 27. Nouns: I/E-Nouns (Third Declension), Masculine and Feminine 72
§ 28. Nouns: I/E-Nouns (Third Declension), Neuter 74
§ 29. Possessive Adjectives: *meus, tuus, suus* 75
§ 30. Conjunctions: *cum, dum,* and *donec* 75
Sententiae Summāriae 76
Cavēte et Mementōte 76

Vocābula Memoranda 76
Fābula Parva 78
Sententiae Interpretandae 79
Sententiae Fictae 80

Chapter 9

§ 31. Verbs: Introduction to Infinitives 81
§ 32. Verbs: Infinitives and Modals, *posse, velle, debēre, nōlle* 82
§ 33. Verbs: Passive Infinitives. 84
§ 34. Lead Verb Forms and Understanding Latin Sentences 84
Sententiae Summāriae 85
Cavēte et Mementōte 85
Vocābula Memoranda 86
Fābula Ficta 87
Sententiae Interpretandae 88
Sententiae Fictae 90

Chapter 10

§ 35. Verbs: Accusative Plus Infinitive Construction 91
§ 36. Verbs: Indirect Statement (*Oratio Obliqua*) 92
§ 37. Syntax: Using *quia, quoniam,* and *quod* in Indirect Speech. . . 93
§ 38. Pronouns: *ipse, ipsa, ipsum* 94
Sententiae Summāriae 95
Cavēte et Mementōte 95
Vocābula Memoranda 95
Fābula Ficta 96
Sententiae Interpretandae 97
Sententiae Fictae 99

Chapter 11

§ 39. Nouns: U-Nouns (Fourth Declension), Masculine and Feminine 100
§ 40. Nouns: U-Nouns (Fourth Declension), Neuter 101
§ 41. Adjectives: I/E-Adjectives (Third Declension) 101
§ 42. Adjectives: Comparative and Superlative 103
Sententiae Summāriae 105
Cavēte et Mementōte 106

Vocābula Memoranda 106
Fābula Ficta 107
Sententiae Interpretandae 108
Sententiae Fictae 110

Chapter 12

§ 43. Nonfinite Verbs: Present Participles 111
§ 44. Nouns: E-Nouns (Fifth Declension) 113
§ 45. Syntax: Adverbial Participles and the Periphrastic 114
§ 46. Conjunctions 114
Sententiae Summāriae 115
Cavēte et Mementōte 115
Vocābula Memoranda 115
Fābulae Excerptae 116
Sententiae Interpretandae 118
Sententiae Fictae 119

Chapter 13

§ 47. Verbs: Impersonal Verbs with a Dative Plus Infinitive Construction 120
§ 48. Verbs: Impersonal Verbs with an Accusative Plus Infinitive
       Construction 121
§ 49. Verbs: Ablative Absolute with Present Participles 122
§ 50. Nouns: Ablative of Time and Accusative of Duration 122
Sententiae Summāriae 123
Cavēte et Mementōte 123
Vocābula Memoranda 123
Fābula Ficta 124
Sententiae Interpretandae 125
Sententiae Fictae 126

Chapter 14

§ 51. Verbs: Passive Personal Endings 127
§ 52. Verbs: *ire* and *fieri* 128
§ 53. Adverbs: Regular, Comparative, and Superlative 129
Sententiae Summāriae 131
Cavēte et Mementōte 132

Vocābula Memoranda	132
Fābula Ficta	133
Sententiae Interpretandae	134
Sententiae Fictae	135

Chapter 15

§ 54. Adjectives: Irregular Adjectives	136
§ 55. Adverbs: Irregular, Comparative, and Superlative	137
§ 56. Verbs: *ferre*	138
§ 57. Indefinite Adjectives: *quīdam, quaedam, quodam*	138
Prefixing Prepositions to Verbs	139
Sententiae Summāriae	140
Cavēte et Mementōte	141
Vocābula Memoranda	141
Excerpta Latina	142
Sententiae Interpretandae	143
Sententiae Fictae	144

Chapter 16

§ 58. Verbs: Deponent Verbs	145
§ 59. Adjectives: *idem, eadem, idem* and *uterque, utraque, utrumque*	147
§ 60. Disjunctive Words: *aut, vel, sive, an*	148
Excursus on Translation	149
Sententiae Summāriae	149
Cavēte et Mementōte	150
Vocābula Memoranda	150
Fābula Latīna	151
Sententiae Interpretandae	152
Sententiae Fictae	153

Chapter 17

§ 61. Verbs: An Overview of Tense and Aspect	154
§ 62. Verbs: *esse* in the Imperfect	157
§ 63. Verbs: Future of *esse* and Morphologically Similar Verbs	158
§ 64. Numerals (Adjectives): Cardinal and Ordinal	159
§ 65. Syntax: Concessive Clauses	161

Sentetiae Summāriae 161
Vocābula Memoranda 162
Sentetiae Interpretandae 163

Chapter 18

Verbs: Imperfect Active and Passive Indicative 165
§ 66. Morphology: Imperfect Active and Passive Indicative 165
§ 67. Meaning: Imperfect Active and Passive Indicative 166
§ 68. Adjectives: *alius, nullus, ullus, totus, solus,* and *unus* 167
§ 69. Verbs: Negative Imperatives 167
Sentetiae Summāriae 168
Cavēte et Mementōte 168
Vocābula Memoranda 168
Fābula Excerpta 169
Sentetiae Interpretandae 171

Chapter 19

Verbs: Future Active and Passive 173
§ 70. Morphology: Future Active and Passive Indicative 173
§ 71. Meaning: Future Active and Passive Indicative 174
§ 72. Indefinite Pronouns and Adjectives 175
Cavēte et Mementōte 176
Sentetiae Summāriae 176
Vocābula Memoranda 177
Fābula Excerpta 178
Sentetiae Interpretandae 178

Chapter 20

Verbs: Perfect Active Indicative, Perfect Infinitive 180
§ 73. Morphology: Perfect Active Indicative 180
§ 74. Meaning: Perfect Active Indicative 182
§ 75. Verbs: Perfect Active Infinitive 183
§ 76. Nouns: Locative 184
Sentetiae Summāriae 185
Cavēte et Mementōte 185
Vocābula Memoranda 185

Fābula Excerpta	187
Furtum Pirorum Sacti Augutini	187
Sententiae Interpretandae	188

Chapter 21

§ 77. Verbs: Morphology of the Perfect Passive Indicative	190
§ 78. Verbs: Meaning of Perfect Passive Participles	191
§ 79. Verbs: Ablative Absolute with Perfect Participles	192
§ 80. Verbs: Perfect Passive Infinitive	193
Sententiae Summāriae	194
Cavēte et Mementōte	195
Vocābula Memoranda	195
Fābula Excerpta	196
Colloquia Ficta ("Imaginary Conversation")	197
Sententiae Interpretandae	197

Chapter 22

Verbs: Future Active Participles and Future Infinitives	200
§ 81. Morphology: Future Active Participle	200
§ 82. Meaning: Future Active Participle	201
§ 83. Future Active Infinitive	202
Sententiae Summāriae	202
Vocābula Memoranda	203
Fābula Excerpta	204
Fābula de Abrahamo et Sara	204
Sententiae Interpretandae	205

Chapter 23

§ 84. Verbs: Morphology of the Pluperfect Active	207
§ 85. Verbs: Meaning of the Pluperfect Active	208
§ 86. Verbs: Morphology of the Pluperfect Passive	208
§ 87. Verbs: Meaning of the Pluperfect Passive	209
§ 88. Syntax: *tantus … quantus* and *tam … quam*	210
Sententiae Summāriae	210
Vocābula Memoranda	211
Fābula Excerpta	212
Sententiae Interpretandae	213

Chapter 24

§ 89.	Verbs: Passive and Deponent Imperatives	215
§ 90.	Verbs: Defective	216
§ 91.	Verbs: Supine	217
§ 92.	Syntax: Verbs of Memory	217
§ 93.	Syntax: Factum	217
	Sententiae Summāriae	218
	Vocābula Memoranda	218
	Fābula Excerpta	220
	Sententiae Interpretandae	220

Chapter 25

§ 94.	Verbs: Morphology of Gerunds	222
§ 95.	Verbs: Meaning of Gerunds	222
§ 96.	Verbs: Semi-Deponent Verbs	223
§ 97.	Verbs: Verbs with Ablative	223
	Sententiae Summāriae	224
	Vocābula Memoranda	224
	Lectum Excerptum	225
	Sententiae Interpretandae	226

Chapter 26

§ 98.	Verbs: Morphology of the Future Perfect Active and Passive	228
§ 99.	Verbs: Meaning of the Future Perfect Active and Passive	229
§ 100.	Verbs: Irregular Imperatives	230
	Sententiae Summāriae	230
	Vocābula Memoranda	231
	Fābula Excerpta	232
	Sententiae Interpretandae	233

Chapter 27

§ 101.	Verbs: Morphology of the Gerundive and Future Passive Participle	235
§ 102.	Verbs: Meaning of the Future Passive Participle	236
§ 103.	Gerunds, Gerundives, and Future Passive Participles	237
	Sententiae Summāriae	238
	Vocābula Memoranda	238
	Fābulaee Excerptae	240
	Sententiae Interpretandae	240

Chapter 28

§ 104. Verbs: Introduction to Subjunctive	244
§ 105. Verbs: Morphology of the Present Subjunctive	247
§ 106. Verbs: Meaning of the Present Subjunctive Indirect Statements	248
§ 107. Verbs: Meaning of the Present Subjunctive Indirect Commands	249
Sententiae Summāriae	250
Cavēte et Mementōte	250
Vocābula Memoranda	251
Fābula Ficta	251
Sententiae Interpretandae	252

Chapter 29

§ 108. Verbs: Morphology of the Imperfect Subjunctive	254
§ 109. Verbs: Meaning of Purpose and Result	255
§ 110. Verbs: Relative Clauses of Characteristic	256
§ 111. Sequence of Tenses Part 1	256
Sententiae Summāriae	258
Vocābula Memoranda	258
Fābula Excerpta	259
Sententiae Interpretandae	260

Chapter 30

§ 112. Verbs: Morphology of Irregular Verbs *nolle, velle, malle*	262
§ 113. Verbs: Meaning of Independent Imperative Subjunctives	263
§ 114. Verbs: Meaning of Optative, Deliberative, and Doubting Words	264
Sententiae Summāriae	264
Vocābula Memoranda	265
Fābula Excerpta	266
Sententiae Interpretandae	267

Chapter 31

§ 115. Verbs: Morphology of the Perfect Subjunctive	270
§ 116. Verbs: Meaning of Fear Clauses	271
§ 117. Verbs: Meaning of Indirect Questions	272
§ 118. Sequence of Tenses Part II	273
Sententiae Summāriae	274
Vocābula Memoranda	275
Fābula Excerpta	276
Sententiae Interpretandae	276

Chapter 32

- § 119. Verbs: Morphology of the Pluperfect Subjunctive 279
- § 120. Verbs: Meaning of the *realis* in the Narrative Subjunctive 280
- § 121. Verbs: Meaning of the *irrealis* in Conditions Contrary to Fact 282
- § 122. Verbs: Meaning of Optative Subjunctives 282
- § 123. Syntax: All the Types of Conditionals. 283
- Cavēte et Mementōte 284
- Sententiae Summāriae 284
- Vocābula Memoranda 285
- Fābula Excerpta 286
- Sententiae Interpretandae 287

Appendices

- Connections to Lingua Latina: Familia Romana and Fābulaee Syrae 289
- Colloquia de Iconibus 292
- Orationes Hebdomadae 297
- Grammar Appendix 318
  - List of Prepositions and Prepositional Prefixes 318
  - Nouns 318
    - First Declension (A-Nouns) 319
    - Second Declension (O-Nouns) Masculine 319
    - Second Declension (O-Nouns) Neuter 319
    - Third Declension Nouns (I/E-Nouns) 320
    - Fourth Declension (U-Nouns) 320
    - Fifth Declension (E-Nouns) 321
  - Pronouns 322
    - Unemphatic Demonstrative Pronouns 322
    - Relative and Interrogative Pronouns 323
    - Emphatic Near Demonstrative Pronouns 324
    - Emphatic Far Demonstrative Pronouns 325
    - Intensive Pronouns or Adjectives 325
  - Adjectives 326
    - Positive Adjectives "A/O" Adjectives 326
    - Positive Adjectives "I/E" Adjectives 327
    - Comparative Adjectives 327
    - Superlative Adjectives 328
  - Adverbs 328
  - Verb Morphology 329
    - Present Indicative 329

Irregular Verbs	330
Imperfect Indicative	330
Future Indicative	332
Perfect Indicative	333
Pluperfect Indicative	335
Future-Perfect Indicative	336
Present Subjunctive	338
Imperfect Subjunctive	339
Perfect Subjunctive	341
Pluperfect Subjunctive	342
Nonfinite Verb Forms	344
Imperatives	344
Present Infinitives	345
Perfect Infinitives	345
Future Infinitives	346
Present Active Participles	346
Perfect Passive Participles	347
Future Active Participles	347
Future Passive Participles (Gerundives)	348
Gerunds	348
Supine	349
Latin to English Vocabulary	350
English to Latin Vocabulary	380
Index	411

ACKNOWLEDGMENTS

This book would not be possible without many people in my life who have encouraged me in the study of Latin and languages in general. I first took Latin with Mrs. Florence Lewis, of blessed memory, who taught me the language in high school. I spent too much time joking with my best friend in class, but on account of her mercy and forbearance, I completed two years of high school Latin. This was to be the basis of the study of many languages and of a burgeoning love for them. I will forever be grateful for her kindness, grace, and passion for Latin and Christian education. I am sure she would be surprised at first to learn that I authored a Latin grammar, but then she would smile delightedly. Thank you, Mrs. Lewis.

When I began teaching Latin to middle school students at the Ambrose School in Boise, Idaho, I had no idea what I was doing. I loved teaching Latin, and I wanted the students to love it too. I am grateful to the Ambrose School for sending me to the Accademia Vivarium Novum to study Latin *viva voce* and revolutionize my understanding and approach to the Latin language and the study of classical languages as living languages.

For the last several years, I have worked through this text at Kenrick-Glennon Seminary. I am grateful to all my students for putting up with errors and corrections and for letting me test out the material on them. Dr. Andrew Chronister taught through the material with his classes and did extensive editing and amending of my many errors. He has put a ton of effort into this book out of his own generosity. Thank you, Andrew. I do not deserve your kindness. Marsha Feingold also gave feedback on the beginning chapters, which was very helpful.

During one phase of the editing of this textbook, I received a very generous Mellon Faculty Development award from Saint Louis University. I am grateful for this additional funding, which allowed me dedicated time for one summer to work on this book.

I want to thank my family. My parents have always encouraged my studies, especially in languages. They have been in my corner, cheering me on in pursuits foreign to them, but made personal because of their love for me. Both my mom and my dad have been a tremendous example to me as I have learned to be a parent. My sister and brother have heard more than their share of odd etymologies and discussion of Latin but have also been supportive of my idiosyncratic work.

Finally, my wife Abby has watched me work on this book and talk about it for years. In the summers when I wrote much of it, she worked a full-time job and took time off to take care of our children. I try my best not to take for granted all the kindness and support you have shown me in our marriage and in our time together. You have always been the definition of grace to me: a gift and kindness undeserved, but lavishly given. We see God and love God in part through the people who love us, and whom we also love. Abby, you have shown me the love of God in more ways than I can ever say.

PREFACE

In his apostolic letter, *Latina Lingua*, Pope Benedict XVI wrote about the necessity for improved didactic methods for the study of Latin: "It therefore appears urgently necessary to support the commitment to a greater knowledge and more competent use of Latin, both in the ecclesial context and in the broader world of culture."[1] While this letter came as part of the beginning of the Pontifical Academy for Latin, it recognizes the need for continued effort towards better methods of teaching "the use of didactic methods in keeping with the new conditions, ... so as to make the most of the rich and multiform patrimony of the Latin civilization." This text was developed with an eye towards better didactic methods to enrich the contemporary world with the great patrimony of the Latin of the Church.

The following primer for Ecclesiastical Latin comes from many years of teaching Latin and other languages, both classical and modern. Over the course of my years teaching classes at a Catholic seminary and university, I realized that I needed a Latin text with clearer grammatical explanations, exercises that matched the covered grammar, and longer selections of text. My students felt that the exercises did not always aid their understanding of the grammar, and, lacking the surrounding context for the sentences, they struggled to see the language as a language.

Although this textbook will have many features that follow the patterns of twentieth-century grammar texts, it moves beyond them by its uses of the advances of Second Language Acquisition Theory. As such, much will be familiar to educators who have used books like Collins and Wheelock's, but much will also be different. I have learned a great deal about second language acquisition and linguistics from teaching from textbooks like Hans Orberg's *Familia Romana*, Rodney Decker's *Reading Koine Greek*, and Cook and Holmstedt's *Beginning Biblical Hebrew*. Following what I have learned from these and other similar works, this text provides comprehensible grammatical explanations, exercises drawn from ecclesiastical literature, and a streamlined approach to complete basic Latin grammar over the course of two college semesters. It will be assumed that the students who use this textbook will want some added background in basic grammatical concepts and will enjoy examples drawn from the literature that they would like to read in larger portions after one year of grammatical preparation.

---

1 Benedict XVI, Motu Proprio *Latina Lingua* (November 10, 2012). Vatican documents are available on the Vatican website, www.vatican.va.

1. Unlike other textbooks, this one will begin by explaining each noun case individually over the course of the first several chapters. The text will eventually present the entire chart of all the forms of the noun, but the intention will be to learn how each case functions on its own. Thus, chapter 1 introduces the nominative as subject for first and second declension nouns, and, as a point of contrast, I do begin introducing the accusative as well. Chapter 2 introduces genitives as possessive for first and second declension nouns. Similarly, verbs are learned first with third person singular and plural, before eventually progressing to first-person singular and plural and second-person singular and plural. This is very deliberate. In the past, students could be expected to know how each case functioned. But I have come to realize it takes time for the student to be familiar with each case. Although the explanation of cases and persons of verbs are slow at the beginning, they do come faster in the latter half of the book as the student already knows how each case works. So while the first several chapters will feel slow as the students gain confidence, the second half will move much more quickly.

2. As far as grammatical explanation is concerned, I live by a dictum I learned and have experienced throughout my Latin studies: "There is no such thing as hard grammar, just grammar you haven't seen enough yet."[2] I will make the explanations of concepts like *ablative absolute* as straightforward as possible. Following the practice in Orberg, I will also explain more "difficult" grammar, with easier grammar in the language. This will solidify the earlier forms and give needed repetition. It will also show that the grammar is not "hard," but rather that the student just has not seen it enough to recognize how it functions and what it does. *Repetitio est mater studiorum*. Repetition is always key for language acquisition.

3. This text will also include several longer form readings in the target language that will get successively more difficult. Every five chapters will have a graded or adapted reading that covers the grammar learned in the previous five chapters; these readings are included in the appendix. All unfamiliar words and vocabulary will be glossed. One frequent difficulty for students is that they only see the vocabulary and grammar in shorter sentences with no context. As students of languages will recall, teachers will say things like "you will figure it out in context." And the student looks bewildered because they don't ever get a chance to really see the language in context. Furthermore, students enjoy seeing everything at once and enjoy reading some longer "real" Latin, or "Latin in the wild" as I frequently call it.

4. As for the example sentences for exercises, they will intentionally be drawn from the roughly one thousand years of Ecclesiastical Latin literature (though of course the language is still used in Vatican documents up until the present day). I will use examples I have written within the text itself to explain to the students the new grammatical concepts, but I would like the students to benefit from seeing the original authors as

---

2 From Justin Slocum Bailey, a Latin educator.

much as possible. Those examples will come frequently from the Vulgate but also from the writings of patristic authors, medieval theologians, and even from saints' lives, so popular in the Middle Ages.

A quick note on the language of "Ecclesiastical Latin." Wheelock has tried to teach the Latin of Cicero. Erasmus wrote intentionally in the Ciceronian style. That said, it would not be a stretch to say that Aquinas, for example, could read Cicero, and certainly vice versa. There are differing emphases, occasional spelling changes, some slight grammatical shifts influenced by Koine Greek, but largely only a change in vocabulary. The vocabulary changes frequently come first from the influence of the Vetus Latina and then from Jerome's Vulgate. Writers like Augustine preached from the Vetus Latina, and those who came after him and Jerome made the Latin scriptures their primary linguistic and theological authority. Thus, the anchor was no longer the classical authors like Cicero but the language of the Vulgate and other luminaries like Augustine or Gregory the Great. As such, the intention of this text is to help students come to read ecclesiastical authors more so than Cicero, but one should not think they are so far apart.

Let me offer a final word and encouragement to students:

I begin my language courses by telling students that learning grammar is like learning what a dog is by another person's description. You can learn much this way, but the descriptions make much more sense when you have seen a dog, heard it bark, and touched its fur. Grammar is quite useful, but it can never replace the actual experience of petting many dogs and learning for yourself what makes a dog a dog. Similarly, the learning of a language requires frequent and spaced-out repetition. Acquiring a language takes time. Rereading older sentences, rereading the long form passages, and beginning by reading a book of the Bible like that of John will help you get those necessary repetitions. This book has also intentionally followed, to some extent, Hans Orberg's *Familia Romana*. Once you finish a chapter in this text, you can go to Orberg and read other selections that roughly follow his grammar presentation. Most students need more repetition at their current level than they realize. The most difficult thing for most institutions or individual attempts to learn a classical language is the well-intentioned desire to get to the "real stuff." You can get there, but do not neglect the practice of rereading simpler things to encourage and remind yourself that you have learned something. Moving too quickly to a difficult ecclesiastical author often makes your knowledge of the language feel insufficient, which it usually is not. Breaking through those mental blocks can be difficult, but the reward is great. Reading Latin gives you the ability to read thousands of years of the greatest intellectual achievements of Western Civilization. You can converse with Augustine, in his own language. Pace yourself and do not lose heart!

CHAPTER LAYOUT

- → **Nova Grammatica:** Three to four sections of new grammar (usually no more than four).
- → **Sententiae Summāriae:** These sentences use familiar vocabulary to illustrate the grammar covered in the chapter in very simple sentences. Students can try and translate them with the provided translations covered to see if they are understanding the grammar of the chapter.
- → **Cavēte et Mementōte:** Summary of important things to remember.
- → **Vocābula Memoranda:** The vocabulary comes from the sentences, some of which come from the longer stories. So, these are not the "most commonly occurring vocabulary" in Ecclesiastical Latin. Rather, they are chosen to help students gain fluency within a specified range. The vocabulary list will never be longer than twenty words.
- → **Sententiae Interpretandae:** Anywhere from fifteen to twenty sentences. It was intended for there to be more exercises than might be necessary for every single student, but I wanted more examples to help students who needed more exercises.
- → There are thirty-two chapters, sixteen per semester in a two-semester Latin course.

NOTE ABOUT USING THIS TEXTBOOK

For learning the endings of the first nouns, and verbs, I recommend not memorizing full charts. Rather, I would have students focus on specific endings for specific meanings. Have them make a flash card of *-us, -a, -um* as possible subjects. Have students learn *-i, -ae, -a* as possible plurals. And then add new ones for every chapter. The downside of this approach is of course that an *-i* ending could be dative in the third declension, genitive in the second declension, or plural nominative. That said, you need to get students looking at those endings as early as possible for their meaning, though they do need to know all the possibilities. I find charts to be helpful, mostly as a reference sheet. If you can get the student to immediately associate an *-us* as a subject, they will have a better time really looking for a subject and looking for an ending. This will be very different from a traditional textbook.

The same will go for verbs. At the beginning, have students look for *-t* and *-nt* as endings for a verb that tell whether the verb is singular or plural. The better the students get at looking for those endings early on, the better they will be later at continuing to look for endings in verbs to assess how the verb is functioning in the sentence. This is just my own strategy, but it comes from many years of teaching students modern and classical languages.

INTRODUCTION: ON PRONUNCIATION AND THE ORATIONES HEBDOMADAE

☙

Before we begin with the grammar itself, I would like to say a few words about pronunciation. Pronunciation is something one must begin with but also something that is not perfected until much later in the learning process. So, the student who reads this work will continue to make mistakes regarding when to use the short or long vowel sound and when to make the "ch" sound or not. That is perfectly normal. It is the perspective of this author that pronunciation is best learned by repeating by someone who speaks the language well.

With that in mind, one function of the *orationes hebdomadae* (prayers of the week) is to help students pronounce the language with the aid of a teacher. When the prayer is first taught, it should be said once by the teacher and then repeated with the entire class slowly. This will help the students develop pronunciation along the way. The prayers also function to help students have Latin in their memories. One way we learn language is just by memorizing songs and stories and set phrases. This helps us develop instincts for the language. That is one reason these prayers are meant to be used every class period. They can sometimes be used to illustrate a minor point of grammar. Finally, the prayers are more than a didactic tool. They are indeed means of communication between humans and God. It is important to remember that Latin remains a language of communication even if it is linguistically dead. Its linguistic death is what makes it a language that can transcend time and still continue to be used as a medium of contact with God through prayer, and with past generations.

There are two primary pronunciation schemes for Latin. This book is a primer on Ecclesiastical Latin, the Latin of the Church. As such, we will teach the Ecclesiastical pronunciation. The easiest way to explain the various ways one can pronounce Latin is to think of the name *Cicero*. In American English, we typically say "sisero," following patterns from England in the nineteenth century. In the Reconstructed Classical Latin pronunciation, we would say, "kikero." In the Ecclesiastical pronunciation we would say, "chichero." Who's correct? Yes. All of those are correct possibilities. Depending on one's place in history and geography, all of those are acceptable pronunciations of that name. Some may wonder how we know the ancient pronunciation at all. Suffice it to say that scholars have ways of figuring out how people pronounced things by how they wrote down the language. Not everyone wrote down the language the same way, and we can tell by their mistakes how they likely pronounced the words. This can also be seen in how Hebrew words were spelled in Latin and similar ways. We actually have a pretty good idea of how Greek, Latin, and Hebrew were historically pronounced. As one final plug for the Ecclesiastical pronunciation, it is drawn primarily from how Latin was pronounced on the Italian peninsula and therefore has many similarities to contemporary Italian. Italian is a beautiful, mellifluous language that is fun to pronounce. I find it much more melodic to pronounce Latin with the Italian flare.

The Alphabet

Ecclesiastical Latin uses the same alphabet as English, with the absence of *k* and *w*.

By and large, Latin has the same vowels, *a, e, i, o, u,* and sometimes *y*. Essentially, Latin just has long and short forms of every vowel, which refer to how long one stresses it.

 ā, as in father; *grātia*
 a, as in at; *aqua*

 ē, as in they; *cēna*
 e, as in bet; *terra*

 ī, as in machine, sheep; *doctrīna*
 i, as in bit; *in*

 ō, as in note; *glōria*
 o, as in not; *dominus*

 ū, as in root; *nātūra*
 u, as in cut; *amābunt*

 y, is pronounced like a short i, as in fit: *hymnus*

Latin has many diphthongs, combinations of two vowel sounds that come together to form one syllable:

 ae, (Classical Latin *ī*) pronounced like the *e* in *they*
 au, pronounced like the *ou* in *snout*
 ei, pronounced like the *ei* in *eight*
 eu, pronounced like the *eu* in *eulogy*
 oe, pronounced like the *e* in *they*
 ui, pronounced like the *wi* in *swift*

Most consonants in Latin will sound exactly like the English equivalents with a few exceptions. *C* is typically hard like *can,* though it can have a "ch" sound. When the letter *c* precedes certain vowels: *e, i, ae, oe,* one makes the "ch-" sound. So the word *coelum* (heaven) is pronounced "chelum," but *cultus* (honor/worship) is pronounced "kultus" with a hard *c*.

> *G* is pronounced like *get* except like a *j* before *e, i, y,* where it is pronounced like the *j* in *juice*. *Gn* is pronounced like in "banyan"; *magnus* like "manyoos."
>
> *H* is pronounced like the *h* in *host*. *Ch* and *th* make a single sound like in *character* or *thyme*.
>
> *J*, which was once just an *i* functioning as a consonant, makes the "y" sound as in *yes*. *Justus* is then pronounced "yoostoos."
>
> *Ph*, makes an "f" sound like in *phalanx*.
>
> The *r* in Latin was trilled like one might find in the Spanish language.
>
> *Sc* together becomes "sh" as in *shout*, when followed by *e* or *i*.
>
> *Su* followed by a vowel makes "sw" sound as in *suavis*.
>
> *Ti*, when followed by a vowel, becomes "tsi" as in *Betsy*. *Laetitia* would be an example of using the "tsi" sound for the second *ti* in the word because it is followed by a vowel.

In some Latin texts, the *u* is used for both vowels and consonants. The *u* in Ecclesiastical Latin when it is a consonantal letter, can be written as an English *v*. It is then pronounced with the hard "v" sound like before *vet*. *Verbum* should be pronounced with the same sound as the *v* in *vet*.

Finally, *z* is "dz" as in *adze*.

You will notice throughout that vowels are marked with what is called a macron. This dash over the vowels indicates that it is a long vowel, as in the examples above.

Another pronunciation rule is that Latin always pronounces its vowels, whether longer or short. For example, in English we have the word bonafide, from the Latin *bonā fide,* which is pronounced "bonah fideh."

All consonants are pronounced and doubled consonants are doubly pronounced, as in *ec-clesia*.

Syllabication

In order to find the number of syllables in a word, the reader needs to count the vowels or diphthongs. The reader can then divide the word into syllables based on whether a vowel is "open," which means it is not followed by a consonant, or whether a vowel is followed by a single consonant.

Me/us. In this case the *e* is open because it is followed by the *u*.
Pi/ra. In this case the *i* is followed by the single consonant *r*.

To know how a noun is accented, one must know the quantity of the syllable. A syllable is long if it contains a long vowel or a diphthong. It can be long by position if a short vowel is followed by two or more consonants or a double consonant. One other rule is that a short vowel made long by position is still pronounced short, like *missa*.

In addition to breaking down the word by its syllables, one also needs to know the quantity of the next to last syllable called the *penult*. Thus, if the penult is long, it takes an accent: *doctrīna*. If the penult is short, then the third syllable from the end, known as the antepenult, gets the accent: *ecclesia*. If a word has two syllables, it is accented on the penult: *cēna*.

A REVIEW OF BASIC GRAMMAR CONCEPTS RELATED TO LATIN[1]

☙❧

Every word in a Latin sentence hangs on or is related to some other word in the same sentence, with the exception of the verb. The verb can exist on its own as a complete sentence. Thus, it will be critical that as a student you identify the verb. All the other words have a function related to the verb, providing a reason for how they function in connection with the verb.

The main possibilities are as follows:

Noun
– subject of the verb or agrees with the verb
  – The *boy* walks.
  – In Latin, the subject is in the **nominative** (nom.) case.[2]
– direct object of the verb
  – The dog loves the *boy*.
  – In Latin, the direct object is in the **accusative** (acc.) case.
– indirect object of the verb (usually with the preposition *to* or *for*)
  – The dog gives the ball *to the boy*.
  – In Latin, the indirect object is in the **dative** (dat.) case.
– genitive or possessive of another noun
  – The dog *of* the *boy*; or the *boy's* dog.
  – In Latin, the possessive is in the **genitive** (gen.) case.

---

1 Based in part on Paula Saffire and Catherine Freis's similar breakdown in *Ancient Greek Alive*, 3rd ed. (University of North Carolina Press, 1999) 74–75.

2 We will learn more about cases in the first few chapters, but a case means that the noun has a certain ending that communicates its function in the sentence. Latin has more cases than English, but as an example, sometimes English does have cases. "He" is in the nominative or subject case. "Him" is in the accusative or direct object case. "His" is in the genitive or possessive case.

– object of the preposition
    – The dog is behind *the boy*.
    – In Latin, the object of the preposition is either in the **ablative** (abl.) or **accusative** (acc.) case.

Pronoun
– can do all the things a noun does but stands in place of the noun
– *he, she, it; hers, his, its; him, her, it*

Article
– can be either definite or indefinite and are a type of adjective
– *a* or *the*

Adjective
– gives more information about a noun (expressed or understood)
– In grammatical terms, we say the adjective "modifies" a noun, which means that it provides more information about the noun.
– the *small* boy; the *tall* boy

Verb
– can be the main verb and exist on its own
– can be a verb in a clause
– A clause is a phrase that is introduced by a conjunction or a relative pronoun and cannot stand alone without a main verb and sentence.
– The dog *loves* the boy.

Infinitive
– completes a verb
    – I want to love.
– completes an adjective
    – That's hard to love.
– acts as a noun
    – To love God is easy.
– used in indirect discourse, stands in the place of a regular verb
    – I believe him to love well, that is, I believe that he praises well.
– *to love* or the bare infinitive *love*

Gerund

– a verb that acts like a noun (I like skiing)

– ski-ing

– can be easily confused with a participle which also ends in -ing but does not give more information about a noun. It is a noun.

Participle

– goes with a noun or a pronoun (either expressed or understood)

– It can give more information about a noun.

– It can provide further information about a circumstance of the verb.

– "lov-*ing*" in English

Preposition

– usually provides more information about a verb, infinitive, or participle

– *behind, above, below, for, to,* etc.

Conjunction

– combines words, phrases, clauses, or sentences

– *while, although, when, and, but,* etc.

Adverb

– modifies, or gives more information about a verb, adjective, or adverb

– *very, quickly, well, better,* etc.

Interjection

– grammatically isolated words

– "*O* Lord! *Behold!*"

CHAPTER 1

☙❧

A quick note about using this textbook. I have rearranged some of the standard ways of presenting the cases (cases are a grammatical description of how a noun appears and works in a sentence: that is, subject, direct object, indirect object) in Latin. This first chapter begins with nouns as subjects and direct objects in their masculine, feminine, and neuter forms. As we proceed, we will come to nouns as objects of prepositions, indirect objects, etc., and their attendant changes in endings. I do this so that the student will become familiar with each case ending and its primary usage, one at a time. Thus, there will not be a complete chart of all the possible endings or uses of a noun until chapter 5.

In a similar way, I do not introduce the *I* and *you* form of the verbs until chapter 10, but I do introduce commands early. This more naturally mimics the way people acquire language, as a language. I have deliberately chosen to focus on the *he/she/it/they* forms of the verbs for the beginning chapters. This again follows the natural pattern of language acquisition.

§ 1. Nouns: Singular and Plural in Masculine, Feminine, and Neuter as Subjects

Nouns in both Latin and English are the names (*Nōmina*) of persons, places, or things. Our focus in chapter 1 will be on nouns as subjects. In English, "the maidservant praises."

Among other functions, nouns can do the action of the verb or receive the action of a verb in a sentence. They can also be found after prepositions. The *boy* walks. The *boy* gives the *girl* a *gift*. The *boy*, the *girl*, and the *gift* are the nouns. The gift is *behind* (*Praepositiō*) the *boy*.

Nouns in Latin, unlike nouns in English, have grammatical gender, which is not the same thing as gender associated with biological sex. There are nouns like *magister*, which is masculine, and *ancilla*, which is feminine, which do have a direct connection to biological gender, but objects and abstract nouns also have gender. Gender functions more like the word *genus*, which means a grouping based on a shared characteristic. That is, they are categorized into three different groups that are called genders. Those are masculine, feminine, and neuter. (*Neuter* literally means in Latin "neither," as in "this word is neither masculine nor feminine.")

discipulus–boy student
ancilla–maidservant
donum–gift

Objects come in the masculine and feminine, in addition to the neuter.

hymnus–hymn; *liber*–book
terra–land; *aqua*–water
canticum–song; *caelum*–heaven

Notice that four of these nouns have feminine and masculine endings -*a* and -*us*. This is how many modern European languages work, but it can feel awkward in English. Ships are often called *she*, but usually English speakers refer to objects as *it*, whereas in Latin it is just as common to found objects as masculine and feminine as neuter.

In English, nouns are either singular or plural, which means the primary way they are spelled differently is with an *s* or without an *s*, and by the position of an apostrophe before and after the *s*.[1] *Student, students; gift, gifts*, etc. Latin, on the other hand, regularly has different endings based on how the word is used in the sentence. There are many different ways to show that nouns are either singular or plural in Latin based on what declension they follow. There are five declensions or patterns, but we will begin with a-nouns and o-nouns.

For this section, we are only learning the endings for singular and plural words that are used as the subject or predicate nominative of a sentence.[2] Latin word endings will change much more frequently than English nouns and verbs. It is much more like German or Greek. The closest similarity is the difference between *he, his,* and *him*. All of those English words have the same root but different endings based on how they function in a sentence. These different functions are called cases. Case allows Latin to convey meaning between nouns and other words, regardless of the order of the sentence. Latin has seven cases, though we will focus on five throughout the book, and only two in the first chapter.

Let's break down a few Latin nouns. You can think of the stem of the word as *discipul-; ancill-; don-*. It will never appear that way in a Latin text, but it is the root of all the possible versions of the word. *Discipulus, ancilla, donum,* etc.[3]

Maria ancilla est. Mary is a maidservant.
Liber donum est. The book is a gift.
Jacobus discipulus est. Jacob is a student.

---

1 I list here the standard English plural, adding an *s*. It should be noted that English, like Latin, has other kinds of plurals: *deer-deer; mouse-mice*, etc.

2 It is worth noting that almost every grammatical term in English comes from a Latin root word. Also, the primary difficulty for many people in learning a language like Latin stems from having to learn another language while learning Latin. The other language is the language of grammar, which is foreign to many students. Thus, at the same time, they have to learn what a "nominative" is and learn what *discipulus* is. This involves learning the language of grammar alongside the language of Latin.

3 We will see in forthcoming chapters that occasionally a first declension noun is masculine and will have an -*a* ending. These typically have to do with occupations: *agricola* (farmer), *nauta* (sailor), *papa* (pope), etc.

We will refer to words that end in *-a* in the nominative singular as a-nouns, or in older grammars, *first declension*. There are five main patterns for nouns, a-nouns, o-nouns, i/e-nouns, u-nouns, and e-nouns. These patterns are traditionally called a declension. If a word is from one pattern, it will not be found in another pattern, except in the case of some words that have masculine and feminine forms. *Discipul-a* is feminine and *discipul-us* is masculine.

Case	Singular	Example Translation	Plural	Example Translation
Nominative	*ancill\a*	handmaid (subject)	*ancill\ae*	handmaids (subject)

We will refer to words that end in *-us* in the nominative singular as o-nouns or *second declension*.

Case	Singular	Example Translation	Plural	Example Translation
Nominative	*discipul\us*	student (subject)	*discipul\ī*	students (sub.)

Finally, we will call words that end in *-um* in the nominative singular, "neuter o-nouns" or "second declension neuter."

Case	Singular	Example Translation	Plural	Example Translation
Nominative	*don\um*	gift (subject)	*don\a*	gifts (sub.)

Latin has many different endings that indicate a word is plural. We have now seen how Latin indicates that a word is the subject of a sentence. This is called the nominative.

Maria et Anna ancillae sunt. Mary and Anna are maidservants.
Petrus et Jacobus discipuli sunt. Peter and Jacob are students.
Libri dona sunt. The books are gifts.

One exception is for words like *magister*, "teacher."

Jesus magister est. Jesus is a teacher.

Right at the beginning, we need to learn one exception, and we will become accustomed to exceptions throughout this book as they tend to be a common feature of learning languages. The typical ending for a masculine nominative is *-us, discipulus*.[4] There are some words, *magister* (teacher), *vir* (man), etc., that end in *-r*.[5] This is only true for singular masculine words that are the subject. There are no exceptions like this for the feminine or neuter.

---

4 We will introduce the other three declensions later.
5 As a general notice to readers and students, there is almost always an exception to any "rule"

§ 2. Nouns: Direct Objects and Accusative

In English, we show the relationship between a subject and a verb by the order of the sentence, that is, syntax. If I say, "the boy throws the ball," no one wonders who is doing the throwing, because the noun *boy* comes before the verb *throws*. The noun *ball* comes after the verb *throw* and is therefore receiving the action of the verb. The word *ball* is the direct object of the verb *throw*. Latin grammar calls this form of the word accusative (*accusativus*).[6]

Latin primarily shows the relationship between a subject, a verb, and a direct object by the ending of the nouns. So, Latin can rearrange the word order without a loss of meaning. I am going to show you what I mean through what I will call "Englatin"—that is, English words with Latin endings. "Boy-us throws ball-um." In this made-up example, our standard English words have Latin endings and can be rearranged without loss of meaning. The *-us* tells us that *boy* is the subject. In addition, the *-um* means that *ball* is the direct object. Thus, we could say, "ball-um throws boy-us," and we know because of the endings that the boy is still the subject and the ball is the direct object. This may seem silly, but it is important to keep in mind that you cannot know what a Latin sentence is saying, simply by translating the words in order from left to right. In English, observing the order of the words is essential for understanding a sentence's meaning. This is not necessarily the case in Latin.

Let's see how direct objects work with our standard verbs:

Ancilla Deum laudat. The maidservant praises God.
Discipulī Deum laudant. The students praise God.

Ancilla dominum monet. The maidservant warns the master.
Discipulī magistrum monent. The students warn the teacher.

Dominus ancillās dūcit. The master leads the maidservants.
Magistrī discipulōs dūcunt. The teachers lead the students.

Ancilla cantica audit. The maidservant hears the songs.
Ancillae cantica audiunt. The maidservants hear the songs.

We could rewrite the first example in several different orders and have the same basic meaning:

Deum ancilla laudat. Laudat deum ancilla. Deum laudat ancilla.
All of these mean the exact same thing: "The maidservant praises God."

---

that is taught in grammar. Rules are given because they offer some generalized prescriptions that are followed most of the time. The hardest part about teaching a foreign language is to constantly remind students about exceptions. There is no way around it, but my general advice is to learn what is most common first and commit that to memory. Then you can worry about the exceptions.

6 We are again not exhausting the possible uses of the accusative. Allen and Greenough have more uses, though only four. *New Latin Grammar* (Dover Press, 2006), § 240–48.

It is important to always keep this in mind when translating Latin sentences: there is no way in English to convey that a word is the subject, except by putting it before the verb. So, when you go to translate, you will have to reorder the sentence on many occasions to put the subject in front of the verb and the direct object after it. There is no preposition or any other word we can add to convey that a noun is a subject or direct object. In English, we usually use word order to convey that a word is a subject or direct object (with the exception of pronouns like *he* and *him* or *she* and *her*). We will learn that Latin has five primary endings for nouns.[7] As we progress into other uses of the nouns, we will find that in English, we can often convey the ending of a noun either with word order, as in subject verb direct object, or through prepositions like *of*, *to*, or *by*.

Here is a final reminder about the difference between English and Latin. Our brains are shaped by the languages we speak, especially our first language. English speakers do not naturally look for gender in most words, or for meaning based on the changing form of the word. Most words in English do not have gender, and we know how a word works in a sentence usually by the order of the nouns and the verb. Latin encodes its meaning through endings, including gender, number, and case. So when you read a Latin sentence, you *must* look at the ending, rather than simply its word order, to discover how a word is functioning. Our English-speaking brains have to be rewired through many repetitions to look for the meaning in a different format than the manner to which we will have to become accustomed in Latin.

A-Nouns / 1st Declension (Usually Feminine)[8]

Case	Singular	Example Translation	Plural	Example Translation
Nominative	*ancill\a*	handmaid (sub.)	*ancill\ae*	handmaids (sub.)
Genitive	Chapter 2			
Dative	Chapter 5			
Accusative	*ancill\am*	handmaid (direct object)	*ancill\ās*	handmaids (d.o.)
Ablative	Chapters 3 and 6			

---

7 Technically Latin has seven cases: vocative, nominative, genitive, dative, accusative, ablative, and locative. We will discuss the vocative case in chapter 3. Locative does not occur frequently enough for it to be memorized in Ecclesiastical Latin.

8 We will call these *a-nouns* after the primary vowel connecting the stem to the ending.

O-Nouns / 2nd Declension (Masculine)[9]

Case	Singular	Example Translation	Plural	Example Translation
Nominative	*discipul|us*	student (sub.)	*discipul|ī*	students (sub.)
Genitive	Chapter 2			
Dative	Chapter 5			
Accusative	*discipul|um*	student (d.o.)	*discipul|ōs*	students (d.o.)
Ablative	Chapters 3 and 6			

O-Nouns / 2nd Declension (Neuter)

Case	Singular	Example Translation	Plural	Example Translation
Nominative	*don|um*	gift (sub.)	*don|a*	gifts (sub.)
Genitive	Chapter 2			
Dative	Chapter 5			
Accusative	*don|um*	gift (d.o.)	*don|a*	gifts (d.o.)
Ablative	Chapters 3 and 6			

§ 3. Verbs: Third Person Singular and Plural in the Four Main Patterns (Conjugations)

One straightforward way to think about verbs (*verba*) is that they express the action of the sentences. "Walks," "give," etc.; *laudat, donant,* etc. This is not exclusively the case, but it is helpful for getting started. Latin, unlike English, can use the verb without an explicit subject.

> *Laudat.* This one word can mean "he walks" or "she walks" or "it walks" depending on the context. Often Latin will have an explicit noun as the subject, but it is not required.

Moving along, we can add nouns to our verbs to make a longer sentence. The ending of the verb changes based on what other words they are working with to make meaning. For now we will just be learning the singular subject (*he, she,* or *it*) plus the verb and plural

---

[9] We will call these *o-nouns* after the vowel in the dative and ablative, learned later.

nouns (*they*) plus verbs. In these two cases, if the subject is singular, then a *-t* is added to the ending, and for the plural an *-nt* is added. The examples below follow the four main patterns of verbs: ā-verbs, ē-verbs, i/e-verbs, and i-verbs. These example verbs will be used throughout the book to illustrate how each pattern of verbs changes based on its usage.

> *Ancilla laudat.* The maidservant praises.
> *Disicpulī laudant.* The students praise.
>
> *Ancilla monet.* The maidservant warns.
> *Discipulī monent.* The students warn.
>
> *Dominus dūcit.* The master leads.
> *Magistrī dūcunt.* The teachers lead.
>
> *Ancilla audit.* The maidservant hears.
> *Ancillae audiunt.* The maidservants hear.

Notice both that the nouns have different endings based on whether they are singular or plural, masculine or feminine, and that the verbs have different endings based on whether or not the subject noun is either singular or plural: for example, *monet* and *monent*. It can be helpful to think of the verb as a stem, a theme vowel, and then a personal ending. *Mon-* is the stem, *e* is the theme vowel, and the personal endings we know at this point are either *-t* or *-nt*. The pattern vowel is how you will know what pattern a verb comes in. When you learn verb forms in the vocabulary, you will learn them with what is called the present infinitive to clarify the pattern in which the verb comes.

There are four main verb patterns based on their pattern vowels. Latin verbs do not have gender. They do have patterns though. Generally speaking, we talk about four main different patterns, ā-verbs, ē-verbs, short ĕ/ĭ-verbs, and ī -verbs.[10] *Laud-**a**-t, mon-**ē**-t, duc-**ĭ**-t, aud-**i**-t*. The vowel pattern is bolded. That vowel pattern presents itself in nearly every form of the verb, and there are many to learn in Latin. The only difficulty is recognizing that the *i* in the third example, *dūcit*, is actually short, *ĭ*.

§ 4. Verbs: Introduction to *esse*, the "to be" Verb

It is also important to know two forms of the verb "to be": *est* and *sunt*. *Est* is used for the singular "he/she/it is," and *sunt* for the plural, "they are." Like we saw in the sentences directly above, often you will find Latin verbs at the ends of sentences.

You can, however, put *est* or *sunt* at the beginning of a sentence and it can mean "it is," "there is" (*est*), or "there are" (*sunt*). Typically, if *est* or *sunt* is going to be used without an

---

10 In older texts, this would be a-verbs, first conjugation; ē-verbs, second conjugation; short i/e-verbs, third conjugation; and ī-verbs, fourth conjugation. The term *conjugation* will become familiar over time, but I will be calling them a-verbs, ē-verbs, i/e-verbs, ī-verbs, and -io-verbs.

explicit subject, it will mean "it/there is" or "there are." It will be at the beginning of the sentence and not have an explicit subject.

Est vir in regno tuo (Dn 5:11). There is a man in your kingdom.

We will work more directly on changes in the verb endings in chapter 7, as well as offer a larger overview of the verb.

§ 5. Syntax: Articles

Some final comments about things that are part of English speech but not Latin speech. English frequently uses what are called articles: *the* and *a*. Latin does not technically have a category called *article*. Most of the time, and for the beginning of the process of learning Latin, the student will have to determine based on context whether an *a* or a *the* or neither is appropriate for a word.

That said, we will learn ways in which Latin replicates the use of the article with adjectives that are functionally articles to create a similar meaning in English. *Quidam vir*, "a man"; or *matrona illa*, "the woman."

Another critical point: Latin word order is more fluid than English. It is not quite right to say, "word order doesn't matter." Word order does matter. It just matters *differently*. We will continue to explore this in the following chapters.

Sententiae Summāriae (Summary Sentences)[11]

Est Deus in caelō.
Est ancilla in aquā.
Sunt cantica in terrā.
Jesus est Deus.

Discipulī volant.
Ancillae dominas vident.
Virī dominos vident.
Dominus virum jubet.
Domina ancillam jubet.
Dominus vincit.
Discipulī audiunt de terrā.

---

[11] These sentences are intended to be used to give a general summary of the grammar covered in each chapter and are created by the author to explicitly demonstrate how the grammar functions using relatively common vocabulary for this book. It might be helpful to work through these with students in class before assigning homework on the later sentences.

CHAPTER 1

Translations

There is a God in heaven.
There is a maidservant in the water.
There are songs on the earth.
Jesus is God.

The students fly.
The maidservants see the ladies.
The men see the masters.
The Lord commands a man.
The lady commands a maidservant.
The Lord conquers.
The students listen from the earth.

Cavēte et Mementōte (Be Aware and Remember)

The *-a* ending can either be feminine singular *or* neuter plural. You will only know by context and whether the verb is singular or plural.

Vocābula Memoranda (Vocabulary to Be Memorized)

Nōmina[12]

ancilla, ancillae (f.): maidservant
aqua, aqua (f.): water
caelum, caelī (n.): heaven[13]
Deus, Deī (m.): God
domina, dominae (f.): lady
dominus, dominī (m.): lord, Lord
ecclēsia, ecclēsiae (f.): church
fēmina, fēminae (f.): woman
lignum, lignī (n.): tree, wood
malum, malī (n.): apple, fruit
mundus, mundī (m.): world
terra, terrae (f.): earth, land
vir, virī (m.): man

---

[12] Each noun is given in the nominative and genitive singular form. The genitive will be explained later.

[13] This noun has many forms. Originally a neuter noun, it is frequently found in the masculine plural nominative form *caeli*. In later medieval Latin, it functions primarily in the plural and is found in the spelling *coeli*, both pronounced "chēli."

Verba[14]

ā-verbs
   laudo, laudare, laudavi, laudatus: praise
     laudat: he/she/it praises
     laudant: they praise
   mandūcō, mandūcāre, mandūcāvī, mandūcātus: eat
     mandūcat: he/she/it eats
     mandūcant: they eat
   volō, volāre, volāvī, volātus: fly, flee
     volat: he/she/it flies, flees
     volant: they fly, flee

ē-verbs
   videō, vidēre, vīdī, vīsus: see
     videt: he/she/it sees
     vident: they see
   jubeō, jubēre, jussī, jussus: order, tell, command
     jubet: he/she/it orders
     jubent: they order

i-verbs
   audiō, audīre, audīvī (audiī), audītus: hear, obey
     audit: he/she/it hears/obeys
     audiunt: they hear/obey

Irregular
   sum, esse, fuī, futūrus: be
     est: he/she/it is
     sunt: they are

---

14 Verbs will be given with their full four principal parts, as they are often presented in a lexicon. Some teachers will want students to memorize all the principal parts at once. Some will prefer just to have the students learn the parts they will be using for the time being, and as such, those forms are provided below the four principal parts. The four principal parts are present, active indicative, first person singular, *laudo*; present active infinitive, *laudare*; perfect active indicative, first person singular, *laudavi*; and perfect passive participle, masculine nominative singular, *laudatus*. None of these forms are covered in the first chapter. All forms of the verb can be derived from these principal parts. This is also how they are traditionally learned in textbooks and lexica. If you were teaching someone the English word *walk*, you could have them learn four principal parts like Latin: "I walk, to walk, walked, walked." For irregular verbs, it would be hard to figure out these other forms: "I broke, to break, broke, broken." This is similar to what is happening with the Latin verbs.

Conjūnctīva

et: and
sed: but

Adverbia

non: not
quoque: also
neque (*nec*): not, neither

Interrogātīva

quem: whom?
quis: who?
quī: who (plural)?

Fābula Parva (Latīna Ficta) (Small Story, Made-up Latin)

Sunt vir et fēmina. Est Deus quoque. Deus non est vir, neque Deus est fēmina. Adamus et Heva sunt vir et fēmina. Deus jubet Adamum et Hevam, sed Heva cibum mandūcat. Heva Adamum jubet. Adamus Hevam audit. Adamus quoque malum mandūcat. Malum Adamus et Heva mandūcant. Heva Deum non audit. Adamus non audit. Heva et Adamus Deum non audiunt.

Respondēte in linguā Latīnā:

1. Quis est Adamus?
2. Quis est Heva?
3. Quis Adamum et Hevam jubet?
4. Quem Adamus audit?

Sententiae Interpretandae (Sentences to be Translated)

1. In ecclesiā et in terrā Dominus rēgnat. (Arnobius Junior, *Commentarii in Psalmos*)

   in: in

2. Sāulus nihil videt. (Acts 9:8)

   nihil: nothing

3. Deus amīcitia est. (Aelred of Rievaulx, *Dē Spīrituālī Amīcitiā*)

   amicitia: friendship

4. Dēus cāritās est. (1 Jn 4:7)
5. Angleī laudant.

6. Verba volant, scrīpta manent.

scrīpta: things written
volant: fly away

7. Sed Dēus videt et Dēus audit. (Hieronymus, *Tractatus in Psalmos* 95)
8. Sunt dei aurei qui non vident, neque audiunt. (Dn 5:23)

aurei: golden

9. Moyses Dominum videt. (Nm 12:8)
10. Terram Dominus non videt. (Ezek 9:9)
11. Discipulī Jēsum vident. (Jn 6:6)
12. Audit verba. (Rv 1:3)
13. Verbum audiunt. (Mk 4:18)
14. Non ubi vir audit, ibi Deus audit. (Augustine, *Enarrationes in Psalmos* 141.2)

ibi: there
ubi: where

15. Dominus est Deus. (1 Kgs 18:21)

Sententiae Fictae Interpretandae (Made-Up Sentences to Be Translated)

(further vocabulary and grammar review with author-created sentences)

1. Quis videt? Christus videt.
2. Quem Christus videt? Virum Christus videt. Feminam Christus videt.
3. Quem vir et femina audiunt? Deum audiunt.
4. Quī vident? Angelī vident.
5. Angelī volant et laudant, sed nōn mandūcant.
6. Fēminae laudant et mandūcant, sed nōn volant.
7. Fēminae nōn sunt angelī, neque deae. Vir nōn est angelus, neque deus.
8. Deus viros et feminas jubet. Sed quoque, Dominus angelos et viros jubet.
9. Dominī et dominae ancillas jubent. Ancillae dominos et dominas audiunt.
10. Viri et angeli Deum laudant.

CHAPTER 2

§ 6. Nouns: Possessive Nouns Singular and Plural in Masculine, Feminine, and Neuter

In the previous chapter, we saw that nouns were spelled in a certain way when they were the subject of a sentence in Latin (*discipulus, ancilla, donum* in the singular; *discipulī, ancillae, dona* in the plural). We also learned that as a direct object they take slightly different endings (*discipulum, ancillam, donum* in the singular; *discipulōs, ancillās, dona* in the plural). Latin also has different endings when the noun is put into a possessive relationship with another noun. We typically call this *possessive*. We might say "the gift of the student" or "the student's gift," in English. In Latin, instead of using *of* or *-s* we added *-ī, -ae, -ī* in the singular or *-ōrum, -ārum, -ōrum* in the plural. The name of this form of the word in Latin grammar is called genitive (*genitivus*).[1] For example,

Singular Possessive (Genitive):
Est donum discipulī. It is a gift of the student.
Est donum ancillae. It is a gift of the maidservant.
Est canticum coelī. It is the song of heaven.

Plural Possessive (Genitive):
Sunt dona discipulōrum. They are the gifts of the students.
Sunt dona ancillārum. They are the gifts of the maidservants.
Sunt cantica coelōrum. They are the songs of heaven.

**If you have learned a language with endings in the past, you might want to see a chart of all the endings of the words we are learning. You can skip ahead to chapter 6 or to the appendix if you would like to see a complete chart.

In general, when you recognize that a noun has the possessive, or genitive (*genitivus*) ending, it is best to translate it as "of" plus the meaning of the stem, or *-'s*.

---

[1] Allen and Greenough, the standard Latin grammar from 1903, lists twelve different uses of the genitive. We are not trying to give an exhaustive account of all the uses of the genitive. See Allen and Greenough, *New Latin Grammar* (Ginn, 1903), § 210–24.

So far, we have seen:

A-Nouns / 1st Declension (Usually Feminine)

Case	Singular	Example Translation	Plural	
Nominative (Nom)	ancill|a	handmaid (sub.)	ancill|ae	handmaids (sub.)
Genitive (Gen)	ancill|ae	of the handmaid	ancill|ārum	of the handmaids
Dative (Dat)	Chapter 5			
Accusative (Acc)	ancill|am	handmaid (d.o.)	ancill|ās	handmaids (d.o.)
Ablative (Abl)	Chapters 3 and 6			

O-Nouns / 2nd Declension (Masculine)

Case	Singular	Example Translation	Plural	Example Translation
Nominative	discipul|us	student (sub.)	discipul|ī	students (sub.)
Genitive	discipul|ī	of the student	discipul|ōrum	of the students
Dative	Chapter 5			
Accusative	discipul|um	student (d.o.)	discipul|ōs	students (d.o.)
Ablative	Chapters 3 and 6			

O-Nouns / 2nd Declension (Neuter)

Case	Singular	Example Translation	Plural	Example Translation
Nominative	don|um	gift (sub.)	don|a	gifts (sub.)
Genitive	don|ī	of the gift	don|ōrum	of the gifts
Dative	Chapter 5			
Accusative	don|um	gift (d.o.)	don|a	gifts (d.o.)
Ablative	Chapters 3 and 6			

§ 7. Relative Pronouns: Nominative and Genitive

When learning a new language, one must learn not only new vocabulary words and endings but patterns of connecting sentences and larger thoughts. Contemporary English favors shorter, punchier sentences rather than longer connected compound sentences. Latin prefers longer, convoluted and compound sentences, sometimes lasting an entire page (or even longer!). One of several ways Latin connects clauses is by relative pronouns. Think of the sentence, "the man, who is the teacher, walks." The relative clause "who is the teacher" gives more information about the man. It answers the question, "which man"? Latin does the same thing, but the relative pronoun has gender, number, and case, like a regular noun. A relative pronoun (*pronomen relativum*) is just a noun that stands in place of (*pro*) a noun and relates it to more information.

> *Discipulus, quī est in ecclesiā, ambulat.* The student, who is in the church, walks.
> *Ancilla, quae est in ecclesiā, ambulat.* The maidservant, who is in the church, walks.
> *Dōnum, quod est poculum, cadit.* The gift, which is a cup, falls.

Slightly harder to follow from Latin to English is the possessive (*genitivus*) form of these relative pronouns. Take for example the sentence, "the student, whose father is in Rome, walks." The phrase that begins with *whose* tells you a bit more about the student, but in this case it does so by relating the subject to another noun. What is the relationship between the student and the father? It is the father, "of the student." As you might recall from above, the standard way to translate a possessive is using *of*. "The father of the student." The word *cuius* relates the subject of the sentence to another noun in the relative clause and can be translated as "whose."

> *Discipulus, cuius magister audit, ambulat.* The student, whose teacher listens, walks.
> *Discipula, cuius magister audit, ambulat.* The student, whose teacher listens, walks.
> *Dōnum, cuius faber audit, cadit.* The gift, whose maker listens, falls.

The last example is a good place to see if we are understanding the use of *whose*. You should ask yourself, "what falls?" Is it the *gift* or the *maker*? This kind of thinking we take for granted in our native tongue, but we become more aware of it when learning a second language. The answer is, *the gift*. The gift falls. The relative clause "whose maker is in Rome," only tells us more about the gift. This kind of reasoning and understanding of how a sentence is constructed will be critical to truly being able to read Latin as Latin.

Singular

Cases	Masculine Singular (M.S.)	Example Translation	Feminine Singular (F.S.)	Example Translation	Neuter Singular (N.S.)	
Nom	*qu|ī*	who	*qu|ae*	who	*qu|od*	what
Gen	*cu|ius*	whose	*cu|ius*	whose	*cu|ius*	of which

Plural

Cases	Masculine Plural (M.P.)	Example Translation	Feminine Plural (F.P.)	Example Translation	Neuter Plural (N.P.)	
Nom	*qu|ī*	who	*qu|ae*	who	*qu|ae*	what
Gen	*qu|ōrum*	whose	*qu|ārum*	whose	*qu|ōrum*	of which

§ 8. Adjectives: An Introduction

Our final bit of grammar for this chapter is a brief introduction to adjectives (*Adjectīva*). Adjectives give more information about a noun: the tall boy, the small girl, the big gift, etc. In English, adjectives tend to come before the noun, but as in other languages derived from Latin, the adjective can come before or after a noun, usually after. Thus, "the boy tall," "the girl small," and "the gift big" could be the order of the words in Latin. Just like nouns have gender, number, and case, so do adjectives. In English, we don't really have agreement between nouns and adjectives. There is no plural form of adjectives in English. So, this is going to feel unnatural at first, but it will make sense over time.

Singular
  Dominus justus: just lord
  Ancilla beata est: the maidservant is blessed
  Dōnum magnum est: big gift

Plural
  Dominī justī sunt. The lords are just.
  Ancillae beatae sunt. The maidservants are blessed.
  Bona magna sunt. The gifts are big.

Notice that the endings of the adjectives match the nouns, in these examples. *discipulī altī, dona magna*, etc. More endings will come as we progress in the language. It is critical that you start remembering this phrase now: "**adjectives agree with nouns in gender, number,** and case, *not* always declension." This will make more sense later when we move into other declensions.[2] Adjectives can have any a noun has.

> *Dōnum discipulī justī magnum est.* The gift of the just student is big.
> *Dōna ancillārum beatārum magna sunt.* The gifts of the blessed maidservants' students are big.
> *Papa nōn magnus est.* The pope is not big.

Notice that *papa* is masculine singular and nominative, though it has an *-a* ending, but the adjective has an *-us*. Technically the adjective and the noun are both masculine singular and nominative, though they don't look like they agree.

Ancilla beata magistrum justum audit. The small maidservant listens to the tall teacher.

Sententiae Summāriae

> Servus vir dominī est.
> Est magister discipulōrum.
> Ancilla jūsta quae quoque manducat laudat.
> Discipulus vērus quī est bonus audit.
> Servī quōrum dominus bonus est laudant.
> Ancillae quārum domina bona est audiunt.

Translations

The servant is a man of the Lord.
He is the teacher of the students.
The just maidservant who also eats praises.
The true student who is good hears.
The servants whose lord is good praise.
The maidservants whose lady is good listen.

Cavēte et Mementōte

The *-ī* ending can either be the genitive singular masculine *or* the nominative plural masculine. You will know by context and whether it is paired with another noun.

Adjectives are paired with nouns and they match those nouns in gender, number, and case *but not* declension or pattern. So they will often have the same letters at the end, but not always.

---

2 Declensions are patterns of endings into which nouns fall. That is, there are five general patterns of nouns and their endings. We have been looking at the first two: *-a, -ae* and *-us, -i/um, i*. For now, we think of feminine words as having an *a* or *ae* ending that matches the first declension. We think of masculine and neuter words as having an *-us, -i/-um* or *-i* ending, which is the second declension. This will become more complicated when we learn a few exceptions.

Vocābula Memoranda

Nōmina

auxilium, -ī (n.): help
Christus, -ī (m.): Anointed One (often translated simply as *Christ*)
misericordia, -ae (f.): mercy
papa, -ae (m.): pope
   Notice this is an a-noun that is masculine.
servus, -ī (m.): servant
via, -ae (f.): way
vita, -ae (f.): life

Adjectīva

aeternus, -a, -um: eternal[3]
beatus, -a, -um: happy, blessed
justus, -a, -um: just
magnus, -a, -um: great, large
multus, -a, -um: many
plenus, -a, -um: full
verus, -a, -um: true

Verba

<u>*ā-verbs*</u>
ambulō, ambulāre, ambulāvī, ambulātus: walk
   ambulat: he/she/it walks
   ambulant: they walk

<u>*ē-verbs*</u>
gaudeō, gaudēre,—, gāvīsus sum: rejoice[4]
   gaudet: he/she/it rejoices
   gaudent: they rejoice

maneo, manēre, mānsi, mānsus: remain
   manet: he/she/it remains
   manent: they remain

---

3 Latin adjectives are listed with the forms of their masculine, feminine, and neuter endings to indicate that this word can be found in all of these forms.

4 There is a dash in the third principal part that means that there is no perfect active indicative for this verb. This will be further explained in chapter 24.

sedeō, sedēre, sēdī, sessus: sit
  sedet: he/she/it sits
  sedent: they sit
timeō, timēre, timuī,—: fear[5]
  timet: he/she/it fears
  timent: they fear

<u>i/e-verbs</u>
dīcō, dīcere, dīxī, dictus: say
  dicit: he/she/it says
  dicunt: they say
intellegō, intellegere, intellēxī, intellexus: to understand
  intellegit: he/she/it understands
  intellegunt: they understand

Interrogātīva

cujus: whose
num: surely not … (introduces a question expecting a negative answer [e.g., "You don't like fish, do you?"])
-ne: (used at the end of a word at the beginning of a sentence, which usually makes the sentence a question)
quālis: what sort, what kind

Coniunctivum

-que: and (added to the end of another word)

Prōnōmina

quī, quae, quod: who, which
cujus: whose

Interjectio

ecce: behold

---

[5] There is no perfect passive participle for this verb.

Fābula Parva (Latīna Ficta)

Deus vir nōn est. Deus fēmina nōn est. Deus dominus virōrum est et Deus dominus fēminārum est. Deus jūstus est. Vir et fēmina, Adam et Hēvā, nōn ambulant in viā dominī. Deus imperat et nōn audiunt. Mandūcant malum lignī bonī et malī. Ergō, vir nōn est jūstus, neque fēmina est jūsta. Vir et fēmina nōn sunt jūstī.

Dominus est deus misericordiae, et plēnus misericordiae. Auxilium Deī venit in terrā. Deus angelōs mittit. Angelī volant, sed virī fēminaeque ambulant, nōn volant. Angelī prope Maria sunt. Maria timet. Angelī dīcunt: "Maria tū eris cum puerō." Maria dīcit: "ancilla deī sum." Beāta Maria est. Maria in viā dominī ambulat, sed nōn Hēva ambulat in viā dominī. Magna est misericordia dominī.

malum: fruit
mittit: sends
in: in (translate the noun that follows with just the gloss)
cum: with
tu eris: you will be
sum: I am
Heva: Eve

1. Estne Deus vir?
2. Quālis est Deus?
3. Quis est Deus?
4. Num vīrī feminaeque volant?
5. Cujus ancilla est Maria?

Sententiae Interpretandae

1. Saūl chrīstus Dominī est. (1 Sm 24:7)
2. Iūstae et vērae sunt viae tuae. (Rv 15:3)
3. Tuī sunt caelī, et tua est terra. (Ps 88:12)

tuus, tua, tuum: yours

4. Multae sunt īnsidiae dolōsī. (Eccl 11:31)

insidia, -ae: traps
dolosus, -i: the crafty one

5. Beāta gēns cuius Dominus est Deus eius. (Ps 32:12)

gens, gentis: the people, nation
eius: its
is can be implied

6. Et dicit quī sedet in thronō. (Venerable Bede, *Sententiae*)

in: in
thronus, thronī: throne

7. Est vērus deus, et vīta aeterna. (1 Jn 5:20)
8. Beātus vir quī spērat. (Venerable Bede, *Sententiae*)

sperat: hopes

9. Misericordia Dominī plēna est terrā. (Venerable Bede, *Sententiae*)
10. Intelligit quod audit. (Anselm, *Proslogion*)
11. Magnum est poenitentiae auxilium, magnum sōlācium. (Lactantius, *Epitomē Īnstitūtiōnum Dīvīnārum*)

solacium, -i: comfort
poenitentia, -ae: penitence

12. Filius tuus vivit. (Jn 4:53)

vivit: lives
tuus: your

13. Ecce ancilla Domini. (Lk 1:38)

Sententiae Fictae

(further vocabulary and grammar review with author-created sentences):

1. Vīa vera plēna misericordiae est. Beati qui Christum timent.
2. Multi quī sunt beātī vincunt, laudant, et gaudent.
3. Servus cujus dominus est Christus nōn timet, sed vincit.
4. Ancillae jūstae quārum domina est Maria intelligunt.
5. Virī justi fēminaeque justae qui ambulant Christum laudant.
6. Servus et ancilla quorum dominus bonus est dominum laudant.
7. Servus et ancilla dominum timent. Dominus nōn jūstus est.
8. Cujus auxilium beātum et aeternum est? Auxilium Christī beatum et aeternum est.
9. Quī sedent? Servī dominōrum sedent.
10. Cujus vīta bona et aeterna est? Vīta ancillārum Deī est beāta.

CHAPTER 3

§ 9. Prepositions: The Ablative and Accusative

A preposition (*praepositiō*) is a word that begins a group of words that indicate direction, time, and relationships between words: "in the house," "from the field," "to the water." Prepositions come with a noun that follows to make the preposition phrase. This is true in English, as well as Latin. Prepositions, and the phrase that follows, cannot stand alone and must be connected to a verb for a complete sentence. We will explain this further when we get to other uses of nouns, but it is important to remember that meaning is created in groups of words and their relationship to each other.

The good news in Latin is that prepositions do not have special endings like verbs or nouns. *In, ex, ad,* and those words never change form. We have learned that nouns have special endings depending on how they are used. If they are the subject, they have the *-us, -a, -um* endings like the nouns *discipulus, ancilla,* and *canticum*. If these words are singular and come after a preposition like *in* or *de*, they have the ending, *discipul-o, ancill-a,* and *cantic-o* in the singular and *discipul-is, ancill-is,* and *cantic-is* in the plural. These endings are simply the form the noun has to take after a preposition. This is called the ablative (*ablativus*). The preposition phrase is simply translated by giving the meaning of the preposition plus the meaning of the noun. So, *in terrā*, means "on the earth" or "in the earth."

We will still learn one other significant use of the ablative in chapter 6. For now, the ablative is one of the two endings we find when nouns come after prepositions. There is no additional English word or change required when a noun is in the ablative case, because it comes after a preposition. We simply translate the preposition and then the noun.

> *Terra bona est.* The earth is good.
> *Vir in terrā est.* The man is on the earth.

Notice that in both of these sentences we do not add a preposition or change the word order to show the importance of the ablative ending. We just translate the word as "earth." Also, this particular preposition can mean, "in," or "on" with the ablative of the noun that follows it. We will learn that the ablative can require us to add another one English in chapter 6, but for now it is just necessary to recognize that the ending changes after a preposition. All we need to do is translate the preposition and then the noun that follows.

CHAPTER 3

So far, we've learned the following cases (we've learned four of the five main ones):

A-Nouns / 1st Declension (Usually Feminine)

Case	Singular	Example Translation	Plural	Example Translation
Nominative	ancill|a	handmaid (sub.)	ancill|ae	handmaids (sub.)
Genitive	ancill|ae	of the handmaid	ancill|ārum	of the handmaids
Dative	Chapter 5			
Accusative	ancill|am	handmaid (direct object)	ancill|ās	handmaids (direct object)
Ablative	ancill|ā	handmaid (object of preposition)	ancill|īs	handmaids (object of preposition)

O-Nouns / 2nd Declension (Masculine)

Case	Singular	Example Translation	Plural	Example Translation
Nominative	discipul|us	student (sub.)	discipul|ī	students (sub.)
Genitive	discipul|ī	of the student	discipul|ōrum	of the students
Dative	Chapter 5			
Accusative	discipul|um	student (d.o.)	discipul|ōs	students (d.o.)
Ablative	discipul|ō	studen (o.p.)	discipul|īs	students (o.p.)

O-Nouns / 2nd Declension (Neuter)

Case	Singular	Example Translation	Plural	Example Translation
Nominative	don|um	gift (sub.)	don|a	gift (sub.)
Genitive	don|ī	of the gift	don|ōrum	of the gifts
Dative	Chapter 5			
Accusative	don|um	gift (d.o.)	don|a	gifts (d.o.)
Ablative	don|ō	the gift (o.p.)	don|īs	the gifts (o.p.)

Above we looked at prepositions with the ablative. In those examples, the nouns that followed the prepositions were in the ablative case (*ablativus*). In this section, we will see prepositions in the accusative case (*accusativus*). So, while it is true that often when we encounter a noun with an accusative ending it will be the direct object, if the noun comes after a preposition and it has the accusative case, it will not be the direct object. The difficulty here for English speakers is that we do not have specific case endings for most of our nouns when they follow prepositions. So we can say "he walks into the store," or "she lives in the house." The words *store* and *house* do not change their endings based on the fact that they follow pronouns.

Discipuli ambulant ad magistrum. The students walk to the teacher.
Turba ambulat prope aquam. The crowd walks near the water.

So there are no new forms to learn for prepositions with the accusatives. We have already learned about the accusative in chapter 1. We have now seen two uses of the accusative: one as the direct object and one as the object of certain prepositions.

§ 10. Demonstrative Pronouns: An Introduction

Simply stated, pronouns are words that stand in place of a noun. We could say, "Peter walks into the room, and he picks up a book and he reads it." The word *he* stands in place of *Peter*, and the word *it* stands in the place of *book*. The definition is not as hard as the many forms these pronouns take in Latin. Just like nouns, pronouns have a subject form, a direct object form, and a possessive form; they can be singular or plural; they can be masculine, feminine, or neuter. That is, they have gender, number, and case. Also, as we stated above, Latin does not have articles *a* or *the*. It does have lots of different pronouns that are used at various points as synonyms or in other specific ways. The English use of pronouns actually comes closest to the way Latin nouns work in general. English has forms of nominative (subject), genitive (possessive), and accusative (direct object). *He, his, him. She, her, her. They, their, them.*

For example,

Is eam laudat. He praises her.
Ea eum laudat. She praises him.
Id eos laudat. It praises them (m.).
Dōnum eius est aqua. The gift of him (or her or it) is water [this translation follows the word order of Latin].

Remember, the endings convey how the pronoun is working in the sentence. They can be the subject, the direct object, and possessive of another noun. As such, they have their own endings much like the nouns and adjectives we have been learning already. Below is a chart of the basic pronouns: *is, ea, id*, which typically means "he," "she," or "it."

Since some Latin nouns have gender that seems unnatural to an English speaker, it can make translating pronouns for objects a bit more challenging.

Terra bona est. Vir sedet in ea. The earth is good, the man sits on it.

In the second sentence, *ea* "literally" means "she." The man sits on "her." If we translated the preposition as "her," though, it would be confusing because in English we don't normally assign gender to the earth. It makes more sense to translate *ea* as "it." So, in the chart below, remember that if the pronoun is referring to an object that is masculine or feminine, we will usually translate that word into English as if it were neuter ("it") rather than giving it the literal gender in Latin.

Cases	M. S.	Example Translation	F. S.	Example Translation	N. S.	Example Translation
Nom	*i|s*	he	*e|a*	she	*i|d*	it (subject)
Gen	*e|ius*	his	*e|ius*	her	*e|ius*	its
Dat	Chapter 5					
Acc	*e|um*	him	*e|am*	her	*i|d*	it (d.o.)
Abl	*e|ō*	him (o.p.)	*e|ā*	her (o.p.)	*e|ō*	it (o.p.)

Cases	M. P.	Example Translation	F. P.	Example Translation	N. P.	Example Translation
Nom	*e|ī (iī)*	they	*e|ae*	they	*e|a*	these
Gen	*e|ōrum*	theirs	*e|ārum*	theirs	*e|ōrum*	of these
Dat	Chapter 5					
Acc	*e|ōs*	them	*e|ās*	them	*e|a*	these (d.o.)
Abl	*e|īs (iīs)*	them (o.p.)	*e|īs (iīs)*	them (o.p.)	*e|īs (iīs)*	them (o.p.)

§ 11. Relative Pronouns: Direct Objects and Accusative and Interrogative Pronouns

Because this can cause confusion later on, it is worth spending some time on how relative pronouns are used as direct objects. This is particularly tricky because in English, we often get the relative pronoun as a direct object wrong. It will also make reading and translating complex Latin sentences difficult if we don't see how the connecting words are relating clauses together. This is a key element of one's ability to read and understand Latin prose.

Take the sentence, "My brother, whom I beat in golf, lives down the street." It is easy in contemporary English to misuse the word *whom*, but it is technically a direct object, relative pronoun. The word *whom* allows the speaker to give more information about the noun *brother* in a shorter clause that is connected to the main clause. The main clause is, "my brother lives down the street." We are adding, "whom I beat in golf." This form makes the relative pronoun technically the direct object of the verb *beat*. In typical Latin prose, authors like to make long interconnected sentences that have these kinds of relative clauses. English also uses the word *whom* as the object of a preposition. We will deal more with that later.

Some examples in Latin are as follows:

Discipulus, quem discipula videt, ambulat. The student (m.), whom the student (f.) sees, walks.
Discipula, quam Dominus amat, canit. The student (f.), whom the Lord loves, sings.
Here are some in the plural:
Discipulae, quās Dominus amat, canunt. The students (f.), whom the Lord loves, sing.

(Notice the verbs: one is singular, *amat*, the other is plural, *canunt*. Who is the subject of each?)

Dōna, quae Dominus dōnat, magna sunt. The gifts, which the Lord gives, are big.

NB. The question word *quis* was introduced in chapter 1 and *cuius* in chapter 2. You might notice that they are similar to the chart below. Technically, *quis* is what we call an interrogative pronoun. It is a pronoun that introduces a question, *quis ambulat?*: "who walks?" The interrogative pronouns that introduce questions are exactly the same as the relative pronouns, except in the nominative singular. So we have *quis* instead of *qui* or *quae* and *quid* instead of *quod*. All the rest are the same whether they relate a noun to another sentence or ask a question about a noun in a sentence.

Cases	M. S.	Example Translation	F. S.	Example Translation	N. S.	Example Translation
Nom	qu|ī / qu|is	who	qu|ae / qu|is	who	qu|od / qu|id	which / what
Gen	cu|ius	whose	cu|ius	whose	cu|ius	of which
Dat	Chapter 5					
Acc	qu|em	whom	qu|ām	whom	qu|od / qu|id	which (d.o.)
Abl	qu|ō	whom (o.p.)	qu|ā	whom (o.p.)	qu|ō	which (o.p.)

Cases	M. P.	Example Translation	F. P.	Example Translation	N. P.	Example Translation
Nom	qu|ī	who	qu|ae	who	qu|ae	what / which
Gen	qu|ōrum	whose	qu|ārum	whose	qu|ōrum	of which
Dat	Chapter 5					
Acc	qu|ōs	whom	qu|ās	whom	qu|ae	what / which (d.o.)
Abl	qu|ibus	whom (o.p.)	qu|ibus	whom (o.p.)	qu|ibus	which (o.p.)

§ 12. Conjunctions: *quia, quod,* and *quoniam*

It is easy to overlook words like *because* or *since* because they seem small and insignificant, but that is a grave mistake. Conjunctions control the flow of thought and can help the reader understand if the author is connecting ideas, contrasting ideas, or comparing ideas. A few will be introduced every chapter. Latin has many of them, and often they look alike. In some ways, conjunctions are more important to memorize than a bunch of nouns and verbs. If you know the flow of the author's thoughts, you will better understand what you are reading.

> *Discipulus fessus est **quia** currit.* The student is tired **because** he runs.
> *Discipula laeta est **quoniam** Deus eam amat.* The student is happy **since** God loves her.

How one chooses to translate these conjunctions does indeed depend on context, as it will with many of the vocabulary words. The word *et* is a great example. Your reflex translation should be "and." That said, *et* can be used to mean "also," "even," "but," etc. One major epochal difference between so-called Ecclesiastical Latin and Classical Latin is the influence of the Vetus Latina and the Vulgate. These Latin translations of the Greek Septuagint and

New Testament became the primary cultural referent for the language of Latin during the first few centuries after Christ. So the word *et* came to be used like the Greek *kai*. We will discuss the phenomenon of the influence of Greek on Latin throughout this book.

Both of these words can also be used to indicate direct speech in Ecclesiastical Latin. This is a direct quotation. In English, we use quotation marks, but Latin, following Greek, often uses *quia* or *quoniam* before whatever are the exact words of a person. When they are used for direct quotation in the Vulgate, they are capitalized. When they are not capitalized, the student must determine how these conjunctions are being used. Context is critical here.

Sententiae Summāriae

> Ancillae bonae Deum vērum quī in caelō est laudant.
> Magister discipulōs bonōs laudat quia audiunt.
> Beātī discipulī Deum vērum quī est in caelō laudant quoniam Deus justus est.
> Ancillae quās Deus audit laudant.
> Discipulī quōs magister audit laudant.

Translations

> The good maidservants praise the true God who is in heaven.
> The teacher praises the good students because they listen.
> The blessed disciples praise the true God who is in heaven since he is just.
> The maidservants whom God hears praise.
> The students whom the teacher hears praise.

Cavēte et Mementōte

Latin word order is not like English word order. Verbs usually go at the end of the sentence. Read the whole sentence first to find the verb and then put the other nouns in place.

Vocābula Memoranda

Nōmina

> *aquila, aquilae* (f.): eagle
> *canticum, cantici* (n.): hymn
> *filia, filiae* (f.): daughter
> *filius, filiī* (m.): son
> *flūvius, flūviī* (m.): river
> *hymnus, hymni* (m.): hymn
> *liber, libri* (m.): book
> *stella, stellae* (f.): star

CHAPTER 3

Verba

ā-verb
  cantō, cantāre, cantāvī, cantātus: sing
  ōrō, ōrāre, ōrāvī, ōrātus: pray
    ōrat: he/she/it prays
    ōrant: they pray

  necō, necāre, necavī, necatus: kill
    nēcat: he/she/it kills
    nēcant: they kill

ē-verbs
  habeō, habēre, habuī, habitus: have
    habēt: he/she/it has
    habent: they have

  taceō, tacēre, tacuī, tacitus: be quiet
    tacēt: he/she/it is quiet
    tacent: they are quiet

i/e-verbs
  āscendō [ad + scando], ascendere, ascendī, ascēnsus: ascend
    ascendit: he/she/it ascends
    ascendunt: they ascend

  dīligō, dīligere, dīlēxī, dīlēctus: cherish, love
    dīligit: he/she/it cherishes, loves
    dīligun: they cherish love

io-verbs
  capiō, capere, cēpī, captus: take, seize
    capit: he/she/it takes, seizes
    capiunt: they take, seize

i-verb
  cūstōdiō, cūstōdīre, cūstōdīvī, cūstōdītus: keep
    cūstōdit: he/she/it keeps
    cūstōdiunt: they keep

  dormio, dormire, dormivi, dormitus: sleep
    dormit: he/she/it sleeps
    dormiunt: they sleep

Conjūnctīva

quoniam: since (or to begin a quotation)
quia: because (or to a begin a quotation)
etiam: also
enim: for

Adverbium

subitō: suddenly

Praepositiōnēs

prope (+acc): near
ad (+acc): to, towards; for the purpose of
de (+abl): from
in (+abl): in
in (+acc): into
ex (+abl): out of

Prōnōmina

quem, quam, quod: whom, which

Interrogātīva

quandō: when
quem: whom (direct object)
cūr: why?

Fābula Parva (Latīna Ficta)

Caīnus et Abēl, Adamī Fīliī.

Adamus est vir prīmus et Hēva est fēmina prīma. Hēva duōs filiōs habet. Iī filiōs multōs habent. Prīmus filius est Caīnus, quī est agricola, et secundus filius est Abēl, quī est pāstor. Agricola est vir quī frūctum terrae habet. Pāstor est vir quī nōn frūctum terrae, sed bēstiās habet. Caīnus et Abel dōna portant ad Deum. Deus dōnum Abēlī, quod est agnus, dīligit, sed Deus dōnum Caīnī, quod est frūctum terrae, nōn dīligit. Caīnus īrātus est. Caīnus et Abel ambulant. Caīnus Abēlum necat. Deus Caīnum non laudat quia Abēlum nōn dīligit et necat. Nunc Caīnus sōlus in terrā ambulat.

pastor: shepherd
fructum: fruit
bēstia, bēstiae: beast, animal

1. Quis est Adamus? Quis est Hēva?
2. Quid habent Adamus et Hēva?
3. Cūr Deus Caīnum pūnit?
4. Quid est dōnum Caīnī? Abēlī?

Ancilla Deī, quae est Ebba, ōrat. Sānctus Cuthbertus, quī est vir Deī, ambulat ad monastērium ancillae. Ancilla, quae est domina monastēriī, Cuthbertum videt. Monastērium situm est prope fluviīum. Dum stēlla et lūna lūcent in caelō, Cuthbertus ambulat in fluviō. Quandō Ebba dormit, monachus monastēriī nōn dormit. Monachus Cuthbertum videt, neque Cuthbertus eum, quī nōn dormit, videt. Quia stēlla et lūna nōn lūcent in caelō, Cuthbertus ascendit ex fluviō. Duo lutrae, quae non dormiunt, digitōs Cutherbertī extergunt. Cuthbertus latraēās dīligit et latraeae eum dīligunt. Cuthbertus ōrat et latraeās benedīcit. Monachus videt et timet. Deinde, monachum Cuthbertus videt. Monachus nōn dīcit sed tacet. Et quia Cuthbertus misericordiam habet, eum benedīcit.

Cf. *Vita Cuthberti* Capitulum X.
quando: when (at the time when)
situm: situated
lutra, lutrae (f.): otter
luna, lunae (f.): moon
lucet: shine
extergunt: dry
digitus, digiti (m.): toe

1. Quis est Sānctus Cuthbertus?
2. Quandō Cuthbertus venit in fluviō?
3. Quem monachus videt in fluviō?
4. Cūr Cuthbertus latraēās benedīcit?
5. Num Cuthbertus eum videt?

Sententiae Interpretandae

1. Beātus vir quī timet Dominum. (Ps 111:1)
2. Magnificat anima mea Dominum. (Lk 1:46)
3. Vīvit in me Christus. (Gal 2:20)

vivit: lives

4. Beātī quī timent Dominum, quī ambulant in viīs eius. (Ps 127:1)
5. Et nōn dīligunt mundum, cuius dominus est diabolus. (Augustine, *De Agōne Chrīstī*)

diabolus: the Devil

6. Beāta gēns cuius est Dominus Deus eius. (Ps 32:12)

gens: people

7. Beātī quī audiunt verbum Deī et custōdiunt. (Lk 11:28)
8. Dīligit Sanctum Cyrillum Dominus, et ōrnat eum quem stōlam glōriae induit eum. (*Breviārium Rōmānum*)

ornat: decorate
Cyrillum: Cyril
induit: puts on
stolam: stole

9. Dīlēctiō Deus est: quī eam habet vīdit Deum. (Augustine, *In Epistolam Ioannis*)

dilectio: love

10. Quī timent Dominum, custōdiunt mandāta. (Eccl 2:21)

mandatum, mandati (n.): commandment

11. Qui credit in Filium, habet vitam aeternam. (Jn 6:47)

credit: believes

12. Quī habet Fīlium, habet vītam: quī nōn habet Fīlium, vītam nōn habet. (1 Jn 5:12)
13. In mundō sunt. De mundō nōn sunt. (Jn 17:16)
14. Quis est, quī vincit mundum, nisi quī credit quoniam Jesus est Fīlius Deī? (1 Jn 5:5)

nisi: except
credit: believes

15. Et nēmō ascendit in caelum, nisi quī descendit de caelō, Fīlius hominis, quī est in caelō. (Jn 3:13)

nemo: no one
nisi: except
hominis: of man

Sententiae Fictae

1. Aquila ascendit in caelō et volat. Aquilae ascendunt in caelo et volant.
2. Fluviī māgnī quoque multam aquam habent.
3. Fīliī filiaeque quī ōrant etiam tacent.
4. Fīlia quae est jūsta Deum audit.
5. Aquila quam Cūthbertus videt volat ad fluvium.
6. Servī vērī deum vērum laudant et cantica multa cantant.
7. Deus cantica servōrum beātōrum et cantica ancillārum beātārum audit in ecclēsiā.
8. Fīliī Deī et filiae Deī hymnōs cantant. Deus enim misericordiam habet.
9. Fīliī et filiae Deum dīligunt, quia Deus filiōs filiāsque dīligit.
10. Fīliī Dominum laudant, et filiae sedent, et stēllae sunt in caelō.

CHAPTER 4

◦⌒◦

§ 13. Nouns: Vocative

This chapter will introduce some elements of direct speech in the Latin language. In many traditional grammars, these are covered near the middle or end of the book. The downside to such an approach is that direct commands come at the early stages of typical language development. One of the first things a child learns is how to respond to a command, and then the child learns to repeat the command. Additionally, the vocative is also fairly common in the prayers of the church. Learning direct speech now aids students in their ability to understand many prayers.

We will begin with how one directly addresses another person in Latin. This is called the "vocative" (*vocativus*). We do not have a vocative in English, except the antiquated phrase "O Lord" or "O Father." So, when it comes to translating the vocative, you can indicate that a noun is in the vocative by adding an *O* before the noun, though in many translations this phrase is no longer used. The good news for Latin is that the vocative case only changes forms for masculine words that end in *-us*. The ending changes to an *-e*, or if the stem has an *-i* before the ending, it changes to a long *-i*. Some words do not change in the vocative, like *Deus* and *agnus*. They retain the same forms as the nominative.

Discipulus becomes *discipule*; *filius* becomes *fili*.
Ancilla does not have a distinct ending for the vocative, like all a-nouns.
Donum does not have a distinct ending for the vocative, like all o-nouns in the neuter.

NB. The word for Jesus, *Jesus*, becomes *Jesu* in the vocative. It is close to the other masculine nouns we have been studying, but it has its own peculiar declension: nominative—*Jesus*; genitive—*Jesu*; dative—*Jesu*; accusative—*Jesum*; ablative—*Jesu*.

§ 14. Verbs: Indicative and Imperative Mood

To this point, we have been using only the *he, she, it* form of the verb or the *they/those* forms. This is what we call in grammatical terms "third person singular" and "third person plural" (i.e., *filius ambulat* and *ancillae ambulant*). Part of learning about the Latin verb is learning the possible *moods* or *modes* in which they can be found. The term *mood* or *mode* might seem unusual because it covers a range of possible changes in the verb.[1] Right now we will contrast two moods that will be primarily used for the next several chapters. In the example above, *filius ambulat*, the verb is found in the "indicative" (*indicativus*) mood. All this means is that the verb is "indicating" something to be the case.[2] The subject does the verb (in the active voice).[3]

What will be new for this chapter is what is called the "imperative" (*imperativus*) mood. In this mood, the verb is not indicating a state of affairs, but it is spoken to tell another person to do something.

ambulā: "you (singular) walk!"
ambulāte: "you all walk!"

In these two examples the verbs do not say what the subject does, in fact, do, but what the speaker of the words wants the subject to do. If the speaker wants a specific person to do something, they might say, *discipule, sta!*: "O student (m.), stand!" This sentence shows how the vocative is used in conjunction with the imperative. If the speaker is speaking to a female person, or a group of people, the noun does not change. *Ancillae, sedēte!*: "O maidservants (f.), sit!"

To form the imperative, you either take the stem of the verb and add the theme vowel for the singular or add the pattern vowel plus *-te* for the plural. (Recall that the stem is just the infinitive form, *sedēre*, minus the pattern vowel and the *-re*; that is, *sed-* is the stem of *sedeo*.)

ambulā, ambulāte
monē, monēte
scrībe, scrībite
audī, audīte

It is important to recall here that Latin verbs generally fall into four patterns that are based around the vowels that are unique to each pattern (or conjugation). Above we see *ambulā*—a-pattern; *monē*—e-pattern; *scrībe*—short i/e-vowel; and *audī*—i-pattern.[4] One should also recognize the change from *-e* to *-i-* in *scrībite*. This short i/e-verb changes vowels when none of the others do.

---

[1] Latin verbs come in many different moods or modes: indicative, imperative, and subjunctive. There are also other nonfinite forms like infinitive, gerundive, gerund, and supine.

[2] Thanks to Andrew Chronister for a better way of explaining this.

[3] We will look at the passive voice in chapter 6.

[4] Traditionally these are called "first, second, third, and fourth" conjugations. I am using their vowel pattern to highlight their unique character that makes them these respective conjugations. It is also worth noting that there are several other classes of verb that do not fit into this pattern, like *est* (is); *vult* (wants); and io-verbs, which fall in between third and fourth conjugation, like *facit* (does/makes).

Some i/e-verbs have irregular imperatives with no vowels that are fairly common: *duc* (lead), *fac* (do), and *dic* (say). In the plural, they have an *-i-* before the *-te*, *ducite, facite, dicite*.

§ 15. Special Uses of Interrogative and Relative Pronouns

As far as relative pronouns are concerned, it is worth noting, as we will see in the example sentences, that sometimes the relative pronoun can introduce a sentence. English prefers a normal *he, she, it,* to start a sentence, but sometimes Latin will begin with *qui* and it can be easiest to translate it as "he." We can call this a *connecting relative*.[5]

We also find that Latin will repeat the relative, and it might be necessary to add some additional English words to make sense of what is happening. We could translate the *qui* as "he who," "the one who," or "whoever."

Qui dicit se in luce esse, et fratrem suum odit, in tenebris est usque adhuc (1 Jn 2:9).
The one who says that he is in the light, but hates his brother, is still in darkness.

Quis est mendax, nisi is qui negat quoniam Jesus est Christus? (1 Jn 2:22)
Who is the liar, except the one who denies that Jesus is the Christ?

Also notice that in the first sentence we have a relative *qui* that begins the sentence because it is not a question. In the second sentence, we have an interrogative *quis* because it is a question.

Cases	M. S.	Example Translation	F. S.	Example Translation	N. S.	Example Translation
Nom	qu|ī / qu|is	who	qu|ae / qu|is	who	qu|od / qu|id	what
Gen	cu|ius	whose	cu|ius	whose	cu|ius	of which
Dat	Chapter 5					
Acc	qu|em	whom	qu|ām	whom	qu|od / qu|id	what (d.o.)
Abl	qu|ō	whom (o.p.)	qu|ā	whom (o.p.)	qu|ō	which (o.p.)

---

5 Thanks to Dr. Chronister for this note.

Cases	M. P.	Example Translation	F. P.	Example Translation	N. P.	Example Translation
Nom	qu|ī	who	qu|ae	who	qu|ae	what
Gen	qu|ōrum	whose	qu|ārum	whose	qu|ōrum	of which
Dat	Chapter 5					
Acc	qu|ōs	whom	qu|ās	whom	qu|ae	what (d.o.)
Abl	qu|ibus	whom (o.p.)	qu|ibus	whom (o.p.)	qu|ibus	which (o.p.)

Notice the difference between the relative pronoun learned in chapter 2 and the interrogative pronoun here. The only significant difference in spelling comes in the nominative singular where you have *quis* vs. *qui*, *quis* vs. *quae*, and *quid* vs. *quod*. The difference in meaning is that these are used when asking a question. These are not used when relating a pronoun to another noun.

Quis ambulat? Vir quī ambulat Jēsus est. Who walks? The man who walks is Jesus.
Quis ambulat? Fēmina quae ambulat Māria est. Who walks? The woman who walks is Mary.
Quid discipulus videt? Dōnum quod discipulus videt pōculum est. What does the student see? The gift which the student sees is a cup.

Sententiae Summāriae

Ancilla lauda!
Ancillae laudāte!
Magister, monē!
Magistrī, monēte!
Domine, dūc!
Dominī, dūcite!
Ō discipule audī!
Ō discipulī audīte!
Quis est Deus?
Quī sunt magistrī?

Translations

Maidservant, praise!
Maidservants, praise!
Teacher, teach!
Teachers, teach!
Lord, lead!

Lords, lead!
O student, listen!
O students, listen!
Who is God?
Who are the teachers?

Cavēte et Mementōte

The *-e* at the end of a noun is the vocative, but it is only used for words that end in *-us*.

Vocābula Memoranda

Nōmina

āger, agrī (m.): field
agricola, agricolae (m.): farmer
anima, animae (f.): soul
discipulus, discipulī (m.): student, disciple
gratia, gratiae (f.): grace
Jēsus, Jēsū (genitive), *Jēsū* (dative), *Jēsum* (accusative), *Jēsū* (ablative): Jesus
turba, turbae (f.): crowd
verbum, verbī (n.): word, verb

Verba[6]

ā-verbs
clāmō, clāmāre, clāmāvī, clāmātus: shout
lavō, lavāre, lavāvī, lāvātus: clean
sānctificō [sanctus + facere], sānctificāre, sānctificāvī, sānctificātus: make holy
sēminō, sēmināre, sēmināvī, sēminātus: sow

ē-verbs
doceō, docēre, docuī, doctus: teach
moneō, monēre monuī monitus: warn, teach

i/e-verbs
cadō, cadere, cecidī, cāsus: fall
dūco, dūcere, dūxisse, ductus: lead
dīmittō [dī + mittō], dīmittere, dīmīsī, dīmissus: send away, forgive
mittō, mittere, mīsī, missus: send

-io-verbs
suscipiō [sub + capio], suscipere, suscēpī, susceptus: undertake, take on

---

[6] As our familiarity with verbs has grown, I will only be offering the four principal parts from this point forward.

Adjectīva

bonus, -a, -um: good
catholicus, -a, -um: universal
vīvus, -a, -um: alive, living

Adverbia

nunc: now
tantum: only

Interrogātivum

quomodō: how?

Coniunctivum

vērō: but, however

Fābula Parva (Latīna Ficta)

Jesus discipulōs docet in parabolīs multa et dīcit: "Audīte: ecce exit semināns quī seminat. Et dum seminat, id cadit circa viam et volatilia veniunt et id mandūcant. Id vērō cadit super terram petrōsam, ubi nōn habet terram multam."

Agricola ex agrīs venit et verbum Jēsū audit. Agricola Jēsum interpellat.

Agricola dīcit: "Salvē, Jēsū!"
Jēsus: "Salvē, Agricola."

Agricola: "Quis est semināns quī seminat circa viam? Nōn est bonus agricola."

Nunc Jēsus nōn tantum turbam docet, sed agricolam quoque.

Jēsus: "Quis est agricola quī magistrum interpellat? Nōn est bonus agricola. Sed, pater meus agricola est. Agricola mittit id in terram et plantat arbūsta. Sīc, Deus grātiam Chrīstī dōnat et animae virōrum fēminārumque accipiunt. Virī fēmināeque agricultūra Deī sunt."

Cf. Mark 4, Matthew 21, John 15.

id: that thing

semināns: one who sows
volatilium, volatilia (n.): flying thing
petrosus, petrosa, petrosum: rocky
dum: while
interpellāre: to interrupt
pater, patris (m.): father
arbūstum, arbūstī: orchard
agricultūra, agricultūre (f.): agriculture
sīc: in the same way

1. Quōmodō Jēsus docet?
2. Quōs Jēsus docet?
3. Quid est agricultūra agricolae?
4. Quae sunt agricultūra Deī?

Sententiae Interpretandae

1. Quī seminat, verbum seminat. (Mk. 4:14)
2. Haec et mea fidēs est, quandō haec est catholica fidēs. (Augustine, *De Trinitate*)

   meus, mea, meum: my
   fides, fidei: faith (f.)

3. Anima Chrīstī, sanctifica mē. O bone Iēsū, exaudi mē. (*Anima Christi*)

   ex-audire: to hear

4. Domine, doce nōs ōrāre, sīcut et Iōannēs docet discipulōs eius. (Lk 11.1)
5. Dīmitte eam, quia clāmat post nōs. (Mt 15:23)

   post nos: after us

6. Cuius fīlius est? (1 Chr 3:23)
7. Dā quod jubēs et jube quod vīs. (Augustine, *Confessions*)

   jubes: you command
   vis: you wish

8. Dilige, et quod vīs fac. (Augustine, *Iōhannīs Epistulam ad Parthōs*)

   vis: you wish

9. Sancta Maria, ōra prō nōbīs. Sancte Petre, ōra prō nōbīs. Omnēs sanctī Discipulī Dominī, ōrate prō nōbīs. Chrīste, audi nōs. Chrīste, exaudi nōs. (*Litaniae Sanctorum*)

   nos, nobis: us

10. Quis est David? et Quis est fīlius Isai? (1 Sm 25:10)
11. Fīlius Deī virum suscipit. Īs suscipit hūmānam creātūram. (Augustine, *De Agōne Chrīstī*)

12. Domine, Jēsū Chrīste, Fīlī Deī vīvī, miserēre meī. (*Oratio Jesu*)

    miserere mei: have mercy on me

13. Tolle grabātum tuum et ambulā! (Jn 5:8)

    grabatum: mat

14. Alius quī sēminat, alius est quī mētit. (Jn 4:37)

    alius: another, one
    metit: reaps

15. Hic est antichristus, quī negat Patrem, et Fīlium. (1 Jn 2:22)

    negat: denies
    Patrem: father

16. Quī facit peccātum, ex diabolō est: quoniam ab initiō diabolus peccat.

    peccatum, peccati (n.): sin (noun)
    initium, initii (n.): beginning
    peccat: sins (verb)

17. Ave Maria grātiā plēna Dominus tecum. Benedicta tū in mulieribus et benedictus frūctus ventrīs tuī Jēsus. Sancta Maria, Mater Deī, ōra prō nōbīs peccātōribus, nunc, et in hōrā mortis nostrae. (Ave Maria)

    fructus: fruit
    mulieribus: women
    ventris: womb
    peccatoribus: sinners
    hora: hour
    mortis: of death
    nostrae: our

Sententiae Fictae

1. O Chrīste, sanctifica mē.
2. Bonī servī, clāmate verba bona.
3. Agricola seminat in agrīs bonīs.
4. Chrīstus Dominus discipulōs docet. Discipulī verō nōn docent.
5. Grātia Deī quae est misericordia de caelō cadit.
6. Bonae ancillae, Deum vīvum laudāte!
7. Deus vīvē, audī! Angelī, audīte!
8. Grātia Deī cadit dē caelō.
9. Turba agricolārum in terrā sēminant.
10. Bonus dominus servōs bonōs dūcit.

CHAPTER 5

§ 16. Nouns: Dative and Indirect Objects

We have covered several different ways nouns function in Latin and the endings that suggest how the word works in the sentence. We discussed the nominative case, which typically functions as the subject; the accusative case, which indicates the noun is the direct object or the object of a preposition;[1] and the genitive case, which is used to show that two nouns are in relation to one another. When we are translating nouns in the nominative, there is no "word" in English that indicates that a noun is the subject; rather it is indicated by where it is placed in the sentence (*discipulus ambulat* becomes "the student walks"). Usually, it is placed before the verb in English. It is also true of accusatives that nouns in this case do not have a specific English preposition that can be attached to them, but rather they must be placed after the verb (*discipula magistrum videt* becomes "the student sees the teacher"). Latin words with a genitive ending can be expressed usually with the word *of* (*donum discipulī* becomes "the gift of the student").

In this section, we will learn the use of the dative case (*dativus*), which most frequently is used as the indirect object of a sentence. As such, it can usually be indicated in English by using the preposition *to*. For example, "the woman gives the fruit to the man." The woman is the subject. The fruit is the direct object. The man is the indirect object, as indicated by the preposition *to*. We could say that the man indirectly receives the action of the verb insofar as he receives the fruit. Latin uses the ending of the noun to show that a noun is the indirect object.

---

[1] We will learn other uses of the accusative that are not always the direct object, but that is what we want to focus on for the moment. Allen and Greenough give nine uses of the dative: *New Latin Grammar*, § 224–39.

In the singular,

Fēmina malum virō dat. The woman gives the apple to the man.
Vir fēminae malum dat. The man gives the apple to the woman.
Fluvius aquam oppidō dat. The river gives water to the town.

In the plural,

Fēmina virīs mala dat. The woman gives apples to the men.
Vir fēminīs mala dat. The man gives apples to the women.
Rīvus aquam oppidīs dat. The river gives water to the towns.

There are also verbs that take a dative as something like their direct object. The verb *credo* can either have a preposition after it, *credit in me* (he believes in me), or a dative, *credit mihi* (he believes me).

We have covered five of the possible six endings for Latin nouns to this point. The last one is called the ablative, which will be learned in the next chapter.

A-Nouns / 1st Declension (Usually Feminine)

Case	Singular	Example Translation	Plural	Example Translation
Nom	*ancill\a*	handmaid (sub.)	*ancill\ae*	handmaids (sub.)
Gen	*ancill\ae*	of the handmaid	*ancill\ārum*	of the handmaids
Dat	*ancill\ae*	to the handmaid	*ancill\īs*	to the handmaids
Acc	*ancill\am*	handmaid (d.o.)	*ancill\ās*	handmaids (d.o.)
Abl	*ancill\ā*	handmaid (o.p.)	*ancill\īs*	handmaids (o.p.)

O-Nouns / 2nd Declension (Masculine)

Case	Singular	Example Translation	Plural	Example Translation
Nom	*discipul\us*	student (sub.)	*discipul\ī*	students (sub.)
Gen	*discipul\ī*	of the student	*discipul\ōrum*	of the students
Dat	*discipul\ō*	to the student	*discipul\īs*	to the students
Acc	*discipul\um*	student (d.o.)	*discipul\ōs*	students (d.o.)
Abl	*discipul\ō*	student (o.p.)	*discipul\īs*	student (o.p.)

CHAPTER 5

O-Nouns / 2nd Declension (Neuter)

Case	Sg.	Translation	Pl.	Translation
Nom	*don|um*	gift (sub.)	*don|a*	gifts (sub.)
Gen	*don|ī*	of the gift	*don|ōrum*	of the gifts
Dat	*don|ō*	to the gift	*don|īs*	to the gifts
Acc	*don|um*	gift (d.o.)	*don|a*	gifts (d.o.)
Abl	*don|ō*	gift (o.p.)	*don|īs*	gift (o.p.)

Unemphatic Pronoun

Cases	M. S.	Example Translation	F. S.	Example Translation	N.S.	Example Translation
Nom	*i|s*	he (sub)	*e|a*	she	*i|d*	it
Gen	*e|ius*	his	*e|ius*	hers	*e|ius*	its
Dat	*e|ī*	to him	*e|ī*	to her	*e|ī*	to it
Acc	*e|um*	him	*e|am*	her	*i|d*	it (d.o.)

Cases	M. P.	Example Translation	F. P.	Example Translation	N. P.	Example Translation
Nom	*e|ī* (iī)	they	*e|ae*	they	*e|a*	these
Gen	*e|ōrum*	theirs	*e|ārum*	theirs	*e|ōrum*	of these
Dat	*e|īs* (iīs)	to them	*e|īs* (iīs)	to them	*e|īs* (iīs)	to these
Acc	*e|ōs*	them	*e|ās*	them	*e|a*	these (d.o.)
Abl	*e|ō*	him (o.p.)	*e|ā*	her (o.p.)	*e|ō*	it (o.p.)

Relative and Interrogative Pronoun

Cases	M. S.	Example Translation	F. S.	Example Translation	N. S.	Example Translation
Nom	*qu|ī / qu|is*	who	*qu|ae / qu|is*	who	*qu|od / qu|id*	what
Gen	*cu|ius*	whose	*cu|ius*	whose	*cu|ius*	of which
Dat	*cu|i*	to whom	*cu|i*	to whom	*cu|i*	to whom
Acc	*qu|em*	whom	*qu|ām*	whom	*qu|od / qu|id*	what (d.o.)
Abl	*qu|ō*	whom (o.p.)	*qu|ā*	whom (o.p.)	*qu|ō*	whom (o.p.)

Cases	M. P.	Example Translation	F. P.	Example Translation	N. P.	Example Translation
Nom	*qu|ī*	who	*qu|ae*	who	*qu|ae*	what
Gen	*qu|ōrum*	whose	*qu|ārum*	whose	*qu|ōrum*	of which
Dat	*qu|ibus*	to whom	*qu|ibus*	to whom	*qu|ibus*	to whom
Acc	*qu|ōs*	whom	*qu|ās*	whom	*qu|ae*	what (d.o.)
Abl	*qu|ibus*	whom (o.p.)	*qu|ibus*	whom (o.p.)	*qu|ibus*	whom (o.p.)

§ 17. Demonstrative Pronouns: *ille, illa, illud* and *hic, haec, hoc*

There are two more pronouns that need to be learned in this chapter. The near demonstrative *hic, haec, hoc* and the far demonstrative *ille, illa, illud*. That said, all it means to be demonstrative is that it demonstrates or points to a particular noun.[2] In English, we use them like this: "this pencil" vs. "that pencil," when you have no other way of identifying the noun. This is going to feel like quite a bit of memorization, which it is to some extent. It is critical, however, to recognize how the endings stay largely the same across the pronouns. After the nominative singular, nearly all the other forms have the same endings: *-ius* for

---

[2] Almost every grammatical term in English comes from its underlying Latin root. The reason for this is how important grammar was to Greek and then Latin speakers. The tradition of learning "grammar" is as old as ancient Greece. This is a particularly Western convention, inherently conservative and perhaps preservative. German has very few Latin cognates in its language, except when it is teaching grammar. As Germany eventually became influenced by Latin culture, it started to use Latin grammatical terms.

genitive, *-i* for dative, an *-m* in the accusative, and *-o, -a, -o* in the ablative. So the good news is that you can discern the cases of nearly all of the pronouns by their endings. We have been working with *is, ea, id* (he, she, it). English has only those pronouns and then the near demonstrative, "this [one]" and the far demonstrative, "that [one]." Latin has about twelve different kinds of pronouns, that is, shorter nouns that stand in the place of other nouns: *is, ille, hīc, iste, ipse, quīdam, īdem, aliquis, alius, meus, quis, qui,* depending on how you count and categorize them. This is extremely frustrating for the beginner, but after the next chapter you will have learned all the endings for these words. It is not required that you learn all of these for this chapter, but eventually all of these words are critical to being able to read well.

This is a good place to remind ourselves that English and Latin are very different languages, which means that to think in one language is different than to think in the other one. So, for a Latin speaker, it was necessary to have access to many different pronouns. One way to explain this feature of Latin is to recall that Latin does not have an article (*a* or *the*). So, in order to communicate something akin to what English does with an article, Latin speakers can use other pronouns. The most familiar example of this might be the title of J. R. R. Tolkien's great work *The Hobbit*. How might a Latin speaker say that? *Hobbitus ille*. It looks like you might want to translate that as "Hobbit, that one." This would not be totally wrong, just overly literal. In the art of translation and interpretation, you have to keep in mind that there are many wrong translations and many correct translations, but there is ***no one single correct translation.***

Near Demonstrative Pronoun

Cases	M. S.	F. S.	N. S.	Example Translation
Nom	*hic*	*haec*	*hoc*	this (one)
Gen	*huius*	*huius*	*huius*	of this (one)
Dat	*huic*	*huic*	*huic*	to this (one)
Acc	*hunc*	*hanc*	*hoc*	this (one) (d.o)
Abl	*hōc*	*hāc*	*hōc*	this (one) (o.p.)

Cases	M. P.	F. P.	N. P.	Example Translation
Nom	*hī*	*hae*	*haec*	these (ones)
Gen	*hōrum*	*hārum*	*hōrum*	of these (ones)
Dat	*hīs*	*hīs*	*hīs*	to these (ones)
Acc	*hōs*	*hās*	*haec*	these (ones)
Abl	*hīs*	*hīs*	*hīs*	those (ones) (o.p.)

Far Demonstrative Pronoun

Cases	M. S.	F. S.	N. S.	Example Translation
Nom	*ill\e*	*ill\a*	*ill\ud*	that (one)
Gen	*ill\ius*	*ill\ius*	*ill\ius*	of that (one)
Dat	*ill\ī*	*ill\ī*	*ill\ī*	to that (one)
Acc	*ill\um*	*ill\am*	*ill\ud*	that (one) (d.o.)
Abl	*ill\ō*	*ill\ā*	*ill\ō*	that (one) (o.p.)

Cases	M. P.	F. P.	N. P.	Example Translation
Nom	*ill\ī*	*ill\ae*	*ill\a*	those (ones)
Gen	*ill\ōrum*	*ill\ārum*	*ill\ōrum*	of those (ones)
Dat	*ill\īs*	*ill\īs*	*ill\īs*	to those (ones)
Acc	*ill\ōs*	*ill\as*	*ill\a*	those (ones) (d.o.)
Abl	*ill\īs*	*ill\īs*	*ill\īs*	those (ones) (o.p.)

These demonstrative pronouns can function alone, like a substantival adjective, or they come paired with another noun.

Ille discipulus et hic discipulus ambulant. That student (m.) and this student (m.) walk.
Ille et hic ambulant. That [one] and this [one] walk.

For these newly introduced demonstrative pronouns, it is ok to think of *hic* as this "this one" and *ille* as "that one" for memorization purposes and to keep them straight in your mind. Most neo-Latin languages (French, Spanish, Italian, etc.) use a shortened form of *ille, illa, illud* as their definite article.

One other important thing to note is that the neuter plural endings of various pronouns are often used to mean "these things" or "those things."

Jēsus haec dīcit. Jesus says these things.

§ 18. Syntax: Dative with *Esse* and without *Esse*

Although the dative functions much more regularly as an indirect object, it can also be used to indicate possession.

Malum discipulo est. The apple belongs to the boy. [*lit.* The apple is to the boy.]

We also find that sometimes a form of *esse* can be omitted for the sake brevity when it is understood.

Gratia vobis, et pax a Deo Patre nostro, et Domino Jesu Christo (Eph 1:2). Grace [be] to you and peace [be] from God our Father and the Lord Jesus Christ.

In some situations, you have to work harder to figure out how to use the dative in situations of reference.

Quid mihi et tibi est, mulier? (Jn 2:4) What does this have to do with me and you, woman? [*lit.* What to me and to you is it, woman?]

Sententiae Summāriae

Hae ancillae cantica illō Deō cantant.
Hī discipulī hymnōs Mariae cantant.
Illī servī cibum hīs dominīs dant.
Illae ancillae cibum hīs dominīs dant.
Hic discipulus illum monet.
Haec ancilla illam audit.
Hoc canticum magnum est.

Translations

These maidservants sing songs to that God.
These students sing hymns to Mary.
Those servants give food to these lords.
Those maidservants give food to these lords.
This student warns that one.
These maidservants hear that one.
This song is great.

Cavēte et Mementōte

English and Latin use pronouns differently. Latin does not have a word for *the*, but it does sometimes use the pronoun as a kind of definite article.

Vocābula Memoranda

Nōmina

āgnus, āgnī (m.): lamb
cibus, cibī (m.): food
cūra, cūrae (f.): care
mandātum, mandātī (n.): commandment
peccātum, peccātī (n.): sin
petra, petrae (f.): rock
prophēta, prophētae (m.): prophet
puella, puellae (f.): girl
puer, puerī (m.): boy
rēgnum, rēgnī (n.): kingdom
synagōga, synagōgae (f.): gathering, synagogue

Verba

ā-verbs
  dō, dare, dedī, datus: give
  interrogō [inter + rogo], interrogāre, interrogāvī, interrogātus: ask
  nūntiō, nūntiāre, nūntiāvī, nūntiātus: announce

ē-verb
  appāreō, appārēre, appāruī, appāritus: appear

-io-verb
  faciō, facere, fēcī, factus: do, make

Adjectīva

aeger, -a, -um: sick
dīlēctus, -a, -um: beloved
fessus, -a, -um: tired
nātus, -a, -um: born
sānātus, -a, -um: healed

Prōnōmina

hic, haec, hoc: this
ille, illa, illud: that
cuī: to whom
quibus: to whom (plural)

Praepositiōnēs

cum (+abl): with (paired with noun in ablatives)
post (+acc): after
super (+acc or +abl): over

Conjūnctīva

cum: when (without a noun in the ablative)
quibus: to whom (plural)

Interrogātīvum

cuī: to whom

Fābula Parva (Latīna Ficta)

Vir Dominī, Sānctus Cūthbertus, et puer ambulant ex monastēriō. Illī sunt fessī neque cibum habent.
Cūthbertus puerum interrogat: "Ubi est cibus?"

Puer ille nescit. Cibus nōn appāret. Cūthbertus puerō dīcit: "Crēde in Deō!" Deinde aquila volat super eōs. Subitō īs, Cūthbertus, videt aquilam in fluviō. Cūthbertus puerō dīcit: "Aquila pisculum habet. Ambulā et cape illum!"

Puer aquilam in fluviō videt. Quī tollit pisculum, quem illa nūper de fluviō capit. Illa illī pisculum dat. Puer pisculum capit. Ille virō dominī pisculum dat. Puer et Cūthbertus grātiās deō agunt.

Cf. *Vita Sānctī Cūthbertī* XII

monasterium, monasteri (n.): monastery
pisculum, pisculī (n.): fish
nuper: recently
gratias agere: to give thanks [*lit.* to do graces]

1. Cur Cūthbertus fessus est?
2. Ubi Cūthbertus cibum videt?
3. Quis pisculum puerō dat?
4. Cuī puer pisculum dat?
5. Quid puer virō dat?

Sententiae Interpretandae

1. Hic est vere propheta, qui venit in mundum. (Jn 6:14)

   vere: truly

2. Agnus deī quī tollis peccāta mundī, dōna nōbīs pācem. (Agnus Dei)

   tollis: you take
   nobis: to us
   pacem: peace

3. Hic est Fīlius meus dīlēctus; illum audīte! (Mt 3:17)
4. Super hanc petram aedificat Chrīstus ecclēsiam. (Cf. Mt 16:18)

   aedificat: build

5. Hī sunt filiī regnī. (Mt 13:38)
6. Haec dīcit in synagōgā. (Jn 6:60)
7. Appāret illī angelus Dominī. (Lk 1:11)
8. Et sānātus est puer in hōrā illā. (Mt 8:15)

   hora, horae: hour

9. Angelus dominī nūntiat Marīae. (Lk 1:26)
10. Et grātia Deī est super illum. (Lk 6:29)
11. Cūram illīus habē. (Lk 10:35)
12. Bene facite hīs quī vōs ōderunt. (Mt 7:12)

> *ōderunt*: hate
> *vos*: you all
> *bene*: well/good

13. Ubi est, quī nātus est, rēx Jūdaeōrum? (Mt 2:2)

> *rex*: king
> *Jūdaeus, Jūdaeī*: Jew, person from Judea

14. Et ille David dīcit in librō Psalmōrum: Dīcit Dominus Dominō meō: sede ā dextrīs meīs. (Lk 20:42)
15. Nōn omnēs capiunt verbum illud. (Mt 19:11)

> *omnes*: all

16. Post hoc, descendit Capharnaum ille et māter eius et discipulī eius. (Jn 2:12)

> *mater*: mother
> *Capharnaum*: to Capharnaum

17. Quī verbum meum audit et crēdit eī, quī mittit mē, habet vītam aeternam et in jūdicium nōn venit. (Jn 5:24)

> *credit*: believes

18. Quid ergō Athēnīs et Hierosolymīs? Quid academiae et Ecclēsiae? Quid haereticīs et Chrīstiānīs? (Tertullian, *Liber de Praescrīptiōnibus*)

> *ergo*: therefore
> *academia, academiae* (f.): academy
> *haereticus, hearetici* (m.): heretic

Sententiae Fictae

1. Ubi est cibus āgnī? Cibus āgnī est in agrīs agricolārum.
2. Quid est mandātum āgnī dominī? Virī cibum puerīs dant.
3. Ecclēsia petrās servīs Deī nōn dat, sed cibum dominī.
4. Puerī quī sunt fessī cibum capiunt.
5. Līber vītae peccāta discipulōrum virīs nūntiat.
6. Angelī mandāta Deī servīs et ancillīs nuniant.
7. Dā cibum illī servō, nōn huic servō!
8. Nūntiātē mandāta Deī illīs ancillīs, nōn hīs ancillīs.
9. Deus fīliīs suīs dīcit. Fīliī Deō cantica cantant.
10. Jēsus fīlium aegrum videt. Jēsus fīliō aegrō dīcit et fīlius sānātus est.

CHAPTER 6

§ 19. Nouns: Ablatives of Means

Although we have already seen one use of the ablative, we have one more common use. After this chapter, there will be no new cases, and you will basically have the tools you need to discern the various possible case endings of nouns (save for three other declensions). The ablative case in Latin is something of a "junk-drawer" case. That is, the ablative (*ablativus*) can be used for several different things and is probably the most versatile and therefore most troublesome case in Latin.[1] We will begin by thinking about it as being translated as the English word "by," as in "by means of."

> *Dominus evangelium verbīs angelī nūntiat.* The Lord proclaims the Gospel by means of the words of an angel.
>
> *Ancilla canticō et hymnō et missā Deum laudat.* The maidservant praises God by means of a hymn and song and the mass.
>
> *Discipulī canticīs et hymnīs et missīs Deum laudant.* The students praise God by means of hymns and songs and masses.
>
> *Aquila ālīs volat.* The eagle flies by means of wings.

A-Nouns / 1st Declension (Usually Feminine)

Case	Singular	Example Translation	Plural	Example Translation
Nominative	*ancill\a*	handmaid (sub.)	*ancill\ae*	handmaids (sub.)
Genitive	*ancill\ae*	of the handmaid	*ancill\ārum*	of the handmaids
Dative	*ancill\ae*	to the handmaid	*ancill\īs*	to the handmaids
Accusative	*ancill\am*	handmaid (d.o.)	*ancill\ās*	handmaids (d.o.)
Ablative	*ancill\ā*	by the handmaid	*ancill\īs*	by the handmaids

---

1 Allen and Greenough provide sixteen uses of the ablative: *New Latin Grammar*, § 248–65.

O-Nouns / 2nd Declension (Masculine)

Nominative	*discipul|us*	student (sub.)	*discipul|ī*	students (sub.)
Genitive	*discipul|ī*	of the student	*discipul|ōrum*	of the students
Dative	*discipul|ō*	to the student	*discipul|īs*	to the students
Accusative	*discipul|um*	student (d.o.)	*discipul|ōs*	students (d.o.)
Ablative	*discipul|ō*	by the student	*discipul|īs*	by the students

O-Nouns / 2nd Declension (Neuter)

Nominative	*don|um*	gift (sub.)	*don|a*	gifts (sub.)
Genitive	*don|ī*	of the gift	*don|ōrum*	of the gifts
Dative	*don|ō*	to the gift	*don|īs*	to the gifts
Accusative	*don|um*	gift (d.o.)	*don|a*	gifts (d.o.)
Ablative	*don|ō*	by the gift	*don|īs*	by the gifts

§ 20. Verbs: Passive Voice

Latin verbs, like English verbs, have different ways the subject relates to the verb. The subject can do the action of the verb, which is called the active voice. Or the subject can receive the action of the verb, which is called the passive voice. To this point, we have only seen active-voice verbs. That is, the subject of the sentence performs the verb. We will now think about the passive voice. Before moving on, it is critical that English speakers not confuse *passive* with *past*. Passive does *not* mean that something happened before now, only that the subject does not perform the action of the verb. We will come to past tense verbs later (I was walking, I walked, etc.).

Subjects of passive-voice verbs receive the action of the verb. For now, we will only be thinking about *he, she, it,* or *they* forms of the verbs. In Latin, these verbs end with *-tur*, and *-ntur*.

Dominus portātur. The master is carried.
Dominī portantur. The masters are carried.
Fīliī videntur. The sons are seen.
Verbum scrībitur. The word is written.
Illae audiuntur. Those ones are heard.

Notice, though, how it is easy to get confused in English over the difference between passive and past. *Carried* can sound like the past tense. "He carried the ball." That is past tense. The difference is how *carried* is used. "The ball is being carried" now conveys that the ball is receiving the action in the present tense. The *-ed* in English can convey either passive or past tense depending on context. There will be a similar feature of Latin we will meet later on, but for now keep in mind that there is an important difference between *passive* and *past*. It is also worth noting that this is an instance where Latin speech patterns are different from English. We tend to resist the passive voice in English, but it is perfectly natural, and indeed even simpler, to convey the passive voice in Latin. It is one of those places where Latin becomes quite different from English.

§ 21. Verbs: Passive Voice with an Agent

We can now put the ablative together with the passive to make a fuller sentence.

Deus cantico laudātur. God is being praised by the song.
Discipulī ab magistrō laudantur. The students are being praised by the teacher.

Ancilla ab servīs monētur. The maidservant is being warned by the servants.
Disicpulī ab magistrīs monentur. The students are being warned by the teachers.

Ancilla ab Deō dūcitur. The maidservant is being led by God.
Discipulī ab magistrīs dūcuntur. The students are being led by the teachers.

Canticum ab Deō audītur. The song is being heard by God.
Cantica ab angelīs audiuntur. The songs are being heard by angels.

You might be wondering why there is a preposition in the second example but not in the first. In Classical Latin, writers like Cicero preferred to have human agents signified by a preposition and objects (or nonpersonal agents) with just ablative. In later Ecclesiastical Latin, this distinction begins to fall away. Eventually of course, the neo-Latin languages use only prepositions and get rid of the case system altogether. Italian does not have case endings and replaces the case endings with prepositions and word order.

We can put the two together.

Haec scrībuntur stȳlō ab illō. These things are written by means of a pen by him.

The last thing to note about true passive verbs—and this will be helpful later—is that passive verbs do not have a direct object. That is, you cannot say *haec stȳlum scrībuntur*. *Stylum* would be in the accusative, and because the verb is passive, there cannot be a direct object. This would be incorrect Latin. So one way you will know you are dealing with a passive voice verb is that there is no direct object.

CHAPTER 6

§ 22. Question Words: *nonne* and *numquid*

We have two new words, which do not decline, and are used to begin a sentence. The word *nonne* begins a question that expects an affirmative answer. "Doesn't a man need water?" The expected answer is "yes." *Numquid* and *num* are sort of the opposite. They are question words that expect a "no" answer. "Surely a man must not kill a harmless animal?" The expected answer is "no, a man shouldn't."

Numquid Paulus in Roma est? Paul is not in Rome, is he?

Sententiae Summāriae

Hī servī Deum illō canticō laudant.
Illae ancillae Mariam hīs hymnīs laudant.
Discipulī ab hōc magistrō monentur.
Ancilla ab hāc fēminā monētur.
Servī ab illō dominō dūcuntur.
Ancillae ab illā fēminā audiuntur.

Translations

These servants praise God by that song.
Those maidservants praise Mary by these hymns.
The students are taught by this teacher.
The maidservant is taught by this woman.
The servants are led by that Lord.
The maidservants are heard by that woman.

Cavēte et Mementōte

Don't confuse *passive* with *past*. Passive just means that the subject receives the action of the verb instead of doing the action of the verb.

Vocābula Memoranda

Nōmina

adversārius, adversāriī (m.): adversary
amīcus, amīcī (m.): friend
hora, horae (f.): hour
inimīcus, inimīcī (m.): enemy
lucerna, lucernae (f.): lamp
oculus, oculī (m.): eye

Verba

ā-verbs
cūrō, cūrāre, cūrāvī, cūrātus: cure, care for
habito, habitare, habitavi, habitatus: live in, well
portō, portāre, portāvī, portātus: carry
servō, servāre, servāvī, servātus: keep, preserve
voco, vocare, vocavi, vocatus: call

ē-verb
teneō, tenēre, tenuī, tentus: hold

i/e-verb
bibō, bibere, bibī, bibitus: drink
pōnō, pōnere, posuī, positus: put
trado [trans + do], tradere, tradidi, traditus: betray, hand over, pass down

io-verbs
accipiō [ad + capio], accipere, accēpī, acceptus: accept
fugiō, fugere, fūgī, fugitus: flee

i-verbs
nescio [ne + scio], nescire, nescivi, nescitus: not know
sciō, scīre, scīvī (sciī), scītus: know
veniō, venīre, vēnī, ventus: come

Adiectivum

malus, -a, -um: evil, bad

Prōnōmina

quo: by whom
quibus: by whom (plural)

Praepositiōnēs

ā/ab (+abl): by, from
sub (+abl): under

Interrogātīva

quibus: by whom (plural)
quō: by whom

Fābula Parva (Latīna Ficta)

Malchus, quī est monachus Syrus, in Graecia habitat. Malchus cum fēminīs virīsque revenit ad familiās eōrum in Syriā. Sed, antequam veniunt in Syriam, Malchus et amīcī eius virōs malōs vident. Malī virī quī vehuntur equīs, eōs capiunt. Malchus et amīcī eius capiuntur ā virīs malīs atque portantur equīs ad erēmum. Neque aquam neque cibum habent. Virī malī Malchō et fēminīs virīsque cibum nōn dant. Malchus et amīcī eius fugiunt ex virīs malīs ad spēluncam. Malchus videt, et timet virōs malōs quī equīs vehuntur et ad eōs veniunt. Ecce per tenebrās leaenae apparent et saliunt et virōs malōs mandūcant. Malchus et amīcī eius equōs virōrum malōrum capiunt et vehuntur ad Syriam.

Cf. *Sanctī Hierōnymī Vīta Malchī Captīvī*

monachus, monachī (m.): monk
Graecia, Graeciae (f.): Greece
reveniō, revenīre: return
antequam: before
vehō, vehere: are carried by (in the passive)[2]
equus, equī (m.): horse
erēmus, erēmī (m.): desert
Syrus: Syrian
leaena, laenae (f.): lioness
saliō, salīre: jump
spēlunca, spēluncae (f.): cave
tenebrae, tenebrārum (f. pl.): darkness

1. Ubi habitat Malchus?
2. Quī virōs malōs portant?
3. Ā quibus vehuntur virī malī?
4. Cūr Malchus et amīcī eius nōn mandūcant?
5. Quae virōs malōs mandūcant?

Sententiae Interpretandae

1. Jēsus, quī vocātur Christus. (Mt 1:16)
2. Maria, quae vocātur Magdalēnē. (Lk 8:2)
3. Quī vocātur ā Deō. (Heb 5:4)
4. Erue eōs quī dūcuntur ad mortem. (Prv 24:11)

erue: deliver
mortem: death

---

[2] The word *vehō, vehere* is tricky when moving from Latin to English. The easiest way is to think of it as another word for "carry." One could convert the passive Latin form in the active English word, "ride," but it creates other the difficulty of figuring out how to make sense of the ablative agent which becomes the direct object.

5. Deus nōn tenētur locō, nōn tenētur spatiō. (Cf. Augustine, *De Genesi contra Manichaeos* 2)

> *locus, locī* (m.): place
> *spatium, spatiī* (n.): time

6. Hoc est enim Corpus meum, quōd prō vōbīs trāditur. (1 Cor 11:24)
7. Et dicit illīs Jesus: Filii hujus saeculi nubunt, et traduntur ad nuptias. (Lk 20:34)

> *saeculum*: age
> *nubunt*: marry
> *ad nuptias*: to marriage

8. Sanctificātur enim per verbum Dei. (1 Tm 4:5)

> *per*: through

9. Quī cum Patre et Fīliō simul adōrātur et cōnglōrificātur. (Symbolum Nicaēnum)

> *patre*: father
> *adorare*: to worship
> *cōnglōrificāre*: to glorify with
> *simul*: at the same time

10. Moritur mendīcus, et portātur ab angelīs in sinum Abrahāē. (Lk 16:22)

> *moritur*: dies
> *mendicus, mendici* (m.): beggar
> *sinum, sini* (n.): bosom

11. Cum videt ergō Jēsus matrem, et discipulum, quem dīligit, dīcit mātrī suae: Mulier, ecce filius tuus. Deinde dīcit discipulō: Ecce māter tua. Et ex illā hōrā accipit eam discipulus. (Jn 20:26–27)

> *matrem*: mother
> *mātrī suae*: to his mother
> *mulier*: woman
> *hora, horae* (f.): hour
> *deinde*: then

12. Sed Deus amandus est, nōn sīcut aliquid quod vidētur oculīs, sed sīcut amātur sapientia, et vēritās et sānctitās et jūstitia et cāritās. (Augustine, *De catechizandis rudibus* 27)

> *amandus*: to be loved
> *aliquid*: something
> *veritas*: truth
> *sanctitas*: holiness
> *justitia, justitiae* (f.): justice
> *caritas*: love

13. Amicus sponsi, qui stat et audit eum, gaudio gaudet propter vocem sponsi. (Jn 3:29)

sponsus, sponsi (m.): bridegroom
propter: on account of
vocem: voice

14. Dominus Jēsus, in quā nocte trāditur, capit panem. (1 Cor 11:23)

nocte: night
panem: bread

15. Nōn est enim aliquid absconditum, quod nōn manifestātur: nec factum est occultum, sed in palam venit. (Cf. Mk. 4:22)

manifestare: to make manifest
aliquid: something
absconditum: hidden
occultum: dark, hidden
in palam: into the open

16. Numquid venit lucerna et sub modiō pōnitur, aut sub lectō? nōnne ut super candelābrum pōnitur? (Cf. Mk 4:21)

modiō: bushel
lectum, lecti (n.): bed

17. Hi autem sunt, qui circa viam, ubi seminatur verbum, et cum [verbum] audiunt, confestim venit Satanas, et portat verbum, quod seminatum est in cordibus eorum. (Mk 4:15)

confestim: immediately
circa: around
seminatum: sown
cordibus: hearts

Sententiae Fictae

1. Illī discipulī Deō bonō clāmant.
2. Quid illī agnī faciunt prope fluvium? Illī agnī aquam bibunt.
3. Aqua ab aquilis bibitur dē pōculīs? Nōn, aquilae aquam dē fluviīs bibunt.
4. Amantur et dīliguntur peccāta virōrum fēminārumque ab Deo? Nōn. Deus peccāta eōrum nōn laudat, sed Deus discipulōs eius amat et dīligit.
5. In ecclēsiā servī et ancillae Deī Christum laudant, glōrificant, et magnificant. Agnī et aquilae etiam Deum laudant, glōrificant, et magnificant in agrīs et in caelō.
6. Illī puerī et illae puellae illī dominō clāmant.
7. Ille puer huic puerō aquam dat.
8. Haec puella illī puellae cibum dat.
9. Illa puella quae nōn amātur ab illō puerō nōn gaudet.
10. Inimīcus quī nōn vidētur ab virīs illam puellam tenet.

CHAPTER 7

☙❧

To this point, we have learned the primary uses of the noun in Latin and the possible cases to which nouns belong. In what follows, we will begin to introduce the verb, but most work on the verb comes in the second half of the book. Chapter 17 provides a more complete introduction to the verb in Latin.

§ 23. Verbs: Full Paradigm for Present Active Indicative

Latin verbs can feel very daunting as there are quite a few different endings and uses that do not always neatly line up with an English equivalent. This book offers more straightforward and literal translations as a kind of scaffolding to learn all the nuances of the verb. But, when the student moves beyond the introductory textbook, it will require recognizing that the straightforward or wooden translation is not always best.

A Latin grammar book like this one offers a systematic approach to the language. There are many categories and subcategories throughout. It is important to remember that this is not how people naturally learn language, nor are languages as regular as we would like them to be. There are strange exceptions that can be quite vexing. So this book will offer much of the standard presentation of Latin grammar in this more systematized way. But it will be important to keep in mind that the language does not always follow the rules we expect.

Now for some categories. Like English, Latin has tenses, voices, and moods. First, *tense* refers to whether events take place in the present, past, and future. In Latin, the tenses are present, imperfect, future, perfect, pluperfect, and future perfect. We will talk more about those in chapter 17 and the latter half of the book.

Voice refers to the relationship of the subject to the verb. We can use the active voice, where the subject does the action. This would be like, "Mike loves the dog." We can also use the passive voice, which would be, "The dog is loved by Mike." In the first example, Mike is the subject who does the action. In the second example, the dog is the subject who receives the action of the verb.

The category of "mood" is likely unfamiliar to many readers. It indicates whether the form of the verb expresses a declaration about an event, a possibility about an event, or a desire that the event occur. We have the indicative mood which is like, "Mike loves the dog." We have the subjunctive mood: "Mike might love the dog." And we have the imperative mood: "Mike, love the dog!" In this sentence, the speaker desires the event to occur.

There are also other kinds of verbs, which we can call *Nonfinite forms*. Nonfinite or indefinite verbs refer to the fact that the subject of the verb is not explicit in the verb form and they cannot create a complete sentence on their own. In these uses of the verb, there is not a personal subject like *I, you, he, she, it, we, you all*, or *they*. These nonfinite forms of the verb are usually used when the verb acts like a noun or adjective. Latin has several of these: infinitive (chapter 9), participle (chapter 12), supine (chapter 24), gerund (chapter 25), and gerundive (chapter 27).

Some Latin verbs do a peculiar thing where they only exist in the form that looks like the passive voice. These are called deponents. We have not yet seen any of these, and we will not until chapter 16.

To this point, all indicative verbs have been either in the third person singular, *filius ambulat*, or in the third person plural, *filii ambulant*. Older English used to have special forms of the verb for every subject: I, you, he, etc. For example, "as thou hast been, thou forever wilt be." The words *hast* and *wilt* go with the second person singular, rather than *will* or *will*, or *have* or *has* for *I* and *he*, respectively. Latin works like older English forms. It has special endings for every single type of subject. Latin, though, does not require an explicit subject. It is perfectly acceptable to have just *videt* and no explicit subject. *Videt* on its own is actually a complete sentence that means "he sees," or "she sees," or "it sees." You might ask, "Why does Latin do both? It can have a subject, but it doesn't have to?" The answer is that Latin speakers like variety and use longer sentences where it might be useful to have the subject as an anchor before the verb. We will now introduce what are called first person and second person, singular and plural, that is, *I, we* and *you, you all*. It is best to memorize these endings first:

	Singular		Plural	
1st Person	*-o / m*	I	*-mus*	we
2nd Person	*-s*	you	*-tis*	you all
3rd Person	*-t*	he / she / it	*-nt*	they

These endings will be repeated in all other tenses (present, imperfect, future, future-perfect, pluperfect), except the perfect active indicative. The first person, *I*, form of the verb has an *-o/-m*. You will not see an *-m* at the end of the first-person singular of the imperfect for regular verbs. It does come up in the first-person singular of *esse*, where it is *sum*. It can be helpful, though, to memorize it now so you are not surprised when it comes up. You will learn how to break down a verb as well, to find out its pattern vowel. Knowing the pattern vowel and the personal endings, you will be able to form any present tense verb in the active voice. In order to find the pattern vowel, you can see it most clearly in the infinitive.

ambul-ā-re, "to walk"; the stem is *ambul*, the pattern vowel is *a*, and the infinitive part is *-re*. Breaking down verbs is straightforward in the beginning, but it will become quite complex. The pattern vowel will not always be long.

vid-ē-re notice here that the *-ē-* has a macron above it because the *e* is long. The pattern vowel will not always be long.

duc-ĕ-re notice here the the *-ĕ-* has a strange mark above it called a breve. That represents that the vowel is "short." This vowel pattern is the "short i/e" vowel pattern. It is the hardest one to remember.

aud-ī-re. Notice here that the *-ī-* has a macron because it is long. This vowel will not always be long, but the *i* is consistently present in the verb.

I will break down all the major verb vowel patterns below:

Active:

Subjects[1]	ā-verb	ē-verb	i/e-verb	i-verb	Example Translation
[ego]	laud|ō	mone|ō	dūc|ō	audi|ō	I hear
[tu]	laudā|s	monē|s	dūci|s	audī|s	you hear
[is / ea][2]	lauda|t	mone|t	dūci|t	audi|t	he hears
[nos]	laudā|mus	monē|mus	dūci|mus	aud|mus	we hear
[vos]	laudā|tīs	monē|tis	dūci|tis	audī|tis	you (pl.) hear
[ii / eae]	lauda|nt	mone|nt	dūcu|nt	audiu|nt	they hear

We should take a look at a few things from this chart. In the first-person singular of the ā-verb and the i/e-verb, the *-o* is stronger than the pattern vowel, so those vowels are not present. In the third person plural of the i/e-verb and the i-verb, there is *-u-* before the *-nt*.

There are a couple of verbs, *faciō, facere; capiō, capere; pariō, parere,* etc., that sort of go in between the short i/e-verbs and the long i-verbs. These *io*-verbs follow the morphologies of *i/e*-verbs and *i*-verbs, depending on the form.

---

1 I will include the common subjects here but remember that a Latin verb is not required to have an explicit or separate subject. The subject can be implied in the verb. It can be helpful to memorize them together, though, so the student remembers both the personal pronoun and the verb forms.

2 In some cases, *ille, illa, illud* can be used as the "he, she, it" form of the third person pronoun. This is what was used in early medieval Latin as a precursor to the Neo-Latin article in languages like French and Italian.

CHAPTER 7

Active:

[ego]	faci|ō	I do
[tu]	faci|s	you do
[is / ea]	faci|t	he does
[nos]	faci|mus	we do
[vos]	faci|tis	you (pl.) do
[ii / eae]	faciu|nt	they do

We have two words in the vocabulary list that come from the root *faciō*: *glōrificō*, *magnificō*. These words are like many words in Latin that are a combination of *facio* plus an adjective or a noun. When the root *facio* takes a prefix like *glori-*, the verb becomes an ā-verb: *glōrificāre*.

Now the "to be" verb, *esse*, has slightly different changes, but you should still be able to recognize the basic personal endings.

[ego]	su|m	I am
[tu]	e|s	you are
[is / ea]	es|t	he / she is
[nos]	su|mus	we are
[vos]	es|tis	you (pl.) are
[ii / eae]	su|nt	they are

Remember that these are only the endings for the active voice, when the subject performs the action of the verb.

A brief recap is provided below:

Amō Deum. I love God.
Egō amō Deum. I love God.

Māriam vidēmus. We see Mary.
Nōs Māriam vidēmus. We see Mary.

Latin often has an explicit subject, but it is not required. Linguists sometimes call this a "null subject." All it means is that the subject is found only in the personal ending of the verb.

§ 24. Pronouns: First and Second Person

I, you, he, she, it, we, you all, they; these are the most standard pronouns in English. They stand in place of a proper noun and are what we think of when we think of pronouns. Although we do not normally put them in this framework, English pronouns have cases, just like Latin. It is incorrect English to say, "me went to the store" or "us go to church." We may not know the rules for why, but we intuitively know that these are not correct. The simplest way to say it is that our pronouns have cases just like Latin. *Me* and *us* are accusative. *I* and *we* are nominative. We do have cases in English, just not nearly as often as Latin. Now it is time to learn all the possible first- and second-person pronouns.

	Singular	Plural
Nominative	*egō*	*nōs*
Genitive	*meī*	*nostri*
Dative	*mihi*	*nobis*
Accusative	*mē*	*nōs*
Ablative	*mē*	*nobis*

	Singular	Plural
Nominative	*tu*	*vos*
Genitive	*tui*	*vestri*
Dative	*tibi*	*vobis*
Accusative	*te*	*vos*
Ablative	*te*	*vobis*

§ 25. Pronouns: Reflexive

We spoke above about the many different kinds of pronouns in Latin. Here, we will look at the reflexive pronoun. This is where the pronoun stands in place of a noun but has a special relationship to the verb, called *reflexive*. I hit myself. You speak to yourself. She dresses herself. These are all English reflexives indicated with the ending *self*.

Nominative	-	-	-
Genitive	*mei*	*tui*	*sui*
Dative	*mihi*	*tibi*	*sibi*
Accusative	*me*	*te*	*se*
Ablative	*me*	*te*	*se*
Nominative	-	-	-
Genitive	*nostri / nostrum*	*vestri / vestrum*	*sui*
Dative	*nobis*	*vobis*	*sibi*
Accusative	*nos*	*vos*	*se*
Ablative	*nobis*	*vobis*	*se*

Ego mē amō. I love myself.
Tū tē amās. You love yourself.
Is sē amat. He loves himself.
Ea sē amat. She loves herself.
Iī sē amant. They love themselves.

For these examples, notice that *se* can be used for "himself," "herself," and "themselves." In a later chapter we will see *se* used in indirect speech.

§ 26. Syntax: et ... et/neque ... neque/non solum ... sed etiam

One other element of language that is not often emphasized enough is how a Latin sentence is structured. That is, you can have memorized all kinds of declensions and meanings of words, but the way Latin combines words can change their meaning beyond just an ending or a dictionary definition. In English, we might say, "the boy is running." But if we add a few words, "Surely the boy is not running?" We have added two words that drastically change the meaning. In the first, we had a declaration, and now we have a question. One states something that is the case, and the other queries whether it is the case. This is pretty simple, but the leading words can help us discern what unique meaning is going on in Latin. So we will occasionally add certain constructions as things to be learned so that reading becomes easier and we can anticipate important changes in meaning from mere declaration.

One common construction in Latin is when an author begins a sentence with *non solum* and then composes a phrase. Then the author will follow it with a coordinating phrase. "Not only (*non solum*) are dogs and cats animals but also (*sed etiam*) people are animals."[3] When we see *non* we tend to think of a negative statement. This construction really just brings together two or more ideas. Almost as if the author is saying, "you already know one thing, and I am going to add one more."

To indicate a list, Latin speakers used certain words that do not always have an English equivalent. If we want to make a list in Latin, we might put *et* before every phrase in a list: *et ambulat et dīcit et audit* (he walks and speaks and listens). We do not need to translate the first *et*. Sometimes *et* and another noun with *et* makes "both ... and."

This goes for the negative as well: *neque ambulat neque dīcit neque audit* (he neither walks nor speaks nor listens). Notice that we have changed the English wording around, even though it is exactly the same word in Latin. This further shows that correct and idiomatic English and Latin are not exactly the same.

Sententiae Summāriae

Ego Deum laudō. Tū Mariam laudās.
Ego ancillās moneō. Tū discipulōs monēs.
Ego filiōs dūcō. Tū filiās dūcās.
Ego Deum audiō. Tū magistrum audīs.

Nōs magistrum laudāmus. Vōs dominum laudātis.
Nōs discipulōs monēmus. Vōs ancillās monētis.
Nōs filiōs dūcimus. Vōs filiās dūcitis.
Nōs magistrum audīmus. Vōs Deum audītis.

Nōn sōlum Deum, sed etiam Mariam laudāmus.
Nōn sōlum ille Deus tuus est, sed etiam Deus meus.
Nōn sōlum magister noster est, sed etiam vester.

---

3 As you read more Latin, you will find many different versions of this basic structure: *nōn tantum ... sed etiam* and *nōn modo ... sed quoque*.

Translations

I praise God. You praise Mary.
I teach the maidservants. You teach the boy students.
I lead the sons. You lead the daughters.
I hear God. You hear the teacher.

We praise the teacher. You all praise the master.
We teach the boy students. You all teach the maidservants.
We lead the sons. You all lead the daughters.
We hear the teacher. You all hear God.

We praise not only God, but also Mary.
Not only is he your God, but also my God.
Not only is he our teacher but your teacher.

Cavēte et Mementōte

Memorizing the personal endings by themselves will help you to be able to identify many different forms.

Looking for the vowel pattern of the verb will also help you to figure out what is happening with every different form of the verb.

Vocābula Memoranda

Prōnōmina

ego: I
tu: you
nos: we
vos: you all
me: myself
te: yourself
se: himself, herself, itself

Nōmina

poculum, poculī (n.): cup
populus, populī, (m.): people
puteus, puteī (m.): well

Verba

ā-verbs
  amō, amāre, amāvī, amātus: love
  baptīzō, baptīzāre, baptīzāvī, baptīzātus: baptize[4]
  glōrificō [gloria + facio], glōrificāre, glōrificāvī, glōrificātus: glorify
  magnificō [mangus + facio], magnificāre, magnificāvī, magnificātus: magnify

ē-verb
  respondeō, respondēre, respondī, respōnsus: respond

i/e-verbs
  agō, agere, ēgī, āctus: do, lead; with *gratias*: give thanks
  crēdō, crēdere, crēdidī, crēditus: believe
  pāscō, pāscere, pāvī, pāstus: feed / give pasture to
  petō, petere, petīvī, petītus: seek
  trahō, trahere, trāxī, tractus: draw, drag

Adjectīva

Iūdaeus, Iūdaea: Jewish person
Samaritānus, Samaritāna: Samaritan

Interrogātīvum

unde: from where

Praepositiō

pro: [+abl] on behalf, before, about

Adverbia

solum: only
tantum: only

Fābulae Parvae

    Ascendit Sīmōn Petrus et trahit pīsculōs in terram. Dīcit discipulīs eius Jēsus: "Venīte, Mandūcate." Et venit Jēsus, et accipit cibum et dat eīs. Cum ergō mandūcant, dīcit Sīmōnī Petrō Jēsus: "Sīmōn Iōannīs, dīligis me plūs hīs?" Dīcit eī: "Etiam Dominē, tū scīs quia amō

---

4 If you find a verb with a *z* in the word, it comes from a Greek word. This word for baptize comes directly from the Greek and is a loan word. It became quite common in Ecclesiastical Latin, but it was not known in Latin before its use in the New Testament.

CHAPTER 7

tē." Dīcit eī: "Pasce agnōs meōs." Dīcit eī iterum: "Sīmōn Iōannis, dīligis mē?" Dīcit illī: "Etiam Domine, tū scīs quia amō tē." Dīcit eī: "Pasce agnōs meōs." Dīcit eī tertium: "Sīmōn Jōannis, amās mē?" Contristātus est Petrus, quia dīcit eī tertium: "Amās mē?" et dīcit eī: "Domine, tū omnia scis, tū scīs quia amō tē." Dīcit eī: "Pasce agnōs meōs."

Cf. John 21

etiam: also, yes
plus his: more than these
iterum: again
contristatus: saddened
nosti: you know
tertium: third time
omnia: all things

1. Quid Jesus accipit?
2. Quibus cibum dat?
3. Cui Jesus dicit?
4. Cur Petrus contristatus est?

Venit ergō Jēsus in cīvitātem Samarīae, quae dīcitur Sichar, juxtā praedium quod dat Jācōb Joseph fīliō suō. Est autem ibi puteus Jācōb. Jēsus ergō fessus sedet suprā puteum. Hōra est quasi sexta. Venit fēmina dē Samarīā capere aquam. Dīcit eī Jēsus: "Dā mihi bibere." Dīcit ergō eī fēmina illa Samarītāna: "Quōmodo tū, Jūdæus cum es, bibere ā mē interrogās, quæ sum fēmina Samarītāna? nōn enim dīcunt Jūdæī Samarītānis." Respondit Jēsus, et dīcit eī: "Scīsne tū quis est quī dīcit tibi: dā mihi bibere? Interrogā mē prō aquā vīvā." Dīcit eī fēmina: "Domine, neque pōculum habēs, et puteus altus est: unde ergō habēs aquam vīvam? Numquid tū major es patre nostrō Jācōb, quī dat nōbīs puteum, et ille ex eō bibit, et fīliī ejus, et agnī ejus?" Respondit Jēsus, et dīcit eī: "Quī bibit ex aquā hāc, sitit iterum; quī autem bibit ex aquā quam ego dabō [future] eī, nōn sitiet [future] in æternum: sed aqua quam ego dabō eī, fīet [will become] in eō puteus aquæ in vītam æternam." Dīcit ad eum fēmina: "Domine, dā mihi hanc aquam." Dīcit eī Jēsus: "Vade, vocā virum tuum, et venī hūc." Respondit fēmina, et dīcit: "Nōn habeō virum." Dīcit eī Jēsus: "Bene dīcis, quia nōn habeō virum; quīnque enim virōs habēs, et nunc, quem habēs, nōn est tuus vir: hoc vērē dīcis." Dīcit eī mulier: "Domine, videō quia prophēta es tū."

Cf. John 4:5–19

quasi sexta: about six
civitatem: city
praedium: farm
sitiet: thirst
major ... patre nostro: greater than our father
huc: here
iuxta: near
vado, vadere: go
quinque: five
vere: truly

1. Quam Jēsus videt iuxtā puteum?
2. Fēmina Jēsū bibere dat?
3. Habetne fēmina ūnum virum?
4. Habetne Jēsus aquam? Quālis est aqua Jēsū?

Sententiae Interpretandae

1. Ego autem si veritatem dico, non creditis mihi. (Jn 8:45)

    veritatem: truth

2. Sed vos non creditis, quia non estis ex ovibus meis. (Jn 10:25)

    ovibus: sheep

3. Laudō et magnificō et glōrificō deum. (Dn 4:37)
4. Verba vītae aeternae habēs. (Jn 6:67)
5. Habēmus Pāpam.

    papa, papae (m.): pope

6. Clāmō ad tē, et nōn exaudīs mē. (Jb 30:20)
7. Et scīmus quoniam Fīlius Deī venit. (1 Jn 5:20)
8. Crēdō in ūnum deum. (Symbolum Nicaenum)
9. Quī vīvis et rēgnās in saecula saeculōrum. (Benedictiō Post Mēnsam)

    saecula saeculorum: forever [*lit.* ages of ages]

10. Nōn sōlum ipse Dominus super aquās ambulat, sed etiam Petrus. (Augustine, *Dē Agōne Chrīstiānō* 24.26)
11. Agimus tibi grātiās, omnipotēns Deus. (Benedictiō Post Mēnsam)

    omnipotēns, omnipotentis: almighty

12. Laudāmus tē, adōrāmus tē, glōrificāmus tē. (Glōria)
13. Ubi vērē discimus, cum stāmus et audīmus eum et gaudiō gaudēmus propter vōcem spōnsī, reddentēs nōs unde sumus. (Augustine, *Confessions* 11)

    vocem sponsi: the voice of the bridegroom
    reddentes: giving back to

14. Sapientia, sapientia ipsa est quae interlūcet mihi. (Augustine, *Confessions* 11)

interlucere: shine forth

15. Nōn sōlum concupīscit carō, sed etiam adversus spīritum concupīscit. (Marius Victorinus, *Commentāriī in Epistulās Paulī ad Galatās* 2.6.17).

carō: flesh
concupīscere: desire
adversus: against

Sententiae Fictae

1. Vōs Pāpam bonum amātis?
2. Pōculum nōn habēmus, neque bibimus. Non solum poculum petimus, sed etiam aquam.
3. Ego neque puteum neque poculum habeō, ergō clāmō Deō, "da mihi aquam ex caelō!" Aqua dē caelō venit! Deum laudō, magnificō, glōrificōque!
4. Vir amīcum interrogat: "Tū aquam bibis? Unde venit aqua tua?" Amīcus respondet: "Aqua mea quae vīvit dē Deō venit. Crēdō in Deō et grātiās deō agō. Crēdisne in Deum quī vīvit?"
5. Dominus servōs interrogat: "Vōs Deum glōrificātis?" Servī dominō respondent: "Nōs Deum glōrificāmus, magnificāmus, laudāmusque."
6. Nōs Deō hymnōs cantāmus, et Deus cantica audit.
7. Vōs Deō vestrō cantica cantātis? Auditne Deus cantica vestra?
8. Ego Deum hymnīs laudō. Quōmodo tū Deum tuum laudās?
9. Nōn sōlum fēminae et virī Deum laudant, sed etiam angelī.
10. Et aquam et cibum habētis, neque illa petitis.

CHAPTER 8

☙❧

§ 27. Nouns: I/E-Nouns (Third Declension), Masculine and Feminine

We are familiar with the primarily feminine words like *ancilla*: maidservant with an a-pattern vowel. The other pattern was the o-pattern with masculine *filius, filii* as boy and boys; and neuter, *donum, dona* as "gift" and "gifts." Nouns that end in -*a* in the nominative singular and -*ae* in the genitive are commonly known as first declension. Nouns that end in -*us* and -*um* and sometimes -*er* or -*ir* in the nominative singular and -*i* in the genitive are known as the second declension. So we have already learned two full declensions, as well as the pronoun endings, which are nearly another full declension.

Now we come to what is called the i/e-nouns, or the third declension out of a total of five. Rather than going through each ending individually as we did to begin the book, we will create one chart for this declension. The cases all function the same as they did in the preceding chapters, they just have different endings. The a-nouns (first declension), o-nouns (second declension), and i/e-nouns (third declensions) are the most common.

I/E-Nouns (Third Declension) (Masculine and Feminine)

Case	Singular	Plural
Nom	*miles*	*milit|ēs*
Gen	*milit|is*	*milit|um*
Dat	*milit|ī*	*milit|ibus*
Acc	*milit|em*	*milit|ēs*
Abl	*milit|e*	*milit|ibus*

One other element of third declension nouns that becomes more pronounced in the i/e-nouns is the fact that sometimes a noun stem changes slightly depending on the case. So, *miles* is nominative masculine singular, but *militis* is the genitive masculine singular. Every ending except the nominative has a *-t-* added. This kind of mutation is common in the third declension. This is why nouns are often listed with the nominative singular and genitive singular forms.

Another strange feature of i/e-nouns (third declension) nouns is that it is not clear based on the endings whether a noun is masculine or feminine. In the first and second declensions, you could often tell the difference by the *-a* forms in the feminine and the *-us/-um* forms in the masculine and neuter. There will be some difference when we move to the neuter forms i/e-nouns in the next section.

Let's look at some examples:

bonus miles: a good soldier
bona uxor: a good woman

bonī militis: of a good soldier
bonae uxoris: of a good woman

We cannot discern in the examples above whether the noun itself is masculine or feminine *except* with the addition of the adjective. The adjective stays in the first or second declension form. Thus, you can figure out that *mulier* is feminine and *homo* is masculine if it has an adjective that comes with it.

These examples elicit another kind of explanation. Early on, we mentioned that an adjective agrees with the noun it modifies in "gender, number, and case, but *not* declension." Now we are seeing a good example of that. *Bonus* agrees with *miles* even though the ending is different. It is critical to remember that nouns and adjectives *always* stay in their original declension. *Bonus, bona, bonum* will never have an *-es* ending. *Miles* will never have an *-us* ending. So they can agree in gender, number, and case, but they will have different endings.

One final exception to be aware of lies in the third declension. There are certain nouns that are called *i-stem* nouns. These nouns have an extra *-i-* before the genitive plural. *Panis, panis, panium*, instead of *panis panis, panum*. They also have an *-i* in the ablative singular rather than an *-e*.

§ 28. Nouns: I/E-Nouns (Third Declension), Neuter

Unlike the previous declensions, where feminine are mostly first declension and masculine and neuter are mostly second, the third declension has many masculine, feminine, and neuter nouns. The good news is that most of the neuters look the same. *Cor, cordis* (n.) means "heart" and looks like the masculine and feminine *except* in the accusative singular and plural. Why? Because all neuters always have the same form in their nominative and accusative. So the accusative singular for *cor* is *cor*. The plural for both is *corda*.

	Singular	Plural
Nom	*cor*	*cord\a*
Gen	*cord\is*	*cord\um*
Dat	*cord\i*	*cord\ibus*
Acc	*cor*	*cord\a*
Abl	*cord\e*	*cord\ibus*

One neuter noun is very common and very irregular. The pattern given below is for all neuter i-stems, based on the noun *mare*, which means "sea."

Neuter

Case	Singular	Plural
Nom	*mar\e*	*mar\ia*
Gen	*mar\is*	*mar\ium*
Dat	*mar\ī*	*mar\ibus*
Acc	*mar\e*	*mar\ia*
Abl	*mar\ī (mar\e)*	*mar\ibus*

CHAPTER 8

§ 29. Possessive Adjectives: *meus, tuus, suus*

We must quickly introduce possessive adjectives. There is nothing new to be learned here except a new stem. *Me-us/-a/-um*; *tu-us/-a/-um*; *su-us/su-a/su-um*. These function just like adjectives with endings that match the nouns they modify in gender, number, and case (but not declension!). *Meus filius* (my son); *tua filia* (your daughter); *suum donum* (his gift).

One important point to clarify before it arises is that the adjective *meus* in the example above is masculine because it matches with the masculine word *filius*. If someone said *mea filia*, *mea* would be feminine because the word *filia* is feminine, not because the speaker is masculine or feminine. It can be easy to think that the *me-* will have a masculine or feminine ending depending on who is speaking, not on the noun with which it is paired.

The full chart for these first and second declension adjectives will be included below.

Cases	Masc. Sing.	Fem. Sing.	Neut. Sing.	Masc. Plur.	Fem. Plur.	Neut. Plur.
Nom	*meus* (*tuus; suus*)	*mea* (*tua; sua*)	*meum* (*tuum; suum*)	*meī* (*tuī; suī*)	*meae* (*tuae; suae*)	*mea* (*tua; sua*)
Gen	*meī*	*meae*	*meī*	*meōrum*	*meārum*	*meōrum*
Dat	*meō*	*meae*	*meō*	*meīs*	*meīs*	*meīs*
Acc	*meum*	*meam*	*meum*	*meōs*	*meās*	*mea*
Abl	*meō*	*meā*	*meō*	*meīs*	*meīs*	*meīs*

§ 30. Conjunctions: *cum, dum,* and *donec*

As we have done in the past, we will continue to introduce important conjunctions that help understand the flow of a sentence. Latin has many ways to convey meaning, which will appear the same in English. Style was an important feature of Latin, and the best Latin speakers would arrange their words in different ways to show their command of the language.

We have already seen the word *cum* as a preposition meaning "with." You will know that it is indeed a preposition in a sentence if the following noun is in the ablative case. If, however, you see the word *cum* beginning a sentence or a clause, it means "when." The noun that will follow it will not be in the ablative, so you will know it means "when" and not "with." For now, when you encounter *cum*, the verb that follows in the phrase will be in the indicative. Later on, we will learn that the verb that follows *cum* is often in the subjunctive (a mood we will meet later).

The same is true for *dum* and *donec*. These words can come with the subjunctive, or they can come with the indicative. The frustrating thing in English is that the meaning does not actually change when the verbs go from indicative to subjunctive. It is a stylistic variation. *Dum* means "while" and *donec* means "until" or "as long as."

Sententiae Summāriae

Bona gēns creātōrī laudem dat.
Malae gentēs animālibus laudēs dant.
Bona gēns ab creātōre monētur.
Malae gentēs ab animālibus nōn monentur.
Milities imāginēs creātōris sunt.
Bona gēns creātōrem audit.
Malae gentēs animalia audiunt.
Cum bonae gentēs creātōrem ōrātiōnibus laudant, cor creātōris gaudet.
Dōnec malae gentēs creātōrem vērum ōrātiōnibus laudant, cor creātōris nōn gaudet.

Translations

The good nation gives praise to the creator.
Evil nations give praise to animals.
The good nation is warned by the creator.
Evil nations are not warned by animals.
Humans are images of the creator.
The good nation listens to the creator.
Evil nations listen to animals.

When good nations praise the creator with prayers, the heart of the creator rejoices.

As long as evil nations do not praise the true creator with prayers, the heart of the creator does not rejoice.

Cavēte et Mementōte

The third declension does not have an easy vowel to associate with it like the first declension or later fourth and fifth. Technically, it is a short i/e. It is much like the third conjugation with its short i/e theme vowel.

Vocābula Memoranda

Nōmina

animal, animālis (n.): animal
aurīs, aurīs (f.): ear
caput, capitis (n.): head

cor, cordis (n.): heart
creātor, creātōris (m.): creator
gēns, gentīs (f.): nation
grex, gregis (m.): flock
homo, hominis (m.): person, human
jānuā, jānuae (f.): door
īdōlum, īdōlī (n.): idol
imāgō, imāginis (f.): image
lūmen, lūminis (n.): light
mare, maris (n.): sea
mīles, mīlitis (m.): soldier
mōns, montīs (m.): mountain
nōmen, nōminis (n.): name, noun
  Often in the expression of someone's name, it will come with the dative of possession.
  Nomen sibi Adamus est. His name is Adam.
opus, operis (n.): work, labor
pānis, pānis (m.): bread
piscis, piscis (m.): fish
plēbs, plēbis (f.): people
sōl, sōlis (m.): sūn
uxor, uxōris (f.): wife

Verba

<u>ā-verbs</u>
  praeparō [prae + parō], praeparāre, praeparāvī, praeparātus: prepare
  salvō, salvāre, salvāvī, salvātus: save
  spīrō, spīrāre, spīrāvī, spīrātus: breathe

<u>ī-verb</u>
  aperiō, aperīre, aperuī, apertus: open

Adjectīva

  meus, tuus, suus: my, your, his/her
  noster, vester: our, your (plural)

Coniunctīva

  autem: but, however
  donec: until
  si: if

Fābula Parva

Placidus est vir, qui est dominus mīlitum multōrum. Quamvīs agit opera misericordiae, sed tamen adōrat īdōla. Chrīstiānī Jēsum Chrīstum adōrant, sed pāgānī īdōla, deōs falsōs, adōrant. Placidus duōs fīliōs et ūnam uxōrem habet. Dum Placidus cum mīlitibus suīs in montibus ambulat, gregem cervōrum invēnit. Prope virōs est silva magna et arborēs magnae. Placidus et mīlitēs suī gregem magnum cervōrum et arborēs magnās spectant. Magnus cervus ab grege ad arborēs magnās discēdit et Placidus eum petit. Mīlitēs multī autem gregem cervōrum petunt. Placidus ergō est sōlus. Cum Placidus prope cervum venit, animal ferum videt. In mediō capitis magnī cervī, vidētur lūmine sōlis imāgō Jēsu Chrīstī, quī per cervum sīcut per asinam Balaam eī dīcit: "Ō Placide, cūr mē petis? Ego apparō tibi in hōc animālī grātiā. Ego sum Chrīstus, quem tū nescīs, sed adōrās. Misericordiae quās tū facīs cōram mē ascendunt et propter hōc veniō tibi per hunc cervum." Placidus vehitur equō et cadit dē equō. Post ūnam hōram ad cervum revēnit et dīcit eī: "Revēlā mihi, quid dīcis, et crēdam [I will believe] in tē." Et ait Chrīstus: "Ego, Placide, sum Chrīstus et creātor caelī et terrae, quī facit sōlem lūcēre et discēdere. Salvāre plēbēs meās, veniō." Haec audit atque iterum cadit in terram. Ait eī: "Crēdō, Domine, quia tū es, quī omnia facit et quī plēbēs salvat." Et dīcit ad eum Dominus: "Sī crēdis, pete ecclēsiam cīvitātis et in ecclēsiā tū baptīzābēris. Nūntia uxōrī tuae et fīliīs tuīs."

Cum ergō Placidus in vīllā eius venit, haec uxōrī renūntiat. Uxor eius clāmat: "Domine, et ego quoque vīdī [I saw] haec. Chrīstus mihi dīcit, "Crās tū et vir tuus et fīliī tuī ad mē venītis." Ille est Jēsus Chrīstus!" Dum sōl nōn lūcet, ecclēsiam Rōmae petunt, cum magnō gaudiō baptīzantur et Placidus quī vocātur Eustachius et eius uxor Teopistin et fīliī eius Agaptium et Theopistum.

Cf. Jacob de Voragine, *De Sancto Eustachio* (nonnullis mutatis)

quamvis: although
antea: before (temporally)
asina, asinae (f.): donkey
transacta: previous
medium, medii (n.): middle
cervus, cervi (m.): deer
ferus, -a, -um: wild
revelare: reveal
coram: before (spatially)
baptizaberis: future and passive
cras: tomorrow
prope: near
silva, silvae (f.): forest
sicut: like or as

CHAPTER 8

1. Quis est Placidus?
2. Estne Placidus vir bonus? Estne Chrīstiānus (in prīmīs, "in the beginning")?
3. Quem Placidus et familiā suā adōrant?
4. Ubi Placidus Chrīstum videt?
5. Quid accidit (happens) in ecclēsiā Rōmae?

Sententiae Interpretandae

1. Deus creātor caelī et terrae est.
2. Ille vērō Abraham stat iūxta eōs sub arbōre. (Gn 18:8)

    iuxta: near

3. Quod oculus nōn vīdet nec auris audīt, nec in cor hominis ascendit, quae praeparat Deus hīs quī dīligunt illum. (1 Cor 2:9)
4. Et venit Jēsus, et accipit panem, et dat eīs. (Jn 21:13)
5. Est autem ibi circa montem grex porcōrum magnus. (Mk 5:11)

    porcus, porci (m.): pig

6. Dum spīrō, spērō.

    spero, sperare: hope

7. Tū autem, cum jejūnās, unge caput tuum, et faciem tuam lavā. (Mt 6:17)

    jejuno, jejunare: fast
    unge: anoint
    faciem: face

8. Ambulat autem Jēsus iūxta mare Galilaeae et vīdet duōs frātrēs, Simōnem, quī vocātur Petrus, et Andrēam frātrem eius, quī mittunt rete in mare (sunt enim piscātōrēs). Et dicit illīs: Venīte post mē, et vōs estis piscātōrēs hominum. (Mt 4:18–19)

    iuxta: near
    rete, retis (n.): net
    piscator, piscatoris (m.): fisherman

9. Est puer unus hic qui habet quinque [5] panes et duos [2] pisces. (Jn 6:9)

    hic: here

10. Nunc dīmittis servum tuum, Domine, secundum verbum tuum in pāce. (Lk 2:29, *Nunc Dimittis*)

    secundum: according to
    pace: peace

11. Lūmen ad revelātiōnem gentium, et glōriam plēbis tuae Israel. (Lk 2:29, *Nunc Dimittis*)

    revelatio, revelotionis (f.): revelation

12. Sī enim bona est vīta creāta; quam bona est vīta creātrīx? (Anselm, *Proslogion* 24)

enim: for
creata: created
quam: how
creatrix: creator

13. Caecī sunt, quia vērum lūmen nōn vīdent. (Francis of Assisi, *Epistola ad Fidēlēs*)

caecī: blind

14. Deus meus, ex tōtō corde amō Tē super omnia, quia es īnfīnītē bonus et īnfīnītē amābilis; et ob amōrem Tuī proximum meum dīligō sīcut meipsum, eīque, sī quid in mē offendit, ignōscō. (*Actus Caritatis*)

infinite: infinitely
amabilis: loveable
ob amorem: on account of love
offendit: offend
ignosco: I forgive

Sententiae Fictae

1. Ubi est grex agnōrum? Illa animālia in montibus sub lūmine sōlis pascunt.
2. Quid est jānua cordis plēbium? Plēbēs panem bonum amant et mandūcant.
3. Suntne animālia imāginēs creātōris? Hominēs sunt imāginēs creātōris, nōn animālia neque piscēs.
4. Quae sunt haec animālia? Sunt opera creātōris, quae creātor amat. Gentēs īdola animālium adōrant.
5. Sī animālia nōn spīrant, nōn vīvunt. Īdola animālium nōn spīrant, neque vīvunt.
6. Piscēs in montibus habitant? Nōn! Piscēs in aquā fluviorum habitant et spīrant.
7. Animālia sunt opera creātōris bonī. Hominēs, quī sunt opera bona creātōris bonī quoque, nōmina animālibus dant.
8. Dum sōl in caelō est, animālia aquam in marī petunt.
9. Plēbēs meae neque īdōla tua neque īdōla sua laudant.
10. Plēbēs bonae Deum jūstum laudant quoniam Deus eās salvant.

CHAPTER 9

§ 31. Verbs: Introduction to Infinitives

To this point, the verbs we have used have been primarily action verbs or linking verbs. This section will introduce verbs that require another verb, called an infinitive, to complete their meaning. *Infinitive* comes from the root *in-* which is used in Latin to negate, so *in-finitus* in Latin means "not finite," or "not definite." Infinitives do not have definite subjects as part of their form. Usually they are associated with the English preposition *to*. In English, though, an infinitive can be in the form of *to praise* or just the bare infinitive *praise*. In English, we can say, "he ought to praise" or "he must praise." In both instances, the verb *praise* is in the infinitive. In Latin, the infinitive will be easier to identify because it has the same form in the present tense: *laudāre*.

The infinitive has many more uses in Latin than in English. We will give an overview of possible uses here, but they will be introduced more in depth as we move along in the following chapters.[1]

1. Infinitive as a noun.
   Laudāre bonum est. To praise is good.

2. Infinitives with modals. Chapter 9.
   Dēbet laudāre. He ought to praise.

3. Infinitive plus accusative subject for indirect speech. Chapter 10
   Dīcit sē laudāre. He says that he praises.

4. Infinitive as the subject of an impersonal. Chapter 13.
   Oportet laudāre. It is necessary to praise.

5. Infinitives of purpose. Chapter 10.
   Venit laudāre. He comes to praise.

---

1 In Classical Latin there are two other uses of the infinitive that are far less common in Ecclesiastical Latin. The first is the historical infinitive, in which case an infinitive functions as a finite main verb. There is also an exclamatory infinitive, where, again, the infinitive functions as a finite verb when the speaker is surprised or wants to demonstrate a heightened sense of emotion about an occurrence. Cf. Allen and Greenough, *New Latin Grammar*, §451–63.

§ 32. Verbs Infinitives and Modals: *posse, velle, debēre, nōlle*

Latin functions similarly to English with respect to modal verbs. When a sentence has a modal verb, it typically requires an infinitive to complete its meaning.

Dēbet laudāre. He ought to praise.

The first word, *debet*, is just a typical present active indicative verb. The second verb, *laudare*, is in an infinitive. We now know three uses of the verb: indicative, imperative, and infinitive.[2] That means we can use verbs to indicate, to command, and in a complement form that is not finite or tied to a specific end or subject. It is thus in-finite. Sometimes we call infinitives verbal nouns. This means they have a verb stem but act more like a noun. When you learn verbs in this book, they are presented with the present active infinitive in the second principal part: *laudō, **laudāre**, laudavī, laudatus.*

laudat: he/she/it praises
laudā!: praise!
laudāre: to praise

valet: he/she/it is well
valē!: be well (idiomatically, "goodbye!")
valēre: to be well

mittit: he/she/it sends
mitte!: send!
mittere: to send

venit: he/she/it comes
venī: come!
venire: to come

These are the three forms of the verb we know in all four patterns. You will notice, though, that the final example is not a complete sentence and needs another verb to complete it. Thus, you usually see the infinitive with another verb, sometimes a modal. The infinitive form always shows the conjugation or vowel pattern by the vowel before the *-re*. You can help yourself by learning to pronounce the second conjugation, long *ē* vowel pattern, with the proper long *ē*. Similarly, you can also help yourself by noticing the short vowel pattern in the third conjugation. The emphasis goes on the syllable before the vowel, not on the vowel, and it is therefore short. Here is where pronunciation can really benefit the learner.

---

[2] Indicative and imperative are moods, while the infinitive is what we call a nonfinite verb form. It is not a mood.

CHAPTER 9

Latin has many different modals. We will focus on five for this chapter:

vult, volunt: he/she/it wants; they want
non vult, nolunt: he/she/it does not want; they do not want
dēbet, dēbent: he/she/it must; they must
potest, possunt: he/she/it can; they can
valēt, valēnt: he/she/it is able; they are able

Notice that *vult* and *volunt* do not look at all like any verb we have done so far. It has its own verb pattern shared by only two other verbs (*malle*, "to prefer, chose," and *nolle*, "to not want"). *Dēbet* and *valet* have a long *ē* verb pattern (second conjugation). Finally, *potest*, you might notice, looks like *est* with a different prefix; this verb will always conjugate like *est*.

Some of these modals with the infinitives produce strange looking translations from Latin to English if one simply thinks of the infinitive in English as "to [verb]."

Debēt mittere. "He must to send."

Does that look like good English? You could change it to say, "he ought to send." That would have the same meaning. You can also just drop the *to*. "He must send." This is still technically an infinitive in English, just without the *to*.

We also have to introduce the irregular verbs *posse* and *velle*. These words have their own peculiar conjugations.

Posse: to be able to		*Velle*: to want to; *nolle*: to not want to	
[ego] possum	"I am able"	[ego] volō / nolo	"I want" / "I do not want"
[tū] potes	"You are able"	[tū] vīs / non vis	"You want" / "You do not want"
[ille, illa] potest[3]	"He / she is able"	[ille, illa] vult / non vult	"He / she wants" / "He / she does not want"
[nōs] possumus	"We are able"	[nōs] volumus / nolumus	"We want" / "We do not want"
[vōs] potestis	"You [pl.] are able"	[vōs] vultis / nultis	"You [pl.] want" / "You do not want"
[illī, illae] possunt	"They are able"	[illī, illae] volunt / nolunt	"They want" / "They do not want"

---

[3] You may notice that sometimes I use *ille, illa, illud* and sometimes *is, ea, id*. Either of these can be used as "he, she, it."

One may notice that *posse* looks very similar to the verb *esse*. The only change is in the prefix. With *posse*, you find either *pos-* or *pot-*. The similarity of *posse* to *esse* will be true for *posse* in all its forms.

§ 33. Verbs: Passive Infinitives

Infinitives, like all verbs, can be active or passive. That is, the subject can do the action of the infinitive or receive the action of the infinitive. In English, this is the equivalent of "to praise" and "to be praised." The first is active, the second is passive. The passive infinitives are less common, but they must be known to understand the language well.

laudāre, laudārī

monēre, monērī

ducere, ducī

audīre, audīrī

The pattern you may notice from all of these is that the active infinitives all have the *-re* form and the passives all have an *-i* at the end. The one that will be the hardest to recognize in context is the third pattern, short i/e-vowel verbs. All of the verbs with long vowels, *ā*, *ē*, and *i* retain the stem plus vowel plus *-r-* form. All of the vowels in the above forms have the markings to show whether they are long or short. For review, long vowels have a longer emphasis in pronunciation.

Here are some examples of these in translation:

Deus laudārī vult. God wants to be praised.
Discipulī monērī nōlunt. The students do not want to be warned.
Servus dūcī dēbet. The servant ought to be led.
Fīlius audīrī potest. The son is able to be heard.

§ 34. Lead Verb Forms and Understanding Latin Sentences

In this section, I want to emphasize and explain how best to work with more complex sentence structures. To this point, we have worked mainly with subject-verb-direct object style sentences, with pronouns added. What is new in this section is the addition of infinitives, that is, verbal nouns. These are words that have verb stems but require another verb in the sentence to make sense. In English, the phrase "to walk over the bridge" is not a complete sentence. You need what I will call a lead verb. A lead verb with this phrase would be "he likes to walk over the bridge," or "he is able to walk over the bridge," or "he comes to walk over the bridge," etc. There are many different kinds of lead verbs. This section focuses on modals: *able, wants, must* etc. We will learn other lead verbs as we go along.

CHAPTER 9

In order to properly follow the syntax of a Latin sentence, it is necessary to identify the lead verb and subject first. Remember in Latin that the subject can be just in the ending of the main verb. In the following sentences, identify the lead verb and subject first, then figure out how to translate the infinitive.

Fīlius ambulāre dēbet. The son must walk.
Laudāre Deum petimus. We seek to praise God.
Discipulī aquilās audīre possunt. They students are able to hear the eagles.

Sententiae Summāriae

Hominēs deum laudāre dēbent, sed nōlunt [non volunt].
Deus laudārī ab hominibus dēbet.
Magistrī discipulōs monēre dēbent, sed nōn possunt.
Discipulī monērī ab magistrō dēbent.
Dominī servōs dūcere dēbent, sed nōlunt.
Servī dūcī ab dominō dēbent.
Ancillae audīre dominōs dēbent, sed nōlunt.
Dominī ab ancillīs audīrī dēbent.

Translations

Humans ought to praise God, but they do not want to.
God ought to be praised by humans.
Teachers ought to warn students but cannot.
Students ought to be warned by the teacher.
Masters ought to lead slaves but do not want to.
Slaves ought to be led by the master.
Maidservants ought to listen to their masters, but they do not want to.
Masters ought to be heard by the maidservants.

Cavēte et Mementōte

The *-re* ending is the standard for the present active infinitive, and the *-rī* is standard for the passive. Be careful, though, of the third conjugation, which only has an *-ī* instead of the *-erī* you might expect.

Vocābula Memoranda

Nōmina

cāritās, cāritātis (f.): love (charity)
corpus, corporis (n.): body
humilitās, humilitātis (f.): humility
lingua, linguae (f.): tongue
multitūdō, multitūdinis (f.): multitude
ovis, ovis, ovium [gen. pl.] (m.): sheep
pactum, pactī (n.): covenant
pāstor, pāstōris (m.): shepherd
resurrēctiō, resurrēctiōnis (f.): resurrection
salvātor, salvātōris (m.): savior
signum, signī (n.): sign
vigilia, vigiliae (f.): the watch, the lookout

Verba

Irregular
possum, posse, potuī,—: be able to
nōlō, nōlle, nōluī,—: not want to; be unwilling to
volō, velle, voluī,—: want to; be willing to

ā-verbs
līberō, līberāre, līberāvī, līberātus: set free, to liberate
mundō, mundāre, mundāvī, mundātus: make clean
peccō, peccāre, peccāvī, peccātus: sin
sānō, sānāre, sānāvī, sānātus: heal

ē-verbs
dēbeō, dēbēre, dēbuī, dēbitus: ought, must, owe
rīdeō, rīdēre, rīsī, rīsus: laugh
valeō, valēre, valuī, valitus: be able, be strong

i/e-verbs
discō, discere, didicī, discitus: learn
ostendō [obs + tendo], ostendere, ostendī, ostēnsus: show
vīvō, vīvere, vīxī, victus: live

i-verbs
inveniō [in + veniō], invenīre, invēnī, inventus: find [*lit.* to come into]
reperiō, reperīre, repperī, repertus: find
sentiō, sentīre, sēnsī, sēnsus: sense, think

Adjectīva

cūnctus, -a, -um: all
stultus, -a, -um: foolish, stupid
novus, -a, -um: new

Fābula Ficta

Abrahamus a deo vocātur et Deus fīlium prōmittit:

Abrahamus gregem ovium dūcit in vallē terrae Chaldaeōrum. Deus Abrahamō vocat: "dīscēde ex terrā patris tuī et pete terram novam. Vide caelum! Potesne tū numerāre stellās? tuī fīliī aequābunt eās numerō." Et Deus pactum facit cum Abrahamō. Abrahamus dēbet audīre Deō. Abrahamus Sarae dīcit de pactō: "Deus nōs prōmittit dare nōbīs fīlium. Nōs autem ambulāre debemus ad terram quam Deus nōbīs ostendit." Abrahamus, ergō, et Sara dīscēdunt de terrā Chaldaeōrum. Ambulant ad terram quam Deus eīs ostendit.

Abrahamus est senex et Sara eius uxor nōn potest habēre neque fīliōs neque fīliās. Abrahamus habēre filium vult et quoque Sara filium habēre vult. Volunt habēre multōs fīliōs fīliāsque. Deus Abrahamō et Sarae fīliōs dare prōmittit. Quōmodo Sara fīliōs habēre potest? Abrahamus et Sara nōn crēdunt Deum et rīdent. Dēbent crēdere Deum.

Abrahamus autem Sarae dīcit: "Egō dēbeō filium habēre. Tū nōn filium habēre potes. Da mihi quaesō ancillam tuam." Sara ancillam, quī potest habēre fīliōs, Abrahamō dat. Ancilla, nōmine Hagar, invenītur cum fīliō, nōmine Ishmael.

vallis, vallis (m.): valley
Chaldaeus: Chaldean, Babylonian
discedo, discedere: leave
numero, numerare: count
aequaro, aequare: equal
senex, senis: old man
quaeso: I beg, I ask
promitto [pro + mitto], promittere: to promise

1. Quem Deus vocat?
2. Unde venit Abrahamus?
3. Ubi ambulant Abrahamus et uxor eius?
4. Habentne Abrahamus et uxor eius fīliōs (in prīmīs, "in the beginning")? Cur nōn?
5. Cur Sara et Abrahamus rīdent?

Nativitas Domini

Nativitas Domini ostenditur creātūris cūnctīs. Est enim creātūra, quae tantum habet esse sīcut pūrē corpōreā; creātūra, quae habet esse et vīvere sīcut vegetābilia; creātūra, quae habet esse, vīvere et sentīre sīcut animālia; creātūra, quae habet esse, vīvere, sentīre, discernere et intelligere sīcut angelus. Per hās creātūrās cūnctās hodiē Christī nativitas ostenditur.

Nativitas ostenditur per creātūram, quae habet esse, vīvere, sentīre et discenere, ut est homō, sīcut per pastōrēs. Nam in illā hōrā, pastōrēs super gregem suum vigilant. Mōs est gentibus in temporibus antīquīs custōdīre vigiliās noctis. Illīs pastōribus igitur angelus domini appāret et Salvātōrem natum adnūntiat, et quōmodō invenītur, et signum dat illam. Et ecce angelus Domini stat iūxta illōs pastōrēs et clāritās Dei circumfulgit illōs, et timent timōre magnō. Et cum angelō multitūdō militiae caelestis vidētur ab pastōribus cantāre "glōria in altissimīs deō et in terrā pāx hominibus bonae voluntātis." Pastōrēs angelōs discēdere spectant et illī veniunt ad Bethlehem et Salvātōrem natum inveniunt.

Cf. Jacob de Voragine, *De nativitate domini* et Lk 2.

nātīvitās, nātīvitātis (f.): nativity
ut: as
pure: purely, only
vegetabilia: vegetative things / things capable of growing
discernere: to discern
hodie: today
mos est: it is the custom
circumfulgit: shines around

Sententiae Interpretandae

1. Quī autem intrat per januam, pastor est ovium. Huic vir aperit, et ovēs vōcem eius audiunt, et ovēs vocantur nōminibus eōrum et dūcit eās. (Jn 10:2–3)
2. Nos autem debemus gratias agere Deo semper pro vobis. (2 Thes 2:12)
3. Viri debent diligere uxores suas ut corpora sua. (Eph 5:28)

ut: as

4. Ego a te debeo baptizari, et tu venis ad me? (Mt 3:14)
5. Sunt autem stultī quī dicunt: Cur nōn potest aliter Sapientia Deī hominēs līberāre? (Augustine, *De Agone Christiano* XI)

aliter: in another way

6. Multī autem dicunt: Quōmodō possumus vincere diabolum quem nōn vidēmus? (Augustine, *De Agone Christiano* XI)

vincere: conquer
diabolus, diaboli (m.): devil
quomodo: how

7. Dīlige, et quod vīs fac. Ama hominem, nōn ejus errōrem. (Augustine, *In Epistolam Ioannis ad Parthos* 7)

error, erroris: error

8. Errāre hūmānum est, persevērāre diabolicum.

errare: to wander, to err
perseverare: persevere

9. Sī portārī vīs, portā et alium. (Thomas a Kempis, *De Imitatione Christi*)

alium: another

10. Nōn potest arbor bona frūctūs malōs facere. (Lk 6:43)

fructūs: accusative masculine plural (matches "malos"); fruit

11. Tunc respondent eī quīdam de scrībīs et pharīsaeīs, "Magister, volumus ā tē signum vidēre." (Mt 12:38)

scriba, scribae (m.): scribe
pharisaeus: Pharisee

12. Fīliī Isrāēl nōlunt audīre tē, quia nōlunt audīre mē. (Ezek 3:7)
13. Vidēre tuum est amāre. (Nicolas of Cusa)
14. Spiritus Sanctus facit nōs rēctē amāre, desiderāre et petere. (Thomas Aquinas *Expositio in Orationem Domincam*)

rēctē: rightly
desiderare: to desire

15. Nam quae superbia sanārī potest, sī humilitāte Fīliī Deī nōn sanātur? Quae avaritia sanārī potest, sī paupertāte Fīliī Deī nōn sanātur? Quae īracundia sanārī potest, sī patientiā Fīliī Deī nōn sanātur? Quae impietās sanārī potest, quae caritāte Fīliī Deī nōn sanātur? Postremō quae timiditās sanārī potest, sī resurrectiōne corporis Christī Dominī nōn sanātur? (Augustine, *De Agone Christiano* XI)

superbia, superbiae (f.): pride
impietas, impietatis (f.): impiety
avāritia, avāritiae (f.): avarice
irācundiā, īrācundiā (f.): anger
patientia, patientiae (f.): patience
paupertas, paupertatis (f.): poverty
timiditas, timiditatis (f.): timidity
postremo: finally

Sententiae Fictae

1. Stultus pāstor quī dēbet tenēre vigiliās nōn vult tenēre vigiliās super gregēs eius. Quid vult? Vult dormīre in terrā.
2. Bonī hominēs peccāre nōn dēbent, sed peccāre volunt.
3. Pāstōrēs bonī invenīre aquam et cibum volunt, sed patientiam habēre dēbent.
4. Sī hominēs peccant, mundārī humilitāte salvātōris et mandūcāre corpus eius dēbent.
5. Homō invenīre resurrēctiōnem corporis vult, sed nōn vult nōn peccāre.
6. Cor eius mundārī cāritāte salvātōris dēbet, deinde resurrēctiōnem habet.
7. Pāstor ovēs ad mare dūcunt, cum eae bibere volunt.
8. Nōn sōlum cibum ovibus pāstōrēs dant, sed etiam aquam.
9. Fessus pastor ambulāre nōn valet.
10. Fessae ovēs dūcī ab malō pāstōre nōn possunt.

CHAPTER 10

§ 35. Verbs: Accusative Plus Infinitive Construction

We learned about the infinitive verb in combination with modal verbs (*potest ambulāre*). This is not the only way Latin uses infinitives. Some Latin verbs require that the infinitive follow in a manner that will not directly correspond to English. The construction we will focus on today is the combination of a lead verb in the indicative, such as *audit, jubet, videt*, with an infinitive and accusative clause. The basic pattern we are looking for in all that follows is this combination of the main indicative verb with connected clause based on an infinitive verb and accusative noun.

As we already know by this point, Latin style differs from English style. Latin sentences tend to be much longer with many different connected phrases, based on one main phrase. The more familiar we become with how Latin works in larger chunks, the better we will be at being able to read more Latin fluently. We started very early with the use of relative clauses to connect phrases. Here we will use the accusative and infinitive construction to connect thoughts. The next big way to connect more clauses is with participles and the ablative absolute. Looking forward, as our reading passages become more complicated, we will eventually see all of these kinds of constructions working together.

When you come across verbs like *audit,* and *videt* in Latin, sometimes you will find a construction of an infinitive with an accusative. The expressions that you learn in this chapter will nearly always feel awkward in English if you translate the Latin literally. It is key to remember how Latin has its own way of composing thoughts that does not always match the English.

Audit filium vocāre. He hears the son call [*lit.* to call].
Videt puellam cadere. He sees the girl fall [*lit.* to fall].

In all the above examples, you have a head verb and then an accusative and infinitive complement to complete the thought. You will notice that in some cases the "literal" translation in the parentheses would not be correct English. It is important to be aware of when this happens because the temptation will be to either go with the woodenly literal translation or to think you do not understand the sentence because it does not fit the rules of good English.

Nouns: Accusatives as Subjects

The last thing to mention about the accusative and infinitive construction is that we will have to amend a principle we learned in the very beginning of the book. In chapter 1, we discussed how the nominative is the subject of the sentence. When we use the accusative and infinitive construction with a head verb, if there is a new subject in the clause created by the accusative and infinitive, it will be in the accusative like the direct object. The first question all students have is, "how will I know which is the subject and which is the direct object?" The answer every teacher gives and every student hates is "you will know in context." The fact is that the grammar of Latin does not always provide a clear answer as to what the subject is.

*Pater videt **filium** pulsāre **filiam**.* The father sees [that] the son punches [*lit.* to punch] the daughter.

Who punches whom (direct object!)? We know the father sees the action, but it is not clear in Latin who did what. Likely the subject will go first, so it is the son who punches the daughter. So the full sentence should read, "the father sees the son punch the daughter" [*lit.* the father sees the son to punch the daughter].

One possible way that Latin will solve this problem is to use the passive infinitive.

*Pater videt **filiam** pulsārī ā filiō.* The father sees [that] the daughter is punched [*lit.* to be punched] by the son.

Now we have no doubt that the father sees the daughter to be punched by the son. But this is not always how Latin is written.

§ 36. Verbs: Indirect Statement (*Oratio Obliqua*)

Another way in which Latin uses the construction of the infinitive plus an accusative is in what is called an indirect statement, or *oratio obliqua*.

Let's take an example in English. If my brother says, "I am good at golf," and I report it to my wife, I will say, "he says that he is good at golf." My brother didn't use the exact words "he is good at golf." They have changed from the original and have become what we call "indirect speech," or in Latin, *oratio obliqua*. This is how we report things. We change the subject and add the word *that*. The first thing my brother says is called direct speech (*oratio recta*).

Let's look at an example in Latin:

Marcus: "Ego sum bonus." Marcus: "I am good."
*Mārcus dīcit sē esse **bonum**.* Marcus says that he is good [*lit.* Marcus says himself to be good].

The first example is direct speech and the second is indirect speech. This form of indirect speech is less common in the Vulgate but still shows up in other Ecclesiastical authors. There are many possible verbs that will introduce indirect speech or the general use of accusative and infinitive.

*Chrīstiānī crēdunt **Jēsum esse Deum**.* Christians believe [that] Jesus is [*lit.* to be] God.

Andreās: "ūnus puer est et habet duo piscēs et quīnque pānēs." Andreas: "there is one boy and he has two fish and five loaves."

*Andreās dīcit **ūnum puerum** esse et habēre duo **piscēs** et quīnque **pānēs**.* Andrew says [that] there is [*lit.* to be] one boy and he has two fish and five loaves.

Jesus: "Veniō dare pācem in terram." Jesus: I have come to give peace to the earth.

Jēsus dīcit sē venīre dare pācem in terram. Jesus says [that] he has come [*lit.* himself to come] to give peace to the earth.

Moving from an infinitive in Latin indirect speech to English is difficult. This is just further evidence of the difficulty of moving from an ancient language to a modern one. It does not always fit nicely. This is why, in many cases, a "literal" translation is not even a translation at all. It does not carry across (*translatio* means to carry across) the meaning of one language into another. All translation requires the translator to do their best to be attentive to the ancient meaning and the modern idiom. I give many quick and simplistic glosses or meanings in this book to help the beginning student get off the ground. Eventually, one must leave these simple glosses behind when the reader has more experience with the language. It is an art and not a science. As the Italians say, *traduttore, traditore*: the translator is a traitor.

§ 37. Syntax: Using *quia*, *quoniam*, and *quod* in Indirect Speech

Latin does not only use the infinitive to create indirect speech. After the translation of the New Testament into Latin, many stylistic features of Koine Greek became common in Latin. Thus, Latin writers began to incorporate the words *quia*, *quoniam*, and *quod* in place of the accusative and infinitive construction we learned above. *Quia* can be used to introduce indirect speech, and the accusative plus infinitive construction does not need to be used.

"*Putātis quia pācem veniō dare in terram?*" (Lk 12:51)
"Do you think that I come to give peace on earth?"

In this quote, Luke could have said, "*Putātis me venīre pacem dare in terram?*" But we often find in the New Testament a construction with *quia* rather than the accusative and infinitive.

Quia and *quoniam* can also be used to introduce indirect speech, primarily in the New Testament. This arises from the early translations of the Greek text into Latin. This is not typically done in non-Christian texts. In the examples below, the *Q* is capitalized, and this indicates where the quote begins. Quotation marks are sometimes added in this text to make this clear, but most versions of the Latin bible do not include them; instead, a capitalized *Q* indicates that the following *Quia* or *Quoniam* present the beginning of a quotation.

> *Quōmodo ergō dīcit hic: Quia dē caelō dēscendī?* (Jn 6:42) "How therefore does he say, [that] 'I have descended from heaven?'"

> "*Rūrsumque concēpit et peperit fīlium, et ait: 'Quoniam audīvit mē Dominus habērī contemptuī.'*" (Gn 29:33) "And again she conceived and bore a son, and said: [that] 'The Lord heard that I was despised.'"

> In these situations, the *quia* or the *quoniam* can be omitted from the translation. The Nova Vulgata has been printed without these additional words.

§ 38. Pronouns: *ipse, ipsa, ipsum*

As there are many pronouns in Latin, it is necessary to present a new one here. This one is called an intensive pronoun. *Ipse, ipsa, ipsum* often intensifies a noun. *Deus ipse* means "God himself." Sometimes the intensive is translated in this way, but also sometimes in the New Testament, it will just be used in place of another pronoun. It is important to remember that it is an intensifier, but it is not always strictly necessary to translate the intensive version.

Cases	M. P.	F. P.	N. S.	Example Translation
Nom	*ips|e*	*ips|a*	*ips|um*	himself
Gen	*ips|ius*	*ips|ius*	*ips|ius*	of himself
Dat	*ips|ī*	*ips|ī*	*ips|ī*	to himself
Acc	*ips|um*	*ips|am*	*ips|um*	himself (d.o.)
Abl	*ips|ō*	*ips|ā*	*ips|ō*	by himself

Cases	M. P.	F. P.	N. S.	Example Translation
Nom	*ips|ī*	*ips|ae*	*ips|a*	themselves
Gen	*ips|ōrum*	*ips|ārum*	*ips|ōrum*	of themselves
Dat	*ips|īs*	*ips|īs*	*ips|īs*	to themselves
Acc	*ips|ōs*	*ips|as*	*ips|a*	themselves (d.o.)
Abl	*ips|īs*	*ips|īs*	*ips|īs*	by themselves

CHAPTER 10

Sententiae Summāriae

Servī filiās filiōsque dominī ambulare putant.
Magister discipulōs librōs scrībere videt.
Discipulus magistrum nōn esse bonum scrībit.
Discipulī magistrōs nōn esse bonōs scrībunt.
Vir dominī plēbēs Deī cantāre Deō audit.
Jēsus dīcit sē esse Fīlium Deī.
Jēsus dīcit quia is est Fīlius Deī.

Translations

Slaves think the master's daughters and sons are walking.
The teacher sees [that] the students write books.
The student writes [that] the teacher is not good.
The students write [that] the teachers are not good.
The man of the Lord hears [that] the common people sing to God.
Jesus says he is the Son of God.
Jesus says that he is the son of God.

Cavēte et Mementōte

Having to look out for accusatives as subjects is a difficult part of indirect speech and the accusative/infinitive construction. That said, remember that the order of the words can clue you in to the subject like English in some cases.

Vocābula Memoranda

Nōmina

dux, dūcis (m.): leader
oppidum, oppidī (n.): town
pater, patris (m.): father
phantasma, phantasmae (f.): ghost, phantasm
praesentia, praesentiae (f.): presence
superbia, superbiae (f.): pride
vestīmentum, vestīmentī (n.): clothes
vīnum, vīnī (n.): wine

Verba

ā-verbs
aedificō [aedis + facere], aedificāre, aedificāvī, aedificātus: build [*lit.* make a building]
ministrō, ministrāre, ministrāvī, ministrātus: serve
putō, putāre, putāvī, putātus: think
temptō, temptāre, temptāvī, temptātus: test, try

ē-verbs
jaceō, jacēre, jacuī, jacitus: lie down
jubeō, jubēre, jussī, jussus: command
perhibeō [per + habeō], perhibēre, perhibuī, perhibitus: present, give

i/e-verbs
colligō [con + ligare], colligere, collēgī, collēctus: collect [*lit.* bind together]
convertō [con + verto], convertere, convertī, conversus: convert, turn around
emō, emere, ēmī, ēmptus: buy
 redēmō [rē-d-emō], redemere, redēmī, redēmptus: buy back
scrībō, scrībere, scrīpsī, scrīptus: write
tollō, tollere, sustulī, sublātus: pick up, take up

io-verb
cupiō, cupere, cupīvī, cupītus: desire

adverbia

ubique: everywhere
dein, deinde: then

coniunctiva

at: but, but yet
atque: and

Fābula Ficta

Post haec, ambulat Jēsus trāns mare Galilaeae, quod est Tiberiadis. Multitūdō magna cum Jēsū venit, quia vident Jēsum sanāre aegrōs. Ascendit ergō in montem Jēsus et ibi sedet cum discipulīs suīs. Jēsus vīdet multitūdinem hominum venīre ad eum et dīcit ad Philippum: "volō emere pānēs. Hominēs volunt mandūcāre." Hoc autem dīcit temptāre eum. Respondit eī Philippus: "Ducentōrum dēnāriōrum pānēs nōn sufficiunt eīs." Dīcit eī ūnus ex discipulīs eius, Andreās, frāter Simōnis Petrī: "Est puer ūnus hīc quī habet quīnque pānēs et duōs piscēs: sed num haec sufficiunt?" Jacōbus, frāter Jōhannis, nōn audit, sed vult intelligere. Jacōbus frātrem eius interrogat: "Quid Andreās dīcit?" Jōhannis dīcit: "Andreās dīcit ūnum puerum esse hīc et eum habēre quīnque pānēs et duōs piscēs." Deinde Jēsus turbae dīcit, "Jacēte." Jacobus Jōhannem interrogat: "Quid Jēsus dīcit?" Jōhannis respondit: "Jēsus jubet hominēs jacere." Hominēs in terrā jacent. Hominēs obēdiunt. Accipit Jēsus pānēs et grātiās patrī agit et hominibus pānēs dat. Quoque Jēsus piscēs accipit et grātiās patrī agit et hominibus piscēs dat. Deinde, Jēsus discipulōs colligere fragmenta ex quīnque pānibus jubet. Jacobus iterum Jōhannem interrogat: "Quid Jēsus jubet?" Et Jōhannem respondit: "Jēsus pānēs et piscēs colligī ā discipulīs jubet." Illī hominēs vident Jēsum facere signum et dīcunt: "Quia hic est vērē prophēta quī venit in mundum."

Cf. John 6:1–14

Tiberiadis: of Tiberias
ducentorum denariorum: 200 denarii worth of bread
sufficiunt: to be sufficient
ibi: there (in that place)

1. Cūr est magna multitudō cum Jēsus? Quid volunt?
2. Quid Jēsus vīdet?
3. Quid Jēsus vult facere prō (for) multitudīne hominum?
4. Discipulī putant se non posse dare cibum hominibus? Cūr?
5. Quid Jēsus hominēs facere jubet?
6. Cūr hominēs dīcunt Jēsum esse vērum prophētam?

Sententiae Interpretandae

1. Sadducaeī enim dicunt nōn esse resurrectiōnem, neque angelum, neque spīritum. (Acts 23:8)

   spiritum: spirit
   Sadducaeus: Sadducee

2. Dicunt eum esse deum. (Acts 28:6)
3. At illī vīdent eum ambulāre super mare et putant phantasma esse et exclāmant. (Mk 6:49)
4. Vōs interrogātis scrīptūrās, quia vōs putātis in ipsīs vītam aeternam habēre, et illae sunt, quae testimōnium perhibent de mē. Sed nōn vultis venīre ad mē habēre vītam. (Jn 5:39–40)

   testimōnium: witness, testimony

5. Et ipse interrogat discipulōs suōs: "Quem mē dicunt esse hominēs?" Quī respondent illī: Joannem Baptīstam, aliī Ēliam, aliī vērō quasi ūnum de prophētīs. Tunc dīcit illīs: Vōs vērō quem mē esse dīcitis? Respondet Petrus, ait eī: Tū es Christus. (Mk 8:27–29)

   quasi unum: as if one
   alius, alia, aliud: other

6. Dīcit autem ad illōs: Quōmodō dicunt Christum fīlium esse Davīd? (Lk 11:41)
7. Cum haec ergō dīcit, ostendit nōbīs sē habēre superbiam. (Regula Benedicti 7)
8. Ubīque crēdimus dīvīnam esse praesentiam. (Regula Benedicti 19)
9. Domus enim, quam cupio aedificāre, magna est. (2 Chr 2:9)

domus, domūs (f.): house

10. Fīlius hominis nōn venit ministrārī sed ministrāre. (Mt 20:28)
11. Rogō ergō tē, pater, mittere eum in domum patris meī.
12. Deī Fīlius crucifīgitur, sed in crūce hominis mortem Deus vincit. Christus Deī Fīlius moritur, sed omnis carō vīvificātur in Christō. (St. Hilary, *De Trinitate* 3.15)

curcifigare: to crucify, torment
crux, crucis: cross
moritur: dies
omnis: all
vivificare: to make alive

13. Sanctus Cuthbertus aquam in vinum convertit. (*Vita Sancti Cutherberti*)
14. In gremiō patris esse fīlium et semper esse Iōhannēs dīcit; nōn sōlum ergō patrem videt, sed etiam in patre semper est. (Marius Victorinus, *Adversus Arium* 1.16)

gremius: lap, bosom

15. Vae vobis scribæ et pharisæi hypocritae, qui aedificatis sepulchra prophetarum. (Mt 23:29)

vae: woe!
scriba, scribae (m.): scribe
pharisaeus, pharisaei (m.): pharisee
hypocrita, hypcoritae (m.): hypocrite
sepulchrum, sepulchri (n.): tombs

16. Qui autem prophetat, ecclesiam Dei aedificat. (1 Cor 14:3)

prophetare: to prophesy

17. Tunc jubet eum mittī in aquam. (Jacobus de Voragine, *De Sancti Blasi*)

Sententiae Fictae

1. Prophēta: "Cum hominēs putant sē esse deōs, ipsa superbia est."
2. Phantasma putat sē esse hominem, sed nōn potest spīrāre atque vestimenta non habet.
3. Discipulī praesentiam hominis sentiunt, sed corpora vidērī nōn possunt.
4. Quid est? Phantasma praesentia hominis est, sed corpus tenērī non potest.
5. Dum ovēs fessī iacent in valle prope fluvium, pāstōrēs cibum petunt in montibus, quia nōn possunt emere cibum.
6. Prophētae ministrāre gentēs volunt, sed multae gentēs audīre nōlunt.
7. Agricolae colligere cibum nōn possunt et cibum invenīre nōn possunt in agrīs.
8. Dominus agricolārum eōs emere cibum jubet.
9. Agricolae autem ambulāre in oppidum nolunt atque putant dominum esse superbum.
10. Agricolae ergō in agrōs jacent et dominum eōs jubēre nōn audiunt.

CHAPTER 11

☙❧

§ 39. Nouns: U-Nouns (Fourth Declension), Masculine and Feminine

It is now time to introduce the fourth declension. This is a pattern for nouns that is less frequent than first, second, or third, but cannot be ignored. Some common words in this declension are *spiritus, -us*; *manus, -us* (f.); and *exercitus, -us*. "Spirit," "hand," and "army" are fairly common. You will notice in how they are written that they look like they could be the second declension pattern like the word *filius*. They are not. It was mentioned that verbs have vowel patterns in their conjugations and some nouns have vowel patterns in their declensions; the *-a-* for feminine first declension is easy to remember. Fourth declension has *-u-* for its pattern. Most u-nouns are masculine or neuter. *Manus* and *domus* are feminine words in this declension.

	Singular	Plural
Nom	spīrit|us	spīrit|ūs
Gen	spīrit|ūs	spīrit|uum
Dat	spīrit|uī	spīrit|ibus
Acc	spīrit|um	spīrit|ūs
Abl	spīrit|ū	spīrit|ibus

Now we can see why so many prayers that include the word *spirit* seem slightly off. *In nōmine Patris, et Fīliī, et Spīritūs Sānctī*. Why doesn't the word *spiritus* agree with the word *sancti*?

Trick question: it does! *Spiritus* just happens to be the fourth declension and not the second declension like the word *sanctus*.

What about this: *glōria patrī et filiō et spīrituī sānctō*? Why does the word *spiritui* have an *i* and not an *o* like *filio* and *sancto*? Because it's the fourth declension!

Spīritus Sānctus Apostolum īnspīrat. The Holy Spirit inspires the Apostle.
Apostolus ab Spīritū Sānctō īnspīrātur. The Apostle is inspired by the Holy Spirit.
Cāritās Spīritūs Sānctī aeterna est. The love of the Holy Spirit is eternal.
Homō laudem Spīrituī Sānctō dat. The person gives praise to the Holy Spirit.
Vir dominī Spīritum Sānctum invocat. The man of the Lord calls upon the Holy Spirit.

§ 40. Nouns U-Nouns (Fourth Declension), Neuter

	Singular	Plural
Nom	*corn|ū*	*corn|ua*
Gen	*corn|ūs*	*corn|uum*
Dat	*corn|ū*	*corn|ibus*
Acc	*corn|ū*	*corn|ua*
Abl	*corn|ū*	*corn|ibus*

When we move to the neuter of the fourth declension, we still have *-u-* as the theme vowel. The other thing to remember here is that it is still neuter so we have *-a-* in the neuter plural nominative and accusative. We also have basically the same form in the singular with just the *-u-*. The only way to know which case the author is using is by context.

§ 41. Adjectives: I/E-Adjectives (Third Declension)

We have seen adjectives that ended in *-us, -a, -um* and look like masculine, feminine, or neuter nouns of the first and second declension. We will now meet adjectives that look like the third declension nouns. The good news is that there are no more declensions for adjectives. They will either follow -a-nouns and -o-nouns (first and second declension) or i/e-nouns (third declension).

The chart for these i/e-adjectives will be listed below. Remember also that adjectives match the nouns they modify in gender, number, and case, *not* declension. So, *fortis puella* says "a strong girl" and it agrees in gender number and case, *not* declension.

	M. S.	F. S.	N. S.	M. P.	F. P.	N. P.
Nom	*acer*	*acr|is*	*acr|e*	*acr|es*	*acr|es*	*acr|ia*
Gen	*acr|is*	*acr|is*	*acr|is*	*acr|ium*	*acr|ium*	*acr|ium*
Dat	*acr|i*	*acr|i*	*acr|i*	*acr|ibus*	*acr|ibus*	*acr|ibus*
Acc	*acr|em*	*acr|em*	*acr|e*	*acr|es*	*acr|es*	*acr|ia*
Abl	*acr|i*	*acr|i*	*acr|i*	*acr|ibus*	*acr|ibus*	*acr|ibus*

Here are all the typical endings for third declension adjectives. This is the chart you should memorize.

	M. S.	F. S.	N. S.	M. P.	F. P.	N. P.
Nom	-	*-is*	*-e*	*-es*	*-es*	*-ia*
Gen	*-is*	*-is*	*-is*	*-ium*	*-ium*	*-ium*
Dat	*-i*	*-i*	*-i*	*-ibus*	*-ibus*	*-ibus*
Acc	*-em*	*-em*	*-e*	*-es*	*-es*	*-ia*
Abl	*-i*	*-i*	*-i*	*-ibus*	*-ibus*	*-ibus*

A few quick things to notice: the ablative ends in *-i* and not *-e*. We have an extra *i* in the genitive plural and the neuter plural nominative and singular. Everything else is fairly regular.

Some third declension adjectives have the same nominative singular in the masculine and feminine like the adjective below: *omnis, omnis, omne*.

	M. S.	F. S.	N. S.	M. P.	F. P.	N. P.
Nom	*omn|is*	*omn|is*	*omn|e*	*omn|es*	*omn|es*	*omn|ia*
Gen	*omn|is*	*omn|is*	*omn|is*	*omn|ium*	*omn|ium*	*omn|ium*
Dat	*omn|i*	*omn|i*	*omn|i*	*omn|ibus*	*omn|ibus*	*omn|ibus*
Acc	*omn|em*	*omn|em*	*omn|e*	*omn|es*	*omn|es*	*omn|ia*
Abl	*omn|i*	*omn|i*	*omn|i*	*omn|ibus*	*omn|ibus*	*omn|ibus*

This word appears very frequently and can mean "every," usually in the singular *omnis homo* (every human), or "all" in the plural *omnia verba* (all words). Also, this word probably appears in what we call the substantive just as often as an actual adjective paired with a noun it modifies to give more information.

Omnēs omnia amant. All people love all things.

Notice in the nominative we have a masculine (or feminine) plural subject that has no noun to pair with it. So we must assume that it means "all people" because it is not neuter. But the second word *omnia* is in the neuter plural accusative. It does not have a noun it matches, so it must mean "all things." These two words will often appear in these substantival forms.

We also have a few third declension adjectives that have the same nominative singular forms in masculine, feminine, and neuter, like the word *felix, felix, felix*. The rest of the chart follows like the ones above. Also, be aware, neuter always has the same forms in the nominative and accusative, so *felix* will be nominative and accusative for neuter singular.

Here are a few examples:

fēlīx culpa: happy fault
felicēs culpae: happy faults

felix verbum: happy word
felicia verba: happy words

We will learn in the next chapter something called a participle, which is like a combination of a verb and an adjective. The adjective part will look exactly like these third declension adjectives, so it is important to remember these.

§ 42. Adjectives: Comparative and Superlative

The adjectives we discussed above are sometimes called the "positive" form of the adjective. That just means that they are not being used in either the comparative or superlative sense. They just describe a noun. But, as in English, we can compare nouns with adjectives. All adjectives have patterns like first declension (like a-nouns), which are feminine; like second declension (like o-nouns), which are masculine or neuter; or like third declension (like i/e-nouns). *Altus, alta, altum* are adjectives from the first and second declension. *Fortis, fortis, forte* are adjectives from the third declension.

When you want to make adjectives from the first group into comparative, they will take an *-ior* ending which is like third declension endings (like i/e-nouns). The same holds true when you want to make third declension adjectives into comparative; you add an *-ior* ending to the adjective and the endings then follow like a third declension adjective. Thus, *altior* and *fortior*. When you want to make superlative adjectives, whether from first and second declension adjectives or third declension adjectives, they get *-issimus, -issima, -issimum* endings: thus, *altissimus* and *fortissimus*.

Frater meus fortior est. My brother is stronger.
Frater meus fortissimus est. My brother is the strongest.

To form the comparative, you take the adjective stem *alt-* or *fort-* and add *-ior*. Whatever case the noun is in, the comparative still has to agree in gender number and case: *manus fortioris fratris* (the hand of the stronger brother). Here, the comparative adjective *fortior* pairs with the noun *fratris*, which is in the genitive, and so it has to agree.

	M. S.	F. S.	N. S.	M. P.	F. P.	N. P.
Nom	*alt|ior*	*alt|ior*	*alt|ius*	*altiōr|ēs*	*altiōr|ēs*	*altiōr|a*
Gen	*altiōr|is*	*altiōr|is*	*altiōr|is*	*altiōr|um*	*altiōr|um*	*altiōr|um*
Dat	*altiōr|ī*	*altiōr|ī*	*altiōr|ī*	*altiōr|ibus*	*altiōr|ibus*	*altiōr|ibus*
Acc	*altiōr|em*	*altiōr|em*	*alt|ius*	*altiōr|ēs*	*altiōr|ēs*	*altiōr|a*
Abl	*altiōr|e*	*altiōr|e*	*altiōr|e*	*altiōr|ibus*	*altiōr|ibus*	*altiōr|ibus*

The one minor thing to note about these third declension adjectives is the *-e* at the end of the ablative singular. These are what are traditionally called *non-i-stem* third declension adjectives, because they do not have an *i* before the *a* in the neuter plural, nor an *i* before the *um* in the genitive plural.

Whenever you see *-ior* near the end of a word, it is a comparative adjective and will be translated in English with either the "-er" form of an adjective or the adverb "more" as in "more beautiful." (Because we don't say "beautiful-er" in English!)

There are two ways to make a comparison with adjectives. You can use *quam* or an ablative of the second noun being compared.

Haec arbor est altior quam illa arbor. This tree is taller than that tree.
Haec arbor est altior illā arbōre. This tree is taller than that tree.

Both of these are "correct" Latin and mean the same thing. Latin has many situations where there are many possibilities for construction but no substantial difference in meaning.

The last thing to know about adjectives is that they can also be superlative: "the strongest brother" or "the very strong brother." In Latin, *frater fortissimus*. The comparative form of the adjective acts like a third declension adjective, *fortior*. The comparative acts like a second or first declension adjective, *fortissima*. This one is very easy to spot as well. Most of the time you will have *-issim-* added to the stem of the adjective, *callidissima puella*, "the smartest girl" or "the very smart girl."

So there are no new endings to learn for either of these. The endings match the nouns we have already seen in previous chapters. They are either third declension, *-ior, -ior, -ius* (m., f., n.), or first and second declension, *-issimus, -issima, issimum*.

We just saw above that *quam* can mean "than." It can also mean "as." *Quam* is one of these words where what it means depends entirely on context, and that can be tricky.

> *Petrus nōn tam callidus est quam Paulus.* Peter is not as smart as Paul [*lit.* Peter not as smart is as Paul].

We will know that the *quam* means "as" in this case because it is coupled with the *tam*. Latin has many of these constructions that combine two words to make a sort of new meaning.

Sententiae Summāriae

> Spīritus sānctus in domō Deī habitat.
> Gladius Spīritūs est verbum Deī.
> Plēbs Deī Spīritum Sānctum laudat.
> Plēbs Deī ab Spīritū Sānctō monētur.
> Plēbs Deī Spīrituī Sānctō dicit.
> Exercitūs angelōrum Deō cantant.
> Exercitūs daemonium exercitūs angelōrum oppugnant. Exercitūs autem angelōrum fortiōrēs sunt.
> Exercitūs angelōrum ab exercitibus daemonium oppugnantur. Exercitūs angelōrum pulchriōrēs sunt.

Translations

> The Holy Spirit lives in the house of God.
> The sword of the Spirit is the word of God.
> The people of God praise the Holy Spirit.
> The people of God are warned by the Holy Spirit.
> The people of God speak to the Holy Spirit.
> The armies of angels sing to God.
> The armies of demons attack the armies of angels. The armies of angels, however, are stronger.
> The armies of angels are attacked by the armies of demons. The armies of angels are more beautiful.

Cavēte et Mementōte

Fourth declension has the theme vowel of *-u*, which is consistent throughout.

Also, *-ior* and *-issim-* are the standard forms for comparative and superlative adjectives. Remember those endings.

Vocābula Memoranda

Nōmina

arma, armōrum (n. pl.): arms, weapons[1]
castra, castrōrum (n. pl.): camp
cōnspectus, cōnspectūs (m.): sight
cornū, cornūs (n.): horn
domus, domūs (f.): home
exercitus, exercitūs (m.): army, host
fructus, fructūs (m.): fruit
gladius, gladiī (m.): sword
lacrima, lacrimae (f.): tears
leō, leōnis (m.): lion
manūs, manūs (f.): hand
proelium, proeliī (n.): battle
soror, sorōris (f.): sister
scūtum, scūtī (n.): shield
spīritus, spīritūs (m.): spirit

Verba

<u>*ā-verb*</u>
 pugnō, pugnāre, pugnāvī, pugnātus: fight

<u>*i/e-verbs*</u>
 cognōscō [con + gnosco], cognōscere, cognōvī, cognitus: know, recognize
 induō, induere, induī, indūtus: put on

<u>*i-verb*</u>
 conveniō [cōn + veniō], convenīre, convēnī, conventūs: come together

---

[1] A few Latin words only exist in the plural; *arma* and *castra* are two good examples.

Adjectīva

altus, alta, altum: high, tall
dulcis, dulcis, dulce: sweet
fortis, fortis, forte: strong
gravis, gravis, grave: heavy
levis, levis, leve: light
omnipotēns, (gen. sing., *omnipotentis*): almighty
pulcher, pulchra, pulchrum: beautiful, handsome
suāvis, suāvis, suāve: agreeable, pleasant

Adverbium

nimis: too (much)

Praepositiōnēs

inter (+acc): between
sine (+abl): without

Fābula Ficta

Philisthiim exercitum suum congregant in proelium atque conveniunt in Sochō Jūdae. Saūl et fīliī Israēl veniunt in vallem Terebinthī, et dūcit exercitum pugnāre contrā Philisthiim. Et Philisthiim stant super montem ex parte hāc, et Israēl stant suprā montem ex alterā parte: vallisque est inter eōs. Et ambulat vir altissimus dē castrīs Philisthinōrum nōmine Goliath, dē Geth. Et galea super caput eius, et lōrīca, quae est gravidissima, induitur. Sūmit manibus scūtum grave et gladium gravem. Clāmat adversum exercitum Israēl, et dīcit eīs: "Cur venītis pugnāre? Numquid ego nōn sum Philisthaeus et vōs servī Saūl? Ego sum altissimus et fortissimus! Quis altior et fortior est? Numquid fīliī Israēl fortiōrēs et altiōrēs sunt? Ēligite ex vōbīs virum sōlum pugnāre mēcum." Fīliī Israēl nōn fortiōrēs neque altiōrēs sunt. Timent altissimum Goliath. Dāvīd autem est filius parvus virōrum Ephrathaēī. Dāvīd pāscit gregem patris suī in Bethlehem. Fīliī Israēl Goliath timent, sed Dāvīd nōn timet, porrō vult pugnāre cum Goliath. Et induit Saūl Dāvīd vestīmentīs suīs, et impōnit galeam gravem super caput eius et vestit eum lōrīca gravis. Dīcit Dāvīd ad Saūl: "Nōn possum sīc ambulāre et pugnāre. Ego nōn sum altus, sed parvus. Arma nimis gravēs sunt. Baculus meus levis est." Arma Saūl Dāvīd dēpōnit. Dāvīd capit sibi quīnque rotundissimās petrās dē fluviō, et mittit eōs in pēram, quam habet, et ambulat levior adversum Philistaeum. Cum Goliath Dāvīd īnspectat et videt, dērīdet eum, quī est pulcher aspectū et parvus. Goliath dīcit: "Numquid ego canis sum, quod tū venīs ad mē cum baculō?" Dāvīd dīcit ad Philisthaeum: "Tū venīs ad mē cum gladiō, et lōrīcā, et scūtō, ego autem veniō ad tē in nōmine Dominī exercituum. Ipsīus enim est bellum, et trādit vōs in manūs nostrās." Cum Goliath currit ad Dāvīd, Dāvīd impōnit manum suum in pēram et sūmit ūnam petram, et jacit. Petra caput Goliath pulsat, et super terram cadit. Dāvīd super Goliath stat et gladium sūmit dē Goliath. Goliath necātur ā Dāvīd gladiō gravī. Philisthiim vident fortissimum eōrum necārī et fugunt.

Cf. 1 Samuel 17

sex cubitorum: six cubits
Socho: town name
Philisithiim: Philistines
Terebinthi: town name
galea, galeae (f.): helmet
lorica, loricae (f.): breastplate
pera, perae (f.): bag
baculus, baculi (m.): staff
porro: rather
sic: in this way

1. Cūr fīliī Isrāēl nōn vult pugnāre cum Philisthiim?
2. Quō induitur Goliath?
3. Estne Dāvīd altior quam (than) Goliath? Parvior? Quis est altior quam Goliath?
4. Fīliī Isrāēl Goliath timent? Cūr?
5. Dāvīd Goliath timet? Cūr?
6. Ā quō Goliath necātur? Quō necātur?

Sententiae Interpretandae

1. Habet sorōrem jūniōrem, quae pulchrior illa est. (Jgs 15:2)

   junior: younger

2. Ūnus est altissimus, creātor omnipotēns. (Sir 1:8)
3. Mittō ad vōs Tīmotheum, quī est fīlius meus cārissimus. (1 Cor 4:17)

   carus, cara, carum: dear

4. Quid dulcius melle, et quid leōne fortius? (Jdt 14:1)

   melle: honey (abl. sing.)

5. Māter pūrissima, ōra prō nōbīs.

   purus, pura, purum: pure

6. Leō fortissimus bēstiārum. (Prv 30:30)
7. Stultissimus sum virōrum, et sapientia hominum nōn est mēcum. (Prv 30:2)
8. Ērēxit cornū salūtis nōbīs in domō Dāvīd puerī suī. (Lk 1:69)

   erexit: he caused to arise

9. Cāritās omnia suffert omnia crēdit omnia spērat omnia sustinet. (1 Cor 13:7)

suffert: an irregular verb that means "suffers" or "endures"

10. Dīlēctiō dulce uerbum est sed dulcius factum. (Augustine, *In Iohannis epistulam ad Parthos* 8)
11. Jugum enim meum suāve est, et onus meum leve. (Mt 11:29)

jugum, jugī (n.): yoke
onus, oneris (n.): burden

12. Pretiōsa in cōnspectū Dominī mors sānctōrum ejus. (Ps 116:15)

pretiōsa: costly, precious

13. Dominus nobiscum. Et cum spīritū tuō.
14. Quam magna porta, et parva via est, quæ dūcit ad vītam: et paucī sunt quī inveniunt eam! Attendite ā falsīs prophētīs, quī veniunt ad vōs in vestīmentīs ovium, intrīnsecus autem sunt lupī rapācēs: ā frūctibus eōrum cognōscitis eōs. Numquid colligunt dē spīnīs ūvās, aut dē tribulīs ficus? Sīc omnis arbor bona frūctūs bonōs facit: māla autem arbor malōs frūctūs facit. Nōn potest arbor bona malōs frūctūs facere: neque arbor mala bonōs frūctūs facere. Omnis arbor, quae nōn facit frūctum bonum, sūmitur, et in ignem mittitur. Igitur ex frūctibus eōrum cognōscētis eōs. (Mt 7:14–20)

quam magna: how great!
attendite: pay attention
intrīnsecus: inside
lupi rapaces: rapacious wolves
sic: such
spina, spinae (f.): thorns
uva, uvae (f.): grapes
tribulus, tribulī (m.): spiny plant
ficus, ficī (m.): fig tree
cognōscētis: you will know

15. SALVĒ RĒGĪNA, Māter misericordiae. Vīta, dulcēdō, et spēs nostra, salvē. Ad tē clāmāmus exsulēs filiī Hēvae. Ad tē Suspīrāmus, gementēs et flentēs in hāc lacrimārum valle. Ēia ergō, Advocāta nostra, illōs tuōs misericordēs oculōs ad nōs converte. Et Jēsum, benedictum frūctum ventris tuī, nōbīs post hoc exsilium ostende. Ō clēmēns, ō pia, ō dulcis Virgō Maria.

spes: hope
exules: exiles
gementes et flentes: groaning and wailing
Advocata: advocate
exilium, exilii (n.): exile

Sententiae Fictae

1. Soror pulchra in castrīs jacet, neque timet quia nōn in cōnspectū proeliī est.
2. Leō fortis autem salit in castra et manūs levēs et crūrēs dulcēs sorōris pulchrae mandūcat.
3. Soror pulchra et dulcis sine baculō leōnem fortem necāre nōn potest.
4. Pater sapiēns fīliam pulchram et dulcem clāmāre audit ex castrīs.
5. Ipse ex exercitū fugit, petit fīliam pulchram et dulcem et fortem leōnem pugnat gladiō et aliīs armīs.
6. Dēnique, pater leōnem necat.
7. Pater vetus lacrimās dulcēs fīliae videt et Deō omnipotentī clāmat, "Ō clēmēns Deus, cūr fīlia dulcis mea suffert?"
8. Deus clēmēns et omnipotēns lacrimās fīliōrum fīliārumque videt et tenet.
9. Gladius gravis est et scūtum gravius est gladiō, sed Goliath gravissimum est!
10. Jēsus suāvior est quam omnēs hominēs.

CHAPTER 12

◇

§ 43. Nonfinite Verbs: Present Participles

We have seen verbs that describe the main action (*indicativus*: *laudānt*); we have seen verbs that command (*imperativus*: *laudāte!*); we have seen verbs that act like nouns (*infinitivus*: *laudāre*); and now we will see verbs that act like adjectives, that is, participles (*participium*: *laudans*). These participles that act like adjectives are called verbal adjectives and cannot stand alone without another main verb in the sentence.[1] In a sentence where you find a participle, you will also have another verb that is the main or lead verb.

As we proceed through the many different forms of the verb, they will be introduced in two ways. There will be the morphology, that is, what the verb looks like in its Latin form, and there will be the meaning, that is, how it functions and how it can be conveyed in English. Usually, the morphology will be straightforward. It will be much harder to figure out how it is working in the sentence and therefore what it "means."

> *Vir ambulāns Deum vīventem laudat.* The walking man praises the living God.
> *Frāter dolēns sorōrem cantantem pulsat.* The hurting brother punches the singing sister.
> *Uxor virī dormientis sedet.* The wife of the sleeping man sits.

In all of these cases, the participle is the verb form, which matches a noun in the same gender, number, and case: *ambulāns, vīventem, dolēns, cantantem, dormientīs*. Each one of these words is made up of a verb stem, *ambula-, vive-, dole-, cant-, dormie-*, and then has -*ns* or -*nt*- plus a third declension adjective ending, -*is*, -*em* etc. So that is how you form the participle. Verb stem + *ns* alone in the nominative, or -*nt*- + third declension (i/e noun) endings for any that are not nominative singular. You might also notice here that verbs in the fourth pattern, like *dormire*, have an -*ie*- before the -*ns* or -*nt*-. The formula translation you will offer is "-ing," knowing that these "-ing" words tell us more about a noun: Which man? The walking man. Which sister? The singing sister; the pattern continues. You can also translate these into more natural-sounding English by saying, "the girl who is singing."[2]

---

[1] In fact, there are four different kinds of participles, but we will only be talking about present active participles for this chapter.

[2] Learning about participles, infinitives, and gerunds can help English speakers understand their

NB. Notice how different the English can be from the Latin when we change a participle into a relative clause: "The singing man" vs. "the man who sings." This can raise questions about all translations. How close does it have to be to the original composition to still be a "good translation"?

	M. S.	F. S.	N. S.	Example Translation
Nom	*laudā\ns*	*laudā\ns*	*laudā\ns*	praising [sub] (one)
Gen	*lauda\nt\is*	*lauda\nt\is*	*lauda\nt\is*	of the praising (one)
Dat	*lauda\nt\ī*	*lauda\nt\ī*	*lauda\nt\ī*	to the praising (one)
Acc	*lauda\nt\em*	*lauda\nt\em*	*lauda\ns*	praising [d.o.] (one)
Abl	*lauda\nt\ī /* *lauda\nt\e*	*lauda\nt\ī /* *lauda\nt\e*	*lauda\nt\ī /* *lauda\nt\e*	by the praising (one)

	M. P.	F. P.	N. P.	Example Translation
Nom	*lauda\nt\ēs*	*lauda\nt\ēs*	*lauda\nt\ia*	praising [sub] (ones)
Gen	*lauda\nt\ium*	*lauda\nt\ium*	*lauda\nt\ium*	of the praising (ones)
Dat	*lauda\nt\ibus*	*lauda\nt\ibus*	*lauda\nt\ibus*	to the praising (ones)
Acc	*lauda\nt\ēs*	*lauda\nt\ēs*	*lauda\nt\ia*	praising [d.o.] (ones)
Abl	*lauda\nt\ibus*	*lauda\nt\ibus*	*lauda\nt\ibus*	by the praising (ones)

This is only the chart for ā-verbs. It is the same for all conjugations, except that the connecting vowel comes from the vowel class *-ā-, -ē-, -e-,* or *-ie-*.

These present participles are much more common in Ecclesiastical Latin than in Classical Latin because the New Testament was written in Koine Greek. Koine Greek relies more on participles, and the early translators of the New Testament from Greek to Latin tried to retain as much of the original syntax as possible.

As we learn more grammar structures, it will be helpful to see how they can be explained using simpler grammar. We will begin with what is called an adjectival use of the participle.

Vir quī ambulat Deum laudat. The man who walks praises God.

---

own language. The "singing girl" is a participle. But if the sentence says, "the girl who likes to sing," the *-ing* word is now in an infinitival form.

In this example, we have used the relative pronoun *qui* to give more information about the man. Which man? The man who walks. We can do the same thing with a present participle.

Vir ambulāns Deum laudat. The walking man praises God.

When students have more time, it can be helpful to review the older grammar and the new grammar by changing them back and forth. So, in this case, if we see a present participle we can change it into a relative clause. *Uxor virī dormientis sedet* becomes *Uxor cujus vir dormit sedet.* These have nearly identical meanings but are expressed in different ways. This is important to remember as we progress into more forms of the verb. Latin loves to have multiple ways to express similar ideas. When ancient Romans learned rhetoric, they were learning how to use differing expressions to make their speech more ornate. Typically, English speakers prefer economy of expression. That is not the standard for most written Latin.

Vir ōrāns in ecclēsiam ambulat. ~ *Vir, quī ōrat, in ecclēsiam ambulat.*
Discipulus sedēns magistrum stantem audit. ~ *Discipulus, quī sedet, magistrum,*
    quī stat, audit.

§ 44. Nouns: E-Nouns (Fifth Declension)

We have finally come to the last possible form of the noun. The fifth declension has a vowel pattern of *-e-*.

Case	Singular	Plural
Nom	*di\ēs*	*di\ēs*
Gen	*di\eī*	*di\ērum*
Dat	*di\eī*	*di\ēbus*
Acc	*di\em*	*di\ēs*
Abl	*di\ē*	*di\ēbus*

While there are not a large number of e-nouns in Latin, some of the most important theological terms come in the fifth declension: *fidēs, fideī* (faith), *rēs, reī* (thing [reality]), *spēs, speī* (hope). They are also typically feminine.

§ 45. Syntax: Adverbial Participles and the Periphrastic

Some participles act like adjectives, which we saw above. That means they modify a noun in the sentence.

Puer cantāns intrat in ecclēsiam. The singing boy enters the church.

The participle can also modify or go with the subject of a sentence and function adverbially. That means you will likely need to add a word to the English translation to make sense of the Latin.

Cantans intrat in ecclesiam. While singing, he enters the church.

When a sentence contains a participle and a form of the verb *to be*, it is called paraphrastic. We use these very often in English. "I am walking" vs. "I walk." The first is a periphrastic construction and is called present progressive. The second is a simple present tense action. We do not typically use periphrastics with present tense participles in Latin. For instance, *laudāns est*, which would mean something like "he is praising," is not preferred in Classical Latin. Classical Latin prefers to just use *laudāt* for both "he is praising" and "he praises."[3]

§ 46. Conjunctions

We have three new postpositive conjunctions to learn. The word *postpositive* simply means that the word is the second word in the sentence. Latin uses many different conjunctions that, while not always necessary to translate, indicate the flow of a paragraph. *Enim* (for) tells us more about a previous sentence. It is explaining something. *Autem* (however), can often go untranslated and is used mainly to connect two thoughts. *Igitur* (therefore), brings a kind of conclusion to a previous thought. In some cases, you will see *igitur* as the first word in the sentence. It is not always postpositive.

"Die autem tertio eductis de carcere," ait: "Facite quae dixi, et vivetis. Deum enim timeo." (Gen 22:4)
"On the third day you will be led from the prison," he said, "Do those things which I said and you will live. For I fear God."

Quid igitur faciam de Jesu, qui dicitur Christus? (Mt 27:22)
What therefore shall I do about Jesus, who is Called Christ?

---

[3] Sometimes the Vulgate will use these phrases, following the syntax of the Greek grammar it is translating. This does not follow the rules of typical Classical Latin, but it is not strictly wrong.

Sententiae Summāriae

Fidēs spem faciēbus hominum dat.
Faciēs hominum illustrantur diē.
Homō laudāns deum ambulat.
Magister dīcēns discipulum audientem monet.
Verba magistrī dīcentis ā discipulō sedente audiuntur.
Dominus ambulāns servō ambulantī dīcit.
Servus fessior est quam dominus. Servus fessior est dominō. Ancilla fessior est quam fēmina. Ancilla fessior est fēmina.

Translations

Faith gives hope to the faces of people.
The faces of humans are enlightened by the day.
The person who is praising God [*lit.* the praising God person] walks.
The teacher speaking teaches his listening student.
The words of the teacher speaking are heard by the student sitting.
The lord walking speaks to the servant walking.
The servant is more tired than the master. The servant is more tired than the master. The maidservant is more tired than the woman. The maidservant is more tired than the woman.

Cavēte et Mementōte

Like the fourth declension uses *-u-* as the theme vowel, the fifth declension uses an easy to remember *-e-* theme vowel.

Present participles have an *-ns*, or *-nt* after the stem and theme pattern vowel, and like the NT (New Testament), they are present and active.[4]

Vocābula Memoranda

Nōmina

diēs, diēī (m./f.): day
facies, faciei (f.): face
fidēs, fideī (f.): faith
glaciēs, glaciēī (f.): ice
intellectus, intellectūs (m.): understanding\
magus, magī (m.): astrologer, magician, "wise man"

---

[4] Thanks to Andrew Chronister for this mnemonic.

missa, missae (f.): mass
mūnus, mūneris (n.): gift, office
pēs, pedis (m.): foot
piscātor, piscātōris (m.): fisherman
prīnceps, prīncipis (m.): prince
prōgeniēs, prōgeniēī (f.): progeny
rēs, reī (f.): thing
rēx, rēgis (m): king
sacerdōs, sacerdōtis (m.): priest
spēs, speī (f.): hope
vōx, vōcis (f.): voice, word, sound

Verba

<u>ā-verb</u>
  adōrō [ad + oro], adōrāre, adōrāvī, ādōrātus: worship, bow down

<u>i/e-verbs</u>
  lēgō, legere, lēgī, lēctus: read
  quaerō, quaerere, quaesīvī, quaesītus: seek

<u>io-verb</u>
  perficiō [per + facio], perficere, perfēcī, perfectus: complete

Adjectīva

  dīves, dīvitis (gen. sing.): wealthy
  pauper, pauperis (gen. sing): poor
  sapiens, sapientis (gen. sing.): wise

Praepositiōnēs

  pro (+abl): instead of, or in the place of
  ante (+acc): in front of, before

Fābulae Excerptae (nōn nūllīs mūtātīs ["with some changes"])

Sīcut legitur, quoniam piscātōrēs sānctī Theobaldī magnum glaciēī prō pisce capiunt ex aquā. Laetiōrēs sunt capere glaciem quam piscem. Epīscopus eōrum malum pedem habet, atque magnum refrīgerium quaerit. Piscātōrēs ergō venientēs in domum epīscopī pōnunt ipsam glaciem sub pedibus epīscopī. Quādam diē, epīscopus sedēns vōcem clāmantis hominis dē glaciē audit. Epīscopus dīcit: "Quis est?!" Et vōx veniēns ex glaciē respondit: "sum anima, quae ego in hāc glaciē prō peccātīs meīs afflīgor. Volō līberārī ex pūrgātōriō. Dīc trīgintā missās prō mē, quaesō." Epīscopus vīgintī missās dīcit, sed hominēs in oppidō pugnāntēs audit. Epīscopus, dēpōnēns vestīmentum clēricum, missam interpellat. Epīscopus discēdit ex domō ad pugnāntēs hominēs. Deinde, epīscopus revēniēns in ecclēsiam omnēs missās perficiunt et glaciēs igne resolvitur. Epīscopus crēdit sē vidēre animam tamquam phanstasmam discēdere dē glaciē.

    Cf. Jacobus dē Vorāgine, *Dē commemorātiōne omnium fidēlium dēfūnctōrum*

refrigerium, refrigerii (n.): cool, rest
affligor: I am afflicted
purgatorium, purgatorii (n.): place of cleansing
quaeso: I beg, I ask
triginta: thirty
viginti: twenty
tamquam: like or as
resolvere: to be released, melted

1. Quid pisactōrēs prēndunt (sūmunt) ex aquā?
2. Suntne piscātōrēs laetī sunt? Cūr?
3. Quid epīscopus dē glaciē audit?
4. Quid Epīscopus crēdit sē vidēre discēdere dē glaciē?

Cum ergō nātus erat [was] Jēsus in Bethlehem Jūdā in diēbus Hērōdis rēgis, ecce magī ab oriente veniunt Jerosolymam, dīcentēs: "Ubi est quī nātus est rēx Jūdæōrum? Vidēmus enim stēllam ejus in oriente, et venīmus adōrāre eum." Audiēns autem Hērōdēs rēx, turbātus est, et omnīs Hierosolyma cum illō. Et congregāns omnēs prīncipēs sacerdōtum, et scrībās populī, vult scīre ab eīs ubi Chrīstus nātus sit (est). At illī dīcunt: In Bethlehem Jūdae: sīc enim scrīptum est per prophētam: Et tū Bethlehem terrā Jūda, nēquāquam parvior es quam prīncipibus Jūda: ex tē enim venit dux, quī regit populum meum Isrāēl. Tunc Hērōdēs vocāns clam magōs ad sē discit ab eīs tempus stēllae, quae appāret eīs: et mittēns illōs in Bethlehem, dīcit: "Ambulāte, et interrogāte dīligenter dē puerō: et cum invenītis, renūntiātē mihi. Ego veniēns volō adōrāre eum." Audientēs rēgem, discēdunt, et ecce stēlla, quam vident in oriente ante eōs ubi est puer. Videntēs autem stēllam gaudent gaudiō magnō valdē. Et intrantēs domum, inveniunt puerum cum Mariā mātre ejus, et ambulantēs adōrant eum: et aperientēs thēsaurōs portant eī mūnera: aurum, thūs, et myrrham. Dormientēs vōcem audiunt, quae eīs nūntiat revēnīre in regiōnem suam per aliam viam.

    Cf. Matthew 2:2–4

turbatus: troubled, disturbed
scriptum: written
nequaquam: by no means
clam: secretly
thēsaurus, thēsaurī (m.): treasure chests
aurum, thus, et myrrham: gold, frankincense, and myrrh

1. Unde veniunt magī?
2. Cūr veniunt Hierosolymam?
3. Quid Hērōdēs jubent magōs?
4. Magī Chrīstum inveniunt? Audiunt Hērōdem?

Sententiae Interpretandae

1. Audiēns sapientī sapientior erit. (Prv 1:5)

   erit: will be

2. Fidēs quaerēns intellēctum. (St. Anselm, *Proslogion Prooemium*)
3. Vidēmus nunc per speculum in ænigmate: tunc autem faciē ad faciem ... Nunc autem manent fidēs, spēs, cāritās, tria hæc: major autem hōrum est cāritās. (1 Cor 13:12)

   aenigma, aenigmatis (n.): enigma, mystery
   major: greater
   speculum, speculi (n.): mirror

4. [clause] Ā prōgeniē in prōgeniēs timentibus eum. (Lk 1:50; *Nunc Dimittis*)
5. Creator rerum omnium visibilium et invisibilium. (Symbolum Nicaeanum)
6. Melior est puer pauper et sapiens, rege sene et stulto. (Eccl 4:13)

   senex, senis: old

7. Et respondens Daniel regi, dicit: Mysterium, quod rex interrogat, sapientes, magi, non possunt indicare regi. (Dn 2:27)

   indicare: to show, point out

8. Unum corpus, et unus Spiritus, sicut vocati estis in una spe vocationis vestræ. Unus Dominus, una fides, unum baptisma. Unus Deus et Pater omnium, qui est super omnes, et per omnia, et in omnibus nobis. (Eph 4:4–6)

   vocati: called (modifying the subject "you" [pl.])

9. Prout potestis legentes intelligere prudentiam meam in mysterio Christi. (Eph 3:4)

   prout: as

10. Certum vērō propriumque fideī catholicae fundāmentum Chrīstus est. (Augustine, *Enchiridion* 1)

    proprium, proprii (n.): fitting
    fundāmentum, fundāmentī (n.): foundation

11. Dā sapientī, et sapientior fiet. (Prv 9:9)

    fiet: will become

12. Ambulāns autem Jēsus juxtā mare Galilææ, vīdit duōs frātrēs, Simōnem, quī vocātur Petrus, et Andream frātrem ejus, mittentēs rēte in mare (erant enim piscātōrēs), et dīcit illīs: Venīte post mē, et faciam vōs piscātōrēs hominum. (Mt 4:18–19)

    erant: they were
    faciam: I will make

13. Ecce ējicis mē hodiē ā faciē terrae. (Gn 4:14)
14. Gaudium ergō nostrum, quod nunc est, in spē est, nōndum in rē ... Salūs vestra in spē est, nōndum in rē. (Augustine, *Sermo* 306B)

nondum: not yet

15. Nōn ēlēgit rēgēs, aut senātōrēs, aut philosophōs, aut ōrātōrēs. Immō vērō ēlēgit plēbēiōs, pauperēs, indoctōs, piscātōrēs. Petrus piscātor, Cypriānus ōrātor ... Nam via nostra humilitās est. (Augustine, *Sermo* 198)

immo vero: rather, on the other hand
plebeius, -a, -um: plebeian

Sententiae Fictae

1. Sacerdōs hominēs legere sacrās scrīptūrās omnibus diēbus monet.
2. Sacerdōs, quī est vōx rēgis, oppidum monet.
3. Piscātōrēs quaerunt tollere piscēs ex mare, sed mare plēnum glaciē est, neque mare pedēs piscātōrum sustinēre potest.
4. Sacerdōtēs piscātōrēs habēre fidem et spem monent, sed faciēs piscātōrum vidēre nōn possunt.
5. Prīncipēs servōs ancillāsque līberant et prōgeniēs servōrum ancilliārumque nōn dominīs serviunt.
6. Venientēs in ecclēsiam filiae Deum vīventem laudant.
7. Servī rēgem jubentem audit, sed mūnerem servōrum nōn faciunt.
8. Magī omnēs rēs sciunt et intellegunt.
9. Mūnus piscātōrum capere piscēs ex aquā est, nōn glaciem.
10. Fīlius vōcem patris nōn audit, sed faciem clāmantem videt.

CHAPTER 13

૱

§ 47. Verbs: Impersonal Verbs with a Dative Plus Infinitive Construction

There will be no new morphology to learn for this section. Instead, we will learn about how Latin authors can arrange verbs and nouns in ways that will not be straightforward to English speakers. We will be learning syntax, not a specific verb or noun form. This is why it is so critical to learn them up front. Learning a language is learning more than all the possible ways a word is formed by memorizing a chart and more still than just looking up words in a dictionary. The meaning of the words can change when combined with other words and in other cases or forms.

We will begin with impersonal verbs that take an infinitive and a dative. These are verbs that have *it* as their subject and so are considered "impersonal." These verbs will not have an explicit subject written in Latin, but it will be understood from their construction.

Necesse est discipulīs discere. It is necessary for students to learn.

Nōn convenit chrīstiānīs peccāre. It is not fitting for Christians to sin.

Facile est ambulāre. It is easy to walk.

Difficile est omnibus discipulīs discere linguam graecam. It is difficult for all students to learn Greek.

Placet magistrīs docēre linguam latīnam. It is pleasing to teachers to teach the Latin language. (Or, more idiomatically, "Teachers like to teach the Latin language.")

Displicet discipulis discere linguam latinam. It is displeasing to students to learn the Latin language. (Or, more idiomatically, "Students don't like to learn the Latin language.")

All of the sentences have a few things in common: impersonal verbs at the front, an infinitive complement, and a noun in the dative. There are more verbs that act like this, but these are a bunch of them. Notice how the translations work. In English, we have to use the phrase "it is." For many of the verbs above, there is no "to be" verb. *Placet magistrīs docere.* There is no *is* here. We have to supply more English words to convey the meaning.

Also, in some cases we translate the dative with the word *to*, but with impersonal verbs, we are now replacing it with the English preposition *for*. We can call this the *dative of agent*. I would just say we are adding another possibility about which English word we can choose to convey the Latin. At this point, many students ask, "how will we know when to use *to* and when to use *for*?" This is a good question. The quick answer is one that students hate: context. The longer answer is you have to look at the other words in the sentence. In all of these cases, we have an impersonal verb. So now we are looking for an agent of the verb. We don't have a nominative, so we will have to look for an agent in the dative or accusative cases. That is when we will substitute *for* in place of *to*. Typically, these impersonal verbs come in the beginning of the sentence to clue us in that there will be no explicit nominative subject.

It is possible to have a different subject with certain verbs that can also be used impersonally. The verb *placet* can have a discreet subject in some case.

placet mihi aqua. Water is pleasing to me.
placent mihi canes. Dogs are pleasing to me.

§ 48. Verbs: Impersonal Verbs with an Accusative Plus Infinitive Construction

Some impersonal Latin verbs do not have the "subject" or the "agent" in the dative case, but in the accusative. This should be somewhat familiar since we have seen these kinds of constructions before. *Pater videt filium pulsāre filiam*, "The father sees [that] the son punches the daughter." *Filium* is in the accusative, as well as *filiam*. One is an accusative subject, and one is an accusative direct object. This infinitive and accusative construction is used with an indicative lead verb with an explicit subject: *pater videt*. Some accusative and infinitive constructions will come with an impersonal lead verb.

Oportet magistrum docēre. It is necessary [that] the teacher teach.

Decet discipulōs discere. It is fitting [that] the students learn.

Mē dēlectat docēre Latīnam. It is delightful [that] I teach Latin.

Taedet tē legere. It is boring for you to read.

Pudet hominēs peccāre. It is shameful for humans to sin.

Paenitet Chrīstiānōs peccāre. It is regretful for Christians to sin.

The question that often arises from what was described here and above is this: Why are there some verbs that take the dative and some that take the accusative in these impersonal constructions? And the answer is this: because these are the conventions.[1] We still have

---

1 Within the history of the language, you will find some writers who use *dative* and *accusative* interchangeably with certain interpersonal verbs.

essentially the same structure as above, though: impersonal verb up front, an agent of the verb not in the nominative—here the accusative rather than the dative—and an infinitive.

The verbs *delectat* and *taedet* can also have a discreet subject like *placet*.

> *Aqua me delectat.* Water delights me.
> *Schola me taedet.* School bores me.

§ 49. Verbs: Ablative Absolute with Present Participles

We began working with participles in the previous chapter. We learned how they can modify a noun like an adjective, matching whatever case the noun is in and how it functions in the sentence. Now we will learn another way to make a subordinate clause with a participle.

Deō volente, māter līberōs parit. God willing, the mother gives birth to children.

Notice that both the *Deō* and *volente* are in the ablative. The two words in the ablative relate to the sentence but are not the subject of the main verb. They are another clause. If you have two words, usually a noun and a participle, in the ablative, you likely have an ablative absolute. There is no English construction that directly matches the ablative absolute construction in Latin. It is a purely Latin way to connect a clause to the main verb adverbially. So usually we have to add an English conjunction like *while*, *if*, *when*, or *since*. Ablative absolutes are quite common and can easily trip up a native English speaker because we don't typically have a way to express them literally in English.

This is another good example of how Latin can express similar meanings in different ways. Instead of *Deō volente*, when we see two ablatives, we can think of it in Latin as *cum Deūs vult*, "when God wills." Either one would be "correct" Latin, they are two ways to say the same thing: *Magistrīs spectantibus, discipulus scrībit*, "while the teachers are watching, the student writes." This could be written, *Dum magister spectat, discipulus scrībit*.

§ 50. Nouns: Ablative of Time and Accusative of Duration

When it comes to words that relate to time, like *dies*, if it is in the ablative, *die*, it does not mean "by means of the day," but rather "on the day." This ablative of time can occur with any word related to time.

Diē dominicā ambulāmus ad ecclēsiam. On the Lord's Day, we walk to church.

Sometimes you will have a word related to time, like *dies*, and it will be in the accusative.

Septem diēs ambulāmus. We walked for seven days.

This is called the accusative of duration. In both cases, the context that helps the reader know that the ablative and the accusative are being used in this slightly different way is that the words in those cases relate to time.

CHAPTER 13

Sententiae Summāriae

Placet magistrō docēre.
Taedet discipulōs audīre.
Nōn licet discipulīs dormīre in scholā.
Discipulīs audientibus magister docet.
Magistrō dīcente discipulī dormiunt.

Translations

It pleases the teacher to teach.
It bores the students to listen.
It is not permitted for the students to sleep in school.
While the students are listening, the teacher teaches.
As the teacher speaks, the students sleep.

Cavēte et Mementōte

Impersonal verbs often come at the beginning of sentences. This can be a clue to distinguish them from regular verbs, which often come at the end of a sentence.

Vocābula Memoranda

Nōmina

convīvium, convīvī(ī) (n.): party
labor, labōris (m.): labor, pain
mēns, mentis (f.): mind
mors, mortis (f.): death
peregrīnātiō, peregrīnātiōnis (f.): pilgrimage
rēgīna, rēgīnae (f.): queen

Verba

ē-verb

compleō, complēre, complēvī, complētus: fill, fulfill
displicet [dis + placere], displicēre, displicuit,—: (impersonal) it is displeasing[2]
licet, licēre, licuit,—: (impersonal) it is allowed/permitted
paenitet, paenitēre, paenituit,—: (impersonal) it is displeasing
placet, placēre,—, *placitus est*: (impersonal) it is pleasing
taedet, taedēre, taeduit,—: (impersonal) it is tiring

i-verb

convenit, convenīre, convenit,—: (impersonal) it is fitting

---

[2] Notice that many of these verbs are in the third personal singular because they are impersonal.

Adjectīva

difficilis, difficilis, difficile: difficult
facilis, facilis, facile: easy
hilarius, -a, -um: merry, drunk
necessis, necessis, necesse: necessary
solus -a, -um: only, alone
speciōsus, -a, -um: beautiful, marvelous
splēndidus, -a, -um: splendid
tōtus, -a, -um: whole

Coninunctivum

ac: and

Praepositiōnēs

per (+acc): through
usque ad (+acc): up to, to

Fābula Ficta

In diēbus rēgis Assuērī, quī rēgnat ab Indiā usque ad Ethiopiam, convīvium habētur cūnctīs prīncipibus fortissimīs Persārum ostendere dīvitiās glōriae rēgnī suī ac magnitūdinem. Cūnctī prīncipēs et Assuerus vīnum bibent aureīs pōculīs et cibum splendidissimum mandūcant. Cum rēx Assuerus hilarior est, placet eī ostendere uxōrem nōmine Vashtī pulchriōrem esse quam cūnctas fēminas. Oportet rēgīnam venīre ad convīvium, sed displicet eī. Rēgīna, manente in convīviō suō, rēx īrātus est et interrogat sapientēs ejus: "Quid oportet mē facere cum rēgīnā Vashtī?" Mamuchan dīcit rēge spectante: "Nōn sōlum rēgem taedet, sed etiam cūnctōs populōs et prīncipēs. Nōn licet rēgīnae nōn audīre rēgem. Necesse est novam rēgīnam pulchriōrem invenīre." Servī rēgis novam virginem speciōsam quaerunt et virginem speciōsissimam ex Jūdaeā nōmine Esther inveniunt.

Cf. Esther 1–2

Assuerus: name of the Babylonian King
Mamuchan: name of Babylonian advisor to the King
Vashti: name of the Queen
Persa, Persae: the Persians

1. Cūr rēx, Assuerus, convīvium habet?
2. Qui sunt ad convivium?
3. Quid agunt in convivio?
4. Quālis est Vashtī, uxor ejus?
5. Cūr Mamuchan vult rēgem quaerere novam rēgīnam?

Sententiae Interpretandae

1. Oportet filium hominis trādī in manūs hominum peccātōrum. (Lk 24:7)
2. Oportet autem eum trānsīre per Samarīam. (Jn 4:4)

   trans-ire: to go across

3. Patrēs nostrī in monte hōc adōrant, et vōs dīcitis, quia Jerosolymis est locus ubi adōrāre oportet. (Jn 4:20)
4. Habēre jam nōn potest Deum Patrem quī Ecclēsiam nōn habet Mātrem. (Cyprian of Carthage, *De Unitate Ecclesiae* V)
5. Deus meus, ex tōtō corde paenitet mē omnium meōrum peccātōrum. (*Actus Contrītiōnis*)[3]
6. Respondēns autem Jēsus, dīcit eī, "Sine modō, sīc enim decet nōs implēre omnem jūstitiam." (Mt 3:15)

   sine modō: without delay

7. Dīc ergō nōbīs quid tibi vidētur; licet cēnsum dare Caesarī, an nōn? (Mt 22:17)

   cēnsum: tax

8. Et in omnēs gentēs prīmum oportet praedicāre ēvangelium. (Mt 13:10)
9. Haec illō loquente ad eōs, ecce prīnceps ūnus accēdit, et adōrat eum. (Mt 9:18)

   accēdit: come towards

10. Et quid est quod mē dēlectat, nisi amāre et amārī? (Augustine, *Cōnfessiōnēs* 2.2)
11. Taedet mihi saepe multa legere et audīre: in tē tōtum est, quod volō et dēsīderō. (Thomas a Kempis, *Imitātiō Chrīstī* 1.3)

    dēsīderō: I desire

12. Quod scīre licet, discutere nōn licet; crēdere convenit, nōn convenit perscrūtāre. (Peter Chrysologus, *Collectio sermonum* 59.38)

    discutere: to discuss
    perscrūtāre: to scrutinize

13. Illud deō Chrīstiānōrum nōn convenit, id est illī quī pater misericordiae dīcitur. (Augustine, *Contra Iulianum opus imperfectum* 5.64)
14. Oportet enim epīscopōs nōn tantum docēre, sed etiam discere, quia et ille melius docet quī cotīdiē crēscit et prōficit discendō meliōra. (Cyprian of Carthage, *Epistula* 74)

    melius: better
    crēscit: grows
    prōficit: advances
    discendō meliōra: by learning better things

---

3 take *omnium meorum peccatorum* as the subject of *paenitet*.

15. Et haec expositiō placet mihi, propter hoc quod dīcit Augustīnus. (Albert the Great, *Commentarii in secundum librum Sententiarum* 14)

    expositio, expositionis (f.): exposition

16. Facile est autem docēre paene ūniversam vēritātem per philosophōs et sectās esse dīvīsam. (Lactantius, *Divinae Institutiones*)

    sectas: sects (groups of philosophers)
    divisam: shared

17. Vōx enim nostra est in illō psalmō: quoniam peregrīnātiō mea longinqua facta est! ergō dē illīs caelīs et mihi difficile est disputāre, sī tamen nōn impossibile, et vōbīs intellegere. (Augustine, *Enārrātiōnēs in Psalmos* 32.2.2)

    longinqua facta est: it is made remote

Sententiae Fictae

1. Licet Deō jubente venīre ad domum Deī.
2. Taedet mē venīre ad convīvium sine multō vīnō bonō.
3. Paenitet mē bibere vīnum malum.
4. Facile est nōbīs invenīre domum rēgīnae coelī Deō adjuvante.
5. Convenit Chrīstiānīs pedibus sōlis facere peregrīnātiōnem.
6. Deō jubente, ad ecclesisam veniō.
7. Mors omnibus nōbīs venit.
8. Jēsus nōbīs mentem Deī ostendit.
9. Placet mihi multōs diēs ambulāre in montibus, sed displicet fīliō meo.
10. Placet Deō ostendere servīs ejus glōriam suam.

CHAPTER 14

§ 51. Verbs: Passive Personal Endings

It is now time to introduce all the personal endings for the passive voice. These will be the endings used for passives (the subject of the verb receives the action of the verb). To compare to the personal endings we have seen so far, here are some examples of active personal endings:

Laudō Deum. I praise God.
Laudās Deum. You praise God.

The subject of the verb does the action of the verb. In the passive voice, the subject of the verb receives the action of the verb.

Laudor a Deō. I am praised by God.
Laudārīs a Deō. You are praised by God.

	ā-verb	
[ego]	laudo|r	I am being praised
[tu]	laudā|rīs	You are being praised
[is / ea / id]	laudā|tur	He is being praised
[nos]	laudā|mur	We are being praised
[vos]	laudā|minī	You all are being praised
[ii / eae / ea]	lauda|ntur	They are being praised

Notice the translation chart on the far right. We have "am being" or "are being," etc., before the verb ending in *-ed*. In one respect, this is an over translation. You do not always need to add *being* in the present passive indicative. It is a good practice in the early stages of learning Latin to have clear delineations between different uses. Students often inquire about the difference. This way, if you follow the practice of translating the present passive with "being," you have a way to keep straight in your mind the difference—even if it is not the most elegant translation.

ā-verb	ē-verb	i/e-verb	i-verb	Example Translation
laudo|r	moneo|r	dūco|r	audio|r	I am being heard
laudā|rīs (laudā|re)	monē|ris (monē|re)	dūce|ris (dūce|re)	audī|ris (audī|re)	You are being heard
laudā|tur	monē|tur	dūci|tur	audī|tur	He is being heard
laudā|mur	monē|mur	dūci|mur	audī|mur	We are being heard
laudā|minī	monē|minī	dūci|minī	audī|minī	You (pl.) are being heard
lauda|ntur	mone|ntur	dūcu|ntur	audiu|ntur	They are being heard

For most of the passive, it is just like the active: you take the stem (*laud-, vid-, duc-, aud-*), the theme vowel (*-a,-e, -i/e, i*), and then add the personal endings (*-r, -ris, -tur, -mur, -mini, -ntur*). Notice the exceptions, though, for the *u* in the third person plural of the i/e-verb and the i-verb, and the *-e-* in *duc-e-ris*. These personal endings will need to be memorized and will recur in the imperfect and future tenses.

§ 52. Verbs: *ire* and *fieri*

It is now time to learn some more irregular verbs. The first is the verb for "to go" which is irregular in several ways, as we will see.

	Verb	Translation
	e|ō	I go
	i|s	You go
	i|t	He / she goes
	ī|mus	We go
	i|tis	You all go
	eu|nt	They go
Infinitive:	ire	to go
Present Active Part.:	iens, euntis	going

Ire is a difficult verb, especially in the present tense with the *eo* form for "I go." It can easily look like a pronoun. This verb is extremely common and is usually prefixed with a directional preposition. *Circumit*, he goes around; *exit*, he goes out; *introit*, he goes in; *adit*, he goes towards; etc. And the participle form looks very different: *iens, euntis*. The good news is that after the present tense, the verb begins to look more like the other standard verbs. You also have the normal personal endings *-o, -s, -t, -mus, -tis, -nt*. One way to explain the difficulty of this verb is to remember that the stem is a short vowel *i/e*.

See the appendix for all the possibilities of prepositions that can come before a verb like *ire*. Usually the student can figure out how the preposition works with the main verb, but for words like *perire*, "to perish," one may not be able to divine just what the word will mean idiomatically.

adeō, adīs, adit. I go to, you go to, he goes to
abeō, abīs, abit. I go away, you go away, he goes away
pereō, perīs, perit. I perish, you perish, he perishes [*lit.* he goes through]

We have one other irregular verb to learn in this chapter: *fieri*. One reason this verb is called irregular is that it has active forms but passive meanings. This often functions as the passive voice of *facio*.

	Verb	Translation
	fi|ō	I become
	fi|s	You become
	fi|t	He / she becomes
	fi|mus	We become
	fi|tis	You all become
	fiu|nt	They become
Infinitive	*fierī*	to become
Present Active Participle	*fiēns, fientīs*	becoming

§ 53. Adverbs Regular, Comparative, and Superlative

An adverb is not a hard thing to explain. It is a word that modifies a verb, an adjective, or another adverb. So, "he walks slowly." How does he walk? Slowly. It tells you more about a verb or an adjective. He is very smart. How smart is he? Very smart. *Very* is the adverb here because it tells you more about the adjective *smart*. What makes adverbs difficult for modern English speakers is that sometimes we don't use adverbs well, and we confuse them with adjectives. What is the answer to the question, "How did you sleep?" If it is positive, we often say "good." The technically correct answer is, "I slept well." Similarly, if you did not have a good night's rest, some people may say, "I slept bad." This is of course incorrect. "I slept poorly." The *-ly* ending is the typical give away for the adverb in English.

Latin has two basic forms for the adverb: *-e* and *-iter*. That is, you can take any adjective that comes from the first or second declension (*-us, -a, -um* ending), put the ending *-e* onto its stem, and it becomes an adverb that can modify a verb. *Scrībit pulchrē*, "she writes beautifully." Or take any adjective from the third declension, attach the suffix *-iter* onto its stem, and you have an adverb. *Pugnat fortiter*, "he fights strongly."

Not only do adverbs modify verbs, but they can be used to compare as well. "The girl writes more beautifully than the boy." *Puella scrībit pulchrius quam puer.* It is important to see that *pulchrius* modifies the verb and not the nouns *puella* or *puer*. The *-ius* ending is the giveaway for the comparative adverb.

One typical way you will find the comparative is in an impersonal construction:

Facilius est discere quam docēre. It is easier to learn than to teach.

Finally, we also have superlatives. These are easy to spot, though, because they are just like the superlative adjective, *fortissimus*, but we will change the ending from the adjectival ending to an *-e*. So *fortissimus* becomes *fortissimē*.

	A/O Adjectives / 1st or 2nd declension adjective	adverb
Positive	*foed|us, -a, -um* ugly	*foed|ē* in an ugly way
Comparative	*foed|ior, -ior, -e* uglier	*foed|ius* in an uglier way
Superlative	*foed|issim|us, -a, um* ugliest	*foed|issim|ē* in the ugliest way

	I/E Adjectives / 3rd declension adjectives	adverb
Positive	*dulc|is, dulc|is, dulc|e*	*dulc|iter*
	sweet	sweetly
Comparative	*dulc|ior, -ior, -e*	*dulc|ius*
	sweeter	in a sweeter way; more sweetly
Superlative	*dulc|issim|us, -a, -um*	*dulc|issim|ē*
	sweetest	in the sweetest way

Sententiae Summāriae

Ego ā magistrō laetē laudor. Tū ā magistrō dulciter laudārīs.
Nōs ā magistrīs laetē laudāmur. Vōs ā magistrīs dulciter laudāminī.
A dominō sevērē moneor. A dominō sevērissimē monēris.
Monēmur fortiter ā patre nostrō. Monēminī ā mātre nostrā.
Ego ā mātre meā dūcor. Tū ā mātre tuā dūceris.
A dominō dūcēmur. A dominā dūcēminī.
A Spīritū Sānctō semper audior. A Spīritū Sānctō semper audīrīs.
A magistrō nōs audīmur. Vōs ā magistrō audīminī.
Ego eō citius quam tū is. Nōs citissimē īmus. Vōs vēlōciter ītis.
Ad ecclēsiam it. Ad ecclēsiam nōn eunt.
Quid fit? Dulcior fit.

Translations

I am happily praised by the teacher. You are sweetly praised by the teacher.
We are happily praised by the teacher. You (pl.) are sweetly praised by the teachers.
I am severely warned by the master. You are most severely warned by the master.
We are strongly warned by our father. You (pl.) are warned by our mother.
I am led by my mother. You are led by your mother.
We are led by the master. You (pl.) are led by the lady.
I am always heard by the Holy Spirit. You are always heard by the Holy Spirit.
We are heard by the teacher. You (pl.) are heard by the teacher.
I go more quickly than you go. We go the most quickly. You (pl.) go very quickly.
He goes to church. They do not go to church.
What happens? It becomes more sweet!

Cavēte et Mementōte

Adverbs often look like adjectives, but have an *-e*, *-iter*, *-ius*, or *-issime* ending.

Vocābula Memoranda

Nōmina

aurum, aurī (n.): gold
calix, calicīs (m.): cup
fenestra, fenestrae (f.): window
mane (n.): morning (indeclinable)
massa, massae (f.): mass
membrum, membrī (n.): member, part of the body
ōsculum, osculī (n.): kiss
parēns, parentīs (m.): parent
pecūnia, pecūniae (f.): money
proximus, proximī (m.): neighbor
urbs, urbis (f.): city
virgō, virginis (f.): virgin

Verba

<u>ā-verbs</u>
excitō [ex + cieo], excitāre, excitāvī, excitātus: be awakened
vigilō, vigilāre, vigilāvī, vigilātus: stay awake

<u>i/e-verb</u>
prōpōnō [pro + pono], prōpōnere, prōposuī, prōpositus: propose, decide

<u>io-verb</u>
jaciō, jacēre, jēcī, jactus: throw

<u>irregular</u>
eō, īre, īvī (iī), itus: go
fīō, fierī,—, factus sum: become, happen

Adjectīvum

vēlōcis, vēlōcis, vēlōce: with haste/speed

Adverbia

cito, citius, citissimē: quickly, more quickly, most quickly
facile, facilius, facillimē: easily, easier
heri: yesterday
hodiē: today
similiter: similarly
vēlōciter, vēlōcius, vēlōcissimē: quickly, more quickly, most quickly, very quickly

Fābula Ficta

Nīcolāus quī est cīvīs Paterae urbis dīvites et sānctos parentes habet. Parentēs ejus moriuntur et Nicolaus fit solus, sed dives, quia magnam pecuniam habet. Nīcolāus, servus Deī, prōpōnit sē posse dare pecuniam magis glōrificāre Deō quam laudārī ā hominibus. Proximus enim Nīcolāī nōn pecūniam habet dare cibum filiābus suīs. Proximus Nīcolāī trēs filiās cōgit prōstituere pro pecuniā. Cum Nīcolāus audit proximum suum pecūniam nōn habēre prō filiābus suīs, Nīcolāus adit ad domum proximī jacēre massam aurī pannō involūtam per fenestram clam et clam abit. Māne surgēns homō massam aurī invenit et Deō grātiam agit. Nōn multō post tempus servus Deī similiter agit. Proximus servī Deī reperiēns massam aurī, prōpōnit vigilāre tōtam noctem. Proximus enim vult vidēre hominem jacere massam aurī per fenestram. Post paucōs diēs massam aurī in domum Nīcolāus prōjacet, ad cujus sonitum proximus excitātur et ad Nīcolāum fugientem vēlōciter adit. Proximus it vēlōcius quam Nīcolāus et eum capit. Vult dare ōsculum pedibus servī Deī, sed nōn placet Deī servō. Servus Deī jubet proximum nōn nūntiāre quod fēcit.

Cf. Iacobus de Voragine, *Historia Sancti Nicolai*

moriuntur: die
cogit: forced
clam: secretly
magis: more than
quam: than
pannus, pannī (m.): cloth
fēcit: did

1. Suntne parentēs Nīcolāī pauperēs?
2. Cūr Nīcolāus vult dare dīvitiās?
3. Cui Nīcolāus dīvitiās dat?
4. Cūr Nīcolāus nōn vult capi?

Sententiae Interpretandae

1. Nunc autem hic cōnsōlātur, tū vērō cruciārīs. (Lk 16:25)
2. Trānsgressor ex uterō vocāris. (Is 48:8)
3. Quī salvāris in Dominō. (Dt 33:29)
4. Et ego tamquam peccātor jūdicor? (Rom 3:7)

   tamquam: as

5. Quī dīceris Paraclītus. (*Veni Creator Spiritus*)
6. Jēsus Chrīstus heri et hodiē īdem, et in saecula! (Heb 13:8)
7. Hic enim vocor et justificor, ibi autem glōrificor. (Augustine, *Enarrationes in Psalmos* 61.12)

   hic: here, meaning "on earth"
   ibi: there, meaning "in heaven"

8. Videō cūncta quae fiunt sub sōle, et ecce ūniversa vānitās et afflīctiō spīritūs. (Eccl 1:13)

   vanitas, vanitatis (f.): vanity
   afflicio, afflictionis (f.): affliction

9. Quōmodo possunt haec fierī? (Jn 3:9)
10. Clāra est sapientia, et facile vidētur ab hīs quī dīligunt eam, et invenītur ab hīs quī quaerunt illam. (Wis 6:13)

    clara: bright

11. Nihil in terra sine causa fit. (Jb 5:6)
12. Sacerdōs īnfundit vīnum et parum aquae in calicem.

    parum: a little

13. Ut cognōscit autem Jēsus cōgitātiōnēs eōrum, respondēns dīcit ad illōs: "Quid cōgitātis in cordibus vestrīs? Quid est facilius dīcere: 'dīmittuntur tibi peccāta tua,' an dīcere: 'Surge, et ambulā.'" (Lk 5:22–23)

    an: or

14. Et iterum dīcō vōbīs: Facilius est camēlum per forāmen acūs trānsīre, quam dīvitem intrāre in rēgnum Deī. (Mt 19:24)

    foramen: eye
    acus, acūs (m.): needle *what case is it in the sentence?*

15. Post paucōs diēs recipimur in carcerem. (*Passiō Perpetuae et Fēlīcitātis*)
16. Hominēs enim cito mūtantur, et dēficiunt vēlōciter, Chrīstus autem manet in aeternum, et adstat usque in fīnem firmiter. (Thomas a Kempis, *Imitātiō Chrīstī* 2.1.1)

    deficiunt: they falter
    firmiter: firmly

17. Fide tantum docēmur Deum vidērī posse. (Augustine, *ep.* 147)
18. "Obsecrō vōs per misericordiam Deī." Rogat Paulus, immō per Paulum rogat Deus, quia plūs amārī vult quam timērī. Rogat Deus, quia nōn tam Dominus esse vult quam pater. (Peter Chrysologus, *Sermō* 108)

> *obsecrō*: I ask
> *immō*: rather
> *nōn tam*: not as much
> *quam*: than

Sententiae Fictae

1. Servus in urbem intrat vēlōciter fugere ex inimīcīs ejus.
2. Quī cōgitat rēctē, aurum proximīs quī sunt sine pecūniā dat.
3. Fīlius quī multa ōscula parentibus dat illōs parentēs amat.
4. Excitārīs ab sōle lūcente manē an ab mātre tuā?
5. Nōnne amāmur ab Deō quī fīlium eius nōbīs dat?
6. Excitāmur ab amōre ejus eum glōrificāre?
7. Ego dūcor ā mātre mea ad ecclēsiam. Tūne dūceris ā mātre tuā?
8. Sapientia Deī tibi facile ostenditur in terrā et caelō.
9. St. Jōhannis pulchrius scrībit quam mē, sed St. Paulus scrībit pulcherrimē.
10. Is vēlōciter, sed eō vēlōcius. Quis it vēlōcissimē?

CHAPTER 15

§ 54. Adjectives: Irregular Adjectives

Latin and English are similar in that the most commonly used adjectives are often the most irregular. So now we will learn some adjectives that are quite common but form their comparative, and superlative, forms in irregular ways.

Positive	Comparative	Superlative	Translations
magnus, -a, -um	maior, maior, maius	maximus, -a, -um	big / great, bigger / greater, biggest / greatest
parvus, -a, -um	minor, minor, minus	minimus, -a, -um	small, smaller, smallest
multus, -a, -um	plus / plūrēs, plūrēs, plūra	plūrimī, -ae, -a	much / many, more, most
paucus, -a, -um	pauciōrēs, pauciōrēs, pauciōra	paucissimī, -ae, -a	few, fewer, least
bonus, -a, -um	melior, melior, melius	optimus, -a, -um	good, better, best
malus, -a, -um	peior, peior, peius	pessimus, -a, -um	bad, worse, worst

Notice that we are still dealing with adjectives—words that give you more information about a noun. As adjectives, they agree with the noun they modify in gender, number, and case, but not declension. Which boy? The big boy. *Puer magnus.* Which book? The better book. *Melior liber.* Which gift? The best gift. *Donum optimum.*

Also notice that the endings for the adjectives are the same as we have seen in the regular adjectives. The positive form has the *-us, -a, -um* endings for masculine, feminine, and neuter. The comparative form has the *-ior, -ior, -ius* for masculine, feminine, and neuter like the third declension. The superlative form has the *-us, -a, -um* again like the first, and second declension for masculine, feminine, and neuter.

I think the hardest ones for students to wrap their heads around are *plures* and *plurimi*, which are both plural in form. These, like many forms of Latin, do not have direct English equivalents. *Plures homines*: "many humans" or "a greater amount of humans." *Plurima verba*: "most words" or "the greatest number of words."

§ 55. Adverbs: Irregular, Comparative, and Superlative

Positive	Comparative	Superlative	Translations
bene	*melius*	*optimē*	well, better, best
male	*peius*	*pessimē*	badly, worse, worst
magnopere	*magis*	*maximē*	greatly, greater, greatest
multum	*plūs*	*plurimum*	more, the most (in quantity)
parum	*minus*	*minimē*	less, least (in quantity)
saepe	*saepius*	*saepissimē*	often, more often, most often
diū	*diūtius*	*diūtissimē*	for a long time, for a longer time, for the longest time
satis			enough
nimis			too much

Maxime can also mean "especially" and *minime* can also mean "not at all."

Here are several examples of how irregular adverbs work:

Quia melior est diēs ūna in ātriīs tuīs super (quam) mīlia alibi. Volo esse ianitorem in domō Deī meī magis quam habitāre in tabernāculīs peccātōrum. (Ps. 83:11)[1]
Because better is one day in your courts than thousands elsewhere. I want to be a doorkeeper in the house of my God, more than to live in the tents of sinners.

Melius est portāre, quam projicere. (Augustine, *Sermo* 9)
It is better to carry, than to throw.

Melius est tē illī crēdere, quam quaerere abīre. (Augustine, *Sermo* 10)
It is better for you to trust him, than to seek to leave.

---

[1] Notice here that sometimes the Vulgate uses *super* in place of *quam*.

§ 56. Verbs: *ferre*

The last thing for this chapter is a new paradigm for an irregular verb.

fero, ferre, tulisse, latus: bear or carry[2]

Active:

[ego] fer|ō	I carry	*[nos] feri|mus*	we carry
[tu] fer|s	you carry	*[vos] fer|tīs*	you [pl.] carry
[is / ea / id] fer|t	he carries	*[ii / eae / ea] feru|nt*	they carry

Passive:

[ego] fero|r	I am being carried	*[nos] feri|mur*	we are being carried
[tu] fer|ris	you are being carried	*[vos] feri|minī*	you [pl.] are being carried
[is / ea / id] fer|tur	he is being carried	*[ii / eae / ea] feru|ntur*	they are being carried

The student should quickly recognize that *ferre* has standard personal endings in the active and passive. It does not have a regular theme vowel. It is also worth adding that Latin words often combine a preposition with certain verbs like *fero*. So, *adfero* means "I bear to" in English. Or *affert*, "he bears away."

§ 57. Indefinite Adjectives: *quīdam, quaedam, quaedam*

The good news about what follows is that you have already learned the basic patterns here. We are just going to take the relative pronoun and add *-dam* to the ending. This creates what is called the indefinite pronoun. In English this will be translated as "a," "one," or "some."

Quīdam vir ambulat. A man walks.

Pater cuiusdam discipulōrum discēdit. The father of one of the disciples left.

Quaedam fēminae cibum petunt. Some women seek food.

---

[2] We have not yet learned what the last two parts of the verb do, but the student might recognize that each stem is different. There aren't many verbs like this in Latin, but this one is common and very irregular.

Cases	M. S.	F. S.	N. S.	M. P.	F. P.	N. P.
Nom	quīdam	quaedam	quoddam	quīdam	quaedam	quaedam
Gen	cuiusdam	cuiusdam	cuiusdam	quōrundam (quōrumdam)	quārundam (quārumdam)	quōrundam (quōrumdam)
Dat	cuidam	cuidam	cuidam	quibusdam	quibusdam	quibusdam
Acc	quendam (quemdam)	quandam (quamdam)	quoddam	quōsdam	quāsdam	quaedam
Abl	quōdam	quādam	quōdam	quibusdam	quibusdam	quibusdam

Prefixing Prepositions to Verbs

Latin verbs can often be deciphered from the combination of the stem of the verb with the prepositional prefix. We just learned the verb *ferre*. On its own, it means "to bear" or "to carry." If you had a prefix, you can change the meaning slightly—*adferre,* which means "to bring towards" or "to carry to." If you add *re-* the verb becomes, *re-ferre*. We get the English word *refer*, and in Latin the word means "to bring back," or "to report." We have several prepositions that are often prefixed to verbs:

a- ab- abs-	(away) from
ad-	to, towards
ante-	before
circum-	around
con-	with, together
contra-	against
de-	down; off, away
di- dis-	apart, asunder
e- ex-	out (of)
extra-	outside
in-	in(to), against; not

inter-	between, among
intra- intro-	within, inside
ob-	against, face-to-face
per-	through; to the bad
post-	after
prae-	before, ahead; surpassing
pro-	before; forward
re- red-	back, again
retro-	back(ward)
se-	apart
sub-	under
super-	over, above
trans-	across

Other verbs like *ferre* can take these prepositional prefixes. Some of the most common are: *ferre, ire, esse, facere*. When a word like *esse* takes a prefix, sometimes the meaning changes and it is straightforward. For instance, *adest* means "he is present." *Deest* means "he is missing." This happens with verbs like *ire*. When you add *per-* to *ire*, it becomes *perire*, "to perish." Literally, it means "to go all the way through." When you add the preposition *re-* to *ire*, Latin adds a consonant in between and thus becomes *redire*, "to return" or "to go back."

Sententiae Summāriae

Goliath maior quam Dāvīd est, quoniam Goliath maximus est omnium hominum.[3] Dāvīd minor est quam Goliath quoniam Dāvīd est minimus frātrum eius.

Cantica Dāvīd meliōra sunt quam Goliath, quoniam cantica Dāvīd optima sunt. Dāvīd cantat melius quam Goliath, quoniam Dāvīd cantat optimē. Cantica Goliath peiōra sunt quam Dāvīd, quoniam cantica Goliath sunt pessima. Goliath cantat peius quam Dāvīd, quoniam Goliath cantat pessimē.

---

[3] The names *David* and *Goliath* are in indeclinable. They only have one form. Thus, the student must infer the case from context.

Ego librum ferō. Tū librum fers. Is librum fert.
Nōs rēs ferimus facilius quam vōs rēs fertīs. Iī nihil ferunt.

Translations

Goliath is bigger than David, for Goliath is the biggest of all people. David is smaller than Goliath, for he is the smallest of his brothers.

The songs of David are better than those of Goliath, for the songs of David are the best. David sings better than Goliath, for David sings in the best way. The songs of Goliath are worse than those of David, for the songs of Goliath are the worst. Goliath sings worse than David, for Golitah sings in the worst way.

I carry the book. You carry the book. He carries the book.
We carry things more easily than you carry things. They carry nothing.

Cavēte et Mementōte

Irregular adjective like the *ferre* sometimes have changes in the stem, but the endings still follow the basic rules for adjectives and verbs.

Vocābula Memoranda

Nōmina

carō, carnīs (m.): flesh, meat
hostīs, hostīs (m./f.): enemy
īnsipiēns, [in-sapiens], īnsipientis (m.): fool [*lit.* without knowing]
intellēctus, intellectūs (m.): understanding
salūs, salūtis (f.): health, salvation

Verba

<u>a-verb</u>
expugnō [ex + pugno], expugnāre, expugnāvī, expugnātus: conquer

<u>Forms of ferre</u>
adferō [ad + fero], adferre, adtulī, adlātus: bring to
auferō [ab + ferro], auferre, abstulī, ablātus: take away
cōnferō [con + fero], cōnferre, cōntulī, collātus: accompany; grant; ponder
ferō, ferre, tulī, lātus: bring, bear, carry
īnferō [in + ferro], īnferre, intulī, illātus: bring in
offerō [ob + ferro], offerre, obtulī, oblātus: offer
prōferō [pro + ferro], prōferre, prōtulī, prōlātus: bring forth, bring forward
referō [re + fero], referre, rettulī, relātus: bring back; yield, render; report

Forms of ire
    praeeō, praeīre, praeīvī, praeitus: go before
    pereo [per + eo], perīre, perīvī [periī], perītus: perish
    redeo [re + d + eo], redīre, redīvī [rediī], reditus: return

Adjectīva

    maior, maioris (gen. sing.): greater
    melior, melioris (gen. sing.): better
    humilis, humilis, humile: humble
    īnfimus, -a, -um: the least
    minimus, -a, -um: the least
    maximus, -a, -um: the greatest
    parvulus, -a, -um: little one
    tālis, tālis, tāle: something, of such a kind

Conjūnctīva

    an: or, whether
    ergo: therefore

Adverbia

    magis: greater
    nondum: not yet
    plūs: more
    satis: enough

Excerpta Latina

Ērgō Domine, quī dās fideī intellēctum, dā mihi scīre, quia es sīcut crēdimus, et hoc es quod crēdimus. Et quidem crēdimus tē esse aliquid quō nihil maius cōgitārī possit (potest). An ergō nōn est aliquā tālis nātūra, quia "dīcit īnsipiēns in corde suō: nōn est Deus" [Ps 13:1; 52:1]? Sed certē ipse īdem īnsipiēns, cum audit hoc ipsum quod dīcō: "aliquid quō maius nihil cōgitārī potest," intelligit quod audit; et quod intelligit, in intellēctū eius est, etiam sī nōn intelligit illud esse. Aliud enim est rem esse in intellēctū, aliud intelligere rem esse. Nam cum pictor praecōgitat quae factūrus [what he is about to do] est, habet quidem in intellēctū, sed nōndum intelligit esse quod nōndum fēcit [done]. Cum vērō iam pīnxit [he has drawn], et habet in intellēctū et intelligit esse quod iam fēcit [made]. Convincitur ergō etiam īnsipiēns esse vel in intellēctū aliquid quō nihil maius cōgitārī potest, quia hoc, cum audit, intelligit, et quidquid intelligitur, in intellēctū est.

Et certē id quō maius cōgitārī nequit [is not able], nōn potest esse in sōlō intellēctū. Sī enim vel in sōlō intellēctū est, potest cōgitārī esse et in rē; quod maius est. Sī ergō id quō maius cōgitārī nōn potest, est in sōlō intellēctū: id ipsum quō maius cōgitārī nōn potest, est quō maius cōgitārī potest. Sed certē hoc esse nōn potest. Existit ergō procul dubiō aliquid quō maius cōgitārī nōn valet, et in intellēctū et in rē.

Cf. Anselm's *Proslogion* (non nullis mutatis)

pictor: painter
praecogitare: to think before
nondum: not yet
convincere: to convince
existere: to exist
procul: far from

1. Quid Anselmus vult scire?
2. Quid est Deus?
3. Estne Deus in intellectu? an in re?

Sententiae Interpretandae

1. Venit fortior mē post mē. (Mk 1:7)
2. Pater maior mē est. (Jn 14:28)
3. Nōn est servus maior dominō suō, neque apostolus maior eō, quī mittit illum. (Jn 13:16)
4. Salūs carnis melior est omnī aurō et argentō. (Sir 30:15)

    argentum, argenti (n.): silver

5. Quī trādit mē tibi, maius peccātum habet. (Jn 19:11)
6. Est Moysēs vir humillimus super omnēs hominēs. (Nm 12:3)
7. Hostis et inimīcus noster pessimus est Amān. (Est 7:6)
8. [fragment] Ā minimō usque ad maximum. (Gen 19:11)
9. Ubi verba sunt plūrima, multiplicant vānitātem. (Eccl 6:11)

    vanitas, vanitatis (f.): vanity

10. Jēsus dīcit: "vērē dīcō vōbīs: Vidua haec pauper plūs quam omnēs mittit." (Lk 21:3)

    vidua, viduae (f.): widow
    mittit: gives

11. Tu es interior intimō meō et superior summō meō. (Augustine, *Confessiones* 3.6)

    intimus, -a, -um: in most, secret

12. Familia mea īnfima est in Mānāsse, et ego minimus in domō patris meī. (Jgs 6:15)
13. Magna est enim miseria superbī hominis, sed maior misericordia humilis Deī. (Augustine, *De Catechizandis Rudibus*)

14. In illā hōrā adeunt discipulī ad Jēsum, dīcentēs: Quis, putās, major est in rēgnō cælōrum? (Mt 18:1)
15. Numquid aliō nōmine vocārī quidam homo potest quam quod est? et quidam homo dicit: Nōn. sīc et egō aliud mē dīcere nōn possum nisi quod sum, Christiāna. (*Perpetua et Felicitas* 3)

alio: another
quam: than
aliud: another thing
nisi: except

Sententiae Fictae

1. Hostēs exercitum nostrum magnopere pugnant, sed nōn expugnant. Ergō, noster exercitus maximē pugnat.
2. Insipiēns cōgitat peius quam sapiēns. Ergō sapiēns melius cōgitat. Deus noster autem optimē cōgitat.
3. Servī ambulant plūs quam dominus eōrum quia saepissimē eum, quī minus ambulat, ferrunt.
4. Mīlitēs rōmānī fortissimī quoque arma leviōra portant. Ergō plūs ambulant quam Germānī quī arma gravissima portant.
5. Salūs Dominī nostrī maior est quam salūs īdōlōrum īnsipientium.
6. Cibum ad convīvium adferō. Quid ad convīvium adfers?
7. Jēsus peccāta nostra aufert ac vītam nostram prōferimus.
8. Quidam sacerdōtēs vīnum et pānem Deō offerunt.
9. Hostēs bellum ad urbem sānctam īnferunt.

CHAPTER 16

☙

§ 58. Verbs: Deponent Verbs

One of the most confusing aspects of classical languages like Greek and Latin are verbs traditionally called *deponent verbs*. These are a class of verbs that have no active personal endings (*-o, -s, -t, -mus, -tis, -nt*). Back in chapter 14, we learned the passive personal endings (*-r, -ris, -tur, -mur, -mini, -ntur*). So *donum datur* means "a gift is given." The subject receives the action of the verb. It would be incorrect to translate *donum datur* as "the gift gives." This incorrect translation assumes that the subject does the action. The deponent verb, or "passive only verb" will operate differently.

Let's take another verb: *timet*, as in *homines Deum timent*, "humans fear God." We could also say, *Deus timētur ā hominibus*, "God is feared by humans." We cannot say, *Homines Deum timēntur*. Why? It is not possible for there to be a direct object with a true passive. Why? The subject receives the action of the verb.

There is a synonym in Latin for *timēt*. It is *verētur*. Notice that the ending of the verb is passive in form. The form is passive, but the meaning is active. It is a deponent.[1] So we can say *homines Deum verentur*, "humans fear God." We cannot say *homines Deum timentur*. Why? Because *verentur* is deponent. It is passive looking but active in meaning; therefore it can have a direct object. The technically correct way to say this is that *verentur* is transitive. It can take a direct object. *Timetur*, as a passive, cannot take a direct object in its passive form. This can happen with all the personal endings, not only the third person.

Here are a few more examples:

*Jesus ei dīcit. ~ Jesus ei **loquitur**.* Jesus says to him. Jesus speaks to him.

They have similar meanings, but one is a regular verb (active and passive), and one is deponent (only passive in form, though usually active in meaning).

---

[1] We will continue to use the language of *deponent* rather than *passive only*. Some linguists think that the right way to classify these types of verbs is *passive only*.

Ego ōro. – *Ego **precor**.* I pray. I beseech.

*Tu filium **spectas**. Tu filium **intueris**.* You look at the son. You behold the son.

How do we know *intuetur* is passive? Well, you could guess because this is what the chapter is about, but also because we have a direct object with a passive ending. That is only acceptable if the verb is deponent.

*Puer <u>ōrāre</u> **temptat**.* – *Puer <u>precārī</u> **cōnātur**.* The boy attempts to pray. The boy tries to pray.

Notice in this example that *precārī* has an *-i* at the end because it is still deponent (passive in form, active in meaning) in the infinitive form. We learned earlier that passive infinitives have an *i* instead of the *e* we expect at the end of an infinitive.

An ā-verb with both active and passive looks like this:

or|ō	I pray	orā|mus	we pray
ora|s	you pray	orā|tis	you (pl.) pray
ora|t	he prays	ora|nt	they pray
oro|r	I am prayed to	orā|mur	we are prayed to
orā|rīs	you are prayed to	orā|minī	you (pl.) are prayed to
orā|tur	he is prayed to	ora|ntur	they are prayed to

An ā-verb that is deponent only has no active voice and looks like this:

precor	I pray	precā|mur	we pray
precā|rīs	you pray	precā|minī	you (pl.) pray
precā|tur	he prays	precā|ntur	they pray

The infinitives are going to be passive only as well. So the verb *precārī* has an *-ari* ending like the passive infinitive *ōrāre*. *Precari* means "to pray," but *ōrāre* means "to be prayed to."

It is one of the great conundrums of the universe as to why classical languages do this. Greek does it too. To some extent, this is how we know that people did not just "create" these languages. No one would have created something as confusing as deponents on purpose, except for maybe J.R.R Tolkien. Many people have argued that language is an epiphenomenon, that is, it is just something that happens on top of the fact that people want to communicate. They started communicating and for whatever reason, these passive looking verbs took on what are active meanings. Furthermore, native speakers would not necessarily even explain them this way. For them, these verbs just adhere to certain rules that are imbibed along with the language. Similarly, most English speakers don't learn to question their own language until much later, and then they wonder why we say "walked" and "punched," but not "goed." We just don't. Deponents are sort of like that. They are an idiosyncrasy of speech that one only realizes is different in the face of a language that doesn't do the same thing.

The last thing to note about deponents is how to classify them. Deponents are not another mood, like imperative or indicative. They are also not nonfinite forms like participles or infinitives. The definition of a deponent is that it has passive forms but usually active meanings. So, when you come across a deponent verb, remember that most deponents are passive in all their forms, unless otherwise noted.

One should be aware, though, that deponents do have a present active participle, as there is no such thing as a present passive participle.

> *Discipulī sequentēs Jēsum intrant in synagōgam.* The disciples, following Jesus, entered into the synagogue.

Here the participle *sequentēs* is present and active, even though this verb is deponent in its other forms.

So, this characterizes the verb in nearly all of its forms. Calling a verb "deponent" means that it looks passive but has an active meaning, except with the present participle.[2]

§ 59. Adjectives: *idem, eadem, idem* and *uterque, utraque, utrumque*

The charts below are two more very specific types of adjectives. The word *same* is typically used as an adjective. This chart looks the same as the regular pronoun we learned earlier (*is, ea, id*). The only difference is the ending *-dem*. This will look much like *quidam, quaedam, quiddam*, the indefinite pronoun. Like all Latin adjectives, it has to agree with the noun it is modifying and so has the following forms:

	M. S.	F. S.	N. S.	M. P.	F. P.	N. P.
Nom	idem	eadem	īdem	iīdem	eaedem	eadem
Gen	eiusdem	eiusdem	eiusdem	eorumdem	earumdem	eorumdem
Dat	eīdem	eīdem	eīdem	eīsdem	eīsdem	eīsdem
Acc	eundem	eandem	idem	eōsdem	eāsdem	eadem
Abl	eōdem	eādem	eōdem	eīsdem	eīsdem	eīsdem

---

[2] You could analyze deponents by their form and call them *passive*. You could analyze them by their meaning and call them *active*. I prefer analyzing them as passive.

Another word, *uterque*, which is often translated as "both," is technically an adjective and so has to have all the forms of a Latin noun.

Uterque, utraque, utrumque: both (of two)

	M. S.	F. S.	N. S.	M. P.	F. P.	N. P.
Nom	*uterque*	*utraque*	*utrumque*	*utrīque*	*utraeque*	*utraque*
Gen	*utrīusque*	*utrīusque*	*utrīusque*	*utrōrumque*	*utrārumque*	*utrōrumque*
Dat	*utrīque*	*utrīque*	*utrīque*	*utrīsque*	*utrīsque*	*utrīsque*
Acc	*utrumque*	*utramque*	*utrumque*	*utrōsque*	*utrāsque*	*utraque*
Abl	*utrōque*	*utrāque*	*utrōque*	*utrīsque*	utrīsque	utrīsque

Eādem fēmina eīsdem fīliīs idem verbum dat. The same woman gives the same word to the same sons.

(*Uterque* means each of two) *Erant autem uterque nudi, Adam scilicet et uxor eius.* They were each naked, Adam and his wife.

§ 60. Disjunctive Words: *aut, vel, sive, an*

Latin has several possibilities for proposing alternatives. *In quā virtūte aut in quō nōmine facitis hoc vōs?* "In what power, or in what name do you do this?" The *or* here in English is not inclusive. Sometimes you will see it twice: *aut in qua virtute aut in quo nomine*, as in "either … or." You did this in either that power or that name—which is it (but not both)?

Vel is inclusive.

Quī maledīxerit patri suō vel matri, morte moriātur. (Ex. 21:17)

Whoever curses his father or his mother [possibly both] will surely die. You could curse one or both of your father or mother, and you will surely die.

Sive is again inclusive.

Magnificābitur Christus in corpore meō, sīve per vitam sīve per mortem. (Phil. 1:20)

Christ will be magnified in my body, whether through life or death [possibly both].

An is usually used in questions to signify a disjunctive like *aut*.

Estne Dominus in nōbīs an nōn? Is the Lord within us or not [not both, it is one or the other]?

CHAPTER 16

Excursus on Translation

The long-term goal of any student learning Latin should be to learn how to read Latin as Latin. This is a difficult goal when most students learn the mechanics of grammar in one year. To meet the demands of a quick course in Latin grammar, many students will have to have aids to read and translate the language at the same time. It is thus important to keep a few things in mind when translating sentences from Latin to English for the sake of understanding what a Latin sentence is saying.

Let's use this sentence as an example:

Is precārī Deum, cuius rēgnum est in aeternum, vult.

1. Remember English word order works differently than Latin word order.
2. Find the subject and the main verb. (Remember the subject could be implied by the verb ending and may not be explicit.) If you get these right, the rest of the sentence will fall into place.
3. Identify the direct object and put it after the verb.
4. Identify any nonfinite verb forms like infinitives, participles, gerunds, etc.
5. Find ways to make smaller clauses into individual units, like relative clauses, conjunctions, and perhaps accusative plus infinitive constructions. Look for key words that begin clauses, like *et, qui, quae, quod, ut, cum, dum, donec, si, etsi, nec, ne*, and similar words that often begin new clauses. In each subordinate clause the grammar "resets." A sentence can have a new subject and a new direct object different from the main sentence.
6. Identify any prepositional phrases (i.e., the preposition and the object of the preposition).
7. Identify genitives, ablatives, and datives that go with the main verb and clause.
8. Translate the smaller clauses using the same steps from 1, 2, 3, 5, and 6 above.
9. Now put it all together.

Sententiae Summāriae

Servus Dominī Deō ōrat. Servus Dominī Deum precātur.
Puerī volāre temptant. Puerī volāre cōnantur.
Fīlius patrem timet. Fīlius patrem verētur.
Hominēs in ecclēsiam ineunt. Hominēs in ecclēsiam ingrediuntur.
Daemonia ex ecclēsiā discēdunt. Daemonia ex ecclēsiā proficīscuntur.

Translations

The servant of the Lord prays to God. The servant of the Lord prays to God.
The boys attempt to fly. The boys try to fly.
The son fears the father. The son fears the father.
People go into the church. People go into the church.
Demons leave from the church. Demons depart from the church.

Cavēte et Mementōte

A deponent verb is a verb that only has a passive form (except with the present participle). Most deponents are translated as active: passive in form, active in meaning.

Vocābula Memoranda

Nōmina

aequitās, aequitātis (f.): equity
fidūcia, fidūciae (f.): faith
fluctus, fluctūs (m.): wave
nāvis, nāvis (f.): boat[3]
nāvicula, nāviculae (f.): small boat
ventus, ventī (m.): wind
vesper, vesperis (m.): evening

Adiectivum

medius, media, medium: middle, means

Verba

<u>ā-verbs</u>
cōnor, cōnārī,—, cōnātus sum: try[4]
laetor, laetārī,—laetātus sum: rejoice, be happy
precor, precārī,—, precātus sum: pray
re-probo [re + probo], reprobāre, reprobāvī, reprobātus: condemn
turbō, turbāre, turbāvī, turbātus: throw into confusion

<u>ē-verbs</u>
cōnfiteor [con + fari], cōnfitērī,—, cōnfessus sum: confess
intueor, intuērī,—, intuitus sum: look at, consider
misereor, miserērī,—, miseritus sum: have mercy on
pareo, parēre, paruī, paritus: appear; obey
vereor, verērī,—, veritus sum: revere, fear

---

3 Adding an *-ul-* to the root of a noun makes it a diminutive. *Navis* becomes *naviculus* (a small ship), *parvus* becomes *parvulus* (very little), etc. If it is a third declension noun, it becomes a first or second declension noun.

4 Notice that there is no third principal part that is normally the *perfect, active, indicative*. This verb, and any other with a —, without the third principal part, are deponents and will not have this perfect active form.

i/e-verbs
    loquor, loquī,—, locūtus sum: say, speak
    morior, mori,—, mortuus sum: die
    occīdo [ob + caedo], occīdere, occīdī, occāsus: go down; kill
    resurgo [re + surgo], resurgere, resurrēxī, resurrectus: arise
    sequor, sequī,—, secūtus sum: follow

-io-verbs
    aggredior [ad + gredior], aggredī,—, aggressus sum: go to
    ingredior, [in + gredior], ingredī,—, ingressus sum: go in
    egredior, [ex + gredior], egredī,—, egressus sum: go out
    com-patior [con + patior], compatī,—, compassus sum: suffer, suffer with

i-verb
    orior, orīrī,—, ortus sum: arise

Adverbium

statim: immediately

Conjūnctīva

vel: either, or (inclusive)
sive: whether, or (inclusive)
an: or (exclusive)

Fābula Latina

Et statim compellit Jēsus discipulōs ascendere in nāviculam, et praeīre eum trāns fretum, cum dīmittit turbās. Ascendit in montem sōlus precārī. Vesper fit et sōlus est ibi. Nāvicula autem in mediō marī jactātur flūctibus: est enim ventus contrārius. Quārta vigilia noctis, venit ad eōs ambulāns super mare. Et vidēntēs eum super mare ambulantem, turbantur, dīcentēs: Phantasma est. Et prae timōre clāmant. Statimque Jēsus loquitur eīs, dīcēns "habēte fidūciam: ego sum, nōlīte timēre." Respondēns autem Petrus, dīcit: "Domine, sī tū es, jubē mē ad tē venīre super aquās." At ipse dicit: "Vēnī." Et dēscendēns Petrus dē nāviculā, ambulat super aquam aggredī ad Jēsum. Vidēns vērō ventum validum, verētur. Cum mergitur, clāmat dīcēns: Domine salvum mē fac! Et statim Jēsus extendēns manum, apprehendit eum et dicit illī: "Modicae fideī, cur dubitās?" Et cum ascendunt in nāviculam, cessat ventus. Quī autem in nāviculā sunt, veniunt, et adōrant eum, dīcentēs: "vērē Fīlius Deī es."

Cf. Matthew 14:22–33

trans fretum: on the other side
validum: strong
modicus, -a, -um: little
cessat: ceases

1. Cūr Jēsus ascendit in montem? Ubi sunt discipulī?
2. Quid accidit in marī?
3. Quid discipulī putant sē vidēre super flūctūs? Quid rē vērā [truly] vident?
4. Mergiturne Jēsus in marī? Mergiturne Petrus?

Sententiae Interpretandae

1. Et ēxiēns videt turbam multam, et miserētur eīs, et cūrat aegrōs.[5] (Mt 14:14)
2. Et palam verbum loquitur. (Mk 6:31–32)

palam: openly

3. Cōnfiteor Deō omnipotentī, quia peccāvī nimis cōgitātiōne, verbō, ōpere et omissione. (Cōnfiteor)

peccavi: I have sinned
omissione: omission

4. Vērē dīcō vōbīs quia, vidua haec pauper plūs quam omnēs mittit. (Lk 18:5)

vidua, viduae (f.): widow
mittit: similar to *dat* here

5. Bonum est cōnfiterī Dominō, et psallere nōminī tuō, Altissime. (Ps 91:2)

psallere: to sing a psalm

6. Oportet Fīlium hominis patī multa, et reprobārī ā seniōribus, et ā summīs sacerdōtibus et scrībīs, et occīdī: et post trēs diēs resurgere. (Lk 9:22)

summus, -a, -um: high, highest

7. Laetantur et exsultant gentēs, quoniam jūdicās populōs in aequitāte, et gentēs in terrā dīrigis. (Ps 66:4–5)

dirigere: to lead

8. Ideō precor beatam Mariam semper Virginem. (Cōnfiteor)
9. Homo videt ea quae apparent, dominus autem intuetur cor. (1 Sm 16:7)
10. Oritur sōl et occidit sōl. (Eccl 1:5)
11. Sīve ergō vīvimus, sīve morimur, Dominī sumus. (Rm 14:8)

---

5 Notice in this sentence we could change "miseretur eis" to "habet misericordiam pro eis" or we could say "aegri sanantur." But we cannot say, "curatur aegros" or "miserit eis." Why not? The first change would not work with *curat* because a true passive cannot have a direct object. The second would not work because a deponent word like *miseri* means that it only has a passive form.

12. Beātī quī persecutionem patiuntur prōpter justitiam: quoniam ipsōrum est rēgnum caelōrum. (Mt 5:10)

propter: (+acc) on account of

13. Et sī quid patitur unum membrum, compatiuntur omnia membra: sīve glōriātur unum membrum, congāudent omnia membra. (1 Cor 12:26)

quid: something
con-gaudere: to delight with

14. Et tamen vadit, redit, descendit, ascendit, et propter tē, homō, Deus patitur, quia tē nimis dīligit, nimis amat. (Peter Chrysologus, *Sermō* 170.8)
15. Quid hic sīc loquitur? blasphēmat. Quis potest dīmittere peccāta, nisi sōlus Deus? (Mk 2:7)

blasphemare: to blaspheme

Sententiae Fictae

1. Magister sōlus in scholam ingreditur.
2. Discipulī ex scholā ēgrediuntur velocius quam magister in scholam ingreditur.
3. Servus et ancilla dominum et dominam, quī sevērī sunt, verentur.
4. Parvulus puer laetārī cōnātur sed nimis trīstis est quia māter ejus ēgreditur.
5. Parvulus puer ad fenestram intuērī mātrem discēdentem aggreditur.
6. Omnēs discipulī Jēsum sequentēs pauperēs amant.
7. Petrus ambulāre super mare similiter Jēsū cōnātur, sed sequī eum nōn potest.
8. Quis nōn morī potest, sī Jēsus ipse moritur.
9. Māter loquitur et īnfāns cōnātur loquī similiter mātrī, sed nōn potest.
10. Sol super mare oritur.

CHAPTER 17

§ 61. Verbs: An Overview of Tense and Aspect

We have been talking about and using verbs for every chapter since the beginning. We have seen verbs in the present tense, whether commanding someone or describing things, or even as a noun. That is, verbs can be used in the indicative mood to talk about something happening or as a fact; verbs can be used as nouns, like infinitives; verbs can be used to command, like imperatives; and verbs can be used as adjectives or adverbs as participles. Latin verbs show all these things through the endings and sometimes by combining a form of *esse* with a regular form of the verb. So everything we have learned to this point has begun with the stem, for example, *laud-*, then the theme vowel, for example, *a*, and then the personal ending or mood formants, *-o, -s, -t, -mus, -tis, -nt* or *-r, -ris, -tur, -mur, -mini, -ntur* or *-re* and *-te* for infinitives and imperatives. This is what we know so far.

The second half of this book will be largely dedicated to seeing the rest of the ways that the verb can change. The verb is going to get more complex. One thing that should always be kept in mind is that there is no such thing as "hard" grammar. It is just grammar you have not seen enough for it to make sense. Language is learned through repetition. What follows will indeed feel "hard," but with enough time and enough repetitions, these new parts of grammar will feel like second nature. This is one reason why this textbook includes stories every few chapters and is written to follow Hans Orberg's *Familia Romana*. It can be quite beneficial to see large chunks of Latin to see how the grammar functions in the broader context of the language.

We will now turn to the various tenses that will appear in the coming chapters. This is a full introduction, but it may not be necessary for every student. The following section and explanations can be used as a reference as students continue.

Before we go through the use of tenses, it is critical to understand one root word that will help you keep straight all the possible tenses in Latin. This word is *perfect*. The word *perfect* in English tends to be used to refer to something without any deficiencies and with all desirable qualities. When we use the word in grammar, it just means "complete." What is a perfect action? It is not one that was done without fault, but one that has been accomplished. So, whenever we see the word *perfect* or any of its related words, we need to think of the English word *complete*. In Latin, we have six tenses: present, imperfect, perfect, pluperfect, future perfect, and future. Notice that the first and the last do not contain the word *perfect*. All the others do, and that will help you remember what they mean. Imperfect means "not completed" and is used for ongoing action or habitual action in the past.[1] Perfect means "complete" and is used for actions done in the past without any more specification. Pluperfect comes from the combination of *plus* with *perfect* to mean "more than completed action." It is thus used for actions that are further in the past from the standpoint of the speaker. Finally, *future perfect* means completed action in the future.

Let's take an example from the sermons of Augustine that shows the differing uses of tenses. In *Sermo* 355, Augustine tells the story of his conversion:

Present (1) I, whom by God's grace you see (*vidētis*) before you as your bishop,

Perfect (2) came (*venī*) to this city as a young man; many of you know that.

Imperfect (3) I was looking for (*quaerēbam*) a place to establish a monastery and live there with my brothers.

Pluperfect (4) I had in fact left behind all (*reliqueram*) worldly hopes, and I did not wish to be what I could have been;

Perfect (5) nor, however, did I seek (*quaesīvī*) to be what I am now.[2]

What this little example shows are the different possible ways to use tenses in Latin. We have four of the six tenses in this example. We can think of the tenses as helping us see what is going on in a story. The present tense is simple enough. When Augustine says, "whom by God's grace you see," he is addressing people who look at him as he speaks. All present tense. Then we move to the perfect tense, the main events of the story. "I came," "I did not seek." He is moving the story along regarding things he did before becoming a priest. He even includes a couple of pluperfect verbs, more than completed action in the past. "I had in fact left behind." Then we have the phrases that give more detail: "I was looking," which is *imperfect.*

There are only two other tenses: future and future-perfect. Future is simple enough, as it is used for situations in the future. The future-perfect—actions completed in the future—tends to be used in conditionals. Our English sentences will probably be translated as the future or present in these cases, "if you will follow me, I will make you fishers of men." Though, in Latin, the first part is in the future-perfect and will look like it should be translated, "if you will have followed me."

---

[1] The Latin suffix *in-* often negates a word *injustus* which means "unjust." And if it is added before certain consonants, it becomes *im*.

[2] The Latin is from *Patralogia Latina*, v.38, and the English is from *Works of Saint Augustine*, v. III/10, 167.

As we have done frequently in this book, I will give you a "quick gloss" to use as a reflex translation. It is of course true that you will not always follow these conventions in a good translation, but these will help you remember what each tense tends to do.

Tense (*Tempus*)	Active	Passive
Present (*Praesens*)	[verb]	is being [verb]-ed
Imperfect (*Imperfectum*)	was [verb]-ing; were [verb]-ing	was being [verb]-ed
Future (*Futurum*)	will [verb]	will be [verb]-ed
Perfect (*Perfectum*)	[verb]-ed; have [verb]-ed	has been [verb]-ed; was [verb]-ed
Pluperfect (*Plusquamperfectum*)	had [verb]-ed	had been [verb]-ed
Future-perfect (*Futurum perfectum*)	will have [verb]-ed	will have been [verb]-ed

Also, when we start adding new tenses, we will often add what I will call *tense formants*. That is, Latin will add a consonant, which indicates that the tense has changed: *-ba-* will indicate imperfect, *-v-/-u-* will indicate perfect, etc. Learning how to break down a Latin verb can be immensely helpful in identification.

Latin forms its tense with verbs differently than English. Often, we have to use a helping verb or a linking verb to make past tense, questions, or possibilities. We can think of a sentence like, "I might have walked to the store." The full verbal phrase "might have walked" can be conveyed in Latin by one word. Also, when English makes questions or negative expressions, it often adds a form of *do*. "Do you walk to the store?" Or, "do not walk to the store!" Latin will do these kinds of sentences with the verb and *non*. Most of the time Latin can communicate all of this in the verb endings. In some cases, Latin does have verbs that include more than one word, but much more is communicated in the main verb form than in English. In these situations, you will not be able to translate Latin into English with the same number of words, and it will begin to get more complicated.

One final concept needs to be introduced about verbs, called aspect. Aspect can be tricky to understand because it is not something most English speakers think about. English tends to focus primarily on the time when the events occur: did they happen before, after, or simultaneously? Latin, as well as Greek, can focus on the event as a whole, not primarily on the sequence of events. We find three aspects in Latin:[3]

---

[3] Drawn largely from Rodney J. Decker, *Reading Koine Greek* (Baker Academic, 2014), 224–25.

Imperfective [Un-completed] Aspect (also called Progressive or Continuous): these are verbs that describe an event or situation as ongoing.

Perfective [Complete] Aspect (also called Simple): these are verbs that describe an event as a complete event.

Stative [Status] Aspect: verbs that describe a state of affairs or status that exists presently as a result of a past action.

Latin has six tenses, but they do not always neatly line up with the aspectual categories.[4]

1. Present tense can convey imperfective (uncompleted) action: *laudo*. "I am praising."
   Present tense can convey perfective (complete) action: *laudo*. "I praise"
2. Imperfect tense conveys imperfective (uncompleted) action: *laudabam*. "I was praising" or "I was in the habit of praising."
3. Perfect tense can convey perfective action: *laudavi*. "I praised."
   Perfect tense can convey stative (status) action: *laudavi*. "I have praised."
4. Future tense can convey perfective action: *laudabo*. "I will praise."
   Future tense can convey imperfective action. *laudabo*. "I will be praising."
5. Pluperfect tense conveys perfective action. *laudaveram*. "I had praised."
6. Future-perfect tense conveys perfective action. *laudavero*. "I will have praised."

While the tense and aspect of Latin verbs might be confusing at first, a study of these uses of the tense will help explain something that occurs with Latin infinitives, and especially the subjunctive, called *sequence of tenses*.

If the main verb of a sentence is present, future, future-perfect, or perfect with stative action (e.g., *have prais-ed*), the sequence is called primary and subjunctives that follow can be only present, perfect, or future participle + *esse* (present subjunctive).

If the main verb of a sentence is imperfect, perfect (with complete action, *I praised*), or pluperfect, the sequence is called secondary, and the subjunctives that follow can be only imperfect, pluperfect, or future participle + *esse* (imperfect subjunctive).[5]

§ 62. Verbs: *Esse* in the Imperfect

We will slowly work our way into the various tenses of Latin verbs by looking at *esse* in the imperfect tense. Latin has several verbs that could be called *past* tense in English: imperfect, perfect, and pluperfect. It has two possible future tenses: future and future-perfect.

---

[4] Cf. Peter Jones, *Reading Latin Grammar and Exercises* (Cambridge University Press, 1998), 287–88.

[5] Jones, *Reading Latin*, 288.

For simplicity's sake, we will offer a go-to translation for the imperfect tense as "was/were." It is of course true that there are other possible ways to construe the imperfect, but for the aid of the beginning student, I think it is best to start here. For each of the tenses in the indicative, I will propose a simple one-to-one translation of the tense, like "was/were" for the imperfect.

esse: to be

[ego] era|m	I was	*[nos] erā|mus*	we were
[tu] erā|s	you were	*[vos] erā|tis*	you (pl.) were
[is / ea / id] era|t	he was	*[ii / eae / ea] era|nt*	they were

Notice that we still have all the standard personal endings: *-m, -s, -t, -mus, -tis, -nt*. Also notice that the imperfect is more regular than the present (*sum, es, est, sumus, estis, sunt*). This also holds true for the verb *posse*. *Poterāmus ambulāre, sed nunc nōn possumus* (we were able to walk, but now we cannot).

[ego] pot|eram	I was able	*[nos] pot|erāmus*	we were able
[tu] pot|erās	you were able	*[vos] pot|erātis*	you (pl.) were able
[is / ea / id] pot|erat	he was able	*[ii / eae / ea] pot|erant*	they were able

§ 63. Verbs Future of *esse* and Morphologically Similar Verbs

We will now add a new tense for the "to be" verb—the future.

ESSE

[ego] er|ō	I will be	*[nos] eri|mus*	we will be
[tu] eri|s	you will be	*[vos] eri|tis*	you (pl.) will be
[is / ea / id] eri|t	he / she / it will be	*[ii / eae / ea] eru|nt*	they will be

You should notice a couple of things here. First, the translation includes the same word: "will," throughout. This will be our "reflex translation" for the future. Like "was/were" was the reflex translation for the imperfect, "will" will be the standard translation for the future. You will notice that it looks almost exactly like the imperfect, except that our vowel has changed to -*i*-, except in the first singular and the third plural. Both the future and imperfect forms of *esse* will show up again in other tenses.

The verb *posse*, "to be able to" has the same forms as *esse* above, with the prefix *pot*-. So, *poterō* means "I will be able to." The verb *posse* will always follow the conjugation of *esse*, though the prefix can change from *pos*- to *pot*-. If it is added to -*e*, the prefix is *pot*-, as in *poterit*. If it is added to -*s*, the prefix is *pos*-, as in *possum*.

§ 64. Numerals (Adjectives): Cardinal and Ordinal

We have seen some numbers on the way, but we will see all of them here. Latin has several ways of counting, some more confusing than others. We will begin with the basic cardinal and ordinal numbers. Cardinal numbers are one, two, three, etc., *unus, duo, tres*; ordinal numbers are first, second, third, etc.: *primus, alter, tertius, quartus, quintus, sextus*.

Only the first three cardinal numbers are declined and therefore match the noun that they modify.

M. S.	F. S.	N. S.	M. P.	F. P.	N. P.	M. P.	F. P.	N. P.
ūnus	*ūna*	*ūnum*	*duō*	*duæ*	*duo*	*trēs*	*trēs*	*tria*
ūnīus	*ūnius*	*ūnīus*	*duōrum*	duārum	duōrum	trium	trium	trium
ūnī	*ūnī*	*ūnī*	*duōbus*	*duābus*	*duōbus*	*tribus*	*tribus*	*tribus*
ūnum	*ūnam*	*ūnum*	*duōs*	*duās*	*duo*	*trēs*	*trēs*	*tria*
ūnō	*ūnā*	*ūnō*	*duōbus*	*duābus*	*duōbus*	*tribus*	*tribus*	*tribus*

unus discipulus, una discipula, unum nomen
duo discipuli, duae discipulae, duo nōmina
tres discipuli, tres discipulae, tria nōmina
quattuor discipuli, quattuor discipulae, quattuor discipula

1	I	*ūnus, ūna, ūnum*	30	XXX	*trīgintā*
2	II	*duo, duae, duo*	40	XL	*quadrāgintā*
3	III	*trēs, tria*	50	L	*quīnquāgintā*
4	IV	*quattuor*	60	LX	*sexāgintā*
5	V	*quīnque*	70	LXX	*septuāgintā*
6	VI	*sex*	80	LXXX	*octōgintā*
7	VII	*septem*	90	XC	*nōnāgintā*
8	VIII	*octō*	100	C	*centum*
9	IX	*novem*	200	CC	*ducentī, -ae, -a*
10	X	*decem*	300	CCC	*trecentī, -ae, -a*
11	XI	*ūndecim*	400	CD	*quadringentī, -ae, -a*
12	XII	*duodecim*	500	D	*quīngentī, -ae, -a*
13	XIII	*tredecim*	600	DC	*sescentī, -ae, -a*
14	XIV	*quattuordecim*	700	DCC	*septingentī, -ae, -a*
15	XV	*quīndecim*	800	DCCC	*octingentī, -ae, -a*
16	XVI	*sēdecim*	900	CM	*nōngentī, -ae, -a*
17	XVII	*septendecim*	1000	M	*mīlle*
18	XVIII	*duodēvīgintī*			
19	XIX	*ūndēvīgintī*			
20	XX	*vīgintī*			

When we move to the ordinal numbers, we will also decline these as adjectives to match the noun they modify in gender, number, and case.

prīmus discipulus, prīma discipula, prīmum nōmen

secundus (alter) discipulus, secunda (altera) discipula, secundum (alterum) nōmen

tertius discipulus, tertia discipula, tertium nōmen

quārtus discipulus, quārta discipula, quārtum nōmen

§ 65. Syntax: Concessive Clauses

Continuing our habit of introducing structures along with the rest of the general grammar, it is important to be familiar with clauses that are easily translated by the English words "although" or "however." These are often called concessive clauses. That is, clauses that begin with a word like *quamquam* or *etsi* in Latin tend to introduce a thought that will provide a contrary opinion. In the example below, some people knew God, but despite this fact, they did not glorify him. The difficulty of introducing these words now is that some of them can take a subjunctive, though we will learn that later. For now, it is important to keep in mind that a word like *quamquam, etsi,* or *tametsi* introduces a contrast between two statements.

Etsī cognōscunt deum, nōn sīcut deum glōrificant aut grātiās agunt, sed ēvānēscunt in cōgitātiōnibus suīs et obscūrātur īnsipiēns cor eōrum. (Rm 1:21)

Although they know God, they do not glorify him as God or give thanks, but they become weak in their thoughts and their foolish hearts become dark.

Sententiae Summāriae

Eramus discipuli et magsitri erimus.
Etsī erit rēx, nēmō eum verētur.
Quamquam erit vir, nunc pugnāre bene nōn potest.

Translations

We were students and we will be teachers.
Although he will be king, no one fears him.
Although he will be a man, now he is not able to fight well.

Vocābula Memoranda

Nōmina

colonus, colonī (m.): settler, farmer
generātiō, generātiōnis (f.): generation
indigena, indigenae (m./f.): native
lex, legis (f.): law
nihil (n.): nothing
operātiō, operātiōnis (f.): work

Verba

<u>ā-verb</u>
peregrīnor, peregrīnārī,—, peregrīnātus sum: sojourn
<u>ē-verb</u>
revereor [re + vereor], reverērī,—, reveritus sum: fear
<u>i/e-verb</u>
expōnō [ex + pono], expōnere, exposuī, expositus: lay out, explain

Numerī

ūnus, ūna, ūnum: 1
duo, duae, duo: 2
trēs, trēs, tria: 3
quattuor: 4
quinque: 5
sex: 6
septem: 7
octō: 8
novem: 9
decem: 10
quadrāgintā: 40

Praepositiō

apud: (+abl) near, in the presence of

Adverbium

mox: soon

Coniunctiva

etsī: even though
nisī: unless, except
quamquam: although

Sententiae Interpretandae

For the following two passages (translated overly literally from the Latin) guess the tense (present, imperfect, perfect, pluperfect, future, future-perfect) and voice (active or passive) of the underlying Latin verb. What does the tense tell you about how the sequence of events work to illuminate the story?

Mark 2:1–6

1) And again he **entered** Capharnaum after some days.
2) And it **was heard** that he **was** in the house. And many **came together**, so that there **was** no room, not even near the door. And he **was speaking** to them the word.
3) And they **came** bringing to him a paralytic who **was being carried** by four.
4) And when they **were not able** to bear him to [Jesus] on account of the crowd, they **uncovered** the roof where he **was**: and opening it, they **put down** the bed where the paralytic **was laying**.
5) And when Jesus **had seen** their faith, he **says** to the paralytic: Son, your sins **are forgiven** from you.
6) And there **were** some of the scribes **sitting** there and **thinking** in their hearts.

Mark 2:15–19

15) And it **happened** when he **was sitting** in the house of [Levi], many publicans and sinners **were reclining** together with Jesus and his disciples. For there **were** many who **were following** him.
16) And the scribes and the Pharisees seeing that they **were eating** with sinners and tax collectors, they **were saying** to his disciples: Why does your teacher **eat** with tax collectors and sinners?
17) Having heard this, Jesus **says** to them: the healthy **have** no need of the doctor but those unwell. For I **have come** not to call the just but sinners.
18) And the disciples of John and the Pharisees **were fasting**. And they **come** to him and **say** to him: Why **do** the disciples of John and the Pharisees **fast**, but your disciples **do not fast**?

19) And Jesus **says** to them, Surely the children of the marriage **cannot** fast while the bridegroom **is** still with them? As long as they **have** the bridegroom with them they cannot fast.

20) But the days **will come** when the bridegroom **will be taken away** from them: and they **will not fast** in those days.

1. Etsī Deum nōn timet nec hominem reverētur. (Lk 18:2)
2. Ego sum resurrēctiō et vīta, quī crēdit in mē, etsī mortuus erit, vīvit. (Jn 11:25)[6]

   mortuus: dead
3. Et nihil impossibile erit vōbīs. (Mt 17:19)
4. Nunc dē operātiōne eōrum satis erit expōnere. (Tertullian, *Apologeticum*)
5. Et erunt duo in carne ūnā. Itaque jam nōn sunt duo, sed ūna carō. (Mk 10:8)
6. Eadem lēx erit indigenae et colōnō, quī peregrīnātur apud vōs. (Ex 12:49)
7. Ā trānsmigrātiōne Babylōnis usque ad Chrīstum generātiōnēs quattuordecim. (Mt 1:17)

   transmigratio, transmigrationis (f.): transmigration
8. Erat in dēsertō diēbus quadrāgintā. (Mk 1:13)
9. Nōn habēmus hīc nisi quīnque pānēs et duōs piscēs. (Mt 14:17)
10. Sex diēbus facit Dominus caelum et terram et mare, et omnia quae in eīs sunt. (Ex 20:11)
11. Nōs erimus servī dominī nostrī. (Gn 44:11)
12. Sānctī eritis, quia ego sānctus sum. (Lv 11:45)
13. Erō illōrum Deus, et ipsī erunt mihi populus. (2 Cor 6:16)

---

6 Technically *erit* + a perfect passive participle is a future perfect. The student should be able to figure out the meaning, though, by translating *mortuus* as "dead."

CHAPTER 18

❧

Verbs: Imperfect Active and Passive Indicative

As we begin to dip our toes into the myriad tenses, moods, and finite and nonfinite forms of the Latin verb, for every tense we will need to think about two things: morphology and meaning. So, we will typically begin with morphology (what it looks like) and then move to meaning (what it does). That is, we will begin with how to make the form or mood in Latin. We will then explain what it does and how it creates meaning.

§ 66. Morphology: Imperfect Active and Passive Indicative

So what is the imperfect active indicative in Latin? *Laudabat. Videbat. Ducebat. Audiebat.* We have already seen the *esse* form of the imperfect tense: *erat, erant*. Notice the vowel here is *a*. We will see that repeated in the regular forms of the other imperfect verbs. The tense formant for this tense will be *-ba-*. So in order to make the imperfect tense in Latin, we will take the stem of the verb *laud-*, add the pattern vowel, *a*, the tense formant, *-ba-*, and then our standard personal endings, *-m, -s, -t, -mus, -tis, -nt*. The same holds true for all pattern vowels. *Mon-e-ba-*, then *-m, -s, -t, -mus, -tis, -nt*. This will also be the case for passive, *laud-a-ba-*, then *-r, -ris, -tur, -mur, -mini, -ntur*.

Active

ā-verb	ē-verb	i/e-verb	i-verb	Example Translation
laudā|ba|m	monē|ba|m	ducē|ba|m	audiē|ba|m	I was hearing
laudā|bā|s	monē|bā|s	ducē|bā|s	audiē|bā|s	You were hearing
laudā|ba|t	monē|ba|t	ducē|ba|t	audiē|ba|t	He was hearing
laudā|bā|mus	monē|bā|mus	ducē|bā|mus	audiē|bā|mus	We were hearing
laudā|bā|tis	monē|bā|tis	ducē|ba|tis	audiē|ba|tis	You (pl.) were hearing
laudā|ba|nt	monē|ba|nt	ducē|ba|nt	audiē|ba|nt	They were hearing

Passive

ā-verb	ē-verb	i/e-verb	i-verb	Example Translation
laudā|ba|r	*monē|ba|r*	*ducē|ba|r*	*audiē|ba|r*	I was (being) heard
laudā|bā|ris (*laudā|bā|re*)	*monē|bā|ris* (*monē|bā|re*)	*ducē|bā|ris* (*ducē|bā|re*)	*audiē|bā|ris* (*audiē|bā|re*)	You were (being) heard
laudā|bā|tur	*monē|ba|tur*	*ducē|ba|tur*	*audiē|ba|tur*	He / She / It was (being) heard
laudā|bā|mur	*monē|bā|mur*	*ducē|bā|mur*	*audiē|bā|mur*	We were (being) heard
laudā|bā|minī	*monē|bā|minī*	*ducē|bā|minī*	*audiē|bā|minī*	You (pl.) were (being) heard
laudā|ba|ntur	*monē|ba|ntur*	*ducē|ba|ntur*	*audiē|ba|ntur*	They were (being) heard

The last thing to note is the exception. In Latin, as in most languages, there's always an exception. For the first three verb patterns (*a, e, i/e*) you will just add the *-ba-* to the vowel. With the final pattern (*i*), you will add an *-e-* before the *-ba-*. Thus we have a-verb, *laudābāt*; e-verb, *vidēbāt*; i/e-verb, *ducēbāt*; then i-verb, *audiēbāt*. The other category of verb is the *-io-* verb. Our representative example is *capio*. This verb in the imperfect looks like an i-verb and looks like this in the imperfect: *capiēbāt*.

§ 67. Meaning: Imperfect Active and Passive Indicative

What does the imperfect do? How does it make meaning? Recall from chapter 17 that imperfect stands for *uncompleted action in the past*. "I was walking," "we were walking," etc. The words we will be using as our reflex translations are "was"/"were," or, in the passive, "was [being]-ed" / "were [being]-ed." It is a tense typically reserved for giving more details about things ongoing in the past. Sometimes it can be translated "used to." Also, when one progresses to more idiomatic and dynamic equivalent translations, one might choose to just use the simple past in English. "They were saying," becomes "they said."

> *Tunc **exī-ba-t** ad eum Jerosolyma, et omnis Judaea, et omnis regiō circā Jordānem; et **baptīzā-ba-ntur** ab eō in Jordāne, cōnfitentēs peccāta sua.* (Mt 3:5–6)

Then all Judea and Jerusalem and all the region around the Jordan, was going out to him; and they were being baptized by him in the Jordan, confessing their sins.

CHAPTER 18

§ 68. Adjectives: *alius, nullus, ullus, totus, solus,* and *unus*

Latin has some adjectives that decline mostly like *parvus, -a, -um* with changes in the genitive and dative. In these instances, the adjectives decline like a pronoun and have *-ius* in the genitive and *-i* in the dative. Otherwise, they decline exactly like first and second declension adjectives.

Cases	M. S.	F. S.	N. S.	M. P.	F. P.	N. P.
Nom	*alius*	*alia*	*aliud*	*alii*	*aliae*	*alia*
Gen	*alius*	*alius*	*alius*	*aliorum*	*aliarum*	*aliorum*
Dat	*alii*	*alii*	*alii*	*aliis*	*aliis*	*aliis*
Acc	*alium*	*aliam*	*aliud*	*alios*	*alias*	*alia*
Abl	*alio*	*alia*	*alio*	*aliis*	*aliis*	*aliis*

The word *nullus* is a little strange. It can mean "no" or "none" depending on context. *Nullus homo,* "no person." *Nullus eorum,* "none of them." *Ullus* means "any," but you will often find it with a negative *nec ullus homo,* "not any person."

Soli deo gloria. Notice here that *soli* and *deo* look like they do not agree because of their different endings. They are both dative singular, though, because *solus* is an adjective like *alius* above.

§ 69. Verbs: Negative Imperatives

We introduced imperatives in chapter 3. We had special endings for these imperatives like *laud-a* and *laud-a-te.* These special endings indicated whether the command was meant for one person, *lauda,* or multiple people, *laud-a-te.* If you want to command people to not do something, you use the phrase *noli* plus the infinitive when speaking to one person, or *nolite* plus the infinitive when speaking to multiple people.

Nōlī audīre. Do not listen!
Nōlīte audīre. Do not listen (plural)!

Notice that the infinitive does not change.

Sententiae Summāriae

Ego Deum laudābam, sed tū daemonia laudābās.
Servī Christī Deum vērum laudābant. Vērus Deus ā servīs Christī laudābātur.
Tū sōlus discipulōs monēbās, sed nōlēbant monērī.
Vōs ā Dominō in coelum dūcēbāminī. Aliī ad mortem dūcēbantur.
Nūllus eōrum ā daemoniō audiēbātur. Nūlla daemonia hominēs audiēbant.

Translations:

I was praising God, but you were praising demons.
The servants of Christ were praising the true God. The true God was being praised by the servants of Christ.
You alone were warning the disciples, but they were not wanting to be warned.
You all were being led by the Lord into heaven. Others were being led to death.
None of them were being heard by the demon. No demons were listening to the humans.

Cavēte et Mementōte

For the imperfect (incomplete) tense, you should memorize the *-ba-* tense formant and then remember to add the normal personal endings.

Watch out though for the *i* pattern verbs where you will see an extra *-e-* after the theme vowel.

Vocābula Memoranda

Nōmina

familia, familiae (f.): family
labium, labiī (n.): lip
līberī, līberōrum (m.): children
os, oris (n.): mouth
parēns, parentis (m.): parent
templum, templī (n.): temple

Verba

<u>*ā-verbs*</u>
complexō [con + plecto], complexāre, complexāvī, complexātus: hug[1]
murmurō, murmurāre, murmurāvī, murmurātus: grumble, complain
stō, stāre, stetī, status: stand

---

1 The classical verb related to this one, *complector, complecti, complexus sum*, is a deponent.

i/e-verbs
   pendō, pendere, pependī, pēnsus: hang
   vadō, vādere, vāsī,—: go

-io-verb
   pariō, parere, peperī, partus: give birth

i-verb
   oboediō, oboedīre, oboedīvī, oboedītus: obey

Irregular
   nōlī: don't (in negative singular commands)
   nōlīte: don't (in negative plural commands)

Adjectīva

adjūnctus, -a, -um: added
alius, -a, -ud: another
dolōrōsus, -a, -um: full of pain or sadness[2]
lacrimōsus, -a, -um: full of tears
leprōsus, -a, -um: full of leprosy
nūllus, -a, -um: no, nothing
trīstis, -is, -e: sad
ūllus, -a, -um: any

Adverbia

cotīdiē; quotīdiē: daily
paene: almost
saepe: often

Fābula Excerpta (nōn nūllīs mūtātīs)

Hebrew names often are indeclinable, but not always. Ephraim, Heli, Elcana, Jeroham, Eliu, Tohu, and Suph are all indeclinable, but Anna and Phennena are declined as first declension.

Est vir ūnus, dē monte Ephraim, et nōmen ejus Elcānā, filius Jeroham, filiī Eliu, filiī Thohu, filiī Suph, Ephrathaeus: et habet duās uxōrēs, nōmen ūnī Anna, et nōmen secundae Phenenna. Sunt Phenennae filiī: Annae autem nōn sunt līberī. Et ascendēbat vir ille dē cīvitāte suā adōrāre et sacrificāre Dominō exercituum in Sīlō. Erant autem ibi duo filiī Hēlī, Ophnī et Phineēs, sacerdōtēs Dominī. Venit ergō diēs, et sacrificat Elcana, datque Phenennae uxōrī

---

[2] As you may recognize here, the noun *dolor* (pain) can become an adjective with *-os-*. The other two words below this one follow the same pattern. As a general rule, you often find that a word with *-os-* attached to the stem, is an adjective meaning "full of" the noun.

suae, et cūnctīs filiīs ejus, et filiābus ūnam partem animālium: Annae autem dat partem ūnam integram trīstīs, quia Annam dīligēbat.³ Nam, nōn potest illa parere līberōs. Afflīgēbat quoque eam inimīca ejus, et vehementer dērīdēbat quia dominus uterum claudēbat. Sīcque faciēbat semper: cum ascendēbant ad templum Dominī: et sīc prōvocābat eam; porrō illa plōrābat, et nōn capiēbat cibum. Dīcit ergō eī Elcana vir suus: Annā, cūr plōrās? et quārē nōn mandūcās? et quam ob rem afflīgitur cor tuum? numquid ego melior tibi sum, quam decem filiī? Surgit autem Annā postquam mandūcābat et bibēbat. Et Hēlī sacerdōte sedente super sellam ante januam templī Dominī, cum erat Annā amārō animō, ōrat ad Dominum, plōrāns valdē, et vōtum vovet, dīcēns: Domine exercituum, sī respiciēns vīdes afflīctiōnem ancillae tuae, dā ancillae tuae filium. Ille erit Dominō omnibus diēbus vītae ejus. Dum illa ōrābat in cōnspectū Dominī, Helī observābat os ejus. Porrō Annā loquēbātur in corde suō, tantumque labiā illīus movēbantur, et vōx nōn audiēbātur. Helī putābat ergō eam inēbriātam esse, dīcit eī: Usquequō ēbria eris? Nōlī bibere nimis vīnum. Respondēns Annā: Minimē, domine mī: nam mulier trīstīs nimis ego sum, vīnumque et omne quod inēbriāre potest, nōn bibēbam, sed effundēbam animam meam in cōnspectū Dominī. Nōlī putāre ancillam tuam quasi ūnam dē filiābus Belial: quia dolōrōsa et lacrimōsa ōrat. Tunc Heli ait eī: Vāde in pāce: et Deus Isrāēl det [may he give] tibi petītiōnem tuam, quam rogābās eum. Et illa ōrat: ego sum ancilla tua, et volō invenīre grātiam in oculīs tuīs. Et abit mulier in viam suam, et manducat, faciēsque illīus nōn est amplius sive dolōrōsa sive lacrimōsa.

Cf. 1 Samuel 1:1–18

votum vovet: vows a vow
quam ob rem: for what reason
dē-rīdēre: to mock
afflīgere: to afflict
uterus, uterī: uterus
provocāre: provoke
inebriatam: drunk
usquequo: for how long
ebrius, ebria: drunk
amplius: any longer

1. Quis est Annā? Cūr trīstis est Annā?
2. Quem Elcāna plūs dīligit, Annam an Phenennēam?
3. Cūr Heli putābat Annam inēbriāre?
4. In fīne fābulae, Annā trīstis est?

---

3 *Trīstīs* here modifies the implied subject of *dat*, *Elcana*.

Sententiae Interpretandae

1. Et accipientēs dēnāriōs, murmurābant adversus patrem familiās. (Mt. 20:11)[4]

    dēnārius: denarius, a coin

2. Mīrābantur, videntēs mūtōs loquentēs, claudōs ambulantēs, caecōs videntēs: Magnificābant Deum Isrāēl. (Mt 15:31)

    mūtus: mute
    claudus: lame (unable to walk)
    caecus: blind

3. Stābat Māter dolōrōsa juxtā crucem lacrimōsa, dum pendēbat Fīlius. (Stābat Māter)
4. Et ecce leprōsus veniēns adōrābat eum, dīcēns: Domine, sī vīs, potes mē mundāre. (Mt 8:2)
5. Quotīdiē sedēbam cum vobis docēns in templō. (Mt 26:55)
6. Sarā oboediēbat Abrahae. (1 Pt 3:6)

    Abraham, Abrahae (m.)

7. Et ībant parentēs Jēsu in Jerusālem. (Lk 2:41)
8. Et complexāns eōs benedīcēbat impōnēns manūs super illōs. (Mk 10:16)
9. Dominus Jēsus, in quā nocte trādēbātur, accēpit pānem. (1 Cor 11:23)
10. Quae moerēbat et dolēbat, pia māter, dum vidēbat, nātī poenās inclytī. (Stābat Māter)

    moerere: to mourn
    natus, nati: son [*lit.* born one]
    inclytus: illustrious

11. Scīmus quia nihil est īdōlum in mundo, et quod nūllus est Deus, nisi ūnus. (1 Cor 8:4)
12. Chrīstum Dominum suīs temporibus ostendet beātus et sōlus potēns, Rēx rēgum, et Dominus dominantium, quī sōlus habet immortālitātem, et lūcem inhabitat inaccessibilem: quem nūllus hominum vīdit, sed nec vidēre potest: cui honor, et imperium sempiternum. Āmēn. (1 Tm 6)

    ostendet: [future] will show
    vidit: [perfect] seen

13. Aliī autem aliud clāmābant. Erat enim ecclēsia cōnfūsa: et plūrēs nesciēbant. (Acts 19:32)
14. Et nōn respondet eī ūllum verbum. (Mt 27:14)
15. Terra autem erat inānis et vacuā, et tenebræ erant super faciem abyssī: et spīritus Deī ferēbātur super aquās. (Gn 1:2; Biblia Vulgata)

    inānis et vacua: hollow and empty

---

4 *Familias* is acting as a genitive.

16. Terra autem erat invīsibilis et incomposita, et tenebrae erant super abyssum. Et spīritus Deī superferēbātur super aquam. (Gn 1:2; Vetus Latina)[5]

invīsibilis et incomposita: invisible and uncomposed

17. Dā mihi castitātem et continentiam, sed nōlī modo. (Augustine, *Confessiōnēs* 8)

castitās, castitātis (f.): chastity
continentia, continententia (f.): continence

---

5 Numbers 15 and 16 are the same verse of two different versions of Genesis 1:2. The first comes from Jerome's Vulgate, and the second is what is known as the Vetus Latina, or the Old Latin version(s). The Vetus Latina is older than Jerome's Vulgate and was used by Latin speakers before Jerome's version was completed.

CHAPTER 19

☙❧

Verbs: Future Active and Passive

In this section, we will follow the pattern established above by beginning with the morphology and then moving to the meaning of the future tense. The future tense is fairly straightforward and much like the English future, as we will see.

§ 70. Morphology: Future Active and Passive Indicative

So what is the future in Latin? *Laudabit, videbit, ducetur, audietur*. You might recall that we have done the future of *esse*: *erit*. We move from the imperfect *a* to the future *i* before the personal endings. This will help you with roughly half of future verbs. The problem is, as you probably noticed in the examples above, the first two patterns have *-bi-* and the second two have *-e-/-ie-*. When you come across a verb you suspect might be future, you will be looking for the *-bi-* or the *-e-*. The future is when we will begin to see the payoff of paying attention to the theme vowels of the verbs. Depending on the verb pattern, the future tense can be formed in one of two possible ways. If the verb has an *a* or an *e* vowel after the stem, it will have the *-bi-* tense formant. If the verb is an i/e-verb or an i-verb, it will have an *-e-* after the stem and before the personal endings. The personal endings will stay the same as they were in the imperfect and the present.

So you have charts for both possibilities. The good news is that the personal endings stay the same. The bad news is that there are variations for the short i/e-verbs and the i-verbs, as well as -io-verbs.

Active

ā-verb	ē-verb	i/e-verb	i-verb	Example Translation
laudā|b|ō	*monē|b|ō*	*dūc|a|m*	*audi|a|m*	I will hear
laudā|b|is	*monē|b|is*	*dūc|ē|s*	*audi|ē|s*	You will hear
laudā|b|it	*monē|b|it*	*dūc|e|t*	*audi|e|t*	He will hear
laudā|b|imus	*monē|b|imus*	*dūc|ē|mus*	*audi|ē|mus*	We will hear
laudā|b|itis	*monē|b|itis*	*dūc|ē|tis*	*audi|ē|tis*	You all will hear
laudā|b|unt	*monē|b|unt*	*dūc|e|nt*	*audi|e|nt*	They will hear

Passive

ā-verb	ē-verb	i/e-verb	i-verb	Example Translation
laudā|b|or	*monē|b|or*	*dūc|a|r*	*audi|a|r*	I will be heard
laudā|b|eris	*monē|b|eris*	*dūc|ē|ris*	*audi|e|ris*	You will be heard
laudā|b|itur	*monē|b|itur*	*dūc|ē|tur*	*audi|e|tur*	He will be heard
laudā|b|imur	*monē|b|imur*	*dūc|ē|mur*	*audi|e|mur*	We will be heard
laudā|b|iminī	*monē|b|iminī*	*dūc|ē|minī*	*audi|e|minī*	You all will be heard
laudā|b|untur	*monē|b|untur*	*dūc|e|ntur*	*audi|e|ntur*	They will be heard

-Io-verbs have the same forms as the i-verbs, for example, *capietur*.

§ 71. Meaning: Future Active and Passive Indicative

What does the future do? How does it create unique meaning? It is fairly simple. The future talks about events in the future. The easy translation is "will," or in the passive, "will be [verb]-ed."

> *Et **cognosc-ē-tis** vēritātem, et vēritās **lībera-bī-t** vōs.* (Jn 8:32)
> And you will know the truth, and the truth will set you free.

> *Vōs enīm estis templum Deī vīvī, sīcut dīcit Deus: "**Inhabitā-bō** in illīs, et **ambulā-bō** inter eōs, et **erō** illōrum Deus, et ipsī **erunt** mihi populus."* (2 Cor 6:16)
> For you all are the temple of the living God, as God says, "I will live in them, and I will walk among them, and I will be their God, and they will be my people."

§ 72. Indefinite Pronouns and Adjectives

What follows is a chart of an indefinite pronoun ("someone" or "something") and an indefinite adjective ("some person" or "some thing"). As far as the Latin forms of these words, indefinite pronouns and adjectives look very similar with four exceptions: masculine nominative singular, the feminine nominative singular, and the neuter nominative and accusative singular because the neuter always has the same endings in the nominative and the accusative. These are indicated in the chart by the different options. The pronoun goes first in the chart, while the adjective comes second if there is a difference.

Cases	M. S.	F. S.	N. S.	M. P.	F. P.	N. P.
Nom	*aliquis / aliquī*	*aliquis / aliqua*	*aliquid / aliquod*	*aliquī*	*aliquae*	*aliquae*
Gen	*alicuius*	*alicuius*	*alicuius*	*aliquōrum*	*aliquārum*	*aliquōrum*
Dat	*alicui*	*alicui*	*alicui*	*aliquibus*	*aliquibus*	*aliquibus*
Acc	*aliquem*	*aliquam*	*aliquid / aliquod*	*aliquōs*	*aliquās*	*aliquae*
Abl	*aliquō*	*aliquā*	*aliquō*	*aliquibus*	*aliquibus*	*aliquibus*

These indefinite pronouns and relatives can be used in three primary ways, though we will see a fourth in chapter 31. They are used just like *qui, quae, quod* and *quis, quis, quid*.

1) Interrogative Indefinite Pronoun (asking a question about a noun): The word *aliquis* can stand alone to begin a question. Thus, it is called an indefinite interrogative pronoun.

> *Aliquis legere vult?* Does someone want to read? (In this situation the *aliquis* is an indefinite pronoun that stands alone.)
>
> *Aliquid in manibus tuīs habēs?* Do you have something in your hands? (In this situation the *aliquid* is an indefinite pronoun that stands alone.)

2) Interrogative Indefinite Adjective (asking a question about an uncertain noun): *Aliqui* or *aliqua* modifies another noun and more generally comes in or as an indefinite adjective.

> *Aliqua fēmina legere vult?* And the *aliqua* changes to an indefinite adjective saying, "does any woman" or "does some woman" want to read?

3) Indefinite Pronoun (used in place of an uncertain noun): We could change it out of a question and say *aliquod poculum in manibus tuis habes.* "You have some cup in your hand." In this case it becomes an adjective that expresses uncertainty about the kind of cup the person has in his hands.

> *Laudat aliquem, sed nescit quem.* "He praises someone, but whom he doesn't know."
> This is an indefinite pronoun.

> *Alicui nōmen Mārcus hīc est, sed quem nesciō.* Someone has the name Marcus here, but whom I don't know.

Similarly, *quicumque, quaecumque, quodcumque* is an indefinite relative pronoun or adjective that follows the above pattern, like *qui, quae, quod [quis, quis, quid]*. As you may recall, *qui, quae, quod* is the adjectival form, and *quis, quis, quid* is the pronominal form. *Quicumque, quaecumque, quodcumque* is usually translated as "whoever" or "whatever."

> *Quīcumque* [here a substantival adjective] *Jēsum sequitur, Chrīstiānus est.* Whoever follows Jesus is a Christian.

Cavēte et Mementōte

For the future we are looking for *-bi-* with a-verbs and e-verbs or an *-e* with i/e-verbs, i-verbs, and -io-verbs. The one irregularity is an *-a-* in the first-person singular before the personal endings that do not change.

Sententiae Summāriae

> Ego filiōs meōs laudābō, sī eī erunt bonī.
> Tū filiās tuās laudābis, sī eae erunt bonae?
> Magister discipulōs semper monēbit et ab eō discipulī semper monēbuntur.
> Nōs exercitus in bellum dūcēmus, sed exercitus hostium in bellum ā duce eōrum dūcentur.
> Vōs exercitūs vestrōs in bellum dūcētis?
> Cantica ecclēsiae ā Deō audientur. Aliquis ex ecclēsiā canticā audiet?

Translations

> I will praise my sons, if they will be good.
> Will you praise your daughters, if they will be good?
> The teacher will always teach the students, and the students will always be taught by him.
> We will lead the armies into war, but the armies of the enemies will be led by their leader into war.
> Will you [pl.] all lead your armies into war?
> The songs of the church will be heard by God. Will someone outside of the church hear the songs?

CHAPTER 19

Vocābula Memoranda

Nōmina

altāre, altāris (n.): altar
cīvitās, cīvitātis (f.): city, commonwealth
cognāta, cognātae (f.): kinsman, someone related by birth
frāter, frātris (m.): brother
illūminātiō, illūminātiōnis (f.): illumination
laus, laudis (f.): praise, merit
medium, mediī (n.): middle
mēnsis, mēnsis (m.): month
requiēs, requiēī (f.): rest
salūs, salūtis (f.): salvation, health
sermō, sermōnis (m.): word, sermon
virtūs, virtūtis (f.): power, virtue
vitium, vitiī (n.): fault, vice, crime

Verba

ā-verbs
cēnō, cēnāre, cēnāvī, cēnātus: dine
creō, creāre, creāvī, creātus: create
juvō, juvāre, jūvī, jūtus: help

ē-verb
fleō, flēre, flēvī, flētus: cry, weep

i/e-verbs
aspergō [ad + spergo], aspergere, aspersī, aspersus: sprinkle, wash
nāscor, nāscī,—, nātus sum: be born
requīrō [rē + quaerō], requīrere, requīsīvī, requīsītus: require, seek, need

-io-verb
concipiō [con + capio], concipere, concēpī, conceptus: to conceive

i-verb
superveniō [super + venio], supervenīre, supervēnī, superventus: to come over

Adjectīva

mundus, -a, -um: clean
aliqui, aliqua, aliquod: some person, some thing

Prōnōmina

aliquis, aliquis, aliquid: someone, something
quīcumque, quaecumque, quidcumque: whoever, whatever

Fābula Excerpta

In mēnse autem sextō, mittitur angelus Gabriel ā Deō in cīvitātem Galilaeae, cui nōmen Nazareth, ad virginem quae prōmittitur virō, cui nōmen erat Joseph, dē domō Dāvīd: et nōmen virginis Maria. Et ingrediēns angelus ad eam dīcit: Avē grātiā plēna: Dominus tēcum: benedicta tū in mulieribus. Quae cum audit, turbātur in sermōne ejus, et cōgitat dē istā salūtātiō. Et dīcit angelus eī: Nōlī timēre, Maria: invenīs enim grātiam apud Deum. Ecce concipiēs in uterō, et pariēs fīlium, et vocābis nōmen ejus Jēsum: hic erit magnus, et Fīlius Altissimī vocābitur, et dabit illī Dominus Deus sēdem Dāvīd patris ejus: et rēgnābit in domō Jācōb in aeternum, et rēgnī ejus nōn erit fīnis. Dīcit autem Maria ad angelum: Quōmodo fīet illud, quoniam virum nōn cognōscō? Et respondēns angelus dīcit eī: Spīritus Sānctus superveniet in tē, et virtūs Altissimī obumbrābit tibi. Ideōque et quod nāscētur ex tē sānctum, vocābitur Fīlius Deī. Et ecce Elisabeth cognātā tuā, et ipsa concēpit fīlium in senectūte suā: et hic mēnsis sextus est illī, quae vocātur sterilis: quia nōn erit impossibile apud Deum omne verbum. Dīcit autem Maria: Ecce ancilla Dominī: fīat mihi secundum verbum tuum. Et discēdit ab illā angelus.

Cf. Luke 1

mulier, mulieris (f.): woman
cognosco: know
concēpit: [perfect] conceived
fit (become/happen), *fīet* (in futuro), *fīat* (subjunctive): let it happen
obumbrābit: overshadow

1. Ā quō angelus mittitur?
2. Quālis erat virgō?
3. In prīncipiō [in the beginning], virgō erat tranquilla? Quōmodo scītur?
4. Cūr virgō est plēna grātiā?
5. Quid fīet virginī?
6. Quālis erit fīlius virginis?
7. Virgō virum cognōscēbat? Quōmodo virgō concipiēs fīlium?
8. In fīne, virgō turbātur? Quōmodo scītur?

Sententiae Interpretandae

1. Intrābō ad illum et cēnābō cum illō. (Rv 3:20)
2. Dabimus eīs mandūcāre. (Mk 6:37)
3. Domine, labia mea aperiēs. Et os meum annūntiābit laudem tuam. (Ps 50:17)
4. Dominus illūminātiō mea et salūs mea, quem timēbō? (Ps 27:1)
5. Gaudēns gaudēbō in Dominō. (Is 61:10)
6. Introībō ad altāre Deī. (Ps 42:10)
7. Domine, ad quem ībimus? Verba vītae aeternae habēs. (Mk 6:68)

CHAPTER 19

8. Inveniētis requiem animābus vestrīs. (Mt 11:29)
9. Beātam mē dīcent omnēs generātiōnēs. (Lk 1:48, *Magnificat*)
10. Aspergēs mē, Domine, hyssōpō, et mundābor. (Ps 50:9)

hyssōpum: hyssop

11. Sānā mē, Domine et sānābor: salvum mē fac, et salvus erō: quoniam laus mea tū es. (Jer 17:14)
12. Effundam super vōs aquam mundam, et mundābiminī ab omnibus inquināmentīs vestrīs, et ab ūniversīs īdōlīs vestrīs mundābō vōs. (Ezek 36:35)

inquināmentum, inquināmentī (n.): impurities

13. Ēmitte Spīritum tuum et creābuntur et renovābis faciem terrae. (Ps 103:30)
14. Salva mē ex ōre leōnis, et ā cornibus ūnicornium humilitātem meam. Nārrābō nōmen tuum frātribus meīs. In mediō ecclēsiae laudābō tē. (Ps 21:22–23)

unicornis, unicornis (m.): unicorn

15. Laudābunt dominum quī requīrunt eum: quaerentēs enim inveniunt eum et invenientēs laudābunt eum. (Augustine, *Confessions* 1.1)
16. Et dīcit eī Nathanaēl: "Ā Nazareth potest aliquid bonī esse?" Dīcit eī Philippus: "Vēnī et vidē." (Jn 1:46)
17. Sed dīcet aliquis: Quōmodo resurgunt mortuī? (1 Cor 15:35)
18. Quīcumque enim Spīritū Deī aguntur, iī sunt fīliī Deī. (Rom 8:14)

agere: lead, do

19. Converte tē ex tōtō corde tuō ad Dominum, et relinque hunc miserum mundum, et inveniet anima tua requiem. (Thomas a Kempis, *Imitātiō Chrīstī* 2.1.1)
20. Cōnantur illī quidem virtūtēs ā vitiīs distinguere: quod est sānē facillimum. (Lactantius, *Dīvīnae Īnstitūtiōnēs* 6.14.1)

sānē: certainly

21. Est quidem jejūnium vitiōrum mors, vīta virtūtum. (Peter Chrysologus, *Sermō* 8)

jejūnium, jejūniī (n.): fasting

22. Bonitās virtūtum māter, malitia orīgō vitiōrum. (Peter Chrysologus, *Sermō* 31)

bonitās, bonitātis (f.): goodness
malitia, malitiae (f.): evil
orīgō, orīginis (f.): orīgīn

CHAPTER 20

❦

Verbs: Perfect Active Indicative, Perfect Infinitive

We are going to split up the active and passive here. We will only be talking about the active in this chapter.

§ 73. Morphology: Perfect Active Indicative

What is the perfect active indicative in Latin? *Laudāvit, monuit, dūxit, audīvit.* You will meet the passive in the following chapter. In many a-verbs, e-verbs, and i-verbs you have either a *-v-* or *-u-* as a tense format after the stem or the theme vowel. All verbs in the vocabulary have been presented with the four principal parts: present active indicative (e.g., *laudo*), present active infinitive (e.g., *laudare*), perfect active indicative (e.g., *laudavi*), and the perfect passive participle (e.g., *laudatus*; chapter 21). The next two chapters will introduce those two latter forms. Also, we will learn a few other forms that use the perfect stem of the verb (e.g., *laudav-; monu-; dux-; audiv-*). There is no sufficiently commonly occurring tense formant for the perfect form of the i/e-verb to be learned on its own. The perfect form of i/e-verb varies depending on the stem. There are some similarities you will learn as you progress, but it is not worth spending too much time on it now.

The perfect form of the verb should be thought of as a new "stem": notice how much *dūxit* changed from *dūcit*. We change a consonant. You would not necessarily recognize *dūxit* as part of *dūcit*. This will get even harder with a verb like *dat* (he gives) when it becomes *dēdit* (he gave). Possibly the most frustrating form in all of Latin is *fert* (he bears) when it becomes *tulit* (he bore) in the perfect. *Fert* has nothing to do with *tulit*. *Ferre* still has one meaning, but the form change is so drastic, and most verbs do not change this drastically. This, though, is why we have learned verbs with their present active indicative, present active infinitive, their perfect active infinitive, and their perfect passive participle (which we will learn more about in the next chapter).

Some more bad news for the perfect active indicative is that this tense has its own peculiar personal endings. The good news is that these hold for all verb patterns of the perfect, including the "to be" form of the perfect in the active (*fuit*).

- ī	I	*- imus*	we
- istī	you	*- istis*	you (pl.)
- it	he / she / it	*- ērunt*	they

Some of the personal endings look the same as ones we have already learned for the first three tenses: the third singular and first plural. The rest must be memorized. One way to remember one of these perfects is the well-known Latin phrase, *veni, vidi, vici*, "I came. I saw. I conquered." Each one of those is perfect and has the new *-i* ending for the first-person singular verb form.

Active

ā-verb	ē-verb	i/e-verb	i-verb	Example Translation
laudāv|ī	*monu|ī*	*dūx|ī*	*audīv|ī*	I have heard
laudāv|istī	*monu|istī*	*dūx|istī*	*audīv|istī*	You have heard
laudāv|it	*monu|it*	*dūx|it*	*audīv|it*	He has heard
laudāv|imus	*monu|it*	*dūx|imus*	*audīv|imus*	We have heard
laudāv|istis	*monu|istis*	*dūx|istis*	*audīv|istis*	You all have heard
laudāv|ērunt	*monu|ērunt*	*dūx|ērunt*	*audīv|ērunt*	They have heard

Below I have given some of the most common ways Latin verbs change into the perfect. The stem is bolded, and what is new for the verb pattern is underlined.

ā-verbs (1st conjugation)

    laudō, laudāre, laud-ā-<u>v</u>-i, laudātus
    amō, amāre, am-ā-<u>v</u>-i, amātus
    dō, dare, <u>dē</u>-d-i, datus

ē-verbs (2nd conjugation)

    moneō, monēre, mōn-<u>u</u>-i, monitus
    habeō, habēre, hab-<u>u</u>-i, habitus
    videō, vidēre, vid-i, vīsus

short i/e verbs (3rd conjugation)

scrībō, scrībere, scrī-ps-i, scriptus
dūcō, dūcere, dū-x-i, ductus
dicō, dīcere, di-x-i, dictus
ferō, ferre, tuli, lātus

i-verbs (4th conjugation)

audiō, audīre, audī-v-i, audītus
dormiō, dormīre, dormī-v-i, dormītus

-io-verbs verbs

faciō, facere, fēcit, factus

Finally, we have to introduce the full paradigm for the perfect active indicative for *esse*:

ESSE

fu|i	I was
fu|isti	you were
fu|it	he was
fu|imus	we were
fu|istis	you (pl.) were
fu|erunt	they were

The only thing to comment on here is that the stem *fu-* will be used for perfect, pluperfect, and future-perfect. It also uses the new personal endings like other perfect verbs.

§ 74. Meaning: Perfect Active Indicative

What does the perfect active indicative do? How does it create unique meaning? The perfect (completed) talks about simple or completed actions in the past. So this will be our second "past tense" in Latin. We are not used to calling things "perfect" in English because of the drift of contemporary English, but we do have it. We usually just want to talk about the "past." The perfect talks about completed actions in the past tense, somewhat like our standard notion of "past" in English.

Latin uses the perfect to convey both "I walked" and "I have walked." Either is correct for *ambulavi*. This holds true for all perfect tense verbs.

There is one further complication here you may notice in the translation of the *esse* in the perfect. Those careful readers will notice that it is translated exactly like the imperfect. Latin makes a distinction between the imperfect and perfect with the "to be" verb, which English does not. Thus, we will translate them the same.

Jesus erat in synagōgā. Jesus was in the synagogue.
Jesus fuit in synagōgā. Jesus was in the synagogue.

The English will be the same, even though the underlying Latin is different. English has no way to distinguish between an imperfect form of the "to be" verb and the perfect form of the "to be" verb. There is not always a strong distinction in meaning between these in Latin, but one possible reason for the difference is that we could say something like "Jesus was habitually in the synagogues" for *erat*. For *fuit*, we would say, "Jesus was once in the synagogue." This is probably over translating, but it gets the point across. This is an example of the difference between tense and aspect.

Et fēcērunt discipulī sīcut cōnstituit illīs Jēsus, et parāvērunt Pascha (Mt 26:19). And the disciples did as Jesus commanded them, and they prepared the Passover.

In this verse, we have three verbs: *fecerunt, constituit,* and *paraverunt*. Each of these is in the perfect tense. *facio*, "I make," becomes *fec-erunt*. The stem changes from *fac-* to *fec-*. Then, the personal ending is added. *Constituo*, "I decide," does not change and looks just like the present. *Paro*, "I prepare," becomes *parav-* and then the new personal ending. The first pattern with the a-vowel will be the easiest to see in this tense because most of the time it just adds a *-v*. The other two are irregular and just have to be memorized.

Moving on in the story, the text reads,

Discumbēbat cum duodecim discipulīs suīs … dixit "amen dico vobis" (Mt 26:20).

He was reclining [at table] with his twelve disciples and he said to them, "truly I say to you."

Here we see more of how the perfect tense differs from the imperfect. "He was reclining [at table] with his twelve disciples. And he *said*: "truly I say to you" The word *dixit* is the only verb in the perfect active indicative. The imperfect presents the background details, and the perfect clues the reader into more of the main action of the story.

§ 75. Verbs: Perfect Active Infinitive

The perfect active infinitive is formed regularly, much like the present active infinitive. Like we have been doing, we will begin with what it looks like: *-isse*. For every perfect active infinitive, you will just have *-isse*. It is formed though by taking the perfect stem *laudav-*, *dux-*, *audiv-*, and adding *-isse*. It is very easy to recognize.

Now what does it do? It is typically used like the present active infinitive, but to describe events in the past. "He said that he came to Rome," *Dīxit sē vēnisse Rōmam.* You may notice that the English is much longer than the Latin. This is because the example is a form of the *ōrātiō oblīqua* or indirect speech. The perfect active infinitive will be used in any kind of construction that takes the accusative and infinitive, which we spent several earlier chapters looking at. In this case, though, it will just take the infinitive portion and put it in the past tense. *Videt puerum pulsāvisse terram*, "he sees that the boy hit the ground." *Placuit Caesarī sē dūxisse exercitum ad Galliam.* In a literal translation, "It pleased Caesar to have led the army to Gaul." In a more idiomatic translation, "It pleased Caesar that he lead his army to Gaul."

Placuit Caesarī Pīlātum Jēsum necāvisse. It was pleasing to Caesar that Pilate killed Jesus.

§ 76. Nouns: Locative

Although less common in Ecclesiastical Latin, city or town names can take special case endings called locatives. These were absorbed into the ablative case in later Latin. For Classical Latin, the locative was common for cities in Italy or Greece. For towns or cities that have a-noun endings, or o-noun endings, we usually see the locative in the genitive. *Rōmae*, "at Rome"; *Tusculī*, "at Tusculum." For place names that were plural in Latin, it is similar to the ablative plural. *Athēnīs*, "at Athens." These same place names can take the accusative if someone is going to them: *Rōmam, Tusuculum, Athēnās.* Place names can take an ablative if it is from where they left: *Rōmā, Ephesō, Athēnīs.*

The word *domus* can also take locatives. *Domī*, "at home"; *domum*: "to home"; *domō*, "from home."

The city Jerusalem can also take locatives, because it was a Hebrew word had several different phonetic spellings: *Hierosolyma, Hierosolymae,* in the singular, as well as *Hiersolyma, Hiersolymorum,* in the plural. Thus, it always looks feminine but is sometimes singular and sometimes plural. It is also sometimes spelled *Jerūsalem, Jerosolyma.*

Et Jēsus et discipulī eius appropinquāvērunt Jerosolymae et Bethāniae (Mk 11:1). Jesus and his disciples approached Jerusalem and Bethany.

CHAPTER 20

Sententiae Summāriae

Angelī Deum semper laudāvērunt, sed gentēs deōs falsōs saepe laudāvērunt.
Ego filiōs meōs cantāre monuī. Tū filiōs tuōs cantāre hymnōs Deō vērō monuistī?
Servus filiōs dominī in scholam dūxit.
Ēva Deō dīxit sē nōn peccāvisse. Petrus dīxit sē nescīvisse Jēsum.
Māter magistrum laudāvisse filiōs suōs in scholā audīvit.

Translations

The angels have always praised God, but the nations often have praised false gods.
I have taught my sons to sing. Have you taught your sons to sing hymns to the true God?
The servant led the sons of the master into school.
Eve said to God that she did not sin [*lit.* Eve said to God herself not to have sinned]. Peter said that he did not know Jesus.
The mother heard [that] the teacher praised her sons in school.

Cavēte et Mementōte

The perfect tense has its own personal endings, which can be hard to remember. The old phrase *veni, vidi, vici* (I came. I saw. I conquered.) can at least help us recall that the perfect is formed very differently, including the first-person singular *I*.

Vocābula Memoranda

Nōmina

abyssus, abyssī (f.): abyss
ars, artis (f.): art
castellum, castellī (n.): castle, town
firmāmentum, firmāmentī (n.): support, prop, firmament
inīquitās, inīquitātis (f.): iniquity, sin
pirum, pira (n.): pear
pullus, pullī (m.): young animal; colt; young chicken

Verba

ā-verbs

appropinquō [ad + propinquo], appropinquāre, appropinquāvī, appropinquātus: approach, draw near towards
gustō, gustāre, gustāvī, gustātus: taste
spērō, spērāre, spērāvī, spērātus: hope

ē-verbs

dēleō, dēlēre, dēlēvī, dēlētus: destroy, delete
horreō, horrēre, horruī,—: be horrified by, despise

i/e-verbs

dērelinquō [dē + relinquō], dērelinquere, dērelīquī, dērelictus: leave behind, discard[1]
pergō pergere, perrēxī, perrēctus: go on, proceed
relinquō, relinquere, relīquī, relictus: leave behind, abandon
sēdūcō [se + duco], sēdūcere, sēdūxī, sēductus: seduce

-io-verb

dēficiō [dē + faciō], dēficere, dēfēcī, dēfectus: die, become defunct

i-verb

pūniō, pūnīre, pūnīvī, pūnītus: punish

Adjectīva

foedus, -a, -um: ugly
turpis, turpis, turpe: ugly

Adverbium

continuō: immediately
foris: outside

Coniunctivum

at: but

Praepositiō

coram: in front of, before

Interrogātīvum

quārē: why

---

1 The prefix *de* does not radically change the meaning of the root word *relinquo*, but it can intensify the meaning.

CHAPTER 20

Fābula Excerpta

Et Jēsus et discipulī eius appropinquāvērunt Jerosolymae et Bethāniae ad montem Olīvārum, et Jēsus mittit duōs ex discipulīs suīs. Et dīcit illīs: Īte in castellum, quod contrā vōs est, et statim introeuntēs illūc, inveniētis pullum ligātum, super quem nēmō adhūc hominum sēdit: solvite illum, et addūcite. Et sī quis vōbīs dīcit: Quid facitis? dīcite, quia Dominō necessārius est: et continuō illum dīmittet hūc. Et abeuntēs invēnērunt pullum ligātum ante jānuam foris: et solvunt eum. Et quīdam dē illīc stantibus dīcēbant illīs: Quid facitis solventēs pullum? Quī dīxērunt eīs sīcut dicebat illīs Jēsus, et dīmīsērunt eīs. Et dūxērunt pullum ad Jēsum: et impōnunt illī vestīmenta sua, et sēdit super eum. Multī autem vestīmenta sua strāvērunt in viā: aliī autem frondēs caedēbant dē arboribus, et sternēbant in viā. Et quī praeībant, et quī sequēbantur, clāmābant, dīcentēs: Hosannā: benedictus quī venit in nōmine Dominī: benedictum quod venit rēgnum patris nostrī Dāvīd: hosanna in excelsīs. Et introīvit Jerosolymam in templum: et circumspectīs omnibus, exiit in Bethāniam cum duodecim.

Cf. Mark 11:1–10

contra: next to
ligatum: tied
illic: there, in that place
sternō, sternere, strāvī, strātus: spread out
frons, frondis (n.): leaves, fronds
caedere: cut down

1. Ubi fuerunt Jesus et discipuli eius?
2. Quid Jesus discipulos facere volebat?
3. Quis super pullum sedebat?
4. Quid multi homines in via agebant, dum Jesus in via ibat?

Furtum Pirorum Sancti Augustini

Fūrtum certē pūnit lēx tua, domine, et lēx scrīpta in cordibus hominum, quam nē (nōn) ipsa quidem dēlet inīquitās. Quis enim fūr aequō animō fūrem patitur? Et ego fūrtum facere voluī et fēcī, nōn quia pirum nōn habuī, sed quia nōn eram iūstus. Nam id fūrābar quod mihi abundābat et multō melius, nec eā rē volēbam fruī quam fūrtō appetēbam, sed ipsō fūrtō et peccātō. Arbor erat pirus in vīciniā nostrae vīneae pirīs onusta nec fōrma nec sapōre inlecebrōsīs. Abportāre pessimī puerī perrēximus nocte intempestā et abstulimus inde onera ingentia, nōn ad nostrās tabulās sed vel iacere porcīs, etiamsī aliquid inde mandūcāvimus.

Ecce cor meum, deus, ecce cor meum, quod misertus es in īmō abyssī. Dīc tibi nunc, ecce cor meum, quid ibi quaerēbat? Eram grātīs malus et malitiae meae causa nūlla erat nisi malitia. Foeda erat, et amāvī eam. amāvī perīre, amāvī dēfectum meum, nōn illud ad quod dēficiēbam, Sed dēfectum meum ipsum amāvī, turpis anima et dissiliēns ā firmāmentō tuō in exterminium, nōn dēdecōre aliquid, sed dēdecus appetēns.

Cf. Augustine, *Confessions* 2.4 (nonnullis mutatis)

aequo animo: in
fur, furis (n.): thief
furtum, furti (n.): theft
furari: to steal
vīcīniā: neighbor
intempestus, -a, -um: dead of night
onusta: laden
nequissimi: most
scriptus, scripta, scriptum: written
inlecebrosus, inlecebrosa, inlecebrosum: enticing
frui, fruisse: to enjoy
porcus, porci (m.): pig
imus, ima, imum: depth
defectus, defectūs (m.): destruction, ruin
dedecus, dedecoris (n.): shame

Sententiae Interpretandae

1. Dīxitque illī Jēsus: Amīce, ad quid vēnistī? Tunc adīvērunt, et manūs injēcērunt in Jēsum, et tenuērunt eum. (Mt 26:50)
2. Petrus vērō sedēbat foris in ātriō: et adīvit ad eum ūna ancilla, dīcēns: Et tū cum Jēsū Galilaeō erās. At ille negāvit cōram omnibus, dīcēns: Nesciō quid dīcis. (Mt 26:69–70)
3. In tē spērāvērunt patrēs nostrī et līberāvistī eōs. (Ps 21:5)
4. Et clāmāvimus ad Dominum, Deum patrum nostrōrum. (Dt 26:7)
5. Nōn horruistī Virginis uterum. (*Tē Deum*)
6. Vīdī cīvitātem sānctam, Jerusālem novam dēscendentem dē caelō ā Deō. (Rv 21:2)
7. Et ut appropinquāvit, vidēns cīvitātem, flēvit super illam. (Lk 19:41)
8. In diē trībulātiōnis meae clāmāvī ad tē, quia exaudīstī mē. (Ps 85:7)
9. Jēsus autem stetit ante praesidem, et interrogāvit eum praes, dīcēns: Tū es rēx Jūdaeōrum? Dīcit illī Jēsus: Tū dīcis. (Mt 25:11)

praeses, praesidis: governer

10. Ego enim accēpī ā Dominō, quod et trādidī vōbīs. (1 Cor 11:23)
11. Deus meus, Deus meus, respice in mē: quārē mē dērelīquistī? Longē ā salūte mea verba dēlictōrum meōrum. (Ps 21:2)

dēlictōrum: sins

NB: The verb *are* can be supplied in the second sentence.

12. Negant hominēs auctōrēs nostrōs secundum artem scrīpsisse. (Ambrose, *Epistulae* 55.1)

secundum artem: according to art; i.e., artfully

13. Item in Epistulā Jōhannis: omnis spīritus, quī cōnfitētur Jēsum Chrīstum in carne vēnisse, dē Deō est. Quī autem negat in carne vēnisse, dē Deō nōn est, sed est dē Antichristī spīritū. (Cyprian of Carthage, *Ad Quirīnum* 2.8.12)
14. Sine dubiō cum gustāvit mulier dē lignō scientiae bonī et malī, peccāvit et sē peccāvisse cognōvit. (Ambrose of Milan, *Dē paradīsō* 6.33)
15. Quam multī sunt enim, quī sciunt sē peccāvisse in frātrēs suōs, et nōlunt dīcere, dīmitte mihi. (Augustine, *Sermō* 211)
16. Cum nōn invēnērunt corpus Jēsu, vēnērunt, dīcentēs sē etiam vīsiōnem angelōrum vīdisse, quī dīcunt eum vīvere. (Lk 24:23)

    vīsiō, vīsiōnis (f.): vīsiōn

17. Simul etiam epīscopus nārrāvit sē quoque parvulum ā sēductā mātre suā datum fuisse Manicaeīs, et omnēs paene nōn lēgisse tantum vērum etiam scrīptitā[vi]sse librōs eōrum, sibique appāruisse nūllō contrā disputante et convincente opporuisse fugisse illam sectam: itaque fūgisse. (Augustine, *Confessions* 3.12)

    Manicaeis: Manichaeans, a heretical sect

CHAPTER 21

What follows reviews much of the grammar seen so far in this text. We have participles, accusative plus infinitive constructions, indirect speech, active and passive voice, and deponent verbs. There are more examples in the story section to provide adequate exposure to the difficulty of building all of these pieces of grammar together. Ultimately, a student's ability to recognize how Latin strings together several different grammatical constructions in different tenses and voices is critical to being able to read original authors. So this chapter is more difficult just because it combines so many elements of what has already been learned, with the only new grammar being the perfect passive indicative.

§ 77. Verbs: Morphology of the Perfect Passive Indicative

We will begin with the morphology of the perfect passive indicative, combining the perfect participle with the simple "to be" verb. The hardest part about how the perfect passive indicative works is that it requires using this participle. Below, we will talk about how this actually makes the Latin much like the English, as shown here:

Passive
The perfect passive requires the perfect passive participle plus a present form of *esse*.

ā-verb	ē-verb	i/e-verb	i-verb	Example Translation
laudātus (-a, -um) sum	*monitus (-a, -um) sum*	*ductus (-a, -um) sum*	*audītus (-a, -um) sum*	I have been / was heard
laudātus (-a, -um) es	*monitus (-a, -um) es*	*ductus (-a, -um) es*	*audītus (-a, -um) es*	You have been / heard
laudātus (-a, -um) est	*monitus (-a, -um) est*	*ductus (-a, -um) est*	*audītus (-a, -um) est*	He has been / was heard
laudātī (-ae, -a) sumus	*monitī (-ae, -a) sumus*	*ductī (-ae, -a) sumus*	*audītī (-ae, -a) sumus*	We have been / were heard
laudātī (-ae, -a) estis	*monitī (-ae, -a) estis*	*ductī (-ae, -a) estis*	*audītī (-ae, -a) estis*	You (pl.) have been / were heard
laudātī (-ae, -a) sunt	*monitī (-ae, -a) sunt*	*ductī (-ae, -a) sunt*	*audītī (-ae, -a) sunt*	They have been / were heard

CHAPTER 21

We should notice that the verb has a typical verb stem in the ā-verbs, though all the other conjugations have a different stem. In this case, we have *laud-*. Then we add the tense formant *-at-*, with the first and second declension adjective endings. For verbs not from the ā-verb conjugation, we have a slightly modified stem, which ends with the first and second declension adjective endings. If the subject is masculine, we have *-us* because the participle (which acts like an adjective) must match the noun it modifies: *Deus laudātus est, Maria laudāta est, donum laudātum est*. The same goes for feminine, neuter, and the plural forms: *Dei laudati sunt, Mariae laudatae sunt, dona laudata sunt*. Remember that a participle shares some verbal qualities and adjectival qualities. You will also notice that I have two Example Translations. This is because it can be hard to make a distinction here in English.

§ 78. Verbs: Meaning of Perfect Passive Participles

In the previous chapter we looked at the perfect active indicative: *veni, vidi, vici*, "I came, I saw, I conquered." Now, we have to learn how to use the passive to be able to say, "I have been seen" or "I have been conquered." Notice how the English phrases there include the participles *seen* and *conquered*. Those are the passive participles for English. In order to make the perfect passive indicative, we have to learn how to make the perfect passive participle.

Vīsus est; vīctus est, laudātus est; ducta est, audītī sunt, etc. These are all perfect passive participles with the "to be" verb, and when considered together, they make the perfect passive indicative. Notice, though, that you could look at that sentence and see *vīsus* as a perfect passive participle and *est* as present active indicative. But when you bring them together, we can call it the *perfect passive indicative* and think of it as one thing. We learned the term periphrastic in chapter 12. A periphrastic is the combination of a participle and a form of the "to be" verb. Latin uses a periphrastic construction to make the perfect passive indicative. You have already been seeing some perfect passive participles (*nātus, sānātus, scrīpta*). Compare those with what you have already learned in the present active participle: *laudāns, vidēns, dūcēns, audiēns*. Now we are going to learn the perfect passive participle. A perfect passive participle is a verb that has characteristics like an adjective, though it describes an action in the past tense.

One thing to notice about the perfect passive participle is that it always has an *-us, -a, -um* ending, like a first or second declension adjective (*parvus, -a, -um*). So, it is a verb in that it describes an action and an adjective in that it agrees with a noun it modifies.

We have only learned two participles so far, and we will add two more in the latter.

	Active	Passive
Present tense	*laudāns, laudāntis*: praising	————————
Perfect tense	————————	*laudātus, laudāta, laudātum*: praised
Future tense	Chapter 22	Chapter 27

So we can use the perfect passive participle alone: *Sānātus puer ambulāvit domum*, "The healed boy walked home." **Cavete**: notice the difference between active and passive here. *Sānāns puer ambulāvit domum*, "The healing boy walked home." *Sānāns*, "healing"; *sānātus*, "healed." We can also use the perfect passive participle with *esse* to make the perfect active indicative, which we will see below.

§ 79. Verbs: Ablative Absolute with Perfect Participles

A common use of the perfect passive participle is to make a subordinate clause to a main verb. We have seen this in the active *deō volente*, "God willing." Now we will see how to do this with a participle that indicates a past tense action, where the noun paired with it receives the action. Compare this sentence: *Et hymnō dictō, exiērunt in montem Olīvētī*, "After the hymn was spoken, they went out into the Mount of Olives." This kind of clause makes it possible to have a separate subject, in this case *hymn*, from the main subject of the main verb, in this case *they*. So the subject of the participle and the participle itself are in the ablative to denote that it is a self-contained clause, that relates to the main verb with a separate subject. This is true of the ablative absolutes in the present tense, but in that case the separate subject does the action of the verb, rather than receiving the action of the verb.

Vōce deī audītā, Thomās discēdit. The voice of God having been heard, Thomas left.

There is no English equivalent of the ablative absolute. So, in order to make it work, we must supply a subordinating conjunction in English. That is, we need to create a separate clause with a word like *while*, *since*, or *after*, which makes the clause depend on the main verb of the sentence. It is best to pick one or two and use those at the beginning; "after" or "since" are good glosses. You can also add the phrase "having been [verb]-ed." All of those are acceptable translations. This is another good place to be reminded that there is no one right answer in a translation. There are wrong answers and there are better answers, but there is not just one right answer. The ablative absolute is one way Latin combines longer interrelated clauses into a whole. It is not uncommon to find sentences with an indicative verb at the end, an absolute at the beginning, and connected relative clauses. So, in order to understand and read Latin as Latin, we have to remember how Latin works differently from English.

One way to think about how an ablative absolute works is to compare it to another way of constructing the sentence in Latin. Below are two sentences that communicate the same idea, with different syntax.

Chrīstō crucifīxātō, omnia peccāta dīmittuntur. After Christ was crucified, all sins are forgiven.
Postquam Chrīstus crucifīxātus est, omnia peccāta dīmittuntur. After Christ was crucified, all sins are forgiven.

The first one uses an ablative absolute and is more typical in well-constructed Latin. The second looks more like what we would understand natively in English.

We should also remind ourselves how present active participles differ from perfect passive participles. The key is to recognize whether the subject does the action of the participle or whether it receives the action of the participle.

Consider this sentence below:

Maria Deum laudāns accēpit verbum angelī. Maria, praising God, accepts the word of the Angel.

The subject, Maria, does the praising, at the same time as the main verb. Now consider the perfect passive participle below:

Deō laudātō, Maria filium concipit. After God was praised, Maria conceived a child.

Notice that God receives the action of participle *praised*. Also because the participle is in the perfect tense, it happens before the verb. The sentence above with an ablative absolute could be converted into another construction more like English: *Postquam Deus laudatus est, Maria filium concipit.* This would still convey nearly the same meaning, but in a different way. Like most languages, there are often many ways to convey similar ideas.

Deponent verbs use the perfect participle differently. Rather than the noun that matches with perfect passive participle in gender, number, and case receiving the action of the verb, the noun matching the perfect passive participle does the action of the verb. Look at this sentence:

Ēgressīs autem illīs, ecce obtulērunt eī hominem mūtum, daemonium habentem. (Mt 9:32)

After they had gone out, look, they brought to him a mute person, having a demon.

The word *illīs*, rather than receiving the action of going, does the action of going. This is an instance where Latin does have a perfect active participle, but the form is passive because it is deponent. Most of the time when reading Latin this will be the intuitive translation, but it is still good to be aware of these unique words.

§ 80. Verbs: Perfect Passive Infinitive

The last piece of grammar is just going to combine things we have already seen. We can take the perfect passive participle and add *esse* to make the perfect passive infinitive. This infinitive is most often used for indirect speech and the construction of an accusative and infinitive.

With our four main verb patterns, we have

laudātus, -a, -um esse
vīsus, -a, -um esse
ductus, -a, -um esse
audītus, -a, -um esse

We can make the following constructions that show the different possibilities of indirect speech, which uses the infinitive plus accusative construction.

Catholicī: "Chrīstiānī Mariam laudāvērunt."
- "Catholics: 'Christians praised Mary.'"
- direct speech in the perfect active voice

Catholicī: "Maria laudāta est ab Chrīstiānīs."
- "Catholics: 'Mary is praised by Christians.'"
- direct speech in the perfect passive voice

Catholicī dīxērunt Chrīstiānōs Mariam laudāvisse.
- "Catholics said [that] Christians have praised Mary."
- indirect speech in the perfect active indicative
- Remember, the word *that*, is implied by the construction of the accusative plus infinitive, but it is not a specific word in the Latin sentence.

Catholicī dīxērunt Mariam laudātam esse ā Chrīstiānīs.
- "Catholics said that Mary was praised by Christians."
- indirect speech in the perfect passive indicative

Sententiae Summāriae

Deus ab omnibus laudātus est. Maria quoque laudāta est.
Ego numquam ā magistrō meō laudātus sum. Tū ā magistrō tuō laudāta es?
Hominēs Deō precātī sunt.
Fīliī monitī sunt ā mātre cantāre in ecclēsiā.
Exercitūs nostrī ductī sunt in bellum.
Jēsus ex synagōgā egreditus est.
Nōs ā Deō nostrō audītī sumus. Vōs ā deīs tuīs audītī estis?
Ōrātiōnibus ab Jēsū audītīs, vir aeger sanatus est.
Omnibus hostibus necātis, exercitūs laetātī sunt.
Ēvangeliō lectō, sacerdōs praedīcere incēpit.

Translations

God was praised by all. Mary was also praised.
I am never praised by my teacher. Are you (f.) praised by your teacher?
Humans prayed to God.
The sons were warned by the mother to sing in church.
Our armies were led into war.
Jesus left the synagogue.
We were heard by our God. Were you heard by your gods?
The prayers having been heard by Jesus, the sick man was healed.
All the enemies having been killed, the armies were happy.
After the Gospel was read, the priest began to preach.

CHAPTER 21

Cavēte et Mementōte

Pay attention to the noun and the participle and whether the participle is active or passive, meaning that it either does the action of the verb or receives the action of the verb.

Vocābula Memoranda

Nōmina

avis, avis (f.): bird
fama, famae (f.): word, fame
poena, poenae (f.): penalty

Verba

ā-verbs

adjuvō [ad + juvō], adjuvāre, adjūvī, adjūtus: help
comminō [cōn + minō], commināre, commināvī, cominātus: threaten
imitor, imitārī,—, imitātus sum: imitate
mīror, mīrārī,—, mīrātus sum: marvel (at)
vexō, vexāre, vexāvī, vexātus: vex, trouble

ē-verb

impleō [in + pleō], implēre, implēvī, implētus: fill in, fulfill

i/e-verbs

accēdō [ad + cēdō], accēdere, accessī, accessus: come near, approach
cēdō, cēdere, cessī, cessus: go[1]
claudō, claudere, clausī, clausus: close
frangō, frangere, frēgī, frāctus: break
persequor [per + sequor], persequī,—, persecutus sum: persecute
scindō, scindere, scidī, scīsum: rend, tear
tangō, tangere, tetigī, tāctus: touch

-io-verbs

ēgredior [ex + gredior], ēgredī,—, ēgressus sum: go out
ējiciō [ē + jaciō], ējicere, ējēcī, ējectus: throw out

Conjūnctīva

adhūc: still, yet
utique: certainly

---

[1] This verb is often prefixed as in the vocabulary word above.

Adjectīva

aeger, -a, -um: sick
dignus, digna, dignum: worthy of (+abl)[2]
indignus, indigna, indignum: unworthy of (+abl)
mūtus, mūta, mūtum: mute

Fābula Excerpta

Et exi[v]it fāma haec in ūniversam terram illam. Et trānseunte inde Jēsū, secūtī sunt eum duo caecī, clāmantēs, et dīcentēs: Miserēre [have mercy] nostrī, fīlī Dāvīd. Cum autem vēnit domum, accessērunt ad eum caecī. Et dīcit eīs Jēsus: Crēditis quia hoc possum facere vōbīs? Dīcunt eī: Utique, Domine. Tunc tetigit oculōs eōrum, dīcēns: Secundum fidem vestram, fiat vōbīs. Et apertī sunt oculī eōrum: et comminātus est illīs Jēsus, dīcēns: Noli nuntiare. Illī autem exeuntēs, nūntiāvērunt eum in tōtā terrā illa. Ēgressīs autem illīs, ecce obtulērunt eī hominem mūtum, daemonium habentem. Et ējectō daemoniō, locūtus est mūtus, et mīrātae sunt turbae, dīcentēs: Numquam appāruit sīc in Israēl. Pharisaeī autem dīcēbant: In prīncipe daemoniōrum ējicit daemonēs. Et circuībat Jēsus omnēs cīvitātēs, et castella, docēns in synagōgīs eōrum, et praedicāns Ēvangelium rēgnī, et cūrāns omnem īnsānum (=non sanum), et omnem īnfirmitātem (=aegrum). Vidēns autem turbās, misertus est eīs: quia erant vexātī, et jacentēs sīcut ovēs nōn habentēs pāstōrem. Tunc dīcit discipulīs suīs: Messis quidem multa, operāriī autem paucī.

Cf. Matthew 9:26–38

utique: certainly
misertus: from *misereri,—, misertum*: have mercy
secuti: *sequi, secutum*
fiat: let it be
aperti: *aperire, aperuisse, apertum*
egressis: *egredi,—, egressum*
eiecto: *eiacere, eieci, eiectum*
miratae: *mirari,—, miratum*
vexati: *vexare, vexavisse, vexatum*
messis: harvest
operarius: worker

1. Cur caecī Jesum secūtī sunt?
2. Quōmodo Jesus caecōs cūrāvit?
3. Quid deinde caecī fēcērunt?
4. Cur mīrātae sunt turbae?
5. Omnes hominēs mīrātae sunt? Cur nōn?

---

2 If you want to say "worthy of" something, you use the ablative. *Fidelis sermo, et omni acceptione* **dignus** (1 Tm 4:9). "This is a trustworthy word and **worthy of** all acceptance." This is called the ablative of description.

Colloquia Ficta ("Imaginary Conversations")

Jēsus ab Jōhanne Baptīzātus est.

Jēsus venit in fluvium Jordānis cum Jōhanne. Jēsus baptīzātus est ab Jōhanne. Avis, quae est columba, dēscendit super Jēsum. Jōhannis spectāvit avem dēscendisse super Jēsum. Nūbēs scīsae sunt et vōx deī audītus est. Jōhannis vīdit nūbēs scīsās esse ab deō. Jōhannis vīdit Deum scidisse nūbēs. Jēsus audīvit vōcem deī sonavisse. Jōhannis vīdit avem datam esse ad Jēsum ab Deō.

Deus: "Hoc est filius meus. Fīlius meus dīlēctus est ab mē."

Puer prope fluvium Jōhannem interrogāvit: "Quid Deus dīxit?"

Jōhannis puerō respondit: "Deus dīxit filium meum dīlēctum esse ab mē."

columba, columbae (f.): dove
dō, dare, dedi, datum: to give

Goliatus Necātus Est a Davidō

Davidus clāmāvit: "Ego necāvī hominem altissimum Goliathum!"
Saulus servum interrogāvit: "Quid Davidus dīxit?"
Servus respondit: "Davidus dīxit sē necāvisse hominem altissimum Goliathum."
Saulus mīrātus est: "Quid? Davidus dīxit Goliāthum necātum esse?"
Servus respondit: "Ita! Goliathus necātus est ā Davidō."

necō, necāre, necāvī, necātum: kill

1. In the colloquia, find two perfect active infinitives and two perfect passive infinitives.
2. How did you recognize them?
3. Why are those forms being used?

Sententiae Interpretandae

1. Omnia mihi trādita sunt ā Patre meō. (Lk 10:22)

   trādita: trādere, trādidī, trāditus

2. Et hymnō dictō, exiērunt in montem Olīvētī. (Mt 26:30)

   dictō: dīcere, dīxī, dictus

3. Vēnit Jēsus jānuīs clausīs. (Jn 20:26)

   clausīs: claudere, clausī, clausus

4. Manē autem jam factō stetit Jēsus in lītore. (Jn 21:4)

   factō: fīo, fierī,—, factus
   litus, litoris (n.): shore

5. Et ascendente Jēsū in nāviculā secūtī sunt eum discipulī ejus. (Mt 8:23)

   secūtī: sequī,—, secūtus

6. Quod vērō sciēbant Chrīstum prō sē esse crucifīxum. (Augustine, *Dē Ūnicō Baptismō*)

   crucifīxum: crufīgāre, crucifīxī, crucifīxus

7. Acceptīs quīnque pānibus et duōbus piscibus aspiciēns in caelum benedīxit et frēgit et dedit discipulīs pānēs. Discipulī autem dedērunt turbīs. (Mt 14:19)

acceptīs: accipere, accēpī, acceptus

8. In Dominō spērāvit cor meum, et adjūtus sum. (Ps 27:7)
9. Et verbum carō factum est, et habitāvit in nōbīs. (Jn 1:14)
10. Per quem omnia facta sunt. (Symbolum Nicaeānum)
11. Nōn sum dignus vocārī apostolus, quoniam persectus sum Ecclēsiam Deī. (1 Cor 15:9)
12. Ego Dominus locūtus sum. (Ezek 17:21)

locūtus: loquī,—, locūtus

13. Tū, Domine, adjūvistī mē et cōnsōlātus es mē. (Ps 18:17)

cōnsōlātus: cōnsōlārī,—, cōnsōlātus

14. Locūtus est per prophētās. (Symbolum Nicaeānum)
15. Praedicātus enim es nōbīs, domine. (Augustine, *Confessions* 1.1)
16. Et nōn inventō corpore ejus, vēnērunt, dīcentēs sē etiam vīsiōnem angelōrum vīdisse, quī dīcunt eum vīvere. Et dīxit ad eōs: Haec sunt verba quae locūtus sum ad vōs cum adhūc sum vōbīscum, quoniam necesse est implērī omnia quae scrīpta sunt in lēge Moȳsī, et prophētis, et Psalmīs dē mē. (Lk 24:44)
17. Peccāvimus quia locūtī sumus contrā tē. (Cf. Num. 21:7)

Quid dīxērunt?

Illī dīxērunt sē peccāvisse quia locūtī sunt contrā Deum.

18. Canticum dīxit: "Illī amāvērunt Chrīstum in vītā suā, imitātī sunt eum in morte. (Cf. *Viri Sancti Gloriosum*)

imitārī,—, imitātus

Quid canticum dīxit?

Canticum dīxit 'illōs amāvisse chrīstum.'[3]

Canticum dīxit 'chrīstum amātum esse ab illīs'[4]

Quid quoque canticum dīxit?

Canticum dīxit 'imitātōs esse eum in morte.'[5]

amāre, amāvisse, amātus

---

[3] indirect speech, active voice, perfect tense
[4] indirect speech, passive voice, perfect tense
[5] indirect speech, passive voice, perfect tense, but deponent

19. Nōlī mē tangere, nōndum ascendī ad Patrem. quārē? nēmō illum tetigit corporāliter, nisi ascendit ad Patrem? adhūc hic erat, palpāvit cicātrīcēs discipulus quī nōn crēdēbat. quōmodo ergō nōlēbat sē tangī, nisi quia hoc figūrātē dictum est? illa mulier ecclēsia erat. et hoc est: nōlī mē tangere, nōlī mē carnāliter tangere, sed quālis sum aequālis Patrī. quamdiū autem nōn mē intellegitis aequālem Patrī, nōlī mē tangere, quia nōn mē, sed carnem meam tangis. (Augustine, *Sermō* 5)

corporāliter: bodily
palpāvit: touch, stroke
cicātrīcēs: scars
figūrātē: figuratively
quamdiu: how long

20. Quod dictum audīvimus ā Dominō Jēsū Chrīstō Nathanaelī, sī bene intellegāmus, nōn ad ipsum pertinet solum. ipse quippe dominus Jēsus sub ficū vīdit omne genus hūmānum. Istō enim locō intellegitur per arborem ficī significāsse peccātum. (Augustine, *Sermō* 122)

quippe: certainly
ficū: ficus tree
significāre: to signify

21. Quid vīdistī? Aquās utique, sed nōn sōlās: levītās illīc ministrantēs, summum sacerdōtem interrogantem et cōnsecrantem. (Ambrose, *Dē mystēriīs*)

lēvīta, lēvītae (m.): decon, lēvītē

22. Deus meus, firmiter crēdō Tē esse ūnum Deum in tribus distīnctīs Persōnīs, Patre, Fīliō et Spīritū Sānctō; et Fīlium propter nostram salūtem incarnātum, passum et mortuum esse, resurrēxisse ā mortuīs, et ūnīcuique prō meritīs retribuere aut praemium in Paradīsō aut poenam in Īnfernō. Haec cēteraque omnia quae crēdit et docet catholica Ecclēsia, crēdō quia Tū ea revēlāstī, quī nec ipse fallī nec nōs fallere potes. (*Āctus Fideī, Catēchismus Catholicus*)

fallo, fallere, fefeli, falsus: deceive

CHAPTER 22

Verbs: Future Active Participles and Future Infinitives

We have discussed present active participles and perfect passive participles in chapters 12 and 21.

§ 81. Morphology: Future Active Participle

You may recall that there are only present active and perfect passive participles and not present passive or perfect active. So in Latin we have *laudāns* (praising) vs. *laudātus* (praised). We will introduce the future participle in this chapter, beginning with the active and leaving the passive for chapter 27.

	Active	Passive
Present tense	*laudāns, laudāntis*: praising	————
Perfect tense	————	*laudātus, laudāta, laudātum*: praised
Future tense	*laudātūrus, laudātūra, laudātūrum*	(Chapter 27)

As you can see in the above chart, we have added the bottom row. The stem is taken from the perfect passive participle form: *laudāt-us, -a, -um*. The only difference is the *-ur-*. That *-ur-* is always part of the future active participle and does not change. You can always spot the future active participle because it has the *-ur-* in it. Actually, the English word future comes from the Latin future active participle *futūrus*, which is the future active participle of *esse*.

One way to think about forming this verb is that you take the perfect participle and insert the *-ur-* in between the perfect stem and the ending. *Laudāt-ūr-us; monit-ūr-us; dūct-ūr-us; audīt-ūr-us.*

CHAPTER 22

§ 82. Meaning: Future Active Participle

So now that we know how to create and recognize a future active participle, what does it mean? The future active participle is used either to create a near future construction in the indicative or used as a participle, typically in indirect speech. What that means is that sometimes the participle can just be used to make a new kind of future.

On its own, a future active participle can just be translated, "about to [verb]."

Discipulus disciturus Latīnam intrat in scholam. The student, about to learn Latin, walks into the classroom.

The verb can also be combined with the "to be" verb in a periphrastic construction:

Laudātūrus sum. I am (m.) about to praise.
Monitūra sum. I (f.) am about to warn.
Ductūrī sumus. We (m.) are about to lead.
Audītūrae estis. You (f. pl.) are about to hear.

In this way, the future active participle is exactly what it says. It is a verb with adjective-like qualities, in that it matches with the noun that is is doing the verb. So, in two of the examples, a woman was speaking those sentences, and they have feminine endings: *monitūra, audītūrae*.

There is also a form of the verb, *esse*, which comes in the future active participle: *futurus*. It is the basis of the English word future and also includes the *-ur-* form that is standard for the future active participle.

*Eritque clāmor magnus in ūniversā terrā Aegyptī, quālis nec ante fuit, nec posteā **fut-ur-us** est.* (Ex 11:6)

There will be a great noise in the entire land of Egypt, of the sort which never was, nor is ever going to be afterwards.

*Āmen dīcō vōbīs, quia ūnus vestrum mē **trādit-ur-us** est.* (Mt 26:21)

Truly I say to you, one of you all is about to betray me.

Finally, the future active participle can also be used with past tense forms of the "to be" verb.

Dīxit ergō ūnus ex discipulīs ejus, Jūdās Iscariōtēs, quī erat eum trāditūrus ... (Jn 12:4)

Therefore, one of his disciples, Judas Iscariot, who was about to betray him, said ...

§ 83. Verbs: Future Active Infinitive[1]

The last form of the infinitive to be learned is what is called the future active infinitive. We don't have a form of this in English. We could use the infinitive *to come* as an illustration. In English, it would be something like "to be about to come" or "to be going to come." We do say "to come" and "to have come," which correspond to the present active infinitive and the perfect active infinitive. In Latin, *venīre, venisse*. So it is hard to translate this into Latin, but this form must also be learned: *ventūrum esse*, "to be about to come" or "to be going to come").

Dīcit sē ventūrum esse. He says that he will come.

Prōmittit sē reditūrum esse. He promises he will return. (*remember that *reditūrum* comes from *re-īre* (lit. "to go back"))

These are not super common but remember that we have combined the future active participle with the present infinitive, *esse*, to create the future active infinitive.

Sententiae Summāriae

Magister discipulōs laudātūrus est, sī eum audītūrī sunt.
Magister dīcit sē laudātūrum esse discipulōs, sī eum audītūrōs esse.
Māter fīliās suās laudātūra est, sī eam audītūrae sunt.
Māter dīcit sē laudātūram esse fīliās suās, sī fīliās audītūrās esse eam.
Mīlitēs nostrōs in bellum ducūtūrus sum quia hostēs castra nostra oppugnātūrī sunt.
    Tū mīlitēs vestrōs in bellum ductūrus es nōbīscum?
Vōs mātrem et patrem audītūrī estis?

Translations

The teacher is about to praise the student, if they are going to listen to him.
The teacher says [that] he will praise [*lit.* to be about to praise] the students, if they will listen to him.
The mother is about to praise the daughters, if they will listen to her.
The mother says [that] she will praise [*lit.* to be about to praise] the daughters, if the daughters will listen to her.
I am about to lead our soldiers into war because the enemies are about to attack our camps. Are you about to lead your soldiers into war with us?
Are you [pl.] about to listen to your father and mother?

---

1 There is a future passive infinitive: *laudātum īrī. Discipulus dīcit 'sē laudātum īrī*, "The student says he is about to be praised." This form appears one time in Jb 22:11 but is extremely uncommon in Ecclesiastical Latin. Cf. Hans Orberg, *Familia Romana* (Accademia Vivarium Novum, 2013), 185.

Vocābula Memoranda

Nōmina

annus, annī (m.): year
carnis, carnis (f.): flesh, meat
holocaustum, holocaustī (n.): sacrifice
hostia, hostiae (f.): victim, sacrifice
iter, itineris (n.): journey
judicium, judiciī (n.): judgment
modicum, modicī (n.): short/small time; little, small amount
oblātiō, oblātiōnis (f.): offering
sanguis, sanguinis (m.): blood
tenebra, tenebrae (f.): darkness, often found in the plural
vānitās, vānitātis (f.): vanity

Verba

<u>*ā-verbs*</u>
acceptō [ad + capio], acceptāre, acceptāvī, acceptātus: accept (repeatedly)
errō, errāre, errāvī, errātus: wander, err
ēxspectō [ex + specto], exspectāre, exspectāvī, expectātus: wait, await
immolō, immolāre, immolāvī, immolātus: sacrifice
memorōr, memorārī, ----, memorātus: remember
prōnūntiō [pro + nuntio], prōnūntiāre, prōnūntiāvī, pronunciātus: pronounce, declare
reservō [re + servo], reservāre, reservāvī, reservātus: save

<u>*i/e-verbs*</u>
reprehendō [re + prehendo], reprehendere, reprehēnsī, reprehēnsus: blame, seize
restituō [re + statuo], restituere, restitui, restitūtus: restore, revive

<u>*-io-verb*</u>
interficiō [inter + facio], interficere, interfēcī, interfectus: to kill

Adverbium

dēnique: finally, in the end

Fābula Excerpta

Quaerēbant ergō [pharisaeī] eum apprehendere: et nēmō mīsit in illum manūs, quia nōndum venit hōra ejus. Dē turbā autem multī crēdidērunt in eum, et dīcēbant: Chrīstus cum veniet, numquid plūra signa faciet quam quæ hic facit? Audī[v]erunt Pharīsaeī turbam murmurantem dē illō haec: et mīsērunt prīncipēs et Phaerisaeī ministrōs apprehendēre eum. Dīxit ergō eīs Jēsus: Adhūc modicum tempus vōbīscum sum: et vādō ad eum quī mē mīsit. Quaerētis mē, et nōn inveniētis: et ubi ego sum, vōs nōn potestis venīre. Dīxērunt ergō Jūdaeī ad illōs: Quō hic itūrus est, quia nōn inveniēmus eum? numquid in dispersiōnem gentium itūrus est, et doctūrus gentēs? quis est hic sermō, quem dīxit: Quaerētis mē, et nōn inveniētis: et ubi sum ego, vōs nōn potestis venīre? In novissimō autem diē magnō fēstīvitātis stābat Jēsus, et clāmābat dīcēns: Sī quis sitit, venī ad mē et bibe. Quī crēdit in mē, sīcut dīcit Scrīptūra, flūmina dē ventre ejus fluent aquae vīvae. Hoc autem dīxit dē Spīritū, quem acceptūrī erant crēdentēs in eum: nōndum enim erat Spīritus datus, quia Jēsus nōndum erat glōrificātus.

Cf. John 7

> *modicum*: short
> *quō*: to where
> *itūrus*: *ire*
> *dispersiō*: diaspora
> *doctūrus*: *docere*
> *sitit*: thirst
> *flūmina*: rivers
> *venter, ventris*: stomach
> *erat Spiritus datus* and *erat glorificatus*: these are pluperfect; translate with "had" for *erat*

1. Pharisaeī Jesum apprehendērunt?
2. Quid dicebant turbae?
3. Quō Jesus itūrus est?
4. Quid crēdentēs acceptūrī erant?

Fābula de Abrahamo et Sara

Abrahāmus jam senuēbat, et Sarā ejus uxor erat sterilis. Quibus tamen Deus prōmīsit filium ex eīs nascitūrum [est]. "Habēbis," inquit, "filium ex Sarā conjuge tuā." Quod audiēns Sarā rīsit, nec statim crēdidit prōmissīs Deī, et ergō reprehēnsa est ā Deō. Abrahamus autem crēdidit Deō prōmittentī.

Et vērō, ūnō post annō, filius nātus est Abrahamō, quī vocāvit eum Isaacum.

Postquam Isaacus juvenis factus est, Deus temptāns fidem Abrahamī, dīxit illī: Abrahame, tolle filium tuum ūnicum quem amās, et immolā eum mihi in monte quem ostendam tibi.

Abrahāmus nōn dubitāvit pārēre Deō jubentī: imposuit ligna holocaustī Isaacō; ipse vērō portābat ignem et gladium. Postquam iter factum est, Isaacus dīxit patrī: mī pater, ecce ligna holocaustī; sed ubinam est hostia quae immolātūra est? Cui Abrahāmus: Deus, inquit, sibi prōvidēbit holocaustum, fīlī mī. Levāvit Abrahāmus oculōs suōs, vīditque bēstiam, quem acceptāvit holocaustum interfectūrum prō fīliō suō.

Cf. Francis Lhomond, *Epitome Historiae Sacrae* (Edizioni Accademia Vivarium Novum, 2009), 25.

sterilis: barren, sterile
ubinam: for where?
senesco, senescere, senui, ---: become old
provideo, providēre, providi, provisus: provide

1. Quid Deus Abrahamō et Sarae prōmīsit?
2. Cur Sara rīsit?
3. Quid Deus Abrahamum jussit?
4. Estne Isaacus holocaustum?
5. Quid Abramus interficiet?

Sententiae Interpretandae

1. Tū es, quī ventūrus es, an alium exspectāmus? (Mt 11:3)
2. Domine, labia mea aperiēs, et os meum annūntiābit laudem tuam. (Ps 50:17)
3. Tunc acceptābis sacrificium jūstitiae, oblātiōnēs et holocausta; tunc impōnent super altāre tuum vitulōs. (Ps 50:21)

vitulus, vitulī: calf

4. At ille respondēns, ait eīs: Ēlias quidem ventūrus est, et restituet omnia. (Mt 17:11)

Ēlias: Elijah

5. Audītūrī enim estis praelia, et opīniōnēs praeliōrum. (Mt 24:6)
6. Vōs ductūrus est Dominus. (Dt 4:27)
7. Nōs quoque resurrēctūrōs esse crēdimus. (Rufinus, *Apologia* 1.4)
8. Potestis bibere ā calice, quem ego bibitūrus sum? (Mt 20:22)
9. Sunt hominēs quī nōn crēdunt diem jūdiciī; istī fidūciam habēre nōn possunt in diē quam ventūram esse nōn crēdunt. (Augustine, *In Jōhannis epistulam ad Parthōs tractātās* 9.5)
10. Et quod cum vidēbunt tē Aegyptiī, dictūrī sunt: Uxor ipsīus est: et interficient mē, et tē reservābunt. (Gn 12.12)
11. Et dīcit, "pāstor animam suam pōnit prō ovibus suīs," hanc utique vītam dīcit, cum sē prō nōbīs moritūrum esse prōnūntiat. (Augustine, *Dē Sermōne Dominī in Monte* 1.42)

translate the second *dīcit* as "means"

12. Errābat Petrus in tenebrīs ignōrantiae, negābat Chrīstum esse moritūrum, quia adhūc nōn vidēbat morī et resurrēctūrum esse prō nōbīs. (Ambrose, *Expositiō Psalmī* 14.10)
13. Benedic, Domine, nōs et haec tua dōna quae dē tuā largitāte sumus sūmptūrī. Per Chrīstum Dominum nostrum. Āmēn. (Ōrātiō ante mēnsam)

largitas, largitatis (f.): bounty

14. Et offerēs oblātiōnēs tuās, carnem et sanguinem, super altāre Dominī Deī tuī: sanguinem hostiārum fundēs in altārī; carnibus autem ipse vēsceris. (Dt 12:27)

vēsceris: you will enjoy, feed on

15. Dīcit Moysēs: Hostiās quoque et holocausta dabis nōbīs, quae offerēmus Dominō Deō nostrō. (Ex 10:25)
16. Pōnetque manum super caput hostiae quae prō peccātō est, et immolābit eam in locō holocaustī. (Lv 4:29)
17. Dēnique apostolī trīstēs erant, cum sē Chrīstum ad patrem reditūrum esse memorābant. (Ambrose, *Explānātiō Psalmōrum* 47.10.3)
18. Īnfīnītus numerus est populī omnium quī fuērunt ante eum, et quī posteā futūrī sunt nōn laetābuntur in eō; sed et hoc vānitās et afflīctiō spīritūs. (Eccl 4:16)
19. Deus meus, cum sīs omnipotēns, īnfīnītē misericors et fidēlis, spērō Tē mihi datūrum, ob merita Jēsu Chrīstī, vītam aeternam et grātiās necessāriās ad eam cōnsequendam, quam Tū prōmīsistī iīs quī bona opera facient, quemadmodum, Tē adjuvante, facere cōnstituō. Āmēn. (*Āctus Speī*, Catēchismus Catholicus)

sīs: you are
ad eam cōnsequendam: in order to obtain it

20. V: Crēdō quod Redēmptor meus vīvit, et in novissimō diē dē terrā surrectūrus sum. Et in carne meā vidēbō Deum Salvātōrem meum.[2]

R: Quem vīsūrus sum ego ipse, et nōn alius; et oculī meī cōnspectūrī sunt in carne meā

21. Crēdō in Deum Patrem omnipotentem, Creātōrem caelī et terrae. Et in Jēsum Chrīstum, Fīlium ejus ūnicum, Dominum nostrum, quī conceptus est dē Spīritū Sānctō, nātus ex Mariā Virgine, passus sub Pontiō Pīlātō, crucifīxus, mortuus, et sepultus, dēscendit ad īnferōs, tertiā diē resurrēxit ā mortuīs, ascendit ad caelōs, sedet ad dexteram Deī Patrīs omnipotentis, inde ventūrus est jūdicāre vīvōs et mortuōs. Crēdō in Spīritum Sānctum, sānctam Ecclēsiam catholicam, sānctōrum commūniōnem, remissiōnem peccātōrum, carnis resurrēctiōnem et vītam aeternam. Āmēn. (Symbolum Apostolōrum)

sepeliō, sepelīre, sepelīvī, sepultus: bury

---

2 V: versiculum; R: responsum

CHAPTER 23

☙❧

§ 84. Verbs: Morphology of the Pluperfect Active

The pluperfect tense is the final past tense in Latin. This tense will follow similar patterns to the perfect, but it will convey events that are more than completed in the past, hence the name pluperfect (*plusquamperfectum*). The pluperfect active is formed by simply adding the perfect stem to the imperfect form of the *esse* verb.

laudav-eram
monū-erās
dux-erat
audiv-erāmus

The name of the tense helps in thinking about how to form it: the perfect plus. So, you need more than just the perfect. You need the perfect plus the imperfect.

ā-verb	ē-verb	i/e-verb	i-verb	Example Translation
laudāv|eram	*monu|eram*	*dūx|eram*	*audīv|eram*	I had praised
laudāv|erās	*monu|erās*	*dūx|erās*	*audīv|erās*	You had praised
laudāv|erat	*monu|erat*	*dūx|erat*	*audīv|erat*	He had praised
laudāv|erāmus	*monu|erāmus*	*dūx|erāmus*	*audīv|erāmus*	We had praised
laudāv|erātis	*monu|erātis*	*dūx|erātis*	*audīv|erātis*	You all had praised
laudāv|erant	*monu|erant*	*dūx|erant*	*audīv|erant*	They had praised

The verb *esse* has a form that combines the perfect stem with the imperfect of *esse*, just like the above forms.

ESSE

fu|eram	I had been	*fu|erāmus*	we had been
fu|erās	you had been	*fu|erātis*	you (pl.) had been
fu|erat	he / she / it had been	*fu|erant*	they had been

§ 85. Verbs: Meaning of the Pluperfect Active

What does it mean? The pluperfect tense in the active indicative is fairly straightforward. It does not feature frequently in Latin prose, but it is quite useful in storytelling. It is the tense of what happened "more than in the completed" past. In Latin, the tense is called *plusquamperfectum*, "more than completed." What happens in the pluperfect tense is some action or state that comes before the main points of a story. "When he had decided to become a priest, he went to the seminary."

Postquam virum necāverat, fugit. After he had killed the man, he fled.

You may recall from chapter 17 when we learned about the way Latin uses the aspect of tenses to convey a sequence of time, the pluperfect is translated by adding the word *had* to the past tense of a verb.

§ 86. Verbs: Morphology of the Pluperfect Passive

What is the pluperfect passive indicative in Latin? It is formed by combining the perfect passive participle with the imperfect form of the *esse* verb or the pluperfect form of the *esse* verb.

laudātus eram or *laudātus fueram*
monitus erās or *monitus fuerās*
ductus erat or *ductus fuerat*
audītī erāmus or *audītī fuerāmus*

If we compare the pluperfect active to the pluperfect passive, you will see that they are very similar, although we have two words for the passive form, called a periphrastic. This will look much like the perfect passive except that it has the imperfect form of *esse* with it.

ductus (-a, -um) eram	I had been led	*ducti (-ae, -a) eramus*	We had been led
ductus (-a, -um) eras	You had been led	*ducti (-ae, -a) eratis*	You all had been led
ductus (-a, -um) erat	He (she, it) had been led	*ducti (-ae, a) erant*	They had been led

§ 87. Verbs: Meaning of the Pluperfect Passive

What does the pluperfect passive indicative mean in Latin? Again, it is very similar to the above, just in the passive voice. Recall that the passive voice means that the subject of the sentence receives the action of the verb if the verb is not a deponent verb.

Postquam necātus erat, nōn vīvit. After he had been killed, he did not live.
Discipulī Jēsūm secūtī erant. The disciples had followed Jesus.

Notice the second sentence includes the often-tricky deponent form.

Just to clarify how Latin forms the passive in several different ways, here is a chart of the possible past tense and passive constructions:

Imperfect Passive Indicative	*dūcēbātur*	he was [being] led
Perfect Passive Indicative	*ductus est*	he was led or he has been led
	ductus fuit	he was led or has been led
Pluperfect Passive Indicative	*ductus erat*	he had been led
	ductus fuerat	he had been led

As a reader and translator, the student will be required to make their own choice as to how to translate these forms of the passive.

§ 88. Syntax: *tantus ... quantus* and *tam ... quam*

Tantus and *quantus* are two adjectives that can be used either independently of each other or together. *Tam* and *quam* are adverbs that can be used together or separately. Since they are adverbs, they do not match the nouns or verbs they modify in gender, number, and case.

First, we will look at *tantus* on its own, in which case it means "so great."

> *Cum autem tanta signa fēcit cōram eīs, nōn crēdēbant in eum* (Jn 12:37).

> When he did such great signs before them, they were not believing in him.

Then we can see *quantus* on its own, in which case it means "how great."

> *Ecce quantus ignis quam magnam silvam incendit!* (Js 3:5)

> Behold, how great is the fire that burns a large forest!

Then we can put them together: *tantus*, "as great as"; *quantus*, "as."

> *Sed mortis metus nōn tantus est, quantus est [metus] tormentōrum* (Tertullian, ad Martyras 4.7).

> But fear of death is not as great as is the fear of torments.

For *tam* and *quam*, we have already seen how to use *quam* on its own, so we will look at what it means when combined with *tam*.

> *Puer autem Samuel prōficiēbat, atque crēscēbat, et placēbat tam Dominō quam hominibus* (1 Sm 2:26).

> The boy Samuel progressed and grew and was as pleasing to the Lord as to people.

Sententiae Summāriae

> Hominēs Deum laudāverant quia Deus eōs audīverat.
> Ego filiōs meōs monueram nōn fugere in bellō, sed filiī tuī ā tē nōn monitī erant.
> Mīlitēs in bellum ductī erant et ōrātiōnēs mīlitum ā Deō audītae erant.
> Dum tantus est timor mortis, quantus est dēsīderium glōriae. Timor mortis nōn tam magnus est quam dēsīderium glōriae.

Translations

> People had praised God because God had heard them.
> I had warned my sons not to flee in war, but your sons had not been warned by you.
> The soldiers had been led into war and the prayers of the soldiers had been heard by God.
> While the fear of death is so great, as great is the desire for glory. Fear of death is not as great as the desire of glory.

CHAPTER 23

Vocābula Memoranda

Nōmina

gallus, gallī (m.): rooster, Gaul
ignis, ignis (m.): fire
lapis, lapidis (m.): stone
monumentum, monumentī (n.): tomb
nēmō, nēminis (m.): no one
ōstium, ōstiī (n.): door
pavor, pavōris (m.): panic
saeculum, saeculī (n.): age
tremor, tremōris (m.): shuddering

Verba

ā-verbs

dignor, dignārī,—, dignātus: deign, condescend
invocō [in-vocō], invocāre, invocāvī, invocātus: invoke, pray
recordor [re + cor + do], recordārī,—, recordātus: call to mind, remember (often comes with a noun in the genitive)

i/e-verbs

benedīcō [bene + dicere], benedīcere, benedīxī, benedictus: bless
parcō, parcere, pepercī, parsus: spare
recumbō [re + cumbo], recumbere, recubī,—: recline
revolvō [re + volvo], revolvere, revolvī, revolūtus: turn, move

-io-verbs

incipiō [in + capio], incipere, incēpī, inceptus: begin
percūtiō [per + quatiō], percutere, percussī, percussus: strike, beat

Adjectīva

quantus, -a, -um: as great, how great
tantus, -a, -um: so great

Adverbium

amplius: greater, furthermore
hīc: here
ibi: there
invicem: one another
quemadmodum: how, in what way
valdē: really, very
verumtamen: although

Fābula Excerpta

Et postquam trānsīverat sabbatum, Maria Magdalēne, et Maria Jacobī, et Salōmē ēmērunt arōmata ungere Jēsum. Et valdē manē ūna sabbatōrum, veniunt ad monumentum, ortō jam sōle.¹ Et dīcēbant ad invicem: Quis revolvet nōbīs lapidem ab ōstiō monumentī? Et respicientēs vīdērunt revolūtum lapidem. Erat quippe magnus valdē. Et introeuntēs in monumentum vīdērunt puerum sedentem, indūtum stolā candidā, et obstupuērunt. Quī dīcit illīs: Nōlīte timēre: Jēsum quaeritis Nazarēnum, crucifīxum: surrēxit, nōn est hic, ecce locus ubi posuērunt eum. Sed īte, dīcite discipulīs ejus, et Petrō, quia praecēdit vōs in Galilaeam: ibi eum vidēbitis, sīcut dīxit vōbīs. At illae exeuntēs, fūgērunt dē monumentō: invāserat enim eās tremor et pavor: et nēminī quidquam dīxērunt: timēbant enim. Surgēns autem manē prīma sabbatī, [Jēsus] appāruit prīmō Mariae Magdālene, dē quā ējēcerat septem daemonia. Illa ambulāns nūntiāvit hīs, quī cum eō fuerant, lūgentibus et flentibus. Et illī audientēs eum vīvere, et vīsus erat ab ea, nōn crēdidērunt. Post hæc autem duōbus ex hīs ambulantibus ostēnsus est in aliā effigiē ēuntibus in vīllam: et illī euntēs nūntiāvērunt cēterīs: nec illīs crēdidērunt.² Novissimē recumbentibus illīs ūndecim appāruit: et exprobrāvit incrēdulitātem eōrum et dūritiam cordis: quia iīs, quī vīderant eum resurrēxisse, nōn crēdidērunt.³

Cf. Mark 16: 1–13

aromata, aromatae (f.): perfume
quippe: indeed
ūna sabbatōrum: first day of the sabbath
euns, euntis: *ire*
stola candida: a bright stole
obstupēscō, obstupēscere, obstupuī: be astounded, be stupefied
quidquam: anything or nothing
exprobavisse: to show
duritia, duritiae (f.): hardness

1. Cur fēminae aromata ēmerunt?
2. Quid vīdērunt fēminae ad monumentum?
3. Ubi fuit Jesus?
4. Cur fūgērunt fēminae?
5. Discipulī fēminās nūntiāvisse illa crēdidērunt? Cur nōn?

---

1 *orīrī, —, ortum*: to arise
2 *effigies, effigiei*: likeness, image
3 *novissimē*: at last, finally

CHAPTER 23

Sententiae Interpretandae

1. Vidēns autem pharisaeus, quī vocāverat eum, dīxit. (Lk 7:39)
2. Erant, quī mandūcāverant, quatuor mīlia hominum. (Mt 15:38)

   mīlia: thousand

3. Locūtusque est Aarōn omnia verba quae dīxerat Dominus ad Moysēn. (Ex 4:30)
4. Ecce stēlla, quam vīderant in oriente, antecēdēbat eōs. (Mt 2:9)
5. Et recordātus est Petrus verbī Jēsū, quod dīxerat: Priusquam gallus cantat, ter mē negābis. Et ēgressus forās, flēvit amāre. (Mt 24:75)

   ter: three times
   amāre: bitterly

6. Coeperat esse jam alicujus mōmentī inter deī servōs fāma mea. (Augustine, *Sermō* 355)

   alicujus mōmentī: of some importance

7. Secūtae autem mulierēs, quae cum eō vēnerant dē Galilaeā, vīdērunt monumentum, et quemadmodum positum erat corpus ejus. (Lk 23:55)
8. Ūnā autem sabbatī vēnērunt ad monumentum, portantēs quæ parāverant arōmata. (Lk 24:1)

   arōmatum: spices
   ūnā sabbatī: first day of the week (sabbath - 7)

9. Et ecce cadāver in marī necātum prōjectum erat ante pedēs Apostolī. (Alexander of Ashby, *Dē artificiōsō modō praedicandī sermō* 1)

   cadāver: dead body
   prōjectum: thrown

10. Quia hic mortuus erat et revīxit, perierat et inventus est. (Ambrose, *Dē paenitentiā* 2:7)
11. Grandō et ignis erant in terrā. Tantaeque fuit magnitūdinis, quanta ante numquam appāruit in ūniversā terrā Aegyptī.

    grando: hail

12. Spem quippe omnem saeculī relīqueram. (Augustine, *Sermō* 355)

    quippe: certainly

13. Etenim jūstitiā nōn tantum valet quantum fidēs; etenim jūstus ex fide vīvit. (Marius Victorinus, *In Ep. ad Ephesiōs* 2.6.13)
14. Quantō minus crēditur piscātōrī, tantō amplius crēditur, quia nōn sua, sed dīvīna sunt, quae locūtus est. (Ambrose, *Dē virginitāte* 20.133)
15. Dē dīvite quid dīcam? quī quantum habet amplius, tantō amplius dēbet. (Peter Chrysologus, *Sermō* 26)

16. Nihil itaque tam magnum atque venerandum quam quod līberat morte et facit vīvere et dat perpetuō rēgnāre. (Pseudo-Cyprian of Carthage, *Dē laude martyriī* 23.1)

   venerandum: venerable

17. Et dīxit Dāvīd ad Nathan: Peccāvī Dominō. Dīxitque Nathan ad Dāvīd: Dominus quoque trānstulit peccātum tuum: nōn moriēris. Vērumtamen, quoniam blasphēmāre fēcistī inimīcōs Dominī, propter verbum hoc, fīlius, quī nātus est tibi, morte moriētur. Et revēnit Nathan in domum suam. Percussit quoque Dominus fīlium, quem pepererat uxor Uriae Dāvīd, et turbātus est. (2 Sm 12:13)

18. Parcīs autem omnibus, quoniam tua sunt. Domine, quī amās animās. (Wis 11:27)

CHAPTER 24

◦◦

§ 89. Verbs: Passive and Deponent Imperatives

Deponent verbs will have a slightly different imperative, as the student might guess. Recall that deponent verbs are verbs that are passive in form and active in meaning. In order to learn the deponent imperatives, you have to know the passive imperative forms of regular verbs. A regular passive imperative is very uncommon but does appear in the Gospels. Jesus says, "be healed!" This is a situation where the subject receives the action of the imperative. In Latin, it is written *sanāre* in the singular and *sanāminī* in the plural. So the first one means "you [sing] be healed," and the second, "you [plural] be healed." The singular imperative is very tricky because it looks like an infinitive, but it is not. The only way you will know is by context. So the deponent imperative is just the passive form like we saw with *sanāre*, but it is active in meaning.

Laetāre, Jerusalem. Rejoice, Jerusalem.

This looks like "to rejoice" because we are used to seeing the *-re* form as an infinitive. With deponent verbs, this is the form of the singular imperative.

Memorāre, Ō piissima Virgō Maria. Remember, O most pious Virgin Mary.

Scrūtāminī scrīptūrās. Study the scriptures.

When one is speaking to more than one person, one uses just the typical passive second person plural *-mini* form of the verb.

In sum, the two options for deponent verbs are the verb stem plus *-re* for the singular command or the verb stem plus *-mini* for the plural command.

We now know three possible endings that look the same:

Potest sanāre. He is able to heal.
sanāre! Be healed!
Tu sanāre. You are being healed.

The only way to tell which way to translate it will be context. The most common is the present active infinitive.

§ 90. Verbs: Defective

There are several verbs that are often described as "defective," which in the broadest sense means that these verbs are not used in all tenses. One kind of defective verb, *ait*, has present tense forms that can be used in the past tense. The verb itself only exists in the present. Also, the verb usually comes before direct speech, as in this case where Jesus speaks:

> *Et clāmāns vōce magnā Jēsus ait: "Pater, in manūs tuās commendō spīritum meum." Et haec dīcēns, expīrāvit.* (Lk 23:46)

> And shouting with a great voice, Jesus says, "Father, into your hand I commend my Spirit." Saying these things, he breathed out.

Notice the two words that relate to speaking, *ait* and *dīcēns*. Sometimes *dīcēns* can introduce direct speech, but it does not have to. *Ait* does indicate direct speech will follow.

The other kind of defective verb, of which there are more examples, are verbs that have a perfect form with a present force. *Meminisse* means "to remember" but can be used only in the perfect tense, pluperfect tense, and future perfect tense. In the pluperfect, it is just translated as a simple past tense, like the perfect. For the future, it uses the future-perfect, which we will learn in chapter 26. There are very few of these verbs in Latin, and the only way one can know that a verb is defective is to memorize it. Also, their form in the vocabulary list and in lexicons does not have the first two principal parts, since they do not exist.

- —, *novī, nōtus*: know, be familiar with
- —, *meminī,*—: remember. **This verb can take the genitive, usually with people, rather than the accusative.
- —, *ōdī, ōsus*: hate

Here are a few example sentences:

> *Diabulum nōvī et ōdī.* I know and hate the devil.
> *Nōn nōveram librum illum.* I did not know that book.

Morphology	Meaning	Example	Translation
perfect tense	present tense	*odi*	I hate
pluperfect tense	past tense	*oderam*	I hated
future-perfect tense[1]	future tense	*odero*	I will hate

---

[1] These forms will be learned in chapter 26.

§ 91. Verbs: Supine

The supine is a form of the verb that also acts like a noun. Supines cannot stand on their own to make a complete sentence. Supines rely on another main verb. Spotting a supine is fairly easy: you have a stem *ambulā-* then *-t-* and then either *-um* or *-u*. *Ambulātum* or *factū*. You can also think of it as the perfect passive participle with either a *-u* or *-um* ending.

*Est facile **dictū** et difficile **factū**.* It is easy to say and difficult to do.

*Venit in montem **ambulātum**.* He came into the mountains to walk.

*Properat tibi in **occursum*** (Mt 25:10). He is hastening to meet you.

As you can see in these examples, it is easiest to translate these as English infinitives. Supines become far less common in later Latin, but it is worth being aware of them. Many Latin verbs do not have a supine.

§ 92. Syntax: Verbs of Memory

In this chapter we have several verbs of "memory": *memoror, meminī, oblīviscor, recordor*. As may be evident from their endings, *oblīviscor* and *recordor* are deponent, and *meminī* is a defective verb, only appearing in the perfect. Latin verbs that relate to recalling or forgetting take the genitive rather than the accusative.

Oblīta es lēgis Deī tuī, oblīvīscar fīliōrum tuōrum et ego (Hos 4:6). You have forgotten the law of your God. And, I will forget your sons.

§ 93. Syntax: Factum

Often in the biblical text, one will find the phrase *factum est* at the beginning of a narrative. It is usually a translation of the Greek word, ἐγένετο. This word is usually translated as "it happened."

Factum est autem in sequentī diē, dēscendentibus illīs dē monte, occurrit illīs turba multa (Lk 9:37).

It happened, however, in the following day, when they were descending from the mountain, a crowd ran into them.

As in this example, which is just one of many, it marks a transition from one story to the next within the larger narrative. It can be translated as if it were impersonal. This will also help distinguish this usage from other uses of *factum est* as in *verbum carō factum est*. In this instance, it means "the Word became flesh." Usually, when the phrase means "and it happened," it comes at the beginning of a sentence. The other way one can tell the difference is that the word *verbum* is the subject of *factum* rather than a kind of impersonal construction.

This formula occurs frequently with the narrative subjunctive or *ut* clauses, which will be learned at the end of the book.

Sententiae Summāriae

Vir aeger servō deī dīcit, "sāna mē!" Servus Deī virō aegrō dīcit, "sānāre!" et vir sānātus est.

Jēsus discipulīs suīs dīcit, "imitāminī mē et laetābiminī, imitāminī alium et moriēminī!"

Illum hominem nōn nōvī. Tū illum hominem nōstī?

Nōs vīdisse illam fēminam in ecclēsiā nōn meminimus. Vōs illam fēminam vīdisse meministis?

Hominēs veniunt in ecclēsiam salūtātum Deum et salūtātum populum eius.

Translations

The sick man says to the servant of God, "heal me!" The servant of God says to the sick man, "be healed," and the man was healed.

Jesus says to his disciples, "imitate me and you will be happy, imitate another, and you will die!"

I do not know that person. Do you know that person?

We do not remember having seen that woman in the church. Do you remember having seen that woman in church?

People come into the church for the purpose of greeting God and greeting his people.

Vocābula Memoranda

Nōmina

benedictiō, benedictiōnis (f.): *blessing*
circus, circī (m.): circus
jūrāmentum, jūrāmentī (n.): oath
mystērium, mystēriī (n.): mystery
testāmentum, testāmentī (n.): covenant

Verba

defective verbs
aiō,—,—,—: say (defective verb that typically only appears in the third person: *ait* and *aiunt*)
inquam,—,—,—: say (postpositive and defective verb, usually in the third person singular: *inquit*)
—, *meminī,—*: (+gen or +acc) remember[2]
—, *nōvī, nōtus*: know
—, *ōdī, ōsus*: hate

ā-verbs
dēprecor [de + precor], dēprecārī,—, dēprecātus: entreat, pray
jūrō, jurāre, juravī, juratus: swear
memoror, memorārī,—, memorātus sum: (+gen or +acc) be mindful of, remember
operor, operārī,—, operātus: work
tractō, tractāre, tractāvī, tractātus: draw, pull, discuss, preach

ē-verb
reflōreō [rē + flōreō], reflōrēre, reflōruī,—: flourish

i/e-verbs
agnōscō [ag + nōscō], agnōscere, agnōvī, agnitus: acknowledge, recognize
incēdō [in + cēdō], incedere, incessī, incessus: advance, march
oblīvīscor, oblīvīscī, oblītus sum: to forget

Adverbia

forās: outside
pusillum: a little bit

Adjectīva

dominicus, -a, -um: dominical, relating to the Lord
fidēlis, fidēlis, fidēle: faithful
mīrābilis, mīrābilis, mīrābile: wonderful, marvelous
pusillus, pusilla, pusillum: little

Conjūnctīva

tandem: finally, at last
aliquandō: sometime, finally, at last

---

[2] Verbs of memory often have the object of the verb in the genitive if it is a person being remembered or recalled.

Fābula Excerpta

Petrus vērō sedēbat foris in ātriō: et accessit ad eum ūna ancilla, dīcēns: Et tū cum Jēsū Galilaeō erās. At ille negāvit cōram omnibus, dīcēns: Nesciō quid dīcis. Exeunte autem illō jānuam, vīdit eum alia ancilla, et ait hīs quī erant ibi: Et hic erat cum Jēsū Nazarēnō. Et iterum negāvit cum jūrāmentō: Quia nōn nōvī hominem. Et post pusillum accessērunt ad illum quī stābant, et dīxērunt Petrō: Vērē et tū ex illīs es: nam et verbum tuum manifēstum tē facit. Tunc coepit dētestārī et jūrāre nōn nōvisse hominem. Et continuō gallus cantāvit. Et meminit Petrus verbī Jēsū, quod dīxerat: Priusquam gallus cantat, ter mē negābis. Et ēgressus forās, flēvit amārē.

Cf. Matthew 26

juramentum: oath
verbum tuum manifēstum tē facit te: your word makes manifest [who] you [are]
detestari: to swear
ter: three times

1. Petrus Jesum nōverat?
2. Cur Petrus dīxit sē nōn nōvisse Jesum?
3. Postquam Petrus negāverat sē nōvisse Jesum, quid dēinde factum est?

Sententiae Interpretandae

1. Ōrāte et dēprecāminī Dominum Caelī. (Tb 6:18)
2. Cōnfitēminī Dominō, invocātē nōmen ejus. Annūntiāte inter gentēs opera ejus. (Ps 104:1)
3. Dignāre, domine, diē istō sine peccātō nōs cūstōdīre. (Tē Deum)
4. Cōnfitēminī invicem peccāta vestra et ōrāte prō invicem. (Jos 5:16)
5. Mariam, ō fidēlis anima, imitāre! (Fatima)
6. Vestrī honōris et benevolentiae memineram cum affectiōne. (2 Macc 9:21)
7. Nōn potest mundus ōdisse vōs; mē autem ōdit. (Jn 7:7)
8. Nōn enim quod volō bonum hoc agō, sed quod ōdī malum illud faciō. (Rom 7:15)
9. Ōdistī omnēs, quī operantur inīquitātem. (Ps 5:7)
10. Quī mē ōdit, et Patrem meum ōdit. (Jn 15:23)
11. Ōderat Esau Jācōb prō benedictiōne, qua benedīxerat eī pater. (Gn 27:41)
12. Et nōs, quī crēdimus, nōvimus cāritātem, quam habet Deus in nōbīs.
13. "Nihil est nōbīs dictū, vīsū, audītū cum īnsāniā circī, cum inpudīcitiā [impurity] theātrī, cum atrōcitāte [atrocity] arēnae, cum xystī [colonnade] vānitāte." (Tertullian, *Apologeticum* 38)

circus, circī (m.): circus
theatrus, theātrī (m.): theatre
arēna, arēnae (f.): arena

14. Sed carō nunc verbum factum—mīrābile dictū! (John Scotus Eriugena, *Carmen* 8)
15. Sed hoc habēs, quia ōdistī facta Nicolaītārum, quae et ego ōdī. (Rv 2:6)

Nicolaīta: Nicolatian

16. Dīcam Deō: Susceptor meus es; quārē oblītus es meī? et quārē contrīstātus incēdō, dum afflīgit mē inimīcus? (Ps 41:10)
17. Miserēre meī, Deus, secundum magnam misericordiam tuam; et secundum multitūdinem miserātiōnum tuārum, dēlē inīquitātem meam. (Ps 50:3)
18. Ego dīxī: Domine, miserēre meī; sānā animam meam, quia peccāvī tibi. (Ps 40:5)
19. Et, cum trānsīvit inde [there] Jēsus, vīdit hominem sedentem in telōniō, Matthaeum nōmine. Et ait illī: Sequere mē. Et surgēns, secūtus est eum. (Mt 9:9)

telōnium, telōniī (n.): tax collector's booth

20. Accipe oblātiōnem plēbis sānctae Deō offerendam [about to be offered]. Agnōsce quod agis, imitāre quod tractābis, et vītam tuam mystēriō dominicae crucis cōnfōrmā. (*Pontificāle Rōmānum*, "Dē ōrdinātiōne Diāconī et Epīscopī")

oblatio, oblationis (f.): offering

21. Vir plēnus leprōsa Jēsum videt et eum rogat, "Sī vīs, potes mē sānāre." Jēsus tangit illum et respondit: "Volō. Sānāre!" (Lk 5:13)

leprōsus, -ā, -um: leprosy

CHAPTER 25

§ 94. Verbs: Morphology of Gerunds

As we have done in the past, we will talk about the morphology of the gerund first and then move into the meaning. Gerunds are like the infinitive insofar as they are verbal nouns. That means a gerund combines elements of verbs and nouns. It will be easy to confuse these with present active particifples that have an *-ing* in English and also in Latin have an *-nd-*. We will talk about the distinction below. They all have endings like o-nouns.

	ā-verb	ē-verb	i/e-verb	i-verb	Example Translation
Nom	*laudā|re*	*monē|re*	*duce|re*	*audī|re*	to hear
Gen	*laudand|ī*	*monend|ī*	*ducend|ī*	*audiend|ī*	of hearing
Dat	*laudand|ō*	*monend|ō*	*ducend|ō*	*audiend|ō*	to hear / for hearing
Acc	*laudand|um*	*monend|um*	*ducend|um*	*audiend|um*	hearing (d.o.)
Abl	*laudand|ō*	*monend|ō*	*ducend|ō*	*audiend|ō*	by hearing

Notice that there is no nominative. The nominative would just be the present active infinitive. The gerunds are also always singular and never plural. They are also considered neuter. All the forms have *-nd-* which ought not be confused with the present active participle, *-nt-*.

§ 95. Verbs: Meaning of Gerunds

As you may have guessed from the table, these gerunds can stand alone in a sentence, but they are never the main verb of a sentence. Gerunds are often coupled with a preposition or paired with another noun in the genitive.

Tempus audiendī est. It is the time of listening.
Causa vīvendī laudāre deum est. The reason for living is to praise God.
Parātus sum ad volandum. I am ready to fly!
Amittit in volandō. He is lost in flying.

One has to be careful to recognize the difference between a participle that ends in *-ing* and the gerund that often ends in *-ing*. A participle typically modifies a noun as it is an adjective, whereas a gerund is a noun and can stand alone. The English participle is illustrated in this sentence, "a singing boy (*puer cantāns*) walked down the street." Here *singing* is the participle because it modifies the boy. You could also say, "a boy has a reason for singing" (*puer habet causam cantandī*). In the second case, we have a gerund because it is not directly modifying a noun but is instead standing alone indicating an action that is not finite or the main verb in the sentence. We should think of the *ad* + accusative gerund and *causa* + genitive gerund as purpose clauses.

§ 96. Verbs: Semi-Deponent Verbs

There are a small number of verbs that have active and passive forms in the present, imperfect, and future tenses but are deponent in the perfect, pluperfect, future perfect.

gaudeō, gaudēre,—, gāvīsus sum: delight
audeō, audēre,—, ausus sum: dare
cōnfīdō, cōnfīdere,—, cōnfīsus sum: trust

Look at the two sentences below:

Vir gaudet. A man rejoices.
Vir laetatur. A man is happy.

The first example has a normal verb in the present active indicative, and the second has a verb with passive endings, but which functions as an active verb.

Vir gāvīsus est. A man rejoiced.
Vir laetātus est. A man was happy.

This second example shows these two verbs in the perfect tense where they both have passive endings, but function actively.

§ 97. Verbs: Verbs with Ablatives

So far, we have become accustomed to verbs that have an accusative as the direct object, a dative as the indirect object, and so on. Certain verbs, though, are paired with the ablative and do not take an accusative. The verb *uti* is both a deponent—it has only passive forms—and it takes the ablative.

Magister verbīs ūtitur docēre discipulōs. The teacher uses words to teach the students.
Hominēs hymnīs ūtuntur laudāre Deum. People use hymns to praise God.

There are several verbs of this kind: *uti, frui, carēre,* are several frequent ones. Notice that only the last one in that group is a regular, non-deponent verb.

Sententiae Summāriae

Cāritās est causa laudandī Deum.
Magister in scholam intrat ad monendum.
Docendō discimus.
Ōrāmus audiendō.
Deus gāvīsus est laudandō populī suī.
Maria ausa est facere voluntātem deī.
Pauper cibō caret. Omnēs hominēs cibō et aquā fruuntur.

Translations

Love is the reason for praising God.
The teacher comes into the school to teach.
By teaching we learn.
We pray by listening.
God delighted in the praise of His people.
Mary dared to do the will of God.
A poor person lacks food. All people enjoy food and water.

Vocābula Memoranda

Nōmina

jūdex, jūdicis (m.): judge
mōtiō, mōtiōnis (f.): motion, movement
potens, potentīs (f.): power, ability
ratiō, ratiōnis (f.): reason, rationality
similitūdō, similitūdinis (f.): likeness, resemblance
trībulātiō, tribulationis (f.): tribulation
volucer, volucris (f.): flying thing, bird

Verba

<u>ā-verbs</u>

dēsīderō [de + sidus], dēsīderāre, dēsīderāvī, dēsīderātus: desire[1]
ēvītō [ex + vito], ēvītāre, ēvītāvī, ēvītātus: avoid
ōrdinō, ōrdināre, ōrdināvī, ōrdinātus: order, arrange
resignō [re + signo], resignāre, resignāvī, resignātus: resign

<u>ē-verb</u>

audeō, audēre, —, ausus sum: dare
careō, carēre, caruī, caritus: (+abl) lack, be without

---

[1] *Sidus* is a word for "star." Perhaps this word meant something like "wish upon a star."

i/e-verbs

appetō [ad + petere] appetere, appetīvi, appetītus: seek
condō [cōn + dō], condere, condidī, conditus: put, build, found
cōnfīdō [cōn + fīdō], cōnfīdere,—, cōnfīsus: trust
corrumpō [cōn + rumpō], corrumpere, corrūpī, corruptus: corrupt
fruor, fruī,—, frūctūs: (+abl) enjoy
gignō, gignere, genuī, genitus: give birth to
maledico [male + dico], maledīcere, maledīxī, maledictus: curse
ūtor, utī,—, ūsus: (+abl) use

Adjectīva

tardus, -a, -um: slow

Adverbia

exterius: outside
interius: inside

Lectum Excerptum

Omnia tempus habent, et suīs spatiīs trānseunt ūniversa sub caelō.
Tempus nāscendī, et tempus moriendī; tempus plantandī, et tempus ēvellendī quod plantātum est.
Tempus occīdendī, et tempus sānandī; tempus dēstruendī, et tempus aedificandī.
Tempus flendī, et tempus rīdendī; tempus plangendī, et tempus saltandī.
Tempus spargendī lapidēs, et tempus colligendī, tempus amplexandī, et tempus longē fierī ab amplexibus.
Tempus acquīrendī, et tempus perdendī; tempus cūstōdiendī, et tempus abjiciendī.
Tempus scindendī, et tempus cōnsuendī; tempus tacendī, et tempus loquendī.
Cf. Ecclesiastes 3

spatium: space, area
plantāre: to plant
ēvellere: to pluck
dēstruere: to destroy
plangere: to wail
saltāre: to dance
spargere: to sow seeds
amplexāre: to embrace
scindere: to cut
cōnsuēre: to sow (clothes)

Sententiae Interpretandae

1. Lēx ōrandī, lēx crēdendī [est].[2]
2. Quī habet aurēs audiendī, audiat. (Mt 11:15)
   audiat: a subjunctive form of *audire*, translate with "let him"
3. Pānem ad mandūcandum multiplicābit. (2 Cor 9:10)
4. Āctus fideī est cōnfitērī Deō, vel in corde crēdendō, vel exterius laudandō, factīs approbandō. (Thomas Aquinas, *In Psalmōs* 15)
   approbāre: to approve, prove
5. Ratiō est mentis mōtiō ea quae discuntur distinguendī et connectendī potēns. (Augustine, *Dē Ōrdine* 2.11.30)
   distinguere: to distinguish
   connectere: to connect
6. Et adhūc ascendēbāmus, interius cōgitandō et loquendō et mīrandō opera tua. (Augustine, *Confessions* 9.10)
7. Ausus est maledīcere exercitum Deī. (1 Sm 17:36)
8. Gāvīsī sunt discipulī vīsō dominō. (Jn 20:20)
   video, vidēre, vīdī, vīsus
9. Numquid domōs nōn habētis ad mandūcandum et bibendum? (1 Cor 11:1)
10. Domine, ad adjuvandum mē festīnā. (Ps 69:2)
11. Ēvītandō vīvit anima quae appetendō moritur. (Augustine, *Confessions* 13.21)
12. Frātrēs meī, volucrēs, multum dēbētis laudāre creātōrem vestrum et ipsum dīligere semper, quī dēdit vōbīs plūmās ad induendum, pennās ad volandum. (Thomās of Celānō, *Vīta Prīma S. Francisci Assisiēnsis* 21.58)
    plūma, plūmae (f.): plume
    penna, pennae (f.): feather
13. Ipse Deus nōvit tempus, et modum līberandī tē, et ideō dēbēs tē illī resignāre. (Thomas a Kempis, *Imitātiō Chrīstī* 2.2.1)
14. Līberat ergō Deus hominem ā malō et trībulātiōnibus, eās in bonum convertendō; quod est signum maximae sapientiae, quia sapientis est malum ōrdināre in bonum; et hoc fit per patientiam, quae habētur in trībulātiōnibus. (Thomas Aquinas, *Expositio in Orationem Dominicam* 7)
15. Et ipse dīxit ad eōs: Ō stultī, et tardī corde ad crēdendum in omnibus quæ locūtī sunt prophētæ! (Lk 24:25)

---

[2] This is a summary of traditional Christian teaching which is hard to locate in one particular author. A search of the Library of Latin Texts database suggests perhaps something akin to this phrase appears in Gennadius Massiliensis in the 7th century. The literal phrase does not appear in the Brepols Library of Latin Texts.

16. Vīdit suum dulcem Nātum; moriéndo desolátum, dum emísit spíritum. (Stābat Māter, stanza 8)

festīna: hurry

17. Adam quidem creātus est ad imāginem et similitūdinem Deī, quia immortālis est in animā et carne conditus. Postquam vērō imāginem in sē Deī ac similitūdinem peccandō corrūpit, genuit ad similitūdinem et imāginem suam fīlium, id est mortālem, corruptibilem, ratiōnis capācem, reātū suae praevāricātiōnis adstrictum. (Venerable Bede, *In Genesim* 5:3)

capāx, capācīs (f.): large, capable
conditor, conditoris (m.): creator, founder
reātus, reātūs (m.): accusation, charge
praevāricātiō, praevāricātiōnis (f.): lie

18. Gāvīsus sum autem in Dominō vehementer, quoniam tandem aliquandō reflōruistis prō mē sentīre. (Phil 4:10)

refloreo, reflorere, reflorui: floruish again, be prosperous again

CHAPTER 26

§ 98. Verbs: Morphology Future Perfect Active and Passive

The last indicative verb tense to be learned is the future perfect. So far, we have learned the present, imperfect, future, perfect, and pluperfect tenses. We have one final tense, which is another future tense. It is used most frequently in conditionals ("if someone will have done *x*, then *y* …"). We will begin as always with the morphology. So what does a future perfect look like? You might have guessed from the name that it is a combination of a future form with a perfect form. The future perfect active looks like this:

laudāv-erit. He will have praised.
docu-erimus. We will have taught.
dūx-eritis. You will have led.
audīv-erint. They will have heard.

You will notice that we have the perfect stem of the verb with the future form of *esse* added to the end. The only difference is that in the very last form, instead of *erunt*, we find *erint*.

In the passive voice, we have nearly the same construction, except that the third person plural form returns to the original future *erunt*. You might also find the future perfect form of *esse*.

laudātus erit or *fuerit.* He will have been praised.
doctī erimus or *fuerimus.* We will have been educated.
ductī eritis or *fueritis.* You (pl.) will have been led.
audītī erunt or *fuerunt.* They will have been heard.

Active

ā-verb	ē-verb	i/e-verb	i-verb	Example Translation
laudāverō	*monuerō*	*dūxerō*	*audīverō*	I will have heard
laudāveris	*monueris*	*dūxeris*	*audīveris*	You will have heard
laudāverit	*monuerit*	*dūxerit*	*audīverit*	He will have heard
laudāverimus	*monuerimus*	*dūxerimus*	*audīverimus*	We will have heard
laudāveritis	*monueritis*	*dūxeritis*	*audīveritis*	You (pl.) will have heard
laudāverint	*monuerint*	*dūxerint*	*audīverint*	They will have heard

Passive

The future perfect passive requires the perfect passive participle, plus a future or future perfect form of *esse*.[1]

ā-verb	ē-verb	i/e-verb	i-verb	Example Translation
laudātus (-a, -um) [fu-]ero	*monitus (-a, -um)* [fu-]ero	*ductus (-a, -um)* [fu-]ero	*audītus (-a, -um)* [fu-]ero	I will have been heard
laudātus (-a, -um) [fu-]eris	*monitus (-a, -um)* [fu-]eris	*ductus (-a, -um)* [fu-]eris	*audītus (-a, -um)* [fu-]eris	You will have been heard
laudātus (-a, -um) [fu-]erit	*monitus (-a, -um)* [fu-]erit	*ductus (-a, -um)* [fu-]erit	*audītus (-a, -um)* [fu-]erit	He will have been heard
laudātī (-ae, -a) [fu-]erimus	*monitī (-ae, -a)* [fu-]erimus	*ductī (-ae, -a)* [fu-]erimus	*audītī (-ae, -a)* [fu-]erimus	We will have been heard
laudātī (-ae, -a) [fu-]eritis	*monitī (-ae, -a)* [fu-]eritis	*ductī (-ae, -a)* [fu-]eritis	*audītī (-ae, -a)* [fu-]eritis	You (pl.) will have been heard
laudātī (-ae, -a) [fu-]erunt	*monitī (-ae, -a)* [fu-]erunt	*ductī (-ae, -a)* [fu-]erunt	*audītī (-ae, -a)* [fu-]erunt	They will have been heard

§ 99. Verbs: Meaning of the Future Perfect Active and Passive

As we have already seen, we have a combination of the future and the perfect. So, this tense is used to describe actions that will be completed in the future. Our reflex translation for the active voice is "will have [verb]-ed." The future perfect is not all that complicated in terms of figuring out the forms.

The hardest part is how it is used. In English, when we make an if-then statement, we more commonly use the simple future or present: "If he will be baptized, he will be saved." In Latin, we will use the future perfect. This is also called the *future more vivid*. We will see a full chart of all the possible conditional constructions after we have learned the subjunctive in chapter 32.

Sī baptīzātus erit, salvus erit. If he will have been baptized, he will be saved.

Sī quis mihi ministrāverit, honōrificābit eum Pater meus. (Jn 12:26)

If someone will have served me, my father will honor him.

---

[1] The parentheses indicate the possible endings for masculine, feminine, or neuter. The brackets indicate a possible prefix to change the tense from future to future perfect.

Latin authors tend to use a few context clues that can help the reader know when to expect a future-perfect. These will not always require the future-perfect, but the future-perfect tends to go with them.

- *si* and its variants, *nisi, etiamsi*
- relative pronouns like *quicumque, quaecumque, quodcumque*
- More regular pronouns that begin a sentence, *qui, quae, quod*; and so these are often translated as "someone" or "whoever."
- other conjunctions added to *-cumque*, for example, *ubicumque, quodcumque*

A full chart of all the possible ways to construct conditional statements comes in chapter 32.

§ 100. Verbs: Irregular Imperatives

There are a few irregular imperatives, which are typically called future imperatives. There are not very many, and they do not come up very often. The endings are simple: *-to* and *-te*. Not all verbs have a future imperative. Some representative and common examples are given.

Irregular imperatives:

Mementō homō quia pulvis es et in pulverem reverterīs. (*Liber Ordinarius Montis Cassini* 328)

Remember that you are dust and into dust you shall return.

Mementō (*mementōte*: plural) *morī*. Remember to die.

Ēstō (*ēstote*: plural) *vir*. Be a man.

Sententiae Summāriae

Etiamsī vōs intrāverīmus in ecclēsiam, nōn salvī eritis.
Nisi baptīzātus erō, nōn salvus erō.
Sī monitus eris, nōn intrābis in oppidum illum.
Nisi doctrīnam vēram audīverīmus, iūstitiam nōn faciēmus.

Translations

Even if you will have entered in the church, you will not be saved.
Unless I will have been baptized, I will not be saved.
If you will have been warned, you will not enter that town.
Unless we will have heard the true teaching, we will not do justice.

CHAPTER 26

Vocābula Memoranda

Nōmina

cōnsuētūdō, cōnsuētūdinis (f.): custom, habit
ēsca, ēscae (f.): food
opus, operis (n.): work
vestīgium, vestīgiī (n.): footprint

Verba

ā-verbs
adōrō [ad + oro], adōrāre, adōrāvī, adōrātus: worship, bow down
honōrō, honōrāre, honōrāvī, honōrātus: honor
ligō, ligāre, ligāvī, ligātus: bind
scandalizō, scandalizāre, scandalizāvī, scandalizātus: tempt to evil, cause to stumble

ē-verbs
mīsceō, miscēre, miscuī, mixtus: mix
vidēor, vidērī,—, vīsus: seem, think

i/e-verbs
colō, colere, coluī, cultus: worship, cultivate
comedō, comedere, comēdī, comestus: eat

-io-verb
recipiō [re + capio], recipere, recēpī, receptus: receive

i-verb
mentior, mentīrī,—, mentītus: lie

irregular
prōsum [pro + sum], prōdesse, prōfui, prōfutūrus: profit, benefit

Adjectīva

necessārius, -a, -um: necessary
singulus, -a, -um: each, every

Adverbia

hūc: here
hinc: from here
illūc: over there
nam: for
quōcumque: to wherever
ubicumque: wherever

Prōnōmina

quīcumque, quaecumque, quodcumque: whoever, whatever
iste, ista, istud: this one, that one (of yours)[2]

Fābula Excerpta

Bel 1 [Dn. 14:1] Erat autem Daniēl convīva rēgis, et honōrātus super omnēs amīcōs ejus. Erat quoque īdōlum apud Babylōniōs nōmine Bel: et portābantur ad īdōlum per diēs singulōs pānēs, et ovēs quadrāgintā, vīnīque amphorae sex. Rēx quoque colēbat eum, et ībat per singulōs diēs adōrāre eum: porrō Daniēl adōrābat Deum suum. Dīxitque eī rēx: Quārē nōn adōrās Bel? Quī respondēns ait eī: Quia nōn colō īdōla manufacta, sed vīventem Deum, quī creāvit cælum et terram, et habet potestātem omnis carnis. Et dīxit rēx ad eum: Nōn vidētur tibi esse Bel vīvēns deus? an nōn vidēs tam multum eum comedere et bibere quotīdiē? Et ait Daniēl rīdēns: Nōlī errāre, rēx: iste enim intrīnsecus lūteus est, et forīnsecus aureus, neque comēdit aliquandō. Et īrātus rēx vocāvit sacerdōtēs ejus, et ait eīs: Nisi dīxerītis mihi quī comēdit escās eās, moriēminī. Sī autem ostenderītis quoniam Bel comedere hæc, moriētur Daniēl, quia blasphēmāvit in Bel. Et dīxit Daniēl rēgī: Fīat juxtā verbum tuum. Erant autem sacerdōtēs Bel septuāgintā, exceptīs uxōribus, et parvulīs, et filiīs. Et venit rēx cum Daniēle in templum Bel. Et dīxērunt sacerdōtēs Bel: Ecce nōs ēgredimur forās: et tū, rēx, pōne ēscās, et vīnum miscē, et claudē ōstium: et cum ingressus fuerīs mane, nisi invēnerīs omnia comesta ā Bel, morte moriēmur, vel Daniēl quī mentītus est adversum nōs. Sacerdōtēs īrātī erant autem, quia fēcerant sub mēnsā absconditum introitum, et per illum ingrediēbantur semper, et dēvorābant ea. Factum est igitur postquam ēgressī sunt illī, rēx posuit ēscās ante Bel: imperāvit Daniēl puerīs suīs, et attulērunt pulverem, et jacuērunt pulverem per tōtum templum cōram rēge: et ēgressī clausērunt ōstium, et abiērunt. Sacerdōtēs autem ingressī sunt nocte juxtā cōnsuētūdinem suam, et uxōrēs et filiī eōrum, et comēdērunt omnia, et bibērunt. Surrēxit autem rēx mane, et Daniēl cum eō. Statimque aperuērunt ōstium, rēx mēnsam vīdit, exclāmāvit vōce magnā: Magnus es, Bēl, et nōn mentītus es. Et rīsit Daniēl, et jussit rēgem nōn intrāre: et dīxit: Ecce terram: vidēte cujus vestīgia hæc. Et dīxit rēx: Videō

---

2 *Iste, ista, istud* declines like *ille, illa, illud* and is typically classified as an unemphatic demonstrative pronoun. It often just means "that one." *Iste liber est malus* (That book is bad).

vestīgia virōrum, et mulierum, et īnfantium. Et īrātus est rēx. Tunc apprehendit sacerdōtēs, et uxōrēs, et fīliōs eōrum: et ostendērunt eī ōstium sub mēnsā, per quod ingrediēbantur, et comedēbant quae erant super mēnsam. Occidit ergō illōs rēx, et trādidit Bēl in potestātem Daniēlis: quī dēstrūxit eum et templum ejus.

quare: why, for what reason
conviva, convivae (f./m.): guest
amphora, amphorae (f.): jug, vessel
porro: rather
manufactum: made by hands
intrinsecus, -a, -um: inside
forinsecus, -a, -um: outside
luteus, -a, -um: clay
aureus, -a, -um: gold
fiat: let it be
septuaginta: seventy
foras: outside
pulvis, pulveris: dust

1. Quis fuit deus Babyloniōrum?
2. Omnēs hominēs in Babylōniā deum eōrum adōrābant?
3. Cur Daniel nōn deum, nōmine Bēl, colēbat?
4. Cur rēx putābat deum eius vīvum esse?
5. Quōmodo Daniel monstrāvit deum rēgis īdolum fuisse?
6. Cur rēx īrātus erat?

Sententiae Interpretandae

1. Quid prōderit, frātrēs meī, sī fidem quis dīcit sē habēre, opera autem nōn habet? numquid poterit fidēs salvāre eum. (Js 2:14)
2. Et sī quis vōbīs dīxerit: Quid facitis? dīcite, quia Dominō necessārius est: et continuō illum dīmittet hūc. (Mk 11:3)
3. Quīcumque suscēperit puerum istum in nōmine meō, mē recipit: et quīcumque mē recēperit, recipit eum quī mē mīsit. Nam quī minor est inter vōs omnēs, hīc major est. (Lk 9:48)
4. Factum est autem: ambulantibus illīs in viā, dīxit quīdam ad illum: Sequar tē quōcumque ierīs. (Lk 9:57)
5. Tū ergō sī adōrāverīs cōram mē, erunt tua omnia. (Lk 4:7)
6. Āmēn quippe dīcō vōbīs, sī habueritis fidem sīcut grānum sināpis, dicētis montī huic: Trānsī hinc illūc, et trānsībit, et nihil impossibile erit vōbīs. (Mt 17:19)

quippe: certainly, truly
grānum sināpis: mustard seed [*lit.* a grain of a mustard plant]

7. Dīcēbat ergō Jēsus ad eōs, quī crēdidērunt eī, Jūdæōs: Sī vōs mānseritis in sermōne meō, vērē discipulī meī eritis. (Jn 8:31)
8. Sī ergō vōs fīlius līberāverit, vērē līberī eritis. (Jn 8:36)
9. Tunc dīcit illīs Jēsus: Omnēs vōs scandalum patiēminī in mē in istā nocte. Scrīptum est enim: Percutiam pāstōrem, et dispergentur ovēs gregis. Postquam autem resurrēxerō, praecēdam vōs in Galilaeam. Respondēns autem Petrus, ait illī: Et sī omnēs scandalizātī fuerint in tē, ego numquam scandalizābor. Ait illī Jēsus: Āmēn dīcō tibi, quia in hāc nocte, antequam gallus cantat, ter mē negābis. Ait illī Petrus: Etiamsī oportuerit mē morī tēcum, nōn tē negābō. Similiter et omnēs discipulī dīxērunt. (Mt 25:31–35)

percūtō, percutere, percussī, percussus: strike
dispergō, dī-spergere, dispersī, dispersus: disperse
praecēdō, praecēdere, praecessisse, praecessus: go before

10. Nōn habēs hīc manentem cīvitātem, et ubicumque fueris, extrāneus es et peregrīnus, nec requiem aliquandō habēbis, nisi Chrīstō intimē fueris ūnītus. (Thomas a Kempis, *Imitātiō Chrīstī* 2.1.1)

ūnītus: united

11. Et dīxit eī: Hæc omnia tibi dabō, sī cadēns adōrāveris mē. (Mt 4:9)
12. Et tibi dabō clāvēs rēgnī cælōrum. Et quodcumque ligāveris super terram, erit ligātum et in cælīs: et quodcumque solvēris super terram, erit solūtum et in caelīs. (Mt 16:19)
13. Quī autem persevērāverit in fīnem, hīc salvus erit. (Mt 24:13)
14. In illā hōrā accessērunt discipulī ad Jēsum, dīcentēs: Quis, putās, major est in rēgnō cælōrum? Et advocāns Jēsus parvulum, statuit eum in mediō eōrum, et dīxit: Āmēn dīcō vōbīs, nisi conversī fueritis, et efficiāminī sīcut parvulī, nōn intrābitis in rēgnum cælōrum. Quīcumque ergō humiliāverit sē sīcut parvulus iste, hic est major in rēgnō cælōrum. Et quī suscēperit ūnum parvulum tālem in nōmine meō, mē suscipit: quī autem scandalizāverit ūnum dē pusillīs istīs, quī in mē crēdunt, expedit eī ut suspendātur mola asināria in collō ejus, et dēmergātur in profundum maris. (Mt 18:1–6)

molā (f.) *asināria*: millstone
suspendātur: be suspended
dēmergatur: be sunk

15. Haec est fidēs catholica, quam nisi quisque fidēliter firmiterque crēdiderit, salvus esse nōn poterit. Āmēn. (Quīcumque Vult)

CHAPTER 27

§ 101. Verbs: Morphology of the Gerundive and Future Passive Participle

Just reading the phrase *future passive participle* or the term *gerundive* is likely to make this form of the verb in Latin feel very daunting. We have used simpler terms where possible to explain the complicated language of grammar. Let's begin with some review to put this complicated sounding form into perspective. We have already seen the present active participle, *ambulans*, "going." The noun that goes with this participle does the action of the verb. *Vir ambulans*, "the walking man." We have seen the perfect passive participle, *auditus*, "heard." The noun that goes with this verb form receives the action. *Verbum auditum est*, "the word is heard." Finally, we have seen the future active participle *ambulaturus*, "about to walk." *Vir ambulaturus est*, "the man is about to walk." The subject is doing the action of the verb in the future. The last participle we have to learn is the future passive participle, *laudandus*, "ought to be praised." *Deus laudandus est*, "God ought to be praised."

	Active	Passive	Key Change	Meaning
Present	*laudāns*	—	*-ns* and *-nt-*	"-ing"
Perfect	—	*laudātus*	*-t-* or perfect stem change	"-ed"
Future	*laudātūrus*		*-ūr-*	"about to"
Future		*laudandus*	*-nd-*	"must be [verb]-ed"

The morphology here is the addition of the *-nd-* to the present stem of the verb: *necandus, docendus, dūcendus, sciendus*. All of these have the *-nd-* added to the stem. Both i-verbs and -io-verbs add the *-e-*. This form is in some ways easy to recognize and is fairly regular; the difficulty will be distinguishing it from the gerund, which we will discuss below.

One question students often have is, "What is the difference between a gerund and a future passive participle?" We will talk about the meaning in the next section, but in terms of how we will spot it in Latin, the future passive participle always has a noun it modifies in gender, number, and case. Remember, the future passive participle is still a participle. So it has to have a noun, or an implied noun, with which it pairs. If you see a verb form with the *-nd-* after the stem, check to see if it has a noun that it agrees with in gender, number, and case (but maybe not declension). Also, the gerund is never in the nominative. The future passive participle is often in the nominative (though not exclusively).

The last thing to remember about the future passive participle is that it is an adjective, so it can end in all the possible endings of a first and second declension adjective. Thus, *audiendus, -a, -um* covers all the gender endings in the singular, and *audiendi, -ae, -a* covers the plural. But it can also come in any of the other cases.

To recap, gerunds have verb stems and noun endings that have the *-nd-* form and do not modify another noun. Future passive participles have verb stems and adjective endings that have the *-nd-* form and modify a noun that it will agree with in gender number and case.

Here is a representative morphology of the future passive participle, minus the permutations for plural and the possible cases:

M. F. and N. Present Forms	Example Translation
lauda|nd|us, -a, -um	ought to be praised
vide|nd|us, -a, -um	ought to be warned
dūce|nd|us, -a, -um	ought to be led
audie|nd|us, -a, -um	ought to be heard
capta|nd|us, -a, -um	ought to be captured
fere|nd|us, -a, -um	ought to be carried

§ 102. Verbs: Meaning of the Future Passive Participle

As far as the difference in meaning between the gerund and the future passive participle, we often see the future passive paired with a noun that "must be done" by the verb. *Maria laudanda est*, "Mary must be praised." This is called the periphrastic. Remember that the future passive participle is passive, so the noun that agrees with the future passive participle receives the action of the participle.

> *Salūs autem est ab omnibus dīligenda* (Thomas Aquinas, *Exposition in Orationem Dominicam* 1). Salvation however ought to be loved by all.

In some cases there will be no explicit agent of the future passive participle, for example, *Deus laudandus est*. In other cases, the agent of the future passive participle will be indicated by the dative case, the dative of agent.

> Sacerdōtī missa celebranda est. The mass must be celebrated by the priest. (Or, simply if you flip the voice from passive to active, "the priest must celebrate the mass.")

CHAPTER 27

§ 103. Gerunds, Gerundives, and Future Passive Participles

What follows will be a highly technical division of a very vexed problem in the grammar of Latin. The differences are slight and nuanced. It is not necessary that introductory students concern themselves too much with these distinctions.[1]

There are two different uses of the form we have been calling the *future passive participle*, which looks like this: *laudandus*, as in *Deus laudandus est*. That same form, *laudandus, -a, -um*, can also be used for something called the gerundive. The gerundive typically gets used in cases other than the nominative. To illustrate the difference, here are two related sentences: *Deus laudandus est* (God is to be praised) and *Sacerdos venit in ecclesiam ad Deum laudandum*. Thus, we could translate it as, "the priest came into the church for the purpose of praising God." The astute reader will notice that we have essentially changed the future passive participle into a kind of active participle with the direct object being in the same case as *laudandum*. We can think of the gerundive as a gerund that takes a direct object. It is possible for a gerund to have an accusative, but good Latin style will prefer a gerundive where the gerundive takes the case of the noun and becomes more like an adjective. It will be translated with *-ing* like a verbal noun, even though it resembles a verbal adjective, the future passive participle.

The gerund and the gerundive function very similarly, only the gerundive has *case* endings like an adjective.

Future passive participle:
Epistulae scribendae sunt. The letters ought to be written.

* The future passive participle matches the noun *epistulae*. Typically, a true future passive participle will be found in the nominative and agree with the noun it modifies.

---

[1] Various scholars of the Latin language have had different things to say about the difference between a future passive participle and the gerundive. Reginald Foster, "the Pope's Latinist," prefers to separate the future passive participle into two different forms, which he calls the participle of "passive futurity" and the "passive obligation." The difficulty is that there is one form being used in two different ways. That is, we might say that the morphology is the same, but the meaning is different. *Liber legendus est* means, "the book is needing to be read." Here we have a participle of passive obligation, or a future passive participle. *Legendus* acts like an adjective that modifies book and signifies that something ought to be done, namely, "reading the book." But we could also say, "vir venit huc ad libros legendos." Here we have a gerundive *legendos*, which doesn't really tell us what "ought to happen" but merely states "the man came here for the purpose of reading books." We could try to say something like "the man here for the purpose of the books to be read." But, that kind of stilted English doesn't make much idiomatic sense. No one talks like this. See Reginald Foster, *Ossa Latinitas* (The Catholic University of America Press, 2016) 323–25, 484–88. *Wheelock's Latin* does not separate out these two uses (Harper Perennial, 2011) 147–50, 276–78; Allen and Grenough, § 503–7. *Learn to Read Latin* (Yale University Press, 2015), 369, separates them out like Reggie Foster, but without his language.

Gerund:
Venit in cubiculum ad epistulās scrībendum. He came into the room for the purpose of writing letters.

* The Gerund here takes a direct object, *epistulas*, but does not match it. It is a verbal noun which can take a direct object, but it does not match it.

Gerundive:
Venit in cubiculum ad epistulās scrībendās. He came into the room for the purpose of writing letters (or, more idiomatically, "he came into the room to write letters")

* The gerundive participle takes on the ending of the noun it modifies. It looks like the future passive participle, but it is not the same. It is closer to the gerund, from which it takes its name.

Sententiae Summāriae

Maria laudanda est. Deus laudandus est omnibus.
Ancillae monendae sunt dominīs.
Dux parātus est ad dūcendum mīlitēs in bellum.
Hominēs in ecclēsiam veniunt ad Ēvangelium audiendum.
Latina docenda erat magistro.

Translations

Mary is to be praised. (*Or* Mary must be praised.) God is to be praised by all.
The maidservants are to be warned by the masters.
The leader was ready to lead the soldiers into war.
The people come into the church to hear the Gospel.
Latin needed to be taught by the teacher.

Vocābula Memoranda

Nōmina

ambitiō, ambitiōnis (f.): ambition, desire
ascēnsiō, ascēnsiōnis (f.): ascent, progress
cōnscientia, cōnscientiae (f.): knowledge, conscience
dīluvium, dīluviī (n.): flood
foedus, foederis (n.): treaty, covenant
gradus, gradūs (m.): step

orbis, orbis (m.): sphere
  orbis terrārum: the world [*lit.* the globe of the lands]
scientia, scientiae (f.): knowledge
sīdus, sīderis (n.): star, constellation
strepitus, strepitūs (m.): racket, noise
transitus, transitūs (m.): passage

Verba

ā-verbs
cōnsīdō [con + sedeo], cōnsīderāre, cōnsīderāvī, cōnsīderātus: examine, reflect on
culpō, culpāre, culpāvī, culpātus: blame
illūminō, illūmināre, illūmināvī, illūminātus: illuminate
levō, levāre, levāvī, levātus: lift up
vēnerō, venerāre, venerāvī, venerātus: venerate, worship

ē-verb
devovō [de + vovo], dēvovēre, dēvōvī, dēvōtus: devote

i/e-verbs
adhibeō [ad + habeo], adhibēre, adhibuī, adhibitus: employ, adhere to, summon
perdō [per + do], perdere, perdidī, perditus: ruin, destroy

irregular
praeferō [prae + fero], praeferre, praetulī, praelātus: carry in front, give preference to
subeo [sub + eo], subire, subivi, subitus: go under

Adjectīva

quilibet, quaelibet, quidlibet: whomever you please, what you please, anyone/anything whatever
simplex, simplicis (gen. sing.): simple
ūtilis, ūtilis, ūtile: useful

Conjūnctīva

sīcut[i]: just as, like
umquam: ever

Fābulaee Excerptae

Rēx ipse nomine Eupator venit in Jūdaeam causa oppugandorum exercituum Judaeorum.

Rēx ipse Eupator, ad necandum Jūdam Machabaeum, omnēs rēgnī suī vīros collēgit: itaque cum centum mīlitibus peditum, et vīgintī mīllibus equitum in Jūdaeam ingressus est. Praeībant elephantī, magnitudine corporis et horrendō strepitu terribilēs; elephantibus impositae erant ligneae turrēs, ex quibus pugnābant mīlitēs armātī. Sed Jūdās, quī potentiae dīvīnae magis quam numerō mīlitum cōnfīdēbat, in videndis elephantis nōn fuit commōtus, in eam castrōrum hostīlium partem cucurrit, ubi erat tabernāculum rēgis, et occīsīs quatuor hominum mīllibus, omnibus militibus desiderium erat fugiendi. Memoranda est haec pugna pro fortitūdine et morte Eleāzarī: is vīderat bestiam ūnam caeterīs majōrem: exīstimāns illā rēgem vehī, sē prō salutanda patria dēvōvit: per mediōs hostēs ad bestiam necandam cucurrit, sub illīus ventrem subi[v]it, repetītīs ictibus elephantum occīdit. Sed Eleazarus elephante cadente occisus est.

Cf. Francis Lhomond, *Epitome Historiae Sacrae*, 145.

Juda Machabeus: Judas Maccabeus
peditis, peditis (m.): foot soldier
equitis, equitis (m.): cavalryman
elephantus, elephanti (m.): elephant
ligneus, -a, -um: wooden or related to wood
turris, turris: tower
desiderium, desiderii (n.): desire
commotus, -a, -um: excited, nervous; moved (usually related to emotions)
cucurrit: perfect form of *currere* (to run)
ictus, ictus (m.): strike, blow

1. Cur rēx Eupātor collēgit vīrēs regnī? (utere infinitīvō, gerundiō, gerundīvō, et supīnō).
2. Quae erant super elephantōs? Cur?
3. Quōmodo Eleazārus occīsus est?

Sententiae Interpretandae

1. Fīlius hominis trādendus est in manūs hominum. (Mt 17:21)
2. In caelestibus dēbet esse habitātiō tua et sīcut in trānsitū cūncta sunt aspicienda. (Thomas a Kempis *Imitātiō Chrīstī* 2.4)

trānsitus, trānsitus: trānsit

3. Ad tē, domine, anima levanda erat et cūranda. (Augustine, *Confessions* 4.7.12)
4. Ad aedificandum domum, omnia praeparāvī. (1 Chr 28:2)
5. Peccāvimus deō nostrō nōn oboediendō vōcī ejus. (Bar 2:5)

6. Sāncta cōnfitētur Ecclēsia ... Venerandum tuum vērum et ūnicum Fīlium. (Tē Deum)
7. Tū ad līberandum susceptūrus hominem, nōn horruistī Vírginis uterum. (Tē Deum)
8. Ecce angelus Dominī appāruit in somnīs Joseph, dīcēns: Surge, et accipe puerum, et mātrem ejus, et fuge in Aegyptum, et estō ibi usque dum dīcam tibi. Hērōdēs quaerit puerum ad perdendum eum. (Mt 2:13)
9. Recordābor foederis meī, nec unquam dīluvium erit ad perdendum orbem terrārum. (Llhomnd, *Epitomē Historiae Sacrae* 14)
10. In hāc ōrātiōne ōrandō illūminātur ad cognōscendum dīvīnae ascēnsiōnis gradūs. (Bonaventure, *Itenerārium Mentis In Deum* 1.2)
11. Nōn est culpanda scientiā, aut quælibet simplex reī nōtitia, quæ bona est in sē cōnsīderāta, et à Deō ōrdināta: sed praeferenda est semper bona cōnscientia et virtuōsa vīta. (Thomas a Kempis, *Imitātiō Chrīstī* 1.3)
12. Adhibitē dīligentiam, ad extirpanda vitia, et virtūtēs īnserendās. (Thomas a Kempis *Imitātiō Chrīstī* 1.4)

> *extirpāre*: root out
> *īnserere*: tō plant

13. Cāritās est habenda ad omnēs, sed familiāritās nōn expedit. (Thomas a Kempis *Imitātiō Chrīstī* 1.8)

> *familiāritās*: intimacy
> *expedēre*: to be expedient; obtain

14. Nōn est magna fidūcia pōnenda in homine fragilī et mortālī etiamsī ūtilis fit et dīlēctus, neque trīstitia multa capienda ex hōc. (Thomas a Kempis *Imitātiō Chrīstī* 2.1.1)
15. Et ambitiō quid nisi honōrēs quaerit et glōriam, quamquam tū es prae cūnctīs honōrandus ūnus et glōriōsus in aeternum? Et ... saevitia potestātum timērī vult: quis autem timendus nisi ūnus Deus? (Augustine, *Confessions*, 2.6.13)
16. Omnēs dēclīnāvērunt, simul inūtilēs factī sunt. Nōn est quī faciat bonum, nōn est usque ad ūnum. Sepulchrum patēns est guttur eōrum; linguīs suīs dolōsē agēbant. Venēnum aspidum sub labiīs eōrum, quōrum os maledictiōne et amāritūdine plēnum est; vēlōcēs pedēs eōrum ad effundendum sanguinem. Contrītiō et īnfēlīcitās in viīs eōrum, et viam pācis nōn cognōvērunt; nōn est timor Deī ante oculōs eōrum. (Ps 13:3)

> *dēclīnāre*: to avoid, to turn astray
> *inūtilēs*: useless
> *faciat*: translate like *facit*
> *guttur*: throat
> *patēns*: open
> *venēnum aspidum*: poison of asps
> *amāritūdine*: bitterness

17. Benedīcite Dominō, omnēs angelī ejus, potentēs virtūte, facientēs verbum illīus, ad audiendam vōcem sermōnum ejus. (Ps 102:20)
18. Parabolae Salomōnis, filiī Dāvīd, rēgis Isrāēl, ad sciendam sapientiam et disciplīnam; ad intelligenda verba prūdentiae, et suscipiendam eruditiōnem doctrīnae, jūstitiam, et jūdicium, et aequitātem. (Prv 1:1–3)

ērudītiō, ērudītiōnis (f.): erudition, learning

19. Duae sunt rēs quibus nītitur omnis tractātiō scrīptūrārum: modus inveniendī quae intellegenda sunt, et modus prōferendī quae intellēcta sunt. (Augustine, *Dē doctrīnā Chrīstiānā* 1.1.1)

nītitur: depends on

20. Aliās dīxī vōbīs dē lēge decalogī, et modo dīcam vōbīs dē grātiā; et magis necessāria est nōbīs grātia quam Lēx; ad quam grātiam frūctuōsē recipiendam hortātur nōs māter Ecclēsia et apostolus Paulus. (Bonaventure, *Collātiōnēs dē dōnīs Spīritus Sānctī*)

decalogus, decalogī: decalogue, the ten commandments
frūctuōsē: fruitfully

21. Vocās itaque nōs ad intellegendum verbum, Deum apud Tē Deum. (Augustine, *Confessions* 11)

CHAPTER 28

☙❧

We will begin our discussion of the subjunctive by reading a passage from the New Testament that offers some examples of the way that Latin uses the subjunctive. Those situations are indicated by giving the Latin in the parentheses.

John 11 — Notice the latin subjunctives in parentheses

(1) Now a certain man was ill, Lazarus of Bethany, the village of Mary and her sister Martha.
(2) Mary was the one who anointed the Lord with perfume and wiped his feet with her hair; her brother Lazarus was ill.
(3) So the sisters sent a message to Jesus, "Lord, he whom you love is ill."
(4) But when Jesus heard it, he said, "This illness does not lead to death; rather it is for God's glory, so that [*ut,* result] the Son of God may be glorified through it."
(5) Accordingly, though Jesus loved Martha and her sister and Lazarus,
(6) after having heard that Lazarus was ill, he stayed two days longer in the place where he was.
(7) Then after this he said to the disciples, "Let us [*eamus,* hortatory] go to Judea again."
(8) The disciples said to him, "Rabbi, the Jews were just now trying to stone you, and are you going there again?"
(9) Jesus answered, "Are there not twelve hours of daylight? Those who walk during the day do not stumble, because they see the light of this world.
(10) But those who walk at night stumble, because the light is not in them."
(11) After saying this, he told them, "Our friend Lazarus has fallen asleep, but I am going there in order that I might awaken him [*ut ā somnō excitem eum,* purpose]."
(12) The disciples said to him, "Lord, if he has fallen asleep, he will be alright."
(13) Jesus, however, had been speaking about his death, but they thought that he was referring merely to sleep [*quia dē dormītiōne somnī dīceret,* indirect statement].
(14) Then Jesus told them plainly, "Lazarus is dead.

(15) For your sake I am glad I was not there, so that [*ut*, purpose] you may believe. But let us go [*eāmus*, hortatory] to him."
(16) Thomas, who was called the Twin, said to his fellow disciples, "Let us also go [*eāmus*, hortatory], that we may die with him."
(17) When Jesus arrived, he found that Lazarus had already been in the tomb for four days.
(18) Now Bethany was near Jerusalem, some two miles away,
(19) and many of the Jews had come to Martha and Mary in order that they might console them [*ut cōnsōlārentur eās dē frātre suō*, purpose] about their brother.
(20) When Martha heard that Jesus was coming, she went and met him, while Mary stayed at home.
(21) Martha said to Jesus, "Lord, if you had been here [*sī fuissēs*, contrary to fact], my brother would not have died [*nōn fuisset mortuus*, contrary to fact] …
(28) When she had said this [*Et cum haec dīxisset*, narrative], she went back and called her sister Mary, and told her privately, "The Teacher is here and is calling for you."

In the above paragraph, we had nine uses of the subjunctive. Notice all the different ways it is used. It is used to express the result, "so that" the Son of Man may be glorified. It is used as a command "let us go." It used to express purpose "in order that." It is used in indirect speech, "they thought that." It can be used to express something that didn't happen, but could have, "if you had been here," where it is implied that you weren't. Finally, it can be used in the sequence of actual events, "when she said these things."

§ 104. Verbs: Introduction to Subjunctive

We have finally come to the last section of the book. We will spend the last five chapters thinking about the subjunctive (*conjunctivus*) in Latin. To start thinking about the subjunctive, it might be helpful to think about what the word means in Latin: "join under" or "join together." The subjunctive is usually a way to join one clause with another clause. From all the way back at the beginning of the book, we talked about ways that Latin likes to join together phrases. We have seen relative clauses, infinitive clauses, conjunctions, participles, and other means to bring together disparate clauses. The last way to join them together is the subjunctive.

The subjunctive feels scary to English speakers because we do not typically use the subjunctive. It exists in the language, but it is not as common or as elegant as it is in Latin. In the previous sections, I have tried to give easy, "go-to," English phrases for translation from Latin to English. I will caution against this practice with the subjunctive. Because we do not have a natural way to do all the subjunctive forms in English, we will have to make do with many alternatives when we translate into English. Many people will encourage you to use *may* or *might* because often the subjunctive has a modal or possible character. That is often true, but it is not always true. It is almost just as likely that the subjunctive will be used in a narrative describing actual events, not ones that "might" occur. In this case, it is misleading to say that the subjunctive describes "possibility." From the above story, it would be strange if we translated the final subjunctive as, "When she might have said these things" rather than "when she said these things." The meaning is extremely different, and only the latter is correct.

The good news is that the subjunctive only occurs in the present, imperfect, perfect, and pluperfect tenses. It is limited to four of the six possible tenses. The other good news about the subjunctive is that you can often tell if a subjunctive is coming by certain lead words (*ut, cum, si, donec,* etc.) We will look at all of these in time. As always, there is one category of subjunctive that has no helpful lead word, which will be difficult.

Uses of Subjunctive in Latin (these need not be learned straight away, as they will be covered in the next five chapters)

Dependent (subjunctive means "to join under"; these are subjunctives that join under a main clause):

1. Indirect Speech
   a. Form in Latin: lead verb of thinking, asking, requesting, commanding, or saying + *ut, quis, quae, quid, ubi, cur,* etc. + subjunctive verb.
   b. Types:
      i. Indirect Statements (Chapter 28)
         *Putant **ut dīceret** dē morte eius.* They thought that he was speaking about his death. (He may or may not have been speaking about his death, we only know they thought he was.)
      ii. Indirect Commands (Chapter 28)
         *Precorque **ut impleat** Dominus verbum suum* (1 Sm 1:23). And I request that the Lord fulfills his word.
      iii. Indirect Questions (Chapter 31)
         Interrogābat sī homō Galilaeus esset (Mk 15:44). He was asking if he was a Galilean?"
2. Result (or consecutive) clauses (Chapter 29): "so ... that," "so ... as to"
   a. Form in Latin: lead verb + *adeo, ita, tam, sic, eo, tot, tantum, tam* + *ut, qui, quae, quod,* etc. + subjunctive verb.
      i. Adverbial
         *Sīc deus dīlēxit mundum sīc **ut** filium suum ūnigenitum **daret*** (Jn 3:16). God so loved the world so that [*sic ut*] he gave his only Son.

ii. Relative

*Deus mundum sīc dīlēxit, **quī** Fīlium **mitteret**.* God so loved the world, the one who sent his son.

3. Purpose (or final clauses) (Chapter 29): *in order to/that, to*
    a. Form in Latin: lead verb + *ut* + subjunctive verb.
        i. Adverbial

            *Venit **ut laudet** Deum.* He came into the church [for the purpose] that [*ut*] he praise God.
        ii. Relative

            *Pater fīliōs mittit ad scholam **quī** amīcōs eōrum **videant**.* The father sent his sons to school so that they might seed their friends.
4. Relative clauses (Chapter 30) (characteristic, or hiding purpose)
    a. Form in Latin: *esse* + *qui, quae, quod*, etc + subjunctive verb.
        i. Characteristic

            *Ille est **quī** cīvitātēs **dēleat**.* He is the sort who destroys cities.
5. Fear Clauses (Chapter 31)
    a. Form in Latin: Verbs of fearing + *ne*, or *ut* + subjunctive verb.

        *Timeō **nē** mē **necās**.* I fear lest you kill me (or, "I am afraid that you might kill me").
6. Doubting (Chapter 30)
    a. Form in Latin: Verbs or phrase of doubting + *quin* + subjunctive verb.

        *nulla est **dubitatio quin** de Deo vero et mundi creatore **dicatur*** (Origen, In Numeros Homiliae). There is no doubt whether it was speaking about the true God and Creator of the world.
7. Conditional Sentences: "If" (Chapter 32)
    a. Form in Latin: *Nisi, si, qui, quicumque*, etc. + subjunctive verb.

        *Sī **veniat**, salvet nōs.* If he should come, he will save us.
8. Temporal Clauses (Chapter 32)
    a. Form in Latin: *cum, dum, donec,* + subjunctive verb.

        ***Cum** Jēsus **vēnisset** Hierusalem, crucifixus erat.* When Jesus came to Jerusalem, he was crucified.

Independent (Chapter 30 and 32)

1. Imperatives (Chapter 30)
    a. Order, "Let them ... "
        i. Form: subjunctive

            Gaudent populi. Let the people rejoice.
    b. Prohibition, "Do not ..."
        i. Form: *ne* + subjunctive

            Ne timeas. You ought not fear.

c. Jussive subjunctive, "Let us ... "
     Ōrēmus. Eāmus. Let us pray. Let us go.
2. Deliberative (Chapter 30)
   a. Form: Interrogative + subjunctive:
      Quid faciam? What should I do?
3. Wishes, Optative (Chapter 32)
   a. Form: [*Utinam*] + subjunctive.
      Utinam tu sis salvus. I wish that you are saved.

§ 105. Verbs: Morphology of the Present Subjunctive

As a general note, in the following chapters we will continue the practice of learning morphology and meaning. With the subjunctive, however, we will need to keep in mind that whatever "meaning" we learn, it can be applied to any tense of the subjunctive. So the "meaning" of the present subjunctive is not only indirect commands, but it can be used for result, purpose, commands, etc. I will also intentionally avoid providing a "fixed formula" for translation, because the subjunctive depends so heavily on context.

You will notice in the table that the most important indicator of the present subjunctive is the presence of the *-e-* in place of the *-a-* in the first conjugation and then the presence of an *-a-* in the other three conjugations. Other than that, it looks very similar to the present active indicative and passive. For ē-verbs, i-verbs, and -io-verbs, you will have another vowel before the *-a-*: either *e*, for ē-verbs, or *-i-* for i-verbs and -io-verbs.

Active

ā-verb	ē-verb	i/e-verb	i-verb	io-verb	ESSE
laud|e|m	mone|a|m	duc|a|m	audi|a|m	capi|a|m	si|m
laud|ē|s	mone|ā|s	duc|ās	audi|ā|s	capi|a|s	sī|s
laud|e|t	mone|a|t	duc|a|t	audi|a|t	capi|a|t	si|t
laud|ē|mus	mone|ā|mus	duc|ā|mus	audi|ā|mus	capi|a|mus	sī|mus
laud|ē|tis	mone|ā|tis	duc|ā|tis	audi|ā|tis	capi|a|tis	sī|tis
laud|e|nt	mone|a|nt	duc|a|nt	audi|a|nt	capi|a|nt	si|nt

Passive

ā-verb	ē-verb	i/e-verb	i-verb	io-verb
laud|e|r	mone|a|r	duc|a|r	audi|a|r	capi|a|r
laud|ē|ris	mone|ā|ris	duc|ā|ris	audi|ā|ris	capi|ā|ris (capiāre)
laud|ē|tur	mone|ā|tur	duc|ā|tur	audi|ā|tur	capi|ā|tur
laud|ē|mur	mone|ā|mur	duc|ā|mur	audi|ā|mur	capi|ā|mur
laud|ē|minī	mone|ā|minī	duc|ā|minī	audi|ā|minī	capi|ā|minī
laud|e|ntur	mone|a|ntur	duc|a|ntur	audi|a|ntur	capi|a|ntur

§ 106. Verbs: Meaning of the Present Subjunctive Indirect Statements

We have already covered indirect statements and commands with the infinitive. These are situations where we have a lead verb that relates to saying, thinking, reporting, etc. In English, this would be something like, "I think that …" or "He said that …" or "We believe that …" etc. In Latin, *puto, dixit, credimus,* etc. These verbs can take the accusative plus infinitive.

Sciō tē esse bonum. I know that you are good.

We can also do indirect statements with *quia, quoniam,* and *quod* plus the indicative, just like English.

Sciō quia tū es bonus. I know that you are good.

Finally, Latin can make indirect statements with the subjunctive.

Sciō quia tū sīs bonus. I know that you are good.

We find all three of these in Ecclesiastical Latin:

Magister, scīmus quia rēctē dīcis et docēs (Lk 20:21). Teacher, we know that you speak and teach correctly.

Vīventēs enim sciunt sē esse moritūrōs (Eccl 9:5). For living they know that they are about to die.

Et nunc quia sciō quod certissimē rēgnātūrus sīs (Sm 24:21). And now I know that you will most certainly reign.

Sometimes the indirect statement has a relative clause containing the content of what is known or thought.

Cui Hazaël ait: "Quārē dominus meus flet"? At ille dīxit: "Quia sciō quae factūrus sīs fīliīs Israël mala." (2 Kgs 8:12)
Hazel said to him, "Why does my lord weep?" And he said, "Because I know those bad things you are about to do to the sons of Israel."

§ 107. Verbs: Meaning of the Present Subjunctive Indirect Commands

As we mentioned at the beginning of this section, the meaning of the subjunctive verb depends entirely on its context. Does it depend on the indicative verb? Does it stand alone? What is the conjunction that comes before it?

For our first consideration of meaning, we will look at subjunctive with indirect commands or requests. These subjunctives will depend on an indicative verb, usually in the first part of the sentence, and the clause with the subjunctive will begin with *ut*. Recall that *ut* means "that," "so that," "for the purpose that," etc.

Petō ut veniās (1 Kgs 15:19). I request that you come.

Notice that we are not using the words "may," "might," or other similar modal words. You could translate this as "I request that you might come," but it would not be good English. All the subjunctive is doing here is giving the content for the request and is so joined to the indicative verb, which is a verb of requesting or commanding. The Latin uses the subjunctive here because it is "joining" one clause with another. Furthermore, the object of the request is the clause that comes after the *ut*.

You might notice as well that we could say in Latin, *petō tē venīre*, "I request that you come." We could use an accusative and infinitive or a subjunctive. Either one is an acceptable Latin construction. They both have effectively the same meaning. In a rhetorical language, it is handy to have many possibilities for translation. Sometimes in Ecclesiastical Latin you will see phrases of indirect speech using *quia* instead of an accusative plus infinitive construction, or a subjunctive: *peto quia tu venis*. The use of *quia* fits more idiomatically into English. It would not have been standard Latin for Cicero, but it is worth pointing out that in many different forms of Ecclesiastical Latin, you will see Latin that is less than what the late ancient grammar manuals would suggest is pure *Latinitas*.

Sententiae Summāriae

Fac ut familia tua Deum laudet.
Magister monet ut nōs deum adōrēmus. Magister tuus monet ut vōs deum adōrētis?
Nōs petimus ut ab optimō duce dūcāmur in bellum.
Ōrāmus ut ab Deō audiāmur. Vōs ōrātis ut ab deīs vestrīs audiāminī?
Scīmus ut Jēsus sit Deus.
Precārīs ut salvus sit?

Translations

Make it so that your family praises God.
The teacher advises that we worship God. Does your teacher advise you that you all worship God?
We request that we are led by a great leader into war.
We pray that we are heard by God. Do you all pray that you all are heard by your gods?
We know that Jesus is God.
Do you pray that you are saved?

Cavēte et Mementōte

Remember that for the present subjunctive you have either an *e* where you would expect an *a* in the first conjugation, or you have an *a* in the other three conjugations. That is the only change from the indicative to the subjunctive.

The other thing to pay attention to is the presence of *ut*. *Ut* is one of the most common conjunctions that precede any use of the subjunctive. If you know that it means "that," it will go a long way to helping you recognize a subjunctive.

CHAPTER 28

Vocābula Memoranda

Nōmina

ēdictum, ēdictī (n.): decree, edict
hiems, hiemis (f.): winter
serpēns, serpentis (n.): snake
somnium, somniī (n.): sleep
vinculum, vinculī (n.): chain
virga, virgae (f.): scepter, rod

Verba

ā-verbs

jūdicō, jūdicāre, jūdicāvī, jūdicātus: judge
obsecrō, obsecrāre, obsecrāvī, obsectrātus: beg
exoptō [ex + optō], exoptāre, exoptāvī, exoptātus: desire, choose
postulō, postulāre, postulāvī, postulātus: ask, request

i/e-verbs

absolvō [ab + solvō], absolvere, absolvī, absolūtus: absolve
dēsinō [de + sinō], dēsinere, dēsīvī, dēsitus: stop
statuō, statuere, statuī, statūtus: establish, set up, decide
ulcīscor, ulcīscī,—, ultus sum: avenge, punish

-io-verb

efficiō [ex + faciō], efficere, effectī, effectūs: bring about, make, effect

Adjectīvum

caelestis, caelestis, caeleste: heavenly, celestial

Fābula Ficta

Ōlim Esther et pater ejus Mordachaeus, et quoque aliī Jūdaeī, fuērunt in exiliō in Babylōniā, Assuerō rēgnante. Esther pulcherrima omnium fēminārum ducta est in mātrimōniō a rēge Assuerō. Erat quīdam homō, nōmine Amān quī patrem Esther ōdit, nam Mordachaeus nōn volēbat adōrāre Amān, ducem prīncipum. Amān causa ulciscendī inimīcī ūniversam Jūdaeōrum gentem perdere statuit. Ēdictō audītō, Mordachaeus compellit Esther obsecrāre a rēge clēmentiam prō Jūdaeīs. Indūta est Esther rēgālibus vestīmentīs, et stetit in ātriō domūs rēgiae. Placuit oculīs rēgis Esther, et extendit contrā eam virgam auream.

Dīxitque ad eam rēx: "Quid vīs, Esther rēgīna? quae est petītiō tua? etiam sī dīmidiam partem rēgnī petīveris, dabitur tibi." Et respondit Esther, "Sī rēgī placet, obsecrō ut veniās ad mē hodiē, et Amān tēcum ad convīvium, quod parāvī." Vēnērunt itaque rēx et Amān ad convīvium, quod eīs rēgīna parāverat. Dīxitque eī rēx, postquam vīnum biberat abundanter: "Quid petis ut dētur tibi? et prō quā rē postulās? etiam sī dīmidiam partem rēgnī meī petierīs, accipiēs." Et respondit Esther, "Petō ut veniātis, rēx et Amān, ad convīvium quod parāvī eīs, et crās aperiam rēgī voluntātem meam." Intrāvit itaque rēx et Amān bibere cum rēgīnā. Dīxitque eī rēx etiam secunda diē, postquam vīnum biberant: "quae est petītiō tua, Esther, ut dētur tibi? et quid vīs fierī? etiam sī dīmidiam partem rēgnī meī petierīs, accipiēs." Ad quem illa respondit: "Sī invēnī grātiam in oculīs tuīs ō rēx, et sī tibi placet, dōnā mihi animam meam prō quā rogō, et populum meum prō quō obsecrō. Quīdam dux tuus imperat ut ego et populus meus interficiamur." Respondēnsque rēx Assuerus ait: "Quis est iste?" Dīxitque Esther: "Hostīs et inimīcus noster pessimus iste est Amān." Servus rēgīnae dīxit, "Ō Rēge, sī placet tibi, rogō ut Amān suspendatur in patibulō." Cui dīxit rēx, "fiat." Suspēnsus est itaque Amān in patibulō quod parāverat Mardochaeō.

Cf. Francis Lhomond, *Epitome Historiae Sacrae*, 185–187.

patibulum, patibulī (n.): gallows
exilium, exiliī (n.): exile
fiat: let it be
dimidia, dimidiae (f.): half
abundanter: abundantlty

1. Cur Amān patrem rēgīnae ōdit?
2. Quid Mordachaeus, pater Esther, eam petere a rēge postulābat?
3. Cur Esther voluit rēgem venīre ad convīvium?
4. Cuius patibulum fuit in quō Amān suspensus est?

Sententiae Interpretandae

1. Nōs quoque ōrāmus ut servīs Deī patris tuī dīmittās inīquitātem hanc. (Gn 50:17)
2. Vocāvit autem Pharaō Moysen et Aarōn, et dīxit eīs: Ōrātē Dominum ut auferat rānās ā mē et ā populō meō. (Ex 8:8)

rāna, rānae (f.): frog

3. Deus, quī per resurrēctiōnem Fīliī tuī Dominī nostrī Jēsu Chrīstī mundum laetificāre dignātus es: praestā, quaesumus, ut per ejus Genetrīcem Virginem Mariam perpetuae capiāmus gaudia vītae. Per eundem Chrīstum Dominum nostrum. (Rēgīna Caelī)
4. Haec enim omnia gentēs mundī quaerunt. Pater autem vester scit quoniam hīs indigētis. (Lk 12:30)
5. Audīvī dē tē, quoniam spīritum deōrum habeās. (Dn 5:14)
6. Irātus Dominus in Moysēn, ait: Aarōn frāter tuus Lēvītēs, sciō quod ēloquēns sit. (Ex 4:14)
7. Haec igitur dīcit Dominus: In hōc sciēs quod sim Dominus. (Ex 7:17)
8. Nunc scīmus quod nōbīscum sit Dominus. (Jos 22:31)

CHAPTER 28

9. Et nunc quia sciō quod certissimē rēgnātūrus sīs, et habitūrus in manū tuā rēgnum Israël. (1 Sm 24:21)
10. Convertiminī itaque peccātōrēs, et facite jūstitiam cōram Deō, crēdentēs quod faciat vōbīscum misericordiam suam. (Tb 13:8)
11. Ōrātē Dominum ut dēsinant tonitrua Deī et grandō. (Ex 9:28)

   tonitruum, tonitruī (n.): thunder
   grandō, grandinis (f.): hail

12. Peccāvimus, quia locūtī sumus contrā Dominum et tē: ōra ut tollat ā nōbīs serpentēs. Ōrāvitque Moysēs prō populō. (Nm 21:7)
13. Obsecrō, Domine, ut vir Deī, quem mīsistī, veniat iterum. (Jgs 13:8)
14. Sciō quia mortī trādēs mē. (Jb 30:23)
15. Scītis quia post bīduum Pascha fiet, et Fīlius hominis trādētur. (Mt 26:2)
16. Ōrāte autem ut nōn fiat fuga vestrā in hieme, vel sabbatō. (Mt 24:20)
17. Vigilāte et ōrāte, ut nōn intrētis in tentātiōnem. (Mk 14:38)
18. Ōrāmus autem Deum ut nihil malī faciātis. (2 Cor 13:7)
19. Petō, Domine, ut dē vinculō improperiī hujus absolvās mē. (Tb 3:15)

   improperium, improperiī: insults

20. Ut enim omnēs vīvant, ārdenter exoptat. (Augustine, *Epistula* 185)

   ardenter: ardently

21. Similiter et hīc nōn deō optāmus ut rēgnet, quī rēx est aeternōrum saeculōrum, cujus rēgnum nec initium habet nec fīnem; sed ut illud rēgnum, id est caeleste quod nōbīs prōmīsit, adveniat. (Chromatius of Aquila, *Tractātus in Mattheum* 28)
22. ipsum enim rēgnum optāmus ut veniat; hoc rēgnum ventūrum sānctī praedicant. (Augustine, *Ēnārrātiōnēs in Psalmōs* 144)
23. Ergō cum facis opera bona, hoc optā ut Deus in tē glōrificētur. (Augustine, *Sermō* 72)

CHAPTER 29

§ 108. Verbs: Morphology of the Imperfect Subjunctive

The important thing to pay attention to here is that the imperfect subjunctive takes the present active infinitive and adds the typical personal endings: *laudare-m, habere-s, dicere-t, audire-mus,* etc. Also, we will not be supplying a typical translation for the imperfect subjunctive. The meaning of the imperfect subjunctive is highly context dependent. We will learn a use of the subjunctive below that will include the imperfect subjunctive, but that is not the only way the imperfect subjunctive can be translated.

Active

ā-verb	ē-verb	i/e-verb	i-verb	-io-verb	esse
laudā|re|m	*monē|re|m*	*dūce|re|m*	*audī|re|m*	*cape|re|m*	*esse|m*
laudā|rē|s	*monē|rē|s*	*dūce|rē|s*	*audī|rē|s*	*cape|rē|s*	*essē|s*
laudā|re|t	*monē|re|t*	*dūce|re|t*	*audī|re|t*	*cape|re|t*	*esse|t*
laudā|rē|mus	*monē|rē|mus*	*dūce|rē|mus*	*audī|rē|mus*	*cape|rē|mus*	*essē|mus*
laudā|rē|tis	*monē|rē|tis*	*dūce|rē|tis*	*audī|rē|tis*	*cape|rē|tis*	*essē|tis*
laudā|re|nt	*monē|re|nt*	*dūce|re|nt*	*audī|re|nt*	*cape|re|nt*	*esse|nt*

Passive

ā-verb	ē-verb	i/e-verb	i-verb	-io-verb
laudā|re|r	monē|re|r	dūce|re|r	audī|re|r	cape|re|r
laudā|rē|ris	monē|rē|ris	dūce|rē|ris	audī|rē|ris	cape|rē|ris
laudā|rē|tur	monē|rē|tur	dūce|rē|tur	audī|rē|tur	cape|rē|tur
laudā|rē|mur	monē|rē|mur	dūce|rē|mur	audī|rē|mur	cape|rē|mur
laudā|rē|minī	monē|rē|minī	dūce|rē|minī	audī|rē|minī	cape|rē|minī
laudā|re|ntur	monē|re|ntur	dūce|re|ntur	audī|re|ntur	cape|re|ntur

Deponent verbs form their subjunctive as if they had a present active infinitive. So *sequerētur* and *precārētur* are imperfect deponent (passive in form, active in meaning) subjunctives.

§ 109. Verbs: Meaning with Purpose and Result

For this chapter, we are going to focus on the imperfect subjunctive in combination with a perfect active indicative as the lead verb. The imperfect subjunctive with purpose and result means that the verb in the subjunctive happens at the same time as the lead or main verb.

There is no specific form that gives you the difference between "purpose" and "result." Most often a subjunctive with result has *sīc* or *ita* with the lead verb.

The new meaning we are learning in this chapter can work with the present and imperfect subjunctive. This new use of the subjunctive express purposes or result. "I came to the house for the purpose of cleaning it." "I gave them bread so that they might eat it." The subjunctive in Latin will come after the purpose or that clause.

> Result: *Sīc enim Deus dīlēxit mundum,* **ut** *Fīlium suum ūnigenitum* **daret** (Jn 3:16).
> For God loved the world in this way [with the result] that he *gave* [*daret*: imperfect subjunctive] his only begotten son.

> Purpose: *Ut omnis quī crēdit in eum, nōn* **pereat***, sed* **habeat** *vītam æternam* (Jn 3:16).
> [With the purpose] that all who believe in him may not perish [*pereat*: present subjunctive] but may have eternal life [*habeat*: present subjunctive].

The primary way to tell the difference between purpose and result is the presence of either the word *sīc* or *ut*.

With respect to the use of the subjunctive with result, we have another case of "joining under" one clause to another. The subjunctive of result joins the secondary clause in the subjunctive to a primary clause.

The subjunctive still works the same with deponent verbs:

Purpose: *Jōannēs prīmum vēnit **ut major sequerētur*** (imperfect passive subjunctive).

We can separate out a more precise example for purpose here. "John came first so that a greater one might follow." The only clue to the different meanings in this verse and in John 3:16 is the presence of the word *sic*. For this reason, we must be very careful about context before we go to translate a subjunctive verb. We cannot assume what helping words we need in English to translate a subjunctive verb until we have considered the whole clause or sentence in which it comes.

We will cover the Sequence of Tenses in two parts. For now, when you come to a sentence with a verb in the subjunctive, translate it in the same tense as the main indicative verb.

§ 110. Verbs: Relative Clauses of Characteristic

These are clauses that will begin with a form *esse* and then be followed by a relative clause and the subjunctive. These are especially difficult because relative clauses to this point have been done in the indicative tense. But there are a subset of relative clauses that can take the subjunctive.

"He is the sort who would save his friends." *Ille est quī amīcōs suōs salvet.* (Notice the *quī* and then the subjunctive *salvet* rather than *salvat*.)

Nōn est quī faciat bonum, nōn est usque ad ūnum (Ps 13:3). There is not any of the sort who does good, not even up to one.

Magister, quid boni faciam, ut habeam vitam aeternam? (Mt 19:16)
Teacher what good must I do so that I may have eternal life?

§ 111. Sequence of Tenses Part 1

This section is entitled "sequence of tenses." This refers to the situation in Latin when a main verb is in one tense, and there is a second verb whose tense depends on that main verb. So the sequence of the tenses names the relationship between the main verb and the secondary verb, and how the time of the verb is understood: before, during, or after. We have now learned two different tenses for the subjunctive: the present tense and the imperfect tense. When we discussed tenses with the indicative verbs, it was fairly straightforward how the tense corresponded to English tenses. It is not straightforward with the subjunctive. A full explanation of the *sequence of tenses* will come in the next chapter. For now, we will talk about the difference between the present subjunctive and the imperfect subjunctive, when they are used in dependent clauses.

The basic rule is that if you have a lead verb (a non-subjunctive verb, typically indicative or possibly imperative) in the present, future, or future perfect, and sometimes the perfect, then you will expect to have a present subjunctive for the clause that follows. If you have a lead verb in the perfect, imperfect, or pluperfect, then you will expect to have an imperfect subjunctive in the clause that follows. The examples are given below.

Look for the changes in the main indicative verb in the primary tenses:

Maria vādit [present indicative] *ad monumentum, ut plōret* [present subjunctive] *ibi.*
Mary goes to the tomb so that she may cry there.

Maria vadet [future indicative] *ad monumentum, ut plōret* [present subjunctive] *ibi.*
Mary will go to the tomb so that she may cry there.

Si Maria vaserit [future-perfect indicative] *ad monumentum, ut plōret* [present subjunctive] *ibi* ... If Mary will have gone to the tomb so that she might cry there ...

Maria vasit [perfect indicative] *ad monumentum, ut plōret* [present subjunctive] *ibi.*
Mary went to the tomb so that she could cry there.

Look for the changes in the main indicative verb in the secondary tenses:

Maria vādēbat [imperfect indicative] *ad monumentum, ut plōrāret* [imperfect subjunctive] *ibi.* Mary was going to the tomb so that she might cry there.

Maria vāsit [perfect indicative] *ad monumentum, ut plōrāret* [imperfect subjunctive] *ibi.* Mary went to the tomb so that she might cry there.

Maria vāserat [pluperfect indicative] *ad monumentum, ut plōrāret* [imperfect subjunctive] *ibi.* Mary had gone to the tomb so that she might cry there.

In the first set of examples, we had the present subjunctive that happens at the same time as the primary verb tense. In the second set of examples, we had the imperfect subjunctive, which occurs simultaneously with secondary tense verbs. This should illustrate how Latin used these different tenses in specific ways.

Sententiae Summāriae

Venīmus in ecclēsiam ut Deum laudārēmus. Vōs venīstis in templum ut deōs vestrōs laudārētis?
Bonī discipulī in scholam veniēbant ut a magistrō docērentur. Aliī discipulī in campum veniēbant ut lūderent.
Ego ductus eram in ecclēsiam ut peccāta mea cōnfitērer.
Sic magister latinam amavit ut semper Latine loqueretur.
Ille est quī dūcat mīlitēs in bellum.

Translations

We came into the church, so that we might praise God. Did you all come into the temple for the purpose of praising your gods?
The good students were coming to school so that they might be taught by the teacher. Other students were coming into the field so that they could play.
I had been led into the church to confess my sins.
The teacher loved Latin so much that he was always speaking Latin.
He is the sort who leads soldiers into war.

Vocābula Memoranda

Nōmina

grabātus, grabātī (m.): mat, cot
īnsidiā, īnsidiae (f.): trap, snare, plot
lūx, lūcīs (f.): light, daylight
mercēs, mercēdis (f.): reward, wage, pay
messis, messis (n.): harvest
nātūra, nātūrae (f.): nature
pūblicānus, pūblicānī (m.): publican, tax collector
rēgiō, regiōnis (f.): region, area
scelus, sceleris (n.): crime, wicked deed

Verba

ā-verb
labōrō, labōrāre, labōrāvi, labōrātus: labor, work
ē-verb
ārdeō, ārdēre, ārsi, ārsus: burn, be on fire
i/e-verb
metō, metere, messui, messus: harvest

Adjectīva

proprius, -a, -um: one's own, own
sollicitus, -a, -um: worry

Adverbia

aliunde: elsewhere, from elsewhere
statim: immediately

Fābula Excerpta

Āmēn, āmēn dīcō vōbīs: quī nōn intrat per ōstium in ovīle ovium, sed ascendit aliunde, ille fūr est et latrō. Quī autem intrat per ōstium, pāstor est ovium. Huic ōstiārius aperit, et ovēs vōcem ejus audiunt, et propriās ovās vocat nōminātim, et ēdūcit eās. Et cum propriās ovēs ēmīserit, ante eās vādit: et ovēs illum sequuntur, quia sciunt vōcem ejus. Aliēnum autem nōn sequuntur, sed fugiunt ab eō: quia nōn nōvērunt vōcem aliēnōrum. Hoc prōverbium dīxit eīs Jēsus: illī autem nōn cognōvērunt quid loquerētur eīs. Dīxit ergō eīs iterum Jēsus: Āmēn, āmēn dīcō vōbīs, quia ego sum ōstium ovium. Omnēs quotquot vēnērunt, fūrēs sunt, et latrōnēs, et nōn audiērunt eōs ovēs. Ego sum ōstium. Per mē sī quis introierit, salvābitur: et ingrediētur, et ēgrediētur, et pāscua inveniet. Fūr nōn venit nisi ut fūrētur, et mactet, et perdat. Ego vēnī ut vītam habeant, et abundantius habeant. Ego sum pāstor bonus. Bonus pāstor animam suam dat prō ovibus suīs. Mercēnārius autem, et quī nōn est pāstor, cujus nōn sunt ovēs propriæ, videt lupum venientem, et dīmittit ovēs, et fugit: et lupus rapit, et dispergit ovēs; mercēnārius autem fūgit, quia mercēnārius est, et nōn pertinet ad eum dē ovibus. Ego sum pāstor bonus: et cognōscō meās, et cognōscunt mē meæ. Sīcut nōvit mē Pater, et ego agnōscō Patrem: et animam meam pōnō prō ovibus meīs. Et aliās ovēs habeō, quæ nōn sunt ex hōc ovīlī: et illās oportet mē addūcere, et vōcem meam audient, et fiet ūnum ovīle et ūnus pāstor. Proptereā mē dīligit Pater: quia ego pōnō animam meam, ut iterum sūmam eam. Nēmō tollit eam ā mē: sed ego pōnō eam ā meipsō, et potestātem habeō pōnendī eam, et potestātem habeō iterum sūmendī eam. Hoc mandātum accēpī ā Patre meō.

John 10:1-18

fur, furis (m.): thief
latro, latronis (m.): robber, brigand
nominatim: by name
macto, mactare, mactavi, mactatus: slaughter
dispergo, dispergere, dispersi, dispersus: scatter, disperse
lupus, lupi (m.): wolf
pascuum, pascui (n.): pasture
propterea: therefore, for this reason
mercenarius, mercenarii (m.): hired worker, laborer
ostiarius, ostiarii (m.): doorkeeper
ovilis, ovilis, ovile: relating to sheep

1. Quid est latro et fur?
2. Quomodo scimus pastorem ab latrone an fure?
3. Ovēs latrōnem sequuntur? Quid agunt?
4. Cūr bonus pastor venit?
5. Quid est discrīmen (the difference) inter pastōrem et mercēnārium?
6. Cūr pater fīlium amat? Quid agit fīlius?

Sententiae Interpretandae

1. Ōrāte prō invicem, ut salvēminī.
2. Fac ut ārdeat cor meum in āmandō Chrīstum Deum. (Stābat Māter)
3. Statimque tunc Paulum dīmīsērunt frātrēs, ut īret usque ad mare. (Acts 11:8)
4. Nōs autem nōn spīritum mundī accēpimus, sed Spīritum, quī ex Deō est, ut sciāmus, quae ā Deō dōnāta sunt nōbīs. (1 Cor 2:12)
5. Fuit homō missus ā Deō, cui nōmen erat Jōannēs; hic venit in testimōnium, ut testimōnium perhibēret dē lūmine ut omnēs crēderent per illum. Nōn erat ille lūx, sed ut testimōnium perhibēret dē lūmine. (Jn 1:6–7)
6. Erat mihi enim meliōrum cōpia, illa autem dēcerpsī, tantum ut fūrārer. (Augustine, *Confessions* 2.6.12)

dēcerpo, dēcerpere, dēcerpsi, dēcerptus: pluck

7. Et abiit, et adhaesit ūnī cīvium regiōnis illīus: et mīsit illum in vīllam suam ut pāsceret porcōs. (Lk 15:15)
8. Erant autem appropinquantēs eī pūblicānī, et peccātōrēs ut audīrent illum. (Lk 15:1)
9. Et nōn respondit eī ad ūllum verbum, ita ut mīrārētur praeses vehementer. (Mt 27:14)
10. Et praecurrēns ascendit in arborem sycomōrum ut vidēret eum: quia inde erat trānsitūrus. (Lk 19:4)

sycomorum, sycomōrī (n.): mulberry, ficus

11. Ego autem nōn ab homine testimōnium accipiō: sed haec dīcō ut vōs salvī sītis. (Jn 5:34)
12. Et statim surrēxit ille: et, sublātō grabātō, abiit cōram omnibus, ita ut mīrārentur omnēs, et honōrificent Deum, dīcentēs: Quia numquam sīc vīdimus. (Mk 2:12)
13. Aufer ā nōbīs, quaesumus, Domīne, iniquitātēs nostrās: ut ad Sāncta sanctōrum pūrīs mereāmur mentibus introīre. (*Ordo Romanus*)
14. Tunc oblātus est eī daemonium habēns caecus et mūtus et cūrāvit eum ita ut loquerētur et vidēret. (Mt 12:22)
15. Et veniēns in patriam suam, docēbat eōs in synagōgīs eōrum, ita ut mīrārentur, et dīcerent: Unde huic sapientia haec, et virtūtēs? (Mt 13:54)
16. Fīlius autem hominis nōn habet, ubi caput reclīnet. (Mt 8:20)

reclinare: to lay, recline

17. Nam et Pater tālēs quaerit, quī adōrent eum. (Jn 4:23)
18. Et mīsērunt nūntiōs ad omnem tribum Benjamin, quī illis dīcerent. (Jgs 20:12)

tribus, tribi (m.): tribe

19. Et mīsit nūntiōs ad rēgem filiōrum Ammōn, quī ex persōnā suā dīcerent: Quid mihi et tibi est, quia vēnistī contrā mē, ut vastārēs terram meam? (Jgs 11:12)

Quid mihi et tibi est: What do I have to do with you?
vastare: destroy

20. Et observantēs mīsērunt īnsidiātōrēs, quī sē jūstōs simulārent, ut capārent eum in sermōne, ut trāderent illum prīncipātuī, et potestātī praesidis. (Lk 20:20)

insidiator, insidiatoris (m.): deciever, attacker, plotter

21. Prope est Dominus, frātrēs meī, ut nihil sollicitī sītis…. Nōlīte dēficere, nōlīte lassārī: quaerite eum dum invenīrī potest, invocāte eum dum prope est. Prope est Dominus hīs quī trībulātō sunt corde: prope est exspectantibus eum, exspectantibus eum in vēritāte. (Bernard of Clairvaux, Sermō IV in *Vigiliā Nātivitātis Dominī*)

sollicitus, -a, -um: concerned, worried
lassāre: to grow weary, tire out

22. Deus homō factus est nātūrā mīrante. (*Gaudēte*)
23. Tālis enim est nātūra corporum ut tempore assūmant perfectiōnem. (Thomas Aquinas, *Catēna Aurea in Jōhannem* 3.2)
24. Et ideō nōn ā prīncipiō generātiōnem ejus coepit dēscrībere, sed posteāquam Baptisma ejus explicuit; ut secundum nātūram et secundum grātiam Deī filium dēmōnstrāret. (Thomas Aquinas, *Catēna Aurea in Lūcam*, 3.8.418)
25. Praetereā, illud quod convenit filiō Deī per nātūram, convenit filiō hominis per grātiam. (Augustine, *Dē Trīnitāte* 3)
26. Sed per orīgināle peccātum nāscimur filiī īrae, ut Eph. 2, 3: erāmus nātūrā filiī īrae; per baptismum autem regenerāmur in filiōs grātiae. (Thomas Aquinas, *In II Sententiarum* 32.1.1.2)
27. Dā nōbīs rēgem, ut jūdicet nōs. Et ōrāvit Samuel ad Dominum. (1 Sm 8:6)
28. Domine, aperī oculōs hujus, ut videat. (2 Kgs 6:17)
29. Ergō nōlī quaerere intellegere ut crēdās, sed crēde ut intellegās; quoniam nisi crēdideritis, nōn intellegētis. (Augustine, *Tractātus CXXIV in Jōhannis ēvangelium*)
30. Appāruit autem Dominus Salomōnī per somnium nocte, dīcēns: Postulā quod vīs ut dem tibi. (1 Kgs 3:5)
31. Quid petis ut dētur tibi? (Est 5:6)
32. Praesta, quaesumus, ut per ejus Genetrīcem Virginem Mariam, perpetuae capiāmus gaudia vītae.

genetrīx, genetrīcis (f.): mother, ancestor

CHAPTER 30

§ 112. Verbs: Morphology of Irregular Verbs *nolle, velle, malle*

There are several modal verbs that have their own unique subjunctives. The forms will be covered below. As with other present and imperfect subjunctives we have used in the previous two chapters, the meaning of the verbs below, when used in the subjunctive, will vary depending on their context.

volō, velle, voluī,—: wish, will, want
nōlō, nōlle, nōluī,—: not want, not will, not wish
mālō, malle, māluī,—: prefer

Present Active Subjunctive:

[ego]	velim, nōlim, mālim
[tu]	velīs, nolīs, malīs
[is / ea]	velit, nōlit, mālit
[nos]	velimus, nōlimus, mālimus
[vos]	velītis, nolītis, mālītis
[ii / eae]	velint, nolint, mālint

The imperfect active subjunctive of these follows the normal pattern of infinitive plus personal endings.

CHAPTER 30

§ 113. Verbs: Meaning of Independent Imperative Subjunctives

This section will focus on possibly the hardest part of the subjunctive: the independent use of the subjunctive. In this case, there are no "clue" words that will help you anticipate a subjunctive. These subjunctives stand alone. These are the kinds of subjunctives you are most likely to see in prayers and invocations. Noticing the genre of what you are reading will help you be on the lookout for possible independent uses of the subjunctive. In what follows, the speaker expresses a command or request.

There are several big words in the section heading: "hortatory subjunctive" and "jussive subjunctive." Hortatory is what we call the independent subjunctive in the first person, "let us go."

Oremus. Let us pray. (compare: *oramus*, "we pray")

Eamus in Judaeam iterum. Let us go into Judaea again. (compare: *imus*, "we go")

The jussive is what we call the independent second and third person subjunctives, "let him go." There is also a jussive use of the future indicative, "you shall love your neighbor." *Dīligēs proximum suum.*

Tollat crucem et sequātur mē. "Let him take up his cross and follow me."
 - Compare this with the indicative: *Tollit crucem et sequitur mē.* "He takes up his cross and he follows me."

Nē timeās. "You should not fear."
 - Compare this with the indicative: *Nōn timēs.* "You do not fear."
 - Sometimes this is called a prohibitive, as the speaker wants to prohibit or stop an action of another person.

Haec hostia fidēlium tuōrum corpora mentēsque santificet. "Let this host sanctify the bodies and minds of your faithful ones."

In this case, we are using the subjunctive as a kind of imperative. So we can use the words *may* or *let* in our translations of these subjunctives.

The expression of commands in the subjunctive come with the word *ne* rather than *non*, if the speaker does not want the verb to occur.

§ 114. Verbs: Meaning of Optative, Deliberative, and Doubting Words

In some cases, Latin can use the subjunctive on its own to express a wish, desire, or deliberation over an action. To begin the desire, sometimes the word *utinam* is added, which makes it easier to translate. It is called the "optative" from the Latin word *optare*, meaning "to wish" or "to desire."

Israël, utinam audiās mē (Ps 80:9). "Israel, would that you listen to me."

Although not very common, on some occasions a speaker will want to deliberate over an action and state it explicitly using the subjunctive. The most common phrases of this are *quid dicam, quid faciam, quid agam.*

Quid faciam populō huic (Ex 17:4)? What shall I do to this people?

If you use a word of doubting *dubitare* or *dubium*, Latin requires the additional word *quin* (that).

Et mandāvit eī (haud dubium quīn esset Mordochaeus) ut ingrederētur ad rēgem, et rogāret prō populō suō et prō patriā suā (Est 15:1). And he commanded her (no doubt that indeed it was Mordechai) that she go to the king and ask for her people and for her country.

Sententiae Summāriae

Laudēmus deum! Ōrēmus deō!
Nē moneāminī ab daemonibus. Nē moneās bonās ancillās.
Audiāmus cantica bona! Nē audiātis cantica mala.
Quid dīcam dē morte Deī? Utinam hominēs vēritātem audiant.

Translations

Let us praise God. Let us pray to God.
Do not be taught by demons. Do not teach good servants.
Let us listen to the good songs. Do not listen to bad songs.
What might I say about the death of God? I wish that people would listen to the truth.

CHAPTER 30

Vocābula Memoranda

Nōmina

jūcunditās, jūcunditātis (f.): charm, pleasantness
fundāmentum, fundāmentī (n.): foundation
offēnsiō, offēnsiōnis (f.): displeasure; accident
nūptiae, nūptiārum (f. pl.): wedding, marriage
pars, partis (f.): part
pontifex, pontificis (m.): bishop, pope [*lit.* "bridge maker"]
perīculum, perīculī (n.): danger, peril

Verba

ā-verbs

abnegō [ab + negō], abnegāre, abnegāvī, abnegātus: deny
īnsonō [in + sonō], īnsonāre, īnsonuī, īnsonitus: resound
jūbilō, jūbilāre, jūbilāvī, jūbilātus: rejoice
mūtō, mūtāre, mūtāvī, mūtātus: change, move, shift
simulō, simulāre, simulāvī, simulātus: imitate

io-verb

ēripiō [ex + rapiō], ēripere, ēripuī, ēreptus: snatch away
perficiō [per + faciō], perficere, perfēcī, perfectus: complete, perfect
prōficiō [pro + faciō], prōficere, prōfēcī, profectus: make, accomplish

Adjectīva

albus, -a, -um: white, ready for the harvest
illicitus, -a, -um: forbidden, illicit

Praepositiō

propter (+acc): on account of

Prōnōmina

semetipsum: himself
temetipsum: yourself
memetipsum: myself

Conjūnctīvum

dōnec: (+subj) until

Adverbia

forsitan: (+subj) perhaps; (*fors-sit-an*, "it would be a chance whether")
fortasse: (+ind) maybe
utinam: (+subj) if only, would that
quin: (+subj) indeed, in fact

Fābula Excerpta

Exiērunt ergō dē cīvitāte et veniēbant ad eum. Intereā rogābant eum discipulī, dīcentēs: "Rabbī, mandūcā." Ille autem dīcit eīs: "Ego cibum habeō mandūcāre, quem vōs nescītis." Dīcēbant ergō discipulī ad invicem: "Numquid aliquis attulit eī mandūcāre?" Dīcit eīs Jēsus: "Meus cibus est ut faciam voluntātem ejus quī mīsit mē, ut perficiam opus ejus. Nōnne vōs dīcitis quod adhūc quattuor mēnsēs sunt, et messis venit? Ecce dīcō vōbīs: levāte oculōs vestrōs, et vidēte regiōnēs, quia albae sunt jam ad messem. Et quī mētit, mercēdem accipit, et congregat frūctum in vītam aeternam: ut et quī sēminat, simul gaudeat, et quī mētit. In hōc enim est verbum vērum: quia alius est quī sēminat, et alius est quī mētit. Ego mīsī vōs metere quod vōs nōn labōrāvistis: aliī labōrāvērunt, et vōs in labōrēs eōrum introistis. Ex cīvitāte autem illā multī crēdidērunt in eum Samarītānōrum, propter verbum mulieris testimōnium perhibentis: Quia dīxit mihi omnia quaecumque fēcī."

Cf. John 4

interea: meanwhile
albus, -a, -um: white, mature
messis, messis (m.): harvest
merces, mercedis (f.): pay

1. Quid erat cibus Jesū?
2. Cur Jesus discipulīs imperāvit ut oculī discipulōrum leverentur?
3. Cur Jesus discipulōs mīsit metere et nōn sēmināre?

CHAPTER 30

Sententiae Interpretandae

1. At ille respondit: Quis est Dominus, ut audiam vōcem ejus, et dīmittam Isrāēl? Nesciō Dominum, et Isrāēl nōn dīmittam. (Ex 5:2)
2. Venīte, exsultēmus dominō et jūbilēmus deō, salūtārī nostrō! (Ps 94:1)
3. Gaudeāmus, et exsultēmus: et dēmus glōriam eī: quia vēnērunt nūptiæ Agnī, et uxor ejus praeparāvit sē. (Rv 19:7)
4. Benedīcat vōs omnipotēns Deus, Pater et Fīlius et Spīritus Sānctus.
5. Et ne velitis dicere intra vos: Patrem habemus Abraham. (Mt 3:9)
6. Sed tē laudet anima mea, ut amet tē. (Augustine, *Confessions* 5)
7. Corpus Dominī nostrī Jēsū Chrīstī cūstōdiat animam tuam in vītam aeternam. (Ordo Missae)
8. Exsultet jam angelica caelōrum: exsultent dīvīna mystēria: et prō tantī [so great] Rēgis victōriā tuba īnsonet salūtāris. (Exsultet)

tuba, tubae (f.): trumpet

9. Misereātur nostrī omnipotēns Deus, et, dīmissīs peccātīs nostrīs, perdūcat nōs ad vītam aeternam. (Cōnfiteor)
10. Tibi serviat omnis creātūra tua. (Jgs 16:17)
11. Quandō fundāmenta ēvertuntur, iūstus quid faciat? (Ps 10:3)

ēvertō, ēvertere: turn upside down

12. Habeās cōnscientiam bonam, et Deus bene tē dēfēnsābit. (Thomas a Kempis, *Imitātiō Chrīstī*, 2.2.1)

dēfēnsāre, dēfēnsāvī, dēfēnsus: defend

13. Per Mariae et omnium sānctōrum intercessiōnem, rogēmus Patrem ut nōs respicere dignētur.
14. V. Domine, exaudī ōrātiōnem meam. R. Et clāmor meus ad tē veniat. V. Benedīcāmus Dominō. R. Deō grātiās. V. Fidēlium animae per misericordiam Deī requiēscant in pāce. R. Āmēn. (Cf. Psalm 101)
15. Dīcēbat autem ad omnēs: Sī quis vult post mē venīre, abneget sēmetipsum, et tollat crucem suam quotīdiē, et sequātur mē. Quī enim voluerit animam suam salvam facere, perdet illam: nam quī perdiderit animam suam propter mē, salvam faciet illam. Quid enim prōficit homō, sī lucrētur ūniversum mundum, sē autem ipsum perdat, et dētrīmentum suī faciat? Nam quī mē ērubuerit, et meōs sermōnēs: hunc Fīlius hominis ērubēscet cum vēnerit in majestāte suā, et Patris, et sānctōrum angelōrum. Dīcō autem vōbīs vērē: sunt aliquī hīc stantēs, quī nōn gustābunt (taste) mortem dōnec videant rēgnum Deī. (Lk 9:23–27)

ērubēscere: to be ashamed of

16. Hīc līber quī attitulātur Rufinī nōn tē sēdūcat, Ō pie lēctor, quia Pelagiānus est et blasphēmiīs Pelagiānōrum plēnus. Simulāns enim contrā Ariānōs disputātiōnem, venēna suae hereseos īnservit. (Scribal Notation from *Dē Fide*)

venēnum, ī: venom, poison
inserere, inservī: sow in

17. Nisi dīxerītis mihi quis est quī mandūcet cibōs hōs, moriēminī. (Dn 14)
18. Ecce ego suscitabo super eos Medos, qui argentum non quaerant, nec aurum velint. (Is 13:17)

suscitāre: encourage, arouse
Medus: Mede
argentum: silver
aurum: gold

19. Quid est, quod nesciat, quī nōvit omnia quae deī sunt? (Ambrose, *Dē Spīritū Sānctō* 2.11.126)
20. Sīc et Chrīstus nōn sēmetipsum clārificāvit ut pontifex fieret: sed quī locūtus est ad eum: Fīlius meus es tū, ego hodiē genuī tē. (Heb 5:5)

clārificāre: to clarify

21. Nam cum in baptismō ūnīcuique peccāta sua remittantur, probat et dēclārat in ēvangeliō suō dominus per eōs sōlōs posse peccāta dīmittī quī habeant spīritum sānctum. (Cyprian of Carthage, *Epistle* 69)
22. Et dedit illī potestātem quōcumque vellet īre. (Tb 1:14)
23. Nec erat quī nōlentēs cōgeret ad bibendum, sed sīcut rēx statuerat, praepōnēns mēnsīs singulōs dē prīncipibus suīs ut sūmeret ūnusquisque quod vellet. (Est 1:8)

cōgō, cōgere, coēgī, coāctus: force, compel

24. Aliī rūrsus praefidentēs dē jūstitiā suā, sīc volunt jūstum ut nōllent misericordem. (Augustine, *Sermō* 22.5)

praefidēns, praefidentis: so confident

25. Sit glōria Dominī in saeculum; laetābitur Dominus in operibus suīs. Quī respicit terram, et facit eam tremere; quī tangit montēs, et fūmigant. Cantābō Dominō in vītā meā; psallam Deō meō quamdiū sum. Jūcundum sit eī ēloquium meum; ego vērō dēlectābor in Dominō. Dēficiant peccātōrēs ā terrā, et inīquī, ita ut nōn sint. Benedic, animā meā, Dominō. (Ps 103:31–35)
26. Nōn est Deus quasi homō, ut mentiātur, nec ut fīlius hominis, ut mūtētur. Dīxit ergō, et nōn faciet? locūtus est, et nōn implēbit? (Nm 23:19)

27. Littera gesta docet
Quid crēdās allēgoriā
Mōrālia quid agās
Quō tendās anagogia.
(*Quadrīgā*)

> *gestum, gestī* (n.): deeds, exploits
> *allēgoria, allēgoriae* (f.): allegory
> *mōrālius, -a, -um*: relating to morals, or philosophy
> *quo*: to which
> *tendō, tendere*: strīve for
> *anagogia, anagogiae* (f.): anagogy, what is above

28. Nōn enim volumus ignōrāre vōs, frātrēs, dē trībulātiōne nostrā, quae facta est in Asiā, quoniam suprā modum gravātī sumus suprā virtūtem, ita ut taedēret nōs etiam vīvere. Sed ipsī in nobismetipsīs respōnsum mortis habuimus, ut nōn sīmus fidentēs in mortuōs, sed in Deō, quī suscitat mortuōs: quī dē tantīs perīculīs nōs ēripuit, et ēruit: in quem spērāmus quoniam et adhūc ēripiet. (2 Cor 1:8–10)

> *gravātus*: pressed
> *suprā*: beyond
> *suscitāre*: revive

29. Visita, quaesumus, Domīne, habitationem istam, et omnēs insidias inimicī ab eā longe repelle: Angelī tuī sānctī habitent in eā, quī nōs in pāce custodiant; et benedictio tua sit super nōs semper.

> *repellere*: to push away

30. Quis enim hoc mortālium? Nam tū semper aderās misericorditer saeviēns, et amārissimīs aspergēns offēnsiōnibus omnēs illicitās jūcunditātēs meās, ut ita quaererem sine offēnsiōne jūcundārī, et ubi hoc possem, nōn invenīrem quidquam praeter tē, Domine? (Augustine, *Confessions* 2.2.4)

> *saeviēns*: severe
> *amārus*: bitter

CHAPTER 31

☙❧

§ 115. Verbs: Morphology of the Perfect Subjunctive

The important thing to notice here is that we essentially have the same chart as the future perfect active indicative. We take the perfect stem and add the future indicative of *esse*. The only change from the future perfect active chart to the perfect subjunctive active chart is the first person singular that changes from *laudāvero* to *laudāverim*, *monuero* to *monuerim*, etc.

Active

ā-verb	ē-verb	i/e-verb	i-verb	-io-verb	esse
laudāv|eri|m	*monu|eri|m*	*dūx|eri|m*	*audīv|eri|m*	*cēp|eri|m*	*fu|eri|m*
laudāv|eri|s	*monu|eri|s*	*dūx|eri|s*	*audīv|eri|s*	*cēp|eri|s*	*fu|eri|s*
laudāv|eri|t	*monu|eri|t*	*dūx|eri|t*	*audīv|eri|t*	*cēp|eri|t*	*fu|eri|t*
laudāv|eri|mus	*monu|eri|mus*	*dūx|eri|mus*	*audīv|eri|mus*	*cēp|eri|mus*	*fu|eri|mus*
laudāv|eri|tis	*monu|eri|tis*	*dūx|eri|tis*	*audīv|eri|tis*	*cēp|eri|tis*	*fu|eri|tis*
laudāv|eri|nt	*monu|eri|nt*	*dūx|eri|nt*	*audīv|eri|nt*	*cēp|eri|nt*	*fu|eri|nt*

Passive

ā-verb	ē-verb	i/e-verb	i-verb
laudātus (-a, -um) sim	*monitus (-a, -um) sim*	*ductus (-a, -um) sim*	*audītus (-a, -um) sim*
laudātus (-a, -um) sis	*monitus (-a, -um) sis*	*ductus (-a, -um) sis*	*audītus (-a, -um) sis*
laudātus (-a, -um) sit	*monitus (-a, -um) sit*	*ductus (-a, -um) sit*	*audītus (-a, -um) sit*
laudātī (-ae, -a) simus	*monitī (-ae, -a) simus*	*ductī (-ae, -a) simus*	*audītī (-ae, -a) simus*
laudātī (-ae, -a) sitis	*monitī (-ae, -a) sitis*	*ductī (-ae, -a) sitis*	*audītī (-ae, -a) sitis*
laudātī (-ae, -a) sint	*monitī (-ae, -a) sint*	*ductī (-ae, -a) sint*	*audītī (-ae, -a) sint*

Now that we have seen the full chart, this chart raises the important question: "How do we know when we have the perfect subjunctive or the future-perfect indicative?" And the answer is context. You will usually have the perfect subjunctive after a conjunction that takes the subjunctive. *Utrum, ut, cum,* etc. You might have the perfect subjunctive after a question, which we will learn below.

The other way you will know is by recalling what you need for the future-perfect indicative. Those are primarily used in conditionals. In practice, it is very unlikely that these two forms will be confused when you take into account the contextual clues. Furthermore, the perfect subjunctive does not get used as frequently as the other subjunctives.

§ 116. Verbs: Meaning of Fear Clauses

With clauses of "fearing" we have the unfortunate task of disentangling some confusing constructions. Verbs like *timēre* and *verērī* often have a subjunctive which follows. "The teacher fears that [*ne*] the students will leave." This is something the teacher does not want to happen. In Latin, the word for "that" in the previous sentence looks like a negation. *Magister timet nē discipulī discēdant.* It is a negation in the sense that it is a negative fear. But the *nē* introduces an affirmative clause. We can turn this sentence around and say, "what the teacher wishes would not happen the teacher fears will happen [*nē*]."

We can also reverse the above construction:

The teacher wishes that the students will remain, but he fears that it will not happen [*ut*]. *Magister timet ut discipulī remānant.*

A frequent student question is how such strange constructions occur. It is important to remember that no one decided "Latin should do this very odd thing." Rather, Latin speakers did this thing that appears odd to English speakers, and possibly even less educated Latin speakers, and it became a rule. It just tells you what you find, not why you find it that way.[1]

This then becomes, "the teacher fears that the students will leave."

Perhaps the most succinct way to explain fears clauses is to translate *ne* as "that" and *ut* as "that ... not." This will of course be counterintuitive to English, but as with many things in Latin, once the student sees many repetitions it will feel more natural.

Vidēns autem Pīlātus, quod multōs sēdūxerat dē tetrarchiā Hērōdis, **timuit, nē** *post eōs sēdūceret eōs quī erant dē tetrarchiā suā* (Bonaventure, *Commentārius in Ēuangelium sānctī* Lūcae 13.1.2).

Pilate, however, seeing that [Jesus] had led many away from the tetrarchy of Herod, feared that he would lead away after them those who were from his own tetrarchy.

---

1 One explanation is that originally Latin had two clauses. *Magister timet. nē discipulī discēdant*, "The teacher fears. If only the students would not leave." Andrew Keller, *Learn to Read Latin Textbook* (Yale University Press, 2004) 473.

§ 117. Verbs: Meaning of Indirect Questions

An indirect question would be a question or statement in reported speech. The wording would not be exactly the same as in the original language but would change slightly because it is being reported. Sometimes in indirect questions what follows the lead verb will be in the subjunctive. So you will have a verb of knowing or questioning, which in classical Latin would be followed either by an accusative plus infinitive or with the subjunctive.

*Invenitque eum vir errantem in agrō, et interrogāvit **quid quaereret*** (Gen 37:15).

And a man found him wandering in the field and asked him what he was seeking.

Notice that the substance of the question begins with *quid* and then is followed by a verb in the subjunctive, *quaereret*.[2]

In the following section will be more examples of indirect questions and how tense works in the subjunctive following the sequence of tenses.

Some words that previously required an accusative plus infinitive can also take a subjunctive.

*Jēsus autem ait eīs: "Nescītis quid **petātis**."* (Mk 10:38).

Jesus however said to them, "You do not know what you are seeking."

The second verb, *petātis*, comes in the subjunctive as it is subordinated to the main verb, *nescītis*. If you recall, early in chapter 10 we learned about using the accusative plus infinitive for head verbs. These can also take the subjunctive, as we saw in the sentence just above. In the Vulgate sometimes you will find a construction that more naturally mimics the English:

*Nōn rogō ut tollās eōs dē mundō, sed ut **servēs** eōs ā mālō* (Jn 17:15).

I am not asking that you take them out of the world, but that you keep them from evil [or the evil one].

*Vigilāte ergō nescītis enim quandō dominus domus **veniat*** (Mk 13:35).

Stay awake therefore for you do not know when the Lord of the house may come.

In Ecclesiastical Latin, this rule is not always followed, and sometimes there will be simply an indicative following a verb of knowing.

*Dīcit eīs: Quia tulērunt Dominum meum: et nesciō ubi **posuērunt** eum* (Jn 20:13).

She says to them: They have taken my Lord and I do not know where they have put him.

---

[2] Occasionally you will find indirect questions that do not take the subjunctive in the Vulgate: *Rogate quae ad pacem sunt Jerusalem, et abundantia diligentibus te* (Ps 121:6).

CHAPTER 31

§ 118. Sequence of Tenses Part II

Now that we have added some more uses of the subjunctive, it will be helpful to review all the possibilities of the sequences of tenses. When you have a main indicative verb that can be followed by a subjunctive, the tense of the main verb will influence which subjunctive follows. Remember that there is no future in the subjunctive and that there is no aspect in the subjunctive. The relationship between the tense of the subjunctive verb with the main verb of the sentence is something that just has to be memorized. It makes sense once you have seen it a few times. Especially in the first year of language study, I would not necessarily require that students know how to predict which tense will be used, but just that they recognize what tense is used.

If the main verb of the lead sentence is in the present, future, or future-perfect (and sometimes perfect), the subjunctive mood verb that follows it can only be in the present, perfect subjunctive, or a future participle with the present subjunctive. It will be in the present if it happens at the same time as the main verb or subsequent to the main verb, the perfect if the second verb happened before the main verb, or the future active participle plus the present subjunctive if the verb would happen in the future. Occasionally you will find the present subjunctive if the verb would happen in the future without the future active participle.

If the main verb of the lead sentence is in the imperfect, perfect, or pluperfect, the subjunctive mood verb that follows it can only be in the imperfect, pluperfect, or future active participle and the imperfect. The following subjunctive verb will be in the imperfect if it happens at the same time as the main verb, the pluperfect if it happens before, and the future participle with the imperfect if it would have happened in the future.

Let's have a look at a few examples.

Here is what happens when we change the tenses of the secondary subjunctive verb.

Direct speech without the subjunctive:
Jēsus interrogat eum, "quid vidēs [present indicative]*" / "quid vīdis* [perfect indicative]*" / "quid vidēbis"* [future indicative]? Jesus asked him what, "What do you see" / "did you see" / "will you see?"

Indirect speech with the subjunctive in the primary tenses (in a similar question):
Jēsus interrogat (interrogābit; interrogāverit; interrogāvit) eum sī quid videat [present subjunctive]. Jesus asked him if he sees something.

Jēsus interrogat (interrogābit; interrogāverit; interrogāvit) eum sī quid vīderit [perfect subjunctive]. Jesus asked him if he saw something.

Jesus interrogat (interrogābit; interrogāverit; interrogāvit) eum sī quid vīsūrus sit [future participle with present subjunctive; or *videat*; present subjunctive]. Jesus asked him if he will see something.

Direct speech without the subjunctive:
> *Jēsus interrogāvit eum, "quid vidēs* [present indicative]*" / "quid vīdis* [perfect indicative]*" / "quid vidēbis* [future indicative]*?*

Indirect speech with the subjunctive in the secondary tenses:
> *Jēsus interrogāvit (interrogabat; interrogaverat) eum sī quid vidērēt* [imperfect subjunctive]. Jesus asked him if he saw something.
>
> *Jēsus interrogāvit (interrogabat; interrogaverat) eum sī quid vīdisset* [pluperfect subjunctive]. Jesus asked him if he had seen something.
>
> *Jēsus interrogāvit (interrogabat; interrogaverat) eum sī quid vīsūrus esset* [future active participle with imperfect subjunctive]. Jesus asked him if he were going to see something.

Sententiae Summāriae

Timeō nē daemonia laudēs.
Timēmus nē moneāminī ab malīs magistrīs.
Tū audīs quae hominēs malī dīxerint? Nōn audiō quae hominēs malī dīxerint.
Vōs scītis quae audīverīmus?
Magister discipulōs interrogāvit ubi illī essent.
Discipulī nescīvērunt ubi essent.

Translations

I am afraid that you praise demons.
We fear lest you be taught by bad teachers.
Did you listen to the things the bad people have said? I do not listen to the things that the bad people have said.
Do you know what we heard?
The teacher asked the students where they were.
The students did not know where they were.

CHAPTER 31

Vocābula Memoranda

Nōmina

animus, animī (m.): mind, intellect, soul, heart[3]
concupiscentia, concupiscentiae (f.): desire (negative since Augustine)
conjūnx, conjugis (m./f.): spouse
ingenium, ingeniī (n.): disposition, ability, talent
mendācium, mendāciī (n.): lie
morbus, morbī (m.): sickness, illness
typus, typī (m.): figure, plan, type
vīs, vīs (f.): strength, force, power

Verba

ē-verbs

admoneō [ad + moneo], admonēre, admonuī, admonitus: warn, admonish
caveō, cavēre, cāvī, cautus: be aware (can be used as a verb of fearing)
praebeō [prae + habeo], praebēre, praebuī, praebitus: supply, provide, present
vereor, verērī,—, veritus: fear

i/e-verbs

adquīrō [ad + quaerō], adquīrere, adquīsīvī, adquīsītus: acquire, obtain
āmittō [ab + mitto], āmittere, āmīsī, amīsus: lose, dismiss (in the passive voice, "missing")
gerō, gerere, gessī, gestus: bear, carry
recēdō [rē + cēdō], recēdere, recessi, recessus: recede, withdraw

-io-verb

rapiō, rapere, rapui, raptus: drag off, snatch, seize

irregular

trānsferō [trāns + fer], trānsferre, trānstulī, trānslātus: carry across

Adjectīva

aliēnus, -a, -um: foreign
dolus, -a, -um: fraud, deceit
ingēns, ingēntis (gen. sing.): not natural, huge

Adverbium

nē (in a fear clause): that

---

[3] Be careful not to confuse this with *anima, animae* (f.): soul; animating principle.

Fābula Excerpta

Magi ab Oriente Hierosolymam veniunt ut Jesum Christum adorent[4]

Nātus est Jēsus in cīvitāte Bethlehem. Magī ab Oriente vēnērunt Hierosolymam ut eum adōrārent. Et stēlla antecēdēbat eōs. Et dīcēbant: "Ubi est rēx Jūdaeōrum? Vīdimus enim stēllam ejus in Oriente." Hērōdēs rēx turbātus est hāc vōce: timēbat enim nē rēgnum āmitteret.

Et cognōvērunt magī ubi Chrīstus nātus sit, abiērunt, et vēnērunt Bethlehem et invēnērunt puerum cum Marīā mātre ejus et adōrāvērunt eum et obtulērunt eī aurum, tūs, et myrrham. Admonitī in somnīs nē redīrent ad Hērōdem, aliā viā revertērunt in regiōnem suam.

Cf. Francis Lhomond, *Epitome Historiae Sacrae*, 156

admonitus, admonitī (m.): warned

Sententiae Interpretandae

1. Et ait: Rogō ergō tē, pater, ut mittās eum in domum patris meī. (Lk 16:27)
2. Erue mē dē manū frātris meī dē manū Esau quia valdē eum timeō nē forte veniēns percutiat mātrem cum filiīs. (Gn 32:11)

   erue: deliver
3. Timēbat Cāīn, nē occīderētur, quia fugere nesciēbat. (Ambrose, *Dē Fugā Saeculī* 7.39)

   nesciēbat: he was not know how...
4. Sed timuī nē honōrem Deī meī trānsferrem ad hominem, et nē quemquam adōrārem, exceptō Deō meō. (Est 13:14)
5. Timuit enim nē forte raperent eum Jūdaeī, et occīderent. (Acts 23:25)

   forte: by chance
6. Et accessit ūnus dē scrībīs, quī audierat illōs conquīrentēs, et vidēns quoniam bene illīs responderit, interrogāvit eum quod esset prīmum omnium mandātum. (Mk 12:28)
7. Et vocāvit ūnum dē servīs, et interrogāvit quid haec essent. (Lk 15:26)
8. Pīlātus autem audiēns Galilaeām, interrogāvit sī homō Galilaeus esset. (Lk 23:6)
9. Invēnitque eum vir errantem in agrō, et interrogāvit quid quaereret. (Gn 37:15)

---

4 Sometimes as additional exercises for purpose clauses, I will have my students practice all the ways to write a purpose statement. Here is a good example with the title of this short story:

Magi ab Oriente Hierosolymam veniunt adorare Jesum.

Magi ab Oriente Hierosolymam veniunt ad adorandum.

Magi ab Oriente Hierosolymam veniunt ad Jesum adorandum.

Magi ab Oriente Hierosolymam veniunt adoratum Jesum.

Jesus crucifixus est pro nobis; mirable adoratu eum.

10. Et ait rēx, "Interrogā tū, cuius fīlius sit iste puer." (1 Sm 17:56)
11. Timeō vōs, nē forte sine causā labōrāverim in vōbīs. (Gal 4:11)
12. Cum Chrīstum habuerīs, dīves es, et sufficit tibi. (Thomās ā Kempīs, *Imitātiō Chrīstī* 2.1.1)
13. Ergō et tū, sī imitātōrem tē praebeās Chrīstī, sīcut ille quī ait: imitātōrēs meī ēstote sīcut et ego Chrīstī, sī dolum nesciās, mendācium ōderīs, vēritātem sequāris, jūstitiam nōn refugiās, dīligās castimōniam, adpropinquāstī Chrīstō et per Chrīstum deō. (Ambrōsē of Milān, Expositiōn Psalmī 22)

castimōnia, castimōniae (f.): chastity

14. Timēbam enim nē mē cito exaudīrēs et cito sānārēs ā morbō concupīscentiae. (Augustine, *Confessions* 8)

morbus: sickness

15. Quid mē interrogās? Interrogā eōs, quī audiērunt quid locūtus sum ipsīs; ecce hī sciunt, quae dīxerim ego. (Jn 18:21)
16. Et ait Samuel: Quid interrogās mē, cum Dominus recesserit ā tē, et trānsierit ad inimīcum tuum? (1 Sm 28:16)
17. Vereor nē rīdiculus videar. (Augustine, *Dē Magistrō* 8.21)
18. Sciēbat enim quisnam esset quī trāderet eum; proptereā dīxit: Nōn estis mundī omnēs. (Jn 13:11)

quis-nam: who indeed

19. Cōgitābat quid Deus facere vellet. (Est 11:12)
20. Innuēbant autem patrī ejus, quem vellet vocārī eum. (Lk 1:62)

innuēre: gesturing, nodding

21. Deinde cōnsīderandum est dē morte Chrīstī, et circā hōc quaeruntur sex: utrum fuerit conveniēns Chrīstum morī; utrum per mortem Chrīstī fuerit sēparāta dīvīnitās ā carne; utrum Chrīstus in trīduō mortis fuerit homō; utrum fuerit īdem numerō corpus Chrīstī vīvum et mortuum; utrum mors Chrīstī sit aliquid operāta ad nostram salūtem. (Thomas Aquinas, *Summa Theologiae* III.50.1)
22. Ille dīxit eīs, Nōn lēgistis quid fēcerit Dāvīd, quandō suriit, et quī cum eō erant? Quōmodo intrāvit in domum Deī et pānēs prōpositiōnis comēdit, quod nōn licēbat eī edere neque hīs, quī cum eō erant, nisi sōlīs sacerdōtibus? (Mt 12:3–4)
23. Nōlīte arbitrārī quia vēnerim mittere pācem in terram; nōn vēnī pācem mittere sed gladium. (Mt 10:34)
24. Quid petō ut veniās in mē, quī nōn essem nisi essēs in mē? (Augustine, *Confessions* 1.2)
25. Optās ut veniat, quem timēs nē veniat. (Augustine, *Enarrationēs in Psalmōs* 97)
26. nōn enim pāx quaeritur, ut bellum excitētur, sed bellum geritur, ut pāx adquīrātur. (Augustine, *Epistula* 189)
27. Beātus quī amat tē et amīcum in tē et inimīcum propter tē. Sōlus enim nūllum cārum āmittit, cui omnēs in illō cārī sunt, quī nōn āmittitur. (Augustine, *Confessions* 4)

28. Cujus typum gerēbat adam, quandō immīsit eī deus sopōrem, ut dē latere illī conjugem faceret. nōn enim nōn poterat uxōrem facere prīmō hominī etiam dē latere vigilantīs? sed quārē volvit dormientī facere? quia dormientī chrīstō in cruce facta est conjunx dē latere. percussum est enim latus pendentis dē lanceā, et prōflūxērunt ecclēsiae sacrāmenta. (Augustine, *Ēnārrātiōnēs in Psalmōs* 56.11)

immīsit (in-mittō): sent in
sopor, sopōris (m.): deep sleep
latus, lateris (n.): sīde, flank
pendeō, pendēre, pependī,—: hang
prōfluō, prōfluere, prōflūxī, profluctus: flow forth

29. Et accessit ūnus dē scrībīs, quī audierat illōs conquīrentēs, et vidēns quoniam bene illīs respondērit, interrogāvit eum quod esset prīmum omnium mandātum. (Mk 12:28)

CHAPTER 32

❧

§ 119. Verbs: Morphology of the Pluperfect Subjunctive

The form of the pluperfect subjunctive is fairly easy to spot. It is the perfect stem of the verb plus *-isse-* and then the regular personal endings: *laudavisse-m, habuisse-s, duxisse-t, audivisse-mus,* etc. The passive form of the pluperfect subjunctive combines the perfect passive participle with the imperfect subjunctive of *esse* or the pluperfect subjunctive of *esse*.

Active

ā-verb	ē-verb	i/e-verb	i-verb	-io-verb	esse
laudāv|isse|m	*monu|isse|m*	*dūx|isse|m*	*audīv|isse|m*	*cēp|isse|m*	*fu|isse|m*
laudāv|issē|s	*monu|issē|s*	*dūx|issē|s*	*audīv|issē|s*	*cēp|issē|s*	*fu|issē|s*
laudāv|isse|t	*monu|isse|t*	*dūx|isse|t*	*audīv|isse|t*	*cēp|isse|t*	*fu|isse|t*
laudāv|issē|mus	*monu|issē|mus*	*dūx|issē|mus*	*audīv|issē|mus*	*cēp|issē|mus*	*fu|issē|mus*
laudāv|issē|tis	*monu|issē|tis*	*dūx|issē|tis*	*audīv|issē|tis*	*cēp|issē|tis*	*fu|issē|tis*
laudāv|isse|nt	*monu|isse|nt*	*dūx|isse|nt*	*audīv|isse|nt*	*cēp|isse|nt*	*fu|isse|nt*

Passive

ā-verb	ē-verb	i/e-verb	i-verb
laudātus (-a, -um) *[fui-]essem*	*monitus (-a, -um)* *[fui-]essem*	*ductus (-a, -um)* *[fui-]essem*	*audītus (-a, -um)* *[fui-]essem*
laudātus (-a, -um) *[fui-]essēs*	*monitus (-a, -um)* *[fui-]essēs*	*ductus (-a, -um)* *[fui-]essēs*	*audītus (-a, -um)* *[fui-]essēs*
laudātus (-a, -um) *[fui-]esset*	*monitus (-a, -um)* *[fui-]esset*	*ductus (-a, -um)* *[fui-]esset*	*audītus (-a, -um)* *[fui-]esset*
laudātī (-ae, -a) *[fui-]essēmus*	*monitī (-ae, -a)* *[fui-]essēmus*	*ductī (-ae, -a)* *[fui-]essēmus*	*audītī (-ae, -a)* *[fui-]essēmus*
laudātī (-ae, -a) *[fui-]essētis*	*monitī (-ae, -a)* *[fui-]essētis*	*ductī (-ae, -a)* *[fui-]essētis*	*audītī (-ae, -a)* *[fui-]essētis*
laudātī (-ae, -a) *[fui-]essent*	*monitī (-ae, -a)* *[fui-]essent*	*ductī (-ae, -a)* *[fui-]essent*	*audītī (-ae, -a)* *[fui-]essent*

§ 120. Verbs: Meaning of the *realis* in the Narrative Subjunctive

One of the most frequent, and at times confusing, aspects of the subjunctive in Latin is that it can be used to explain "real" events. Some refer to this distinction as *realis* and *irrealis*. *Realis* describes actual states of affairs. Some have also termed this a "grammatical" use of the subjunctive. That means that grammatically we have a subjunctive, but the meaning is no different from the indicative. In English we can say, "When I walked to the store, I took my dog with me." There is no subjunctive; it denotes a real state of affairs. In Latin, you can express that same sentence with the subjunctive, *Cum ambulāvissem ad tabernam, canem meam tulī*. Notice that the first verb *ambulāvissem* is in a new form. That is the morphology we are learning in this chapter called the pluperfect subjunctive. We do not translate it, "when I might have walked to the store," "when I would have walked to the store," or anything like that.

When a student is reading Latin, there are important clue words for the narrative subjunctive. *Cum, dum,* and *donec* are three of the most common conjunctions which can have the subjunctive that follows. Usually *cum* can be translated as "since" but sometimes it has the meaning of "although," which is less common. It is simply a convention of Latin to use the subjunctive with the word *cum* in a narrative context.[1] We call this the *narrative subjunctive* and it is critical that the student recognize that the combination of the word *cum*,

---

[1] As a frustrating side note for beginners, it appears that Latin has undergone several changes with the respect to the use of the conjunction and preposition *cum*. *Cum* can be used as a conjunction

or sometimes *dum* and *donec*, can have the subjunctive to follow, but the meaning is still the same as if it were in the indicative. This is purely conventional. It is a form that occurs frequently in the Vulgate, especially the Gospels because they are primarily narrative. Genre, and the larger context of the text in question, can help the student expect certain forms of the language, like the narrative subjunctive. In the narrative subunctive, one simply translates the conjunction and the tense of the verb follows its standard meaning, pluperfect: "had [verb]-ed" and imperfect "was [verb]-ing" or sometimes just the simple past "[verb]-ed."

> *Quī **cum audīssent** rēgem, abiērunt, et ecce stēlla, quam vīderant in oriente, antecēdēbat eōs, usque **dum veniēns stāret** suprā, ubi erat puer* (Mt 2:9).

When they had heard the king, they left, and behold a star, which they had seen in the East, was preceding them, up to the point when, coming, it stood [*lit.* was standing] above where the boy was.

Notice that we have both a pluperfect subjunctive and an imperfect subjunctive used in a narrative, and neither have a meaning of "would" or "might" but merely indicate events. It is the combination of the conjunction *cum* and *dum* with the subjunctive that indicate to the reader that these are factual, real events, not possible states of affairs.

> ***Dum** autem septem diēs **cōnsummārentur**, hī quī dē Asiā erant Jūdæī, **cum vīdissent** eum in templō, <u>concitāvērunt</u> omnem populum, et injēcērunt eī manūs, clāmantēs* (Acts 21:27).

But while the seven days were ending, those Jews who were from Asia, when they saw [*lit.* had seen] him in the temple, stirred up all the people and laid hands upon him, shouting.

One other thing to notice about the narrative subjunctive is that the clause created by the *cum* or the *dum* often pairs with an indicative verb. In this instance, the verb *concitāvērunt* (stirred) is in the indicative and not the subjunctive because it is not governed by a conjunction like *cum* or *dum*.

The narrative subjunctive most frequently uses the pluperfect subjunctive and the imperfect subjunctive, but occasionally it will use the perfect subjunctive.

---

to mean "when" or as a preposition to mean "with." According to Lewis and Short, the most ancient forms of the conjunction were spelled *quom*, which could have been distinguished from the preposition *cum*. This way, it was easier to distinguish between the two possible spellings of a word. In late medieval, early modern Latin, the convention changed again and the form *quum* came into use for the conjunction *cum* to mean "when." So only in the classical, late ancient, and early medieval period do we have the confusion between *cum* as "when" and *cum* as "with." That said, most Latin texts that people regularly read use *cum* for both instances.

§ 121. Verbs: Meaning of the *irrealis* in Conditions Contrary to Fact

We now have to talk about the exact opposite use of the subjunctive—commonly found with the pluperfect or imperfect subjunctive—that is, conditions contrary to fact. Often, if we find the imperfect subjunctive or the pluperfect subjunctive standing alone, they indicate that the speaker is talking about something that did not happen. Occasionally, you will have the imperfect subjunctive on its own, without the word *si*, and this will be translated "were." The contrary-to-fact use of the subjunctive takes the imperfect or pluperfect subjunctive.

Sī apud covivium fuissem, laetus fuissem. Notice here that we have the pluperfect subjunctive. It is translated as "would" in the more typical use of the subjunctive.

"If I was [*lit.* would have been] at the party, I would have been happy." This is a condition contrary to fact. I did not go to the party, so therefore I am not happy.

Sī fuissēmus in diēbus patrum nostrōrum, nōn essēmus sociī eōrum in sanguine prophētārum! (Mt 23:30)

If we were [*lit.* would have been] in the days of our fathers, we would not be sharers with them in the blood of the prophets!

§ 122. Verbs: Meaning of Optative Subjunctives

The subjunctive can be used to speak of attainable and unattainable wishes. We also have a word, perhaps the one enduring optative in Latin, which means "I wish." *Utinam* is found only in this form, when it appears, and it means "I wish" or even just "would."

Utinam tū essēs mēcum. "I wish that you would have been with me." (It is frequently used to introduce an unattainable wish, but it is not always necessary.)

Atque utinam tacērētis, ut putārēminī esse sapientēs! (Job 13:5)

And would that you were silent so that you would be thought to be wise!

CHAPTER 32

§ 123. Syntax: All the Types of Conditionals

	English	Latin	Latin Verb Forms
Simple Present	If he walks, he uses his legs.	*Sī ambulat, crūribus ūtitur.*	Present Indicative
Simple Past	If he walked, he used his legs.	*Sī ambulāvit, crūribus ūsus est.*	Imperfect, Perfect, Pluperfect indicative
Future More Vivid	If he will have walked, he will have used his legs, or he will use his legs.	*Sī ambulāverit, crūribus ūtētur.*	Future or Future-Perfect Indicative
Future Less Vivid	If he might walk, he might use his legs	*Sī ambulet, crūribus ūtātur.*	Present Subjunctive
Present Contrary to Fact	If he were walking, he would use his legs.	*Sī ambulāret, crūribus ūterētur.*	Imperfect Subjunctive
Past Contrary to Fact	If he had walked, he would have used his leg. (But he didn't walk).	*Sī ambulāvisset, crūribus ūsus esset.*	Pluperfect Subjunctive

Present Simple
   Sī Fīlius Deī es, dēscende dē cruce (Mt 27:40).
   If you are the Son of God, get down from the cross.

Past Simple
   Sī ergō ego lāvī pedēs vestrōs, Dominus et Magister, et vōs dēbētis alter alterutrum lavāre pedēs (Jn 13:14).
   If I, Lord and teacher, have washed your feet, and you all must wash the feet of one another.

Future More Vivid (or Future More Vivid with Emphasis)
   Sī vestīmentum ejus tetigerō, salva erō (Mk 5:28).
   If I will [have] touch [-ed] his clothes, I will be saved.

Future Less Vivid
   Sī cōnfiteāmur peccāta nostra: fidēlis est, et jūstus, ut remittat nōbīs peccāta nostra, et ēmundet nōs ab omnī inīquitāte (1 Jn 1:9).
   If we should confess our sins: he is faithful and just, such that he forgives our sins from us and cleanses us from all iniquity.

Present Contrary to Fact
> *Sī scīret paterfamiliās quā hōrā fūr ventūrus esset, vigilāret utique, et nōn sineret perfodī domum suam* (Mt 24:43).

If the head of the house were to know the hour which the thief was to come, he certainly would stay awake, and he would not permit his house to be broken into.

Past Contrary to Fact
> *Vīvit Dominus, quia sī servāssētis eōs, nōn vōs occīderem* (Jgs 8:19).

As surely as the Lord lives, [that] if you all had not saved them, I would not have killed you all.

Cavēte et Mementōte

The key to understanding the difference between the *realis* and *irrealis* in the subjunctive are the context clues. If you begin a sentence with a word like *cum* or *donec*, you have to have a subjunctive that follow, often in the past tense, either imperfect subjunctive or pluperfect subjunctive.

If you have a conditional word, *nisi* or *si* or *etiam si*, you will have a contrary-to-fact conditional and *irrealis*. Also, in some cases, if you have a past tense subjunctive that standing alone, you will have a contrary-to-fact conditional.

Sententiae Summāriae

> Sī discipulōs malōs laudāvissem, nōn didicissent.
> Sī discipulī monitī essent, nōn intrāvissent in silvam.
> Etiamsī ductī fuissent ab optimō duce, tamen mortuī fuissent.
> Cum Jēsus mortuus fuisset, Maria flēvit.

Translations

> If I would have praised the bad students, they would not have learned.
> If the bad students would have been warned, they would not have gone into the forest.
> Even if they were led by a great leader, they still would have died.
> When Jesus had died, Mary wept.

Vocābula Memoranda

Nōmina

aetās, aetātis (f.): age
excūsātiō, excūsātiōnis (f.): excuse
fēlīcitās, fēlīcitātis (f.): happiness
memoria, memoriae (f.): memory
pāx, pācis (f.): peace
supplicium, supplic[i]ī (n.): punishment

Verba

<u>ā-verbs</u>
accūsō [ad + causa], accūsāre, accūsāvī, accūsātus: accuse, blame, charge[2]
excūsō [ex + causa], excūsāre, excūsāvī, excūsātus: excuse, acquit
migrō, migrāre, migrāvī, migrātus: transport, move
praedēstinō [prae + destino], praedēstināre, praedēstināvī, praedēstinātus: determine beforehand, provide beforehand
rogō, rogāre, rogāvī, rogātus: to ask
spectō, spectāre, spectāvī, spectātus: to see, look at, regard

<u>ē-verb</u>
indigeō, indigēre, indiguī,—: need, lack (with gen. or abl.)
soleo, solere,—, solitus: be in the habit of, be accustomed to

<u>i/e-verbs</u>
abscondō [ab + scondo], abscondere, abscondī, absconditus: hide, conceal
cōnsūmō [con + sumo], cōnsūmere, cōnsūmpsī, cōnsūmptus: burn up, use up, expend
dēstruō, dēstruere, dēstrūxī, dēstrūctus: destroy, demolish

<u>io-verb</u>
prōspiciō [prō + specto], prōspicere, prōspexī, prōspectus: foresee, look for

Adjectīva

fēstus, -a, -um: festal day, joyous day
terrenus, -a, -um: earthly

Adverbia

utinam: if only, would that (+subj)

Conjūnctīvum

etenim: indeed, because, as a matter of fact

---

[2] *Causa* in legal Latin has to do with a legal case.

Fābula Excerpta

Ante diem fēstum Paschae, sciēns Jēsus quia venit hōra ejus ut trānseat ex hōc mundō ad Patrem: cum dīlēxisset suōs, quī erant in mundō, in fīnem dīlēxit eōs. Et cēna facta, cum diabolus jam mīsisset in cor ut trāderet eum Jūdās Simōnis Iscariōtae: sciēns quia omnia dēdit eī Pater in manūs, et quia ā Deō exīvit, et ad Deum vādit: surgit ā cēnā, et pōnit vestīmenta sua, et cum accēpisset linteum, praecīnxit sē. Deinde mittit aquam in pēlvim, et coepit lavāre pedēs discipulōrum, et extergere linteō, quō erat praecīnctus. Venit ergō ad Simōnem Petrum. Et dīcit eī Petrus: Domine, tū mihi lavās pedēs? Respondit Jēsus, et dīxit eī: Quod ego faciō, tū nescīs modo: sciēs autem posteā. Dīcit eī Petrus: Nōn lavābis mihi pedēs in aeternum. Respondit eī Jēsus: Sī nōn lāverō tē, nōn habēbis partem mēcum. Dīcit eī Simōn Petrus: Domine, nōn tantum pedēs meōs, sed et manūs, et caput. Dīcit eī Jēsus: Quī lōtus est, nōn indiget nisi ut pedes lavet, sed est mundus tōtus. Et vōs mundī estis, sed nōn omnēs. Sciēbat enim quisnam esset quī trāderet eum; proptereā dīxit: Nōn estis mundī omnēs. Postquam ergō lāvit pedēs eōrum, et accēpit vestīmenta sua, cum recubuisset iterum, dīxit eīs: Scītis quid fēcerim vōbīs? Vōs vocātis mē Magister et Domine, et bene dīcitis: sum etenim. Sī ergō ego lāvī pedēs vestrōs, Dominus et Magister, et vōs dēbētis alter alterutrum lavāre pedēs. Exemplum enim dedī vōbīs, ut quemadmodum ego fēcī vōbīs, ita et vōs faciātis. Āmēn, āmēn dīcō vōbīs: nōn est servus major dominō suō: neque apostolus major est eō quī mīsit illum. Sī haec scītis, beātī eritis sī fēcerītis ea. Nōn dē omnibus vōbīs dīcō: ego sciō quōs ēlēgerim; sed ut adimpleātur Scrīptūra: Quī mandūcat mēcum pānem, levābit contrā mē calcāneum suum. Āmodo dīcō vōbīs, priusquam fiat: ut cum factum fuerit, crēdātis quia ego sum. Āmēn, āmēn dīcō vōbīs: quī accipit sī quem miserō, mē accipit; quī autem mē accipit, accipit eum quī mē mīsit. Cum haec dīxisset Jēsus, turbātus est spīritū: et prōtestātus est, et dīxit: Āmēn, āmēn dīcō vōbīs, quia ūnus ex vōbīs trādet mē.

Cf. John 13

pascha, paschae (f.): Passover, Easter
praecingere, praecīnxī: put around
pēlvis, pēlvis (f.): shallow bowl
linteum, linteī (n.): linen cloth, towel
extergere: to dry
alteruter, -a, -um: ne of two, both
calcāneus, calcāneī (m.): heel
āmodo: henceforth
priusquam fiat: befōre it happēns
prōtestor, prōtestārī, prōtestātus sum: testify

1. Quid diabolus Judae fēcit?
2. Quid Jesus discipulīs suis fēcit?
3. Quī hōc facere solent?
4. Cur Jesus pedēs discipulōrum lavit?
5. Cur Jesus turbātus est spīritū?

CHAPTER 32

Sententiae Interpretandae

1. Sapientiam autem loquimur inter perfectōs: sapientiam vērō nōn hujus saeculī, neque prīncipum hujus saeculī, quī dēstruuntur: sed loquimur Deī sapientiam in mystēriō, quae abscondita est, quam praedēstināvit Deus ante saecula in glōriam nostram, quam nēmō prīncipum hujus saeculī cognōvit: sī enim cognōvissent, numquam Dominum glōriae crucifīxissent. (1 Cor 2:6–8)
2. Sī semel perfectē introīssēs in interiōra Jēsū, et modicum dē ārdentī amōre ejus sapuīssēs, tunc dē propriō commodō, vel incommodō nihil cūrārēs, sed magis dē opprobriō illātō gaudērēs, quia amor Jēsū facit hominem sē ipsum contemnere. (Thomas a Kempis, *Imitātiō Chrīstī* 2.1.6)

> *semel*: once
> *ārdeō, ārdēre, ārsī, ārsus*: burn, be on fire
> *sapiō, sapere, sapīvī*: taste

3. Sī rēctē tibi essēs, et bene pūrgātus essēs, omnia tibi in bonum cēderent, et prōfectum. (Thomas a Kempis, *Imitātiō Chrīstī* 2.1.8)
4. Jūstus essēs, sī tē accūsārēs et frātrem tuum excūsārēs. (Thomas a Kempis, *Imitātiō Chrīstī* 2.3.2)
5. Cum vēnissent ergō ad illum Samarītānī, rogāvērunt eum ut ibi manēret. Et mānsit ibi duōs diēs. (Jn 4:40)
6. Cum ergō vēnisset in Galilaeam, excēpērunt eum Galilaeī, cum omnia vīdissent quæ fēcerat Jerosolymis in diē fēstō: et ipsī enim vēnerant ad diem fēstum. (Jn 4:45)
7. Fīlius quidem hominis vādit, sīcut scrīptum est dē illō: vae autem hominī illī, per quem Fīlius hominis trādētur! bonum erat eī, sī nātus nōn fuisset homō ille. (Mt 26:24)

> *vae*: woe

8. Mementōte sermōnis meī, quem ego dīxī vōbīs: nōn est servus major dominō suō. Sī mē persecūtī sunt, et vōs persequentur; sī sermōnem meum servāvērunt, et vestrum servābunt. Sed haec omnia facient vōbīs propter nōmen meum: quia nesciunt eum quī mīsit mē. Sī nōn vēnissem, et locūtus fuissem eīs, peccātum nōn habērent: nunc autem excūsātiōnem nōn habent dē peccātō suō. (Jn 15:20–22)
9. Et factum est, cum consumāsset Jēsus sermōnēs istōs, migrāvit ā Galilaeā, et venit in fīnēs Jūdaeæ trāns Jordānem, et secūtae sunt eum turbae multae, et cūrāvit eōs ibi. (Mt 19:1–2)
10. Dīxit ergō Martha ad Jēsum: Domine, sī fuissēs hīc, frāter meus nōn fuisset mortuus. (Jn 11:21)
11. Ūna autem sabbatī, Maria Magdalēne venit mane, cum adhūc tenebrae essent, ad monumentum: et vīdit lapidem sublātum ā monumentō. (Jn 20:1)
12. Maria autem stābat ad monumentum foris, plōrāns. Dum ergō flēret, inclīnāvit sē, et prōspexit in monumentum: et vīdit duōs angelōs in albīs sedentēs, ūnum ad caput, et ūnum ad pedēs, ubi positum fuerat corpus Jēsū. (Jn 20:11–12)

> *inclīnō, inclīnāre, inclīnāvī, inclīnātus*: bend, lower

13. Cum ergō sērō esset diē illō, ūna sabbatōrum, et forēs essent clausæ, ubi erant discipulī congregātī propter metum Jūdaeōrum: venit Jēsus, et stetit in mediō, et dīxit eīs: Pāx vōbīs. Et cum hoc dīxisset, ostendit eīs manus et latus. Gāvīsī sunt discipulī, vīsō Dominō. (Jn 20:19–20)

latus: side

14. Sī dē mundō fuissētis, mundus quod suum erat dīligeret: quia vērō dē mundō nōn estis, sed ego ēlēgī vōs dē mundō, proptereā ōdit vōs mundus. (Jn 15:19)
15. Sī enim data esset lēx, quae posset vīvificāre, vērē ex lēge esset jūstitiā. (Gal 3:21)
16. Sī scīrēs dōnum Deī et quis est quī dīcit tibi, "Dā mihi bibere," tū forsitan petīssēs ab eō et dedisset tibi aquam vīvam. (Jn 4:10)
17. Canticum graduum. Nisi Dominus fuisset in nōbīs–dīcat nunc Israēl, nisi Dominus fuisset in nōbīs: cum exsurgerent hominēs in nōs, forte vīvōs dēglūtīssent nōs; cum īrāscerētur furor eōrum in nōs, forsitan aqua absorbuisset nōs; torrentem pertrānsīvit anima nostra; forsitan pertrānsīsset animā nostrā aquam intolerābilem. (Ps 123:1)

forte: perhaps
deglutere, dēglūtī: swallow
īrāscor, īrāscī,—, īrātus: become angry
absorbēre, absorbuī: absorb
pertrānsīre, pertrānsī: go across
intolerābilis, intolerābilis: intolerable

18. "Jacet Petrī corpus Rōmae," dīcunt hominēs, "jacet Paulī corpus Rōmae ... ubi sunt memoriae apostolōrum?" quid dīcis? ecce hoc dīxī: tanta mala Rōma patitur: ubi sunt memoriae apostolōrum? ibi sunt, ibi sunt, sed in tē nōn sunt. utinam in tē essent, quisquis ista loqueris ... utinam in tē essent memoriae apostolōrum, utinam tū cōgitārēs apostolōs. vidērēs utrumnam eīs terrēna fēlīcitās prōmissa fuerit, an aeterna. (Augustine, *Sermō* 296)

APPENDICES

CONNECTIONS TO LINGUA LATINA: FAMILIA ROMANA AND FĀBULAEE SYRAE

The best possible way to improve one's Latin is to practice reading using additional material at the same level or even easier than one's current progression. This grammar has been written in English, but roughly matching the layout of Hans Orberg's *Familia Romana*. As such, when the student has completed a lesson in this textbook, the student should be able to read an accompanying chapter from *Familia Romana*. These connections are not perfect, though, as this book is written with 32 chapters, whereas *Familia Romana* has 34.

Ecclesiastical Latin	Familia Romana	Fābulaee Syrae	Grammar
Chapter 1	*Capitulum Primum / Tertium*		Nominatives / Accusatives
Chapter 2	*Capitulum Alterum*		Genitives
Chapter 3	*Capitulum Quintum*		Ablatives and Prepositions
Chapter 4	*Capitulum Quartum*		Imperatives and Vocatives
Chapter 5	*Capitulum Septimum*		Datives
Chapter 6	*Capitulum Sextum*		Ablatives and Passive Voice
Chapter 7	*Capitulum Quindecimum*		Active Personal Endings for Verbs
Chapter 8	*Capitulum Nonum*		Third Declension Nouns
Chapter 9	*Capitulum Decimum*		Basic Infinitives, Active and Passive

Chapter 10	*Capitulum Undecimum*		Indirect Speech and Accusative as Subject
Chapter 11	*Capitulum Duodecimum*		Forth Declension and Third Declension Adjectives
Chapter 12	*Capitulum Tredecimum et Quattordecimum*		Participles and Fifth Declension
Chapter 13	*Capitulum Quattordecimum et Quindecimum*		Impersonal Verbs and Ablative Absolute
Chapter 14	*Capitulum Quindecimum*		Passive Personal Endings for Verbs
Chapter 15	*Capitulum Septimum et Duodevicesimum*		Irregular Adjectives and Adverbs; *Esse* in the Imperfect
Chapter 16	*Capitulum Sedecimum*		Deponents in the Present
Chapter 17	*Capitulum Vicesimum*		Overview of Verbs; *Esse* in the Future
Chapter 18	*Capitulum Undevicesimum*		Imperfect Active and Passive Indicative
Chapter 19	*Capitulum Vicesimum*		Future Active and Passive Indicative
Chapter 20	*Capitulum Vicesimum et Unum*		Perfect Active Indicative and Infinitives
Chapter 21	*Capitulum Vicesimum et Unum*		Perfect Passive Indicative, Participle, and Infinitive
Chapter 22	*Capitulum Vicesimum Tertium*		Future Active Participle and Infinitive
Chapter 23	*Capitulum Vicesimum et Quartum*		Pluperfect Active and Passive
Chapter 24	*Capitulum Vicesimum et Duo et Capitulum Vicesimum et Quintum*		Passive Imperative, Defective Verbs, and Supines
Chapter 25	*Capitulum Vicesimum et Sextum*	XXVI	Gerunds
Chapter 26	*Capitulum Trecesimum*	XXX	Future Perfect Active and Passive

Chapter 27	*Capitulum Trecesimum Primum*	XXXI	Gerundive and Future Passive Participles
Chapter 28	*Capitulum Vicesimum et Septimum*	XXVII	Present Subjunctive and Purpose Clauses
Chapter 29	*Capitulum Vicesimum et Ocatvum*	XXVIII	Imperfect Subjunctive and Result Clauses
Chapter 30	*Capitulum Trecesimum*	XXIX et XXX	Independent Subjunctives and Sequence of Tenses
Chapter 31	*Capitulum Trecesimum et Duo*	XXXII	Perfect Subjunctive and Clauses of Fearing
Chapter 32	*Capitulum Trecesimum et Tertium*	XXXII et XXXIII	Pluperfect Subjunctive and Narrative Subjunctive

COLLOQUIA DE ICONIBUS[1]

The following section of *colloquia*, or conversations, are intended to be used with icons. These are questions, usually with answers, which the teacher and students can use to be able to look at an image and have a conversation about it in Latin.

Annunciation

Possible script of questions from chapters 1 through 6:

— Quis est? Qui sunt?
— Est Maria. Est angelus. Sunt Maria et Angelus.

— Quid est hoc?
— Ecclesia est.

— Quid agunt?
— Maria sedet. Angelus stat. Angelus volat.

— Quid tu vides?
— Mariam et Angelum video.
— Caelum video. Terram video.

— Quis est Maria?
— Maria est femina.

— Cuius femina est Maria?
— Maria est femina Josephi.

— Cuius vir est Josephus?
— Josephus est vir Mariae.

— Cui angelus apparet?
— Angelus Mariae apparet.

— Apparetne angelus Josepho?
— Angelus quoque Josepho apparet.

— Quem angelus videt?
— Mariam angelus videt.

— Quem Maria videt? Quid Maria videt?
— Angelum Maria videt. Terram Maria videt.

— Ubi sunt angelus et Maria?
— Maria et angelus in terra sunt.

---

1 *icon, iconis* (f.): icon

— A quo angelus videtur?

                                                  — Ab Maria angelus videtur.

— A quo Angelus mittitur?

                                                  — Angelus ab Deo mittitur.

The Labor of the Holy Family—Joseph Working (Chapters 7–11)

Nova Vocābula:
clavus, clavi (m): nail
lignum, ligni (n.): wood, tree
malleus, mallei (m): hammer
percutio, percutere, percussi, percussus: strike, beat, pierce
serra, serrae (f.): saw
secco, seccare, seccavi, seccatus: cut

— Quid est nomen feminae?

                                                  — Nomen feminae Maria est.

— Quid est nomen viro?

                                                  — Nomen viro Josephus est.

— Quis Josephus? Cuius pater est?

                                                  — Josephus est pater Jesu.

— Quis est Maria? Cuius mater est?

                                                  — Maria est mater Jesu.

— Quid agit Josephus?

                                                  — Josephus laborat. Josephus seccat.

— Quis docet quem? Quis docetur? A quo?

— Docet-ne Josephus Jesum? Discitne Jesus ab Josepho?

— Quem Maria videt?

                                        — Josephum Maria videt. Jesum Maria videt.

— Quid Maria videt? (*practice accusative plus infinitive with active and passive voice*)

                                    — Maria videt Josephum et Jesum laborare.
                                    — Maria videt lignum seccare a Josepho.
                                    — Maria videt Jesum pulsare malleo.

— Quid Jesus agit?

                                                  — Jesus malleo pulsat.

— Quid tu vides? Quid vos videtis?

                          — Ego video aedificium et villam et arborem et montem.

— Quid est levior, malleus an lignum?

— Malleus levior est quam lignum (ligneo).

— Quid est gravior, malleus an lignum?

— Lignum gravior est quam lignum (ligneo).

— Quid est longior, malleus an lignum?

— Lignum longior est quam malleus.

— Quis est fortior, filius an pater?

— Pater fortior est filio (quam filius).

Crucifixion (Chapters 12–16)

crucio, cruciare, crucfigi, crucifictus: torment, crucify
crux, crucis (f.): cross
mors, mortis (f.): death

— Quid tu vides? Quid tu intueris?

— Ego video Jesum. Ego Jesum intueor.
— Ego video Jesum crucifigari. Ego Jesum intueor Jesum crucifigari.

— Quid vos videtis? Quid vos intuemini?

— Nos Jesum videmus. Nos Jesum intuemini.
— Nos Jesum videmus Jesum crucifigari. Nos intuemini Jesum crucifigari.

— Potestne Jesus descendere de cruce?

— Jesus descendere potest.

— Vultne Jesus descendere de cruce?

— Jesus non vult descendere de cruce.

— Cur Jesus mori vult?

— Jesus vult mori pro peccatis nostris.

— Quis est major Jesus an mors?

— Jesus major est quoniam mortem expugnat.

— Ubi est Jesus?

— Jesus est in ligno, in cruce.

— Quis est prope Jesum?

— Prope Jesum sunt latrones.

— Quis est procul ab Jesu?

— Deus procul ab Jesu est.

Temptation (Chapters 17–21)

– Quis tempatavit?

– Diabolus temptavit.

– Quem temptavit?

– Jesum Diabolus temptavit.

– A quo Jesus temptatus est?

– A diabolo Jesus temptatus est.

– Quid tu vides (intueris)? (primum in tempore praesente; deinde in tempore perfecto)
– Video Diabolum temptare Jesum.
– Video Jesum temptari a Diabolo.
– Video Diabolum tempativisse Jesum.
– Video Jesum temptatum esse a Diabolo.

Mary at the Tomb; Noli me tangere (Chapters 22–27)

– Cur Maria venit ad monumentum?

– Maria venit ad monumentum plorare.
– Maria venit ad monumentum ploratum.
– Maria venit ad monumentum plorandum.
Maria venit ad corpus Jesu lavandum.

– Ubi est Jesus?

– – Non est in monumento.

– Estne Jesus mortuus?

Non Jesus resurrexit.

– Quid Maria putabat?

– Maria putabat Jesum esse mortuum.

Foot Washing (Chapters 28–32)

pelvis, pelvis (f.): bowl
linteum, lintei (n.): towel
praecingo, praecingere, praecinxi, praecinctus: surround, gird
lavo, lavare, lavavi, lautus (laatus): wash
purus, -a, -um: clean
mundus, -a, -um: clean
impurus, -a, -um: unclean

– Cur Jesus se inclinavit?

– Jesus se inclinavit pedes discipulorum lavare.
– Jesus se inclinavit lavatum.
– Jesus se inclinavit ad lavandum.
– Jesus se inclinavit ad pedes lavandos.
– Jesus se inclinavit ut pedes discipulorum lavaret.

– Petrus Jesum lavare pedes suos voluit?
– Petrus non voluit ut Jesus pedes lavaret.

– Quidnam Petrus Jesu oravit?
– Oravit ut Jesus totum corpus, manus et pedes, lavaret.

– Quid Petrus timuit?
– Petrus timuit ne Jesus non lavaret totum corpus et impurus fuerit.

– Cur Jesus voluit pedes lavare, aut quid Jesus timuit?
– Jesus timuit ne discipuli impuri fuerint.

ORATIONES HEBDOMADAE

These prayers will often contain vocabulary and grammar that have not been covered. It is up to the instructor whether to mention this or just say what it means. If the class seems to be moving quickly, it can be helpful to "pre-teach" some harder grammar. So, with these prayers, you might just mention in class "this is a third declension. Here's what it does, we will see it more in depth later." The idea is that the more a student sees something like the variation in nouns early, it will feel less threatening when it comes along later. Memorization through songs and prayers is one of the best ways to help students get a feel for the language. It has been organized to be introduced with each chapter and the grammar reviewed is noted.

Chapter 1

Sanctus

Sanctus, Sanctus, Sanctus, Dominus Deus Sabaoth.[2] Plēnī sunt caelī et terra glōriā tuā. Hosanna in excelsīs.[3] Benedictus quī venit in nōmine Domīnī. Hosanna in excelsīs.
- Notice the nominatives in the first line.

Chapter 2

Signum Crucis

In nōmine Patrīs, et Fīliī, et Spīritūs Sanctī. Amen
- Notice the genitives for *Filii* and *Sancti*.

Chapter 3

A: Dominus nōbīscum.

R: Et cum spīritū tuo.
- Practice with prepositions.
- The pronoun *cum* can have a personal pronoun precede it and be attached to it.

Chapter 4

Oratio Jesu

Domine, Jēsū Chrīste, Fīliī Deī vīvī, miserēre meī.
- Notice all the vocatives. *Miserere* (have mercy upon) is a deponent imperative, which is learned in chapter 24. It looks like an infinitive, but it is not.

---

[2] *Sabaoth* (pl.): hosts, armies
[3] *excelsum, excelsi* (n.): high place

Anima Chrīstī

Anima Chrīstī, sānctificā mē.
Corpus Chrīstī, salvā[4] mē.
Sanguis Chrīstī, inēbriā[5] mē.
Aqua lateris[6] Chrīstī, lavā mē.
Passiō Chrīstī, cōnfortā[7] mē.
Ō bone Jēsū, exaudī mē.
Intrā tua vulnera, absconde[8] mē.
Nē permittās[9] mē sēparārī[10] ā tē.
Ab hoste malignō[11], dēfende mē.
In hōrā mortis meae, vocā mē.
Et iubē mē venīre ad tē,
Ut cum Sānctīs tuīs laudem[12] tē
In saecula saeculōrum. Āmēn.

- This second prayer that can be used with chapter 5 highlights the imperative in all the conjugations.

Chapter 5

Gloria Patri

Glōria Patrī et Fīliō et Spīrituī Sānctō, sīcut erat in prīncipiō[13] et nunc et semper, et in saecula saeculōrum.

- Notice in this prayer that *Patri, Filio, Spiritui Sancto* are all dative. We will meet these declensions later, but we have already seen the dative singular end with *o* and *i*. We also have *in principio* and *in saecula*. The first is *in* with the ablative, "in the beginning" and the second is *in* with the accusative, "into the ages."

---

4 *salvare*: save
5 *inebriare*: intoxicate, make drunk
6 *latus, lateris* (n.): side
7 *confortare*: comfort
8 *abscondere*: hide
9 *Ne permittas*: do not permit
10 *separari*: to be separated
11 *malignus, -a, -um*: spiteful, evil
12 *ut ... laudem*: that I may praise
13 *principium, principii* (n.): beginning

Chapter 6

Glōria in excēlsīs Deō

et in terra pax hominibus[14] bonae voluntātis.[15]

Laudāmus[16] te,

benedīcimus te,

adorāmus te,

glorificāmus te,

grātiās āgimus tibi propter magnam glōriam tuam,

Dōmine Deus, Rex caelestis,

Deus Pater omnipotens.

- Notice the ablatives with prepositions, as well as a review of vocatives.
- The use of *we* as a subject will be introduced next chapter

Chapter 7

Agnus Dei

Agnus Deī quī tollis[17] peccāta mundī, miserēre nobis.

Agnus Deī quī tollis peccāta mundī, miserēre nobis.

Agnus Deī quī tollis peccāta mundī, dona nobis pācem.[18]

- Notice the relative pronoun working with the subject of *tollis*. This is less explicit in the English translation of this prayer, "who takes away …" This also reviews the new subjects for verbs.

Chapter 8

Nunc Dimittis

Nunc dīmittis servum tuum, Domine, secundum verbum tuum in pāce:

Quia vīdērunt[19] oculī meī salūtāre tuum

Quod parāstī[20] ante faciem omnium populōrum:

Lūmen ad revēlātiōnem gentium, et glōriam plēbis tuae Isrāēl.

- Notice all the third declension nouns and their cases. How do *plēbis* and *tuae* work together?

---

14 *hominibus* (dative): to humans
15 *voluntatis* (genitive): will
16 The *-mus* ending means "we."
17 This is read as *[tu] tollis*.
18 *pacem* (accusative): peace
19 *Viderunt* (perfect tense) is read as *vident*, but just the past tense.
20 *Parasti* is a syncopated or shortened form of *paravisti*. It means, "you have prepared."

Chapter 9

A: Laus tibi Domine

R: Rēx Aeternae Glōriae

- good review of genitives and a dative

Chapter 10

From Psalm 113:9

Nōn nōbīs, Domine, Domine,

Nōn nōbīs, Domine.

Sed nōminī sed nōminī

tuō dā glōriam.

- More review of imperatives and datives.

Chapter 11

Āctus Cāritātis

Domine Deus, amō tē super omnia, et proximum[21] meum propter tē, quia tū es summum initium et perfectissimum bonum, omnī dīlēctiōne[22] dignum.[23] In hāc cāritāte vīvere et morī statuō.[24] Amēn.

- Take note of the adjectives and the superlative; also, the active and passive infinitives after *statuo*.

Arma Dei

Induite vōs arma Deī. Statē ergō succīnctī[25] lumbōs[26] vestrōs in vēritāte, et indūtī[27] lōrīcam[28] iūstitiae. et calceātī[29] pedēs in praeparātiōne Ēvangeliī pācis in omnibus sūmentēs[30] scūtum fideī et galeam[31] salūtis assūmite, et gladium spīritūs (quod est verbum Deī).

- reviews imperatives and fourth declension and military vocabulary

---

21 *proximum, -i* (n.): neighbor
22 *dilectio, dilectionis* (f.): love
23 *dignus, -a, -um:* worthy
24 *statuere*: I decide
25 *succincti*: girded
26 *lumbus, lumbi* (m.): loins
27 *induti*: dressed
28 *lorica, loricae* (f.): breastplate
29 *calceati*: wearing
30 *sumere*: to take up
31 *galea, galeae* (f.): helmet

Chapter 12

Magnificat

Magnificat anima mea Dominum.

Et exultāvit spīritus meus in Deō salūtārī[32] meō,

Quia respexit[33] humilitātem ancillae suae; ecce enim ex hōc beātam mē dicent[34] omnēs generātiōnēs.

Quia fēcit[35] mihi magna[36] quī potēns est, et sānctum nōmen ejus, Et misericordiā ejus ā prōgeniē in prōgeniēs timentibus eum.

Fēcit potentiam brāchiō suō;

Dispersit[37] superbōs[38] mente cordis suī.

Dēposuit[39] potentēs dē sēde, et exaltāvit humilēs.

Ēsurientēs[40] implēvit bonīs, et dīvitēs dīmīsit[41] inānēs.[42]

Suscēpit[43] Isrāēl, puerum suum, recordātus[44] misericordiae suae, Sīcut locūtus est[45] ad patrēs nostrōs, Abraham et sēminī[46] ejus in saecula.

— many present active participles to be reviewed

Chapter 13

Salve Regina

Salvē Rēgīna, Māter misericordiae. Vīta, dulcēdō, et spēs nostra, salvē. Ad tē clāmāmus exsulēs[47] fīliī Hēvae. Ad tē suspīrāmus, gementēs[48] et flentēs in hāc lacrimārum valle. Ēia

---

32 *salutare, salutaris* (n.): salvation; neuter singular ablative in this instance
33 This comes from *respectare*, to regard, look upon. Here it is in the perfect tense.
34 *Dicent* is similar to *dicunt*, but in the future tense.
35 This is the perfect form of *facio*.
36 *Magna* is neuter plural accusative here.
37 *dispergo, dispergere, dispersi, dispersus*: scatter, disperse; here in the perfect tense
38 *superbus, -a, -um*: proud
39 *depono, deponere, deposui, depositum*: put down
40 *esurio, esurire*: be hungry
41 *dimitto, dimittere, dimisi, dimissum*: dismiss, send away
42 *inanis, inanis, inane*: empty, void
43 perfect form of *suscipio, suscipere:* take up, receive
44 *recordatus*: remembered
45 *locutus est*: perfect deponent, "spoke"
46 *semen, seminis* (n.): seed, offspring
47 *exsulis, exsulis* (m.): exile; here it is the nominative and tells more about the implied subject of *clamamus*, "we."
48 *gemo, gemere, gemui, gemitus*: groan

ergō, Advocāta nostra, illōs tuōs misericordēs oculōs ad nōs converte. Et Jēsum, benedictum frūctum ventris[49] tuī, nōbīs post hoc exsilium ostende. Ō clēmēns, ō pia, ō dulcis Virgō Maria.

– reviews fifth declension, imperatives, and first-person subjects

Chapter 14

Oratio Fatimae

Domine Jēsu, dīmitte nōbīs dēbita nostra, salva nōs ab igne[50] īnferiōrī, perdūc in caelum omnēs animās, praesertim[51] eās, quae misericordiae tuae maximē indigent.[52]

– reviews adverbs

Chapter 15

From Bernard of Clairvaux

Jēsus dulcis memoriā, dāns vēra cordī gaudia, sed super mel[53] et omnia Eius dulcis praesentia. Nīl cantātur suāvius, Nīl audītur iūcundius, Nīl cōgitātur dulcius, quam Jēsus, Deī Fīlius. Jēsū, dulcēdō cordium, fōns[54] vīvus, lūmen mentium, excēdēns[55] omne gaudium, Et omne dēsīderium!

– Reviews comparative adverbs. *Nīl* is a shortening of *nihil*.

Chapter 16

Cōnfiteor

Cōnfiteor Deō omnipotentī,
beātae Mariae semper Virginī,
beātō Michaēlī Archangelō,
beātō Iōannī Baptistae,
sānctīs Apostolīs Petrō et Paulō,
omnibus Sānctīs, et vōbīs, frātrēs:
quia peccāvī[56] nimis
cōgitātiōne, verbō et opere:

---

49 *venter, ventris* (m.): stomach
50 *ignis, ignis* (m.): fire
51 *praesertim*: especially
52 *indigeo, indigere, indigui, —* : need (the object of need comes in the genitive)
53 *mel, mellis* (n.): honey
54 *fons, fontis* (m.): spring
55 *excedo, excedere, excessi, excessus*: pass, exceed
56 *peccavi*: I have sinned; it is a perfect active indicative.

mea culpa,[57] mea culpa,

mea maxima culpa.

Ideō precor beātam Mariam semper Virginem,

beātum Michaēlem Archangelum,

beātum Iōannem Baptistam,

sānctōs Apostolōs Petrum et Paulum,

omnēs Sānctōs, et vōs, frātrēs,

ōrāre prō mē ad Dominum Deum nostrum.

    – reviews deponents

Chapters 17 and 27[58]

Tē Deum

Tē Deum laudāmus:

tē Dominum cōnfitēmur.

Tē aeternum Patrem

omnis terra venerātur.[59]

Tibi omnēs Angelī;

tibi caelī et ūniversae Potestātēs;

Tibi Cherubim et Seraphim

incessābilī[60] vōce prōclāmant:

Sānctus, Sānctus, Sānctus, Dominus

Deus Sabaoth.

Plēnī sunt caelī et terra

majestātis glōriae tuae.

Tē glōriōsus Apostolōrum chorus,

Tē Prophētārum laudābilis numerus,

Tē Martyrum candidātus laudat exercitus.

Tē per orbem terrārum

Sāncta cōnfitētur Ecclēsia,

Patrem immēnsae majestātis:

---

  57 *culpa, culpae* (f.): fault, blame
  58 I suggest using the Tē Deum in chapter 17, but only up to the line, *Patrem immensae maiestatis*.
  59 *veneror, venerari, veneratus sum*: adore, revere, venerate
  60 *incessabilis, incessabilis, incessabile*: unceasing

Venerandum tuum vērum et ūnicum Fīlium;

Sānctum quoque Paraclītum[61] Spiritum.

Tū Rēx glōriae, Chrīste.

Tū Patrīs sempiternus[62] es Filius.

Tū ad līberandum susceptūrus hominem,

nōn horruistī Virginis uterum.

Tū, dēvictō[63] mortis aculeō,[64] aperuisti

crēdentibus rēgna caelōrum.

Tū ad dexteram[65] Deī sēdēs, in glōriā Patrīs.

Jūdex[66] crēderis esse ventūrus.

Tē ergō quaesumus, tuīs famulīs subvēnī:[67]

quōs pretiōsō sanguine redēmistī.[68]

Aeternā fac cum sānctīs tuīs in glōriā numerārī.[69]

Salvum fac populum tuum,

Domine, et benedic hērēditātī[70] tuae.

Per singulōs diēs benedīcimus tē;

Et laudāmus Nōmen tuum in saeculum, et in saeculum saeculī.

Dignāre, Domine, diē istō sine peccātō nōs cūstōdīre.

Miserēre nostrī Domine, miserēre nostrī.

Fiāt[71] misericordia tua,

Domine, super nōs, quemadmodum spērāvimus in tē.

In tē, Domine, spērāvī:

nōn cōnfundar[72] in aeternum.

---

61 *paraclitus, paracliti* (m.): advocate; name for Holy Spirit from Greek
62 *sempiternus, sempiterna, sempiternum*: perpetual, eternal
63 *devinco, devincere, devici, devictus*: subdue, defeat
64 *aculeus, aculei* (m.): sting
65 *dextera, dexterae* (f.): right hand
66 *judex, judicis* (m.): judge
67 *subvenio, subvenire, subveni, subventus*: help, rescue
68 *redimo, redimere, redemi, redemptus*: buy back, redeem
69 *numero, numerare, numeravi, numeratus*: number
70 *hereditas, hereditatis* (f.): inheritance
71 *fiat*: let it be
72 *confundo, confundere, confudi, confusus*: dismay confuse

APPENDICES

Chapter 18[73] Chapter 31

Stābat Māter Dolorōsa[74]

1. Stābat Māter dolōrōsa
Juxtā crucem lacrimōsa
Dum pendēbat[75] Fīlius.

2. Cujus animam gementem[77]
Contrīstātam[78] et dolentem
Pertrānsīvit[79] gladius.

3. Ō quam trīstīs et afflīcta[83]
Fuit illa benedicta
Māter ūnigenitī!

4. Quae moerēbat[84] et dolēbat,
Pia Māter, dum vidēbat
Nātī[85] poenās inclytī.[86]

5. Quis est homō quī nōn flēret,
Mātrem Chrīstī sī vidēret
In tantō suppliciō?[88]

Stābat Māter Speciōsa

1. Stābat Māter speciōsa
Juxtā foenum[76] gaudiōsa
Dum jacēbat parvulus.

2. Cujus animam gaudentem
Laetābundam[80] et ferventem[81]
Pertrānsīvit iubilus.[82]

3. Ō quam laeta et beāta
Fuit illa immaculāta
Māter ūnigenitī!

4. Quae gaudēbat et rīdēbat,
Exultābat cum vidēbat
Nātī partum[87] inclytī.

5. Quis est, quī nōn gaudēret,[89]
Chrīstī Mātrem sī vidēret
In tantō sōlāciō?[90]

---

73 I use the first four stanzas for chapter 18 and leave the rest for later.

74 I have included the lesser known Stābat Māter Speciosa. Some have suggested it goes back to the fifteenth century. It is useful to compare it to the Stābat Māter and to practice more Latin. We have two main versions in common usage: one from Franz Liszt, the other from Alphons Johannes Maria Diepenbrock. The Liszt text is used in the main portion with Diepenbrock in footnotes.

75 *pendere*: hang
76 *foenum* (n.): hay
77 *gemere*: groan
78 *contristere*: make sad, afflict
79 *pertransire*: pierce, go through
80 *laetabundus, -a, -um*: greatly rejoicing
81 *fervens, ferventis*: feverish, warmed
82 *jubilus, jubili* (m.): joyful melody
83 *afflictus, -a, -um*: miserable, downcast
84 *maerere*: be sad, grieve
85 *natus, nati* (m.): son [*lit*. born]
86 *inclytus, -a, -um*: famous
87 *partus, parti* (m.): offspring
88 *supplicium supplicii* (n.): pain, punishment
89 Alphons Johannes Maria Diepenbrock: "*qui est homo, quin gauderet.*"
90 *solacium, solaci(i)* (n.): comfort, solace

6. Quis nōn posset contrīstārī,
Chrīstī Mātrem contemplārī⁹¹
Dolentem cum Fīliō?

7. Prō peccātīs suae gentis
Vīdit Jēsum in tormentīs,⁹³
Et flagellīs⁹⁴ subditum.⁹⁵

8. Vīdit suum dulcem nātum
Moriendō dēsōlātum⁹⁸
Dum ēmīsit spīritum.

9. Pia Māter, fōns¹⁰⁵ amōris
Mē sentīre vim¹⁰⁶ dolōris
Fac, ut tēcum lūgeam.¹⁰⁷

6. Quis nōn posset collaetārī,
Piam Mātrem contemplārī
Lūdentem⁹² cum Fīliō?

7. Prō peccātīs suae gentis
Vīdit Jēsum cum jūmentīs,⁹⁶
Et algōrī⁹⁷ subditum.

8. Vīdit suum dulcem nātum
Vagientum⁹⁹ adōrātum
Vīlī dīversōriō.¹⁰⁰

8ā. Nāti Chrīsti in praesēpe¹⁰¹
Coelī cīvēs canunt laetē
Cum immēnsō gaudiō.

8b. Stābat senex¹⁰² cum puella
Nōn cum verbō nec loquēlā¹⁰³
Stupēscentēs¹⁰⁴ cordibus.

9. Pia Māter, fōns amōris
Mē sentīre vim ārdōris¹⁰⁸
Fac, ut tēcum sentiam.

---

91 *contemplari*: to contemplate
92 *ludere*: to play
93 *tormentum, tormenti* (n.): torture, torment
94 *flagellum, flagelli* (n.): scourge, lashing
95 *subditus, -a, -um*: subject, submissive
96 *jumentum, jumenti* (n.): cattle
97 *algor, agloris* (m.): cold, coldness
98 *desolatus, -a, -um*: forsaken
99 *vagire*: wailing, crying
100 *diversorium, diversori(i)* (n.): inn
101 *praesepe, praesepis* (n.): crib; manger
102 *senex, senecis* (m.): old man
103 *loquela, loquelae* (f.): speech, utterance
104 *stupescere*: be stupified
105 *fons, fontis* (f.): fountain
106 *vis* (f.): force, strength
107 *lugere*: mourn, cry out
108 *ardor, ardoris* (m.): fire, love

10. Fac, ut ārdeat[109] cor meum
In āmandō Chrīstum Deum
Ut sibi complaceam.[110]

11. Sāncta Māter, istud agās,
Crucifixī fige[111] plāgās[112]
Cordī meō validē.[113]

12. Tuī nātī vulnerātī,
Tam dignātī prō mē patī,
Poenās mēcum dīvidē.[115]

13. Fac mē tēcum, piē, flēre,
Crucifixō condolēre,
Dōnec ego vīxerō.

14. Juxtā crucem tēcum stāre,
Et mē tibi sociāre[122]
In plānctū[123] dēsīderō.

10. Fac, ut ārdeat cor meum
In āmandō Chrīstum Deum
Ut sibi complaceam.

11. Sānctā Māter, istud agās,
Pōne nostrō dūcās plāgās[114]
Cordī fīxās validē.

12. Tuī nātī coelō lāpsī,[116]
Jam dignātī foenō[117] nāscī,
Poenās mēcum dīvidē.

13. Fac mē tēcum congaudēre
Iesulīnō[118] cohaerēre[119]
Dōnec ego vīxerō.

13a. In mē sistat[120] ārdor tuī
Puerinō[121] fac mē fruī
Dum sum in exiliō.

14. Hunc ārdōrem fac commūnem,
Nē mē faciās immūnem,[124]
Ab hōc dēsīderiō.

---

109 *ardere*: burn
110 *com-placere*: thorough please
111 *figere*: fasten, fix
112 *plaga, plagae* (f.): blow, strike
113 *valide, valde*: really, truly
114 Diepenbrock has "*prone introducas plagas cordi meo valide.*"
115 *dividere*: divide, share
116 *lapsus, lapsi* (m.): fallen
117 *foenum, foeni* (n.): hay
118 *Jesulinus, Jesulini* (m.): little Jesus
119 *cohaerere*: embrace, be connected
120 *sistat*: let your love stand
121 *puerinus, puerini* (m.): little boy
122 *sociare*: share in
123 *planctus, planctus* (m.): weeping
124 *ne facias*: don't make me immune

15. Virgō virginum praeclāra,[125]
Mihi jam nōn sīs amāra[126]
Fac mē tēcum plangere.[127]

16. Fac, ut portem[129] Chrīstī mortem
Passiōnis fac cōnsortem,[130]
Et plāgās recolere.[131]

17. Fac mē plāgīs vulnerārī,
Fac mē cruce inēbriārī,[132]
Et cruōre[133] Fīliī.

18. Flammīs[136] nē ūrar[137] succēnsus
Per tē, Virgō, sim dēfēnsus
In diē jūdiciī.

19. Fac mē cruce cūstōdīrī
Morte Chrīstī praemūnīrī[140]
Cōnfovērī[141] grātia.

20. Quandō corpus moriētur,
Fac, ut animae dōnētur
Paradīsī glōria. Āmēn.

15. Virgō virginum praeclāra,
Mihi jam nōn sīs amāra
Fac mē parvum rapere.[128]

16. Fac, ut portem pulchrum fortem
Quī nāscendō vīcit mortem,
Volēns vītam trādere.

17. Fac mē tēcum satiārī,[134]
Nātō tuō inēbriārī,
Stāns inter tripudia.[135]

18. Īnflammātus et accēnsus
Obstupēscit[138] omnīs sēnsūs
Tālī decommerciō.[139]

19. Fac mē nātō cūstōdīrī
Verbō Chrīstī praemūnīrī
Cōnservārī grātia.

20. Quandō corpus moriētur,
Fac, ut animae dōnētur
Tuī nātī vīsiō.

---

125 *praeclarus, -a, -um*: very beautiful, splendid
126 *amarus, -a, -um*: bitter
127 *plangere*: strike
128 *rapere*: grasp, seize
129 First person singular present active subjunctive of *portare*.
130 *consors, consortis* (f./m.): sharer
131 *recolere*: call to mind
132 *inebriare*: saturate, drunk
133 *cruor, cruoris* (f.): blood
134 *satiare*: satisfy
135 *tripudium, tripudi(i)* (n.): sacred dance
136 *flamma, flammae* (f.): flame
137 *urere*: burn
138 *obstupescere*: be stupified
139 *decommercium, decommerci(i)* (n.): exchange
140 *praemunire*: fortify, make safe
141 *confovere*: cherish assiduously

Chapter 19

Gaudete

Gaudēte, gaudēte! Chrīstus est nātus
Ex Mariā virgine, gaudēte!
Tempus adest grātiae hoc quod optābāmus,[142]
Carmina[143] laetitiae, dēvōtē[144] reddāmus.
Deus homō factus est Nātūrā mīrante,
Mundus renovātus est ā Chrīstō rēgnante.

Chapter 20

V: Chrīstus resurrēxit!
R: Vērē resurrēxit! Allēlūia.

Chapter 21

V: Replētī sumus manē misericoridā tuā.
R: Exultāvimus et dēlectātī sumus.

Chapter 21

Ave Maria

Avē Maria, grātia plēna,
Dominus tēcum.
Benedicta tū in mulieribus,
et benedictus frūctus ventris tuī, Jēsus.
Sānctā Mariā, Māter Deī,
ōra prō nōbīs peccātōribus,
nunc, et in hōrā mortis nostrae.
Āmēn.

---

142 *optare*: desire, wish
143 *carmen, carmins* (n.): song
144 *devotis*: devotedly

Chapter 22

Diēs īrae,[145] diēs illa,
Solvet saeclum in favīllā:[146]
Teste[147] Dāvīd cum Sibyllā.
Quantus tremor[148] est futūrus,
Quandō Iūdex est ventūrus,
Cūncta strictē[149] discussūrus!

Tubā, mīrum spargēns sonum[150]
Per sepulchra[151] regiōnum,
Cōget[152] omnēs ante thronum.

Mors stupēbit, et nātūra,
Cum resurget creātūra,
Iūdicantī respōnsūra.

Līber scrīptus prōferētur,
In quō tōtum continētur,[153]
Unde mundus iūdicētur.

Iūdex ergō cum sedēbit,
Quidquid latet,[154] appārēbit:
Nīl inultum[155] remanēbit.

---

145 *ira, irae* (f.): anger
146 *favilla, favillae* (f.): ashes of the dead
147 *testis, testis* (m.): witness
148 *tremor, tremors* (m.): trembling
149 *strictus, -a, -um*: severe, strict
150 *sonum, soni* (m.): sound
151 *sepulchrum, sepulchri* (n.): grave
152 *cogere*: force, prod
153 *continere (con-teneo)*: contain
154 *latere*: be hidden
155 *inultus, -a, -um*: unpunished

Quid sum miser tunc dictūrus?
Quem patrōnum[156] rogātūrus,
Cum vix[157] iūstus sit[158] sēcūrus?

Rēx tremendae maiestātis,
Quī salvandōs[159] salvās[160] grātīs,
Salvā mē, fōns pietātis.

Recordāre,[161] Jēsu piē,
Quod sum causā tuæ viæ:
Nē mē perdās[162] illā diē.

Quaerēns mē, sēdistī lassus:[163]
Redēmistī[164] Crucem passūs:
Tantus labor nōn sit cassus.[165]

Iūstē Iūdex ultiōnis,[166]
Dōnum fac remissiōnis
Ante diem ratiōnis.

Ingemīscō,[167] tamquam reus:
Culpā rubet[168] vultus meus:
Supplicantī parce,[169] Deus.

---

156 *patronus, patroni* (m.): patron, advocate
157 *vix*: scarcely
158 *sit*: is (present active subjunctive of *esse*)
159 *salvandos* (gerundive): those who ought to be saved
160 *salvas* (from *salvare*): to save
161 *recordare*: remember
162 Negative command: do not make me perish.
163 *lassus, -a, -um*: weary, exhausted
164 *redemere*: to redeem
165 *tantus labor sit cassus*: let not such labor be in vain
166 *ultio, ultionis* (f.): punishing, avenging
167 *ingemiscere*: sigh, groan
168 *rubere*: be red, blush
169 *parcere*: spare

Quī Mariam absolvistī,
Et latrōnem[170] exaudīstī,
Mihi quoque spem dedistī.

Precēs meae nōn sunt dignae:
Sed tū bonus fac benignē,
Nē perennī cremer[171] igne.

Inter ovēs locum praestā,[172]
Et ab haedīs[173] mē sequestrā,[174]
Statuēns in parte dextrā.

Cōnfūtātīs[175] maledictīs,
Flammīs ācribus addictīs,
Vocā mē cum benedictīs.

Ōrō supplex et acclīnis,[176]
Cor contrītum quasi cinis:[177]
Gere[178] cūram meī fīnis.

Lacrimōsa diēs illa,
Quā resurget ex favílla
Iūdicandus homō reus:[179]
Huic ergō parce, Deus:

Piē Jēsu Domine,
Dōnā eīs requiem. Āmēn.

---

170 *latro, latronis* (m.): brigand, thief
171 *cremare*: burn; *cremer*: lest I be burned
172 *praestare*: offer, give
173 *haedus, haedi* (m.): kid, goat
174 *sequestrare*: remove, seperate
175 *confutare*: check, suppress
176 *acclinis, acclinis*: bowing
177 *cinis, cineris* (m.): ashes
178 *gerere*: bear
179 *reus, rei* (m.): guilty person, culprit, sinner

Chapter 22

V: Crēdō quod Redēmptor meus vīvit, et in novissimō diē dē terrā surrectūrus sum. Et in carne meā vidēbō Deum Salvātōrem meum.

R: Quem vīsūrus sum ego ipse, et nōn alius; et oculī meī cōnspectūrī[180] sunt in carne meā.

Chapter 24

Memorāre, Ō piissima Virgō Maria, nōn esse audītum[181] ā saeculō, quemquam ad tua currentem praesidia,[182] tua implōrantem auxilia, tua petentem suffrāgia,[183] esse dērelictum.[184] Ego tālī animātus cōnfidentiā, ad tē, Virgō Virginum, Māter, currō, ad tē veniō, cōram tē gemēns[185] peccātor assistō.[186] Nōlī, Māter Verbī, verba mea dēspicere; sed audī propitia[187] et exaudī. Amen.

Chapter 24

Cōnfiteor Deō et beātae Mariae semper virginī,

et beātō Michaēlī archangelō et beātō Jōhannī baptistae

et sānctīs apostolīs Petrō et Paulō

cum omnibus sānctīs et tibi patrī

mea culpa III vic., peccāvī

per superbiam in multa mea mala inīqua et pessimā cōgitātiōne,

locūtiōne, pollūtiōne,[188] sugestiōne, dēlectātiōne, cōnsēnsū,[189] verbō et opere,

in perjūriō, in adulteriō, in sacrilegiō, homicīdiō, furtū, falsō testimōniō,

peccāvī vīsū, audītū, gustū,[190] odōrātū[191] et tāctū, et mōribus, vitiīs meīs malīs.

Precor beātam Mariam semper virginem et omnibus sānctīs et istī sānctī et tē pater,

ōrāre et intercēdere[192] prō mē peccātōre Dominum nostrum Jēsum Chrīstum.

---

180 *conspectare*: see, regard

181 This is an accusative plus infinitive construction based on the main imperative verb, *memorare*. The subject of *auditum* is an implied "it."

182 *praesidium, praesidi(i)* (n.): protection. This word goes with *tua*.

183 *suffragium, suffragi(i)* (n.): judgment, help

184 *derelinquo, derelinquere, dereliqui, derelictus*: leave behind, abandon

185 *gemere*: groan

186 *assistere*: stand before

187 *propitius, propitia, propitium*: well disposed, favorable. Here it is used substantivealy to refer to Mary.

188 *pollutio, pollutionis* (f.): pollution

189 *consensus, consensus* (m.): agreement

190 *gustare*: taste

191 *oderare*: smell

192 *intercedere*: intercede

Chapter 25
Tē Deum (Second half)

Chapter 26
Psalm 127

Nisi Dominus aedificāverit domum, in vānum labōrāvērunt quī aedificant eam. Nisi Dominus cūstōdierit cīvitātem, frūstrā[193] vigilat quī cūstōdit eam.

Vānum est vōbīs ante lūcem surgere: surgite postquam sēderitis,[194] quī mandūcātis pānem dolōris. Cum dederit dīlēctīs suīs somnum,

ecce haerēditās[195] Dominī, filiī; mercēs, frūctus ventris.

Sīcut sagittae[196] in manū potentīs, ita filiī excussōrum.

Beātus vir quī implēvit dēsīderium suum ex ipsīs: nōn cōnfundētur[197] cum loquētur inimīcīs suīs in portā.

Chapter 27
Benedictus

Benedictus Dominus Deus Isrāēl; quia vīsitāvit et fēcit redēmptiōnem plēbis suae

et ērēxit[198] cornū salūtis nōbīs, in domō Dāvīd puerī suī,

sīcut locūtus est per os sānctōrum, quī ā saeculō sunt, prophētārum ejus,

salūtem ex inimīcīs nostrīs, et dē manū omnium, quī ōdērunt nōs;

ad faciendam misericordiam cum patribus nostrīs, et memorārī testāmentī suī sānctī,

jūsjūrandum,[199] quod jūrāvit[200] ad Abraham patrem nostrum, datūrum sē nōbīs,

ut sine timōre, dē manū inimīcōrum nostrum līberātī, serviāmus illī

in sānctitāte et jūstitiā cōram ipsō omnibus diēbus nostrīs.

Et tū, puer, prophēta Altissimī vocāberis: praeībis[201] enim ante faciem Dominī parāre viās ejus,

---

193 *frustra*: in vain
194 *sederitis*: perfect subjunctive indicative, "after you have sat down."
195 *haereditas, haereditatis* (f.): inheritance
196 *sagitta, sagittae* (f.): arrow
197 *confundo, confundere, confudi, confusus*: confuse, dismay
198 *erigo, erigere, erexi, erectus*: cause to arise
199 *jūsjūrandum, jūsjūrandi* (n.): oath
200 *jurare*: swore
201 *prae-ire*: go before

ad dandam scientiam salūtis plēbī ejus in remissiōnem peccātōrum eōrum,

per vīscera[202] misericordiae Deī nostrī, in quibus vīsitābit nōs oriēns ex altō,

illūmināre hīs, quī in tenebrīs et in umbrā[203] mortis sedent, ad dīrigendōs[204] pedēs nostrōs in viam pācis.

Chapter 28

Rēgīna caelī[205]

V. Rēgīna caelī, laetāre, allēlūja.

R. Quia quem meruistī[206] portāre, allēlūja,

V. Resurrēxit, sīcut dīxit, allēlūja.

R. Ora prō nōbīs Deum, allēlūja.

V. Gaudē et laetāre, Virgō Maria, allēlūja,

R. Quia surrēxit Dominus vērē, allēlūja.

Ōrēmus. Deus, quī per resurrēctiōnem Fīliī tuī Dominī nostrī Jēsu Chrīstī mundum laetificāre dignātus es: praestā, quaesumus, ut per ejus Genetrīcem[207] Virginem Mariam perpetuae capiāmus gaudia vītae. Per eundem Chrīstum Dominum nostrum. R. Āmēn.

Chapter 29

Angelus Domini

V. Angelus Dominī nūntiāvit Mariae,

R. Et concēpit dē Spīritū Sānctō.

Avē Maria, grātia plēna, Dominus tēcum; benedicta tū in mulieribus, et benedictus frūctus ventris tuī, Jēsus. Sānctā Mariā, Māter Deī, ōra prō nōbīs peccātōribus, nunc et in hōrā mortis nostrae. Āmēn.

V. Ecce ancilla Dominī,

R. Fīat mihi secundum verbum tuum.

Avē Maria

V. Et Verbum carō factum est.

R. Et habitāvit in nōbīs.

---

202 *viscer, visceris* (n.): internal organs, mercy
203 *umbra, umbrae* (f.): shade, shadow
204 *dirigere*: lead
205 Liturgically used during Eastertide.
206 *mereo, merere, merui, meritus*: earn, deserve, merit
207 *genetrix, genetricis* (f.): mother, ancesstress

Avē Maria

V. Ora prō nōbīs, sānctā Deī Genitrīx.

R. Ut dignī efficiāmur prōmissiōnibus Chrīstī.

Ōrēmus. Grātiam tuam, quaesumus,[208] Domine, mentibus nostrīs īnfunde; ut, quī, angelō nūntiante, Chrīstī Fīliī tuī incarnātiōnem cognōvimus, per passiōnem ejus et crucem, ad resurrēctiōnis glōriam perdūcāmur. Per eundem Chrīstum Dominum nostrum.

Chapter 30

Pater Noster

Pater noster, quī es in caelīs: Sānctificētur nōmen tuum: Adveniat rēgnum tuum: Fīat voluntās tua, sīcut in caelō, et in terrā. Pānem nostrum quotīdiānum dā nōbīs hodiē: Et dīmitte nōbīs dēbita nostra, sīcut et nōs dīmittimus dēbitōribus nostrīs. Et nē nōs indūcās in tentātiōnem, sed līberā nōs ā mālō. Amen.

Tantum Ergo

Tantum[209] ergō sacrāmentum venerēmur cernuī[210]: Et antīquum documentum novō cēdat rītuī[211]: praestet fidēs supplēmentum sēnsuum dēfectuī[212]. Genitōrī[213], Genitōque[214] laus et jūbilātiō, salūs, honor, virtūs quoque sit et benedictiō: prōcēdentī[215] ab utrōque compār[216] sit laudātiō. Āmēn. V. Pānem dē caelō praestitistī[217] eīs. R. Omne dēlectāmentum[218] in sē habentem. V. Ōrēmus: Deus, quī nōbīs sub sacrāmentō mīrābilī, passiōnis tuae memoriam relīquistī: tribue[219], quaesumus, ita nōs corporis et sanguinis tuī sacra mystēria venerārī, ut redēmptiōnis tuae frūctum in nōbīs jūgiter[220] sentiāmus. Quī vīvis et rēgnās in saecula saeculōrum.

---

208 *quaerere*: beg, ask
209 *tantum*: so great
210 *cernus, -a, -um*: bowed [modifying the subject, "we"]
211 *ritus, ritus*: rite
212 *defectus, defectus*: failing
213 *genitor, genitoris*: begettor
214 *genitus, -a, -um*: begotten
215 *procedere*: proceed
216 *compar*: equal
217 *praesto, praestare, praestiti, praestitus*: provide, give
218 *delectamentum*: delight
219 *tribuere*: give
220 *jugiter*: continually

Chapter 31

Ubi Caritas

Ubi cāritās et amor, Deus ibi est.
Congregāvit nōs in ūnum Chrīstī amor.
Exsultēmus, et in ipsō jūcundēmur.[221]
Timeāmus, et amēmus Deum vīvum.
Et ex corde dīligāmus nōs sincērō.[222]
Ubi cāritās et amor, Deus ibi est.
Simul ergō cum in ūnum congregāmur:
Nē nōs mente dīvidāmur, caveāmus.
Cessent jūrgia maligna, cessent lītēs.
Et in mediō nostrī sit Chrīstus Deus.
Ubi cāritās et amor, Deus ibi est.
Simul quoque cum beātīs videāmus,
Glōrianter vultum tuum, Chrīste Deus:
Gaudium quod est immēnsum, atque probum,
Saecula per īnfīnīta saeculōrum.
Amen.

Stābat Māter (Stanzas 5–20)

Chapter 32

Psalm 51:17, 18

Domine, labia[223] mea aperiēs, et os meum annūntiābit laudem tuam.
Quoniam sī voluissēs sacrificium, dedissem utique; holocaustīs nōn dēlectāberis.

---

221 *jucundari*: please, take delight
222 *sincero*: sincerely
223 *labium, labii* (n.): lip

GRAMMAR APPENDIX

List of Prepositions and Prepositional Prefixes

Latin uses a common list of prepositions that will, for the most part, be familiar to English speakers. That said, it will take some time to get used to breaking up words. For verbs like *ire*, where the stem is really just *i-*, it will often be difficult to recognize that it is a compound word.

a/ab (abs): by, from
    ** this preposition changes based on whether a vowel comes before or a consonant

ad: towards

ante: before

circum: around

con: with; also completion

contra: against

de: about, concerning

e/ex: from, out of
    ** this preposition changes based on whether a vowel comes before or a consonant

extra: outside of

in: into, onto, against; in

intra: within

ob: on account of, according to

per: through; also entirely

post: after, behind

pro: for, in behalf of, before, instead of

sub: under, beneath

super: above, beyond

supra: above, over

Nouns

Quick Definition: In English, nouns are persons, places, or things whose function in the sentence is determined either by where they occur in the sentence (before or after the verb) or by additional prepositions. So the translation of a noun from Latin to English requires placing the noun either before a verb to make it the subject, or after the verb to make it the direct object. Alternatively, you will need to add a preposition to make sense of how it is being used in Latin.

A-Nouns / 1st Declension Feminine (and sometimes Masculine)

Case	Singular	Example Translation	Plural	Example Translation
Nom	ancill\a	handmaid (sub.)	ancill\ae	handmaids (sub.)
Gen	ancill\ae	of the handmaid	ancill\ārum	of the handmaids
Dat	ancill\ae	to the handmaid	ancill\īs	to the handmaids
Acc	ancill\am	handmaid (d.o.)	ancill\ās	handmaids (d.o.)
Abl	ancill\ā	by the handmaid	ancill\īs	by the handmaids

O-Nouns / 2nd Declension Masculine

Case	Singular	Example Translation	Plural	Example Translation
Nom	discipul\us	student (sub.)	discipul\ī	students (sub.)
Gen	discipul\ī	of the student	discipul\ōrum	of the students
Dat	discipul\ō	to the student	discipul\īs	to the students
Acc	discipul\um	student (d.o.)	discipul\ōs	students (d.o.)
Abl	discipul\ō	by the student	discipul\īs	by the students

O-Nouns / 2nd Declension Neuter

Case	Singular	Example Translation	Plural	Example Translation
Nom	don\um	gift (sub.)	don\a	gifts (sub.)
Gen	don\ī	of the gift	don\ōrum	of the gifts
Dat	don\ō	to the gift	don\īs	to the gifts
Acc	don\um	gift (d.o.)	don\ōs	gifts (d.o.)
Abl	don\ō	by the gift	don\īs	by the gifts

I/E-Nouns / 3rd Declension

Masculine/Feminine

Case	Singular	Plural
Nom	*homō*	*homin|ēs*
Gen	*homin|is*	*homin|em*
Dat	*homin|ī*	*homin|ibus*
Acc	*homin|em*	*homin|ēs*
Abl	*homin|e*	*homin|ibus*

Neuter

Case	Singular	Plural
Nom	*mar|e*	*mar|ia*
Gen	*mar|is*	*mar|ium*
Dat	*mar|ī*	*mar|ibus*
Acc	*mar|e*	*mar|ia*
Abl	*mar|ī (mar|e)*	*mar|ibus*

U-Nouns / 4th Declension Masculine and Feminine

Case	Singular	Plural
Nom	*spirit|us*	*spirit|ūs*
Gen	*spirit|ūs*	*spirit|uum*
Dat	*spirit|uī*	*spirit|ibus*
Acc	*spirit|um*	*spirit|ūs*
Abl	*spirit|ū*	*spirit|ibus*

Neuter

Case	Singular	Plural
Nom	corn|ū	corn|ua
Gen	corn|ūs	corn|uum
Dat	corn|ū	corn|ibus
Acc	corn|ū	corn|ua
Abl	corn|ū	corn|ibus

E-Nouns / 5th Declension

Case	Singular	Plural
Nom	di|ēs	di|ēs
Gen	di|eī	di|ērum
Dat	di|eī	di|ēbus
Acc	di|em	di|ēs
Abl	di|ē	di|ēbus

Pronouns

Quick Definition: In English, pronouns take the place of an implied noun. Usually English pronouns only use gender when referring to humans or animals; otherwise English typically turns the pronouns into neuter. Latin pronouns often function similarly, but they have an expanded role in Latin. They can also be used in place of an article.

(These act like regular first and second declension nouns, except in the genitive and dative.)

Unemphatic Demonstrative Pronouns

Cases	M. S.	Example Translation	F. S.	Example Translation	N.S.	Example Translation
Nom	i|s	he (sub)	e|a	she	i|d	it
Gen	e|ius	his	e|ius	hers	e|ius	its
Dat	e|ī	to him	e|ī	to her	e|ī	to it
Acc	e|um	him	e|am	her	i|d	it (d.o.)
Abl	e|ō	by him	e|ā	by her	e|ō	by it

Cases	M. P.	Example Translation	F. P.	Example Translation	N.P.	Example Translation
Nom	e|ī (iī)	they	e|ae	they	e|a	these
Gen	e|ōrum	theirs	e|ārum	theirs	e|ōrum	of these
Dat	e|īs (iīs)	to them	e|īs (iīs)	to them	e|īs (iīs)	to these
Acc	e|ōs	them	e|ās	them	e|a	these (d.o.)
Abl	e|īs (iīs)	by them	e|īs (iīs)	by them	e|īs (iīs)	by these

Cases	M. S.	Example Translation	F. S.	Example Translation	N. S.	Example Translation
Nom	*ist|e*	he (sub)	*ist|a*	she	*ist|ud*	it
Gen	*ist|ius*	his	*ist|ius*	hers	*ist|ius*	its
Dat	*ist|ī*	to him	*ist|ī*	to her	*isti|ī*	to it
Acc	*ist|um*	him	*ist|am*	her	*isti|ud*	it (d.o.)
Abl	*ist|ō*	by him	*ist|ā*	by her	*ist|ō*	by it

Cases	M. P.	Example Translation	F. P.	Example Translation	N.P.	Example Translation
Nom	*ist|ī*	they	*ist|ae*	they	*ist|a*	these
Gen	*ist|ōrum*	theirs	*ist|ārum*	theirs	*is|tōrum*	of these
Dat	*ist|īs*	to them	*ist|īs*	to them	*ist|īs*	to these
Acc	*ist|ōs*	them	*ist|ās*	them	*ist|ae*	these (d.o.)
Abl	*ist|īs*	by them	*ist|īs*	by them	*ist|īs*	by these

Relative and Interrogative Pronouns

Only nominative singular masculine and neuter differ for the relative and interrogative singular, and this difference is indicated with a forward slash.

Cases	M. S.		F. S.		N. S.	
Nom	*qu|ī / qu|is*	who	*qu|ae / qu|is*	who	*qu|od / qu|id*	what
Gen	*cu|ius*	whose	*cu|ius*	whose	*cu|ius*	of which
Dat	*cu|i*	to whom	*cu|i*	to whom	*cu|i*	to whom
Acc	*qu|em*	whom	*qu|ām*	whom	*qu|od / qu|id*	what (d.o.)
Abl	*qu|ō*	by whom	*qu|ā*	by whom	*qu|ō*	by which

Cases	M. P.		F. P.		N. P.	
Nom	*qu|ī*	who	*qu|ae*	who	*qu|ae*	what
Gen	*qu|ōrum*	whose	*qu|ārum*	whose	*qu|ōrum*	of which
Dat	*qu|ibus*	to whom	*qu|ibus*	to whom	*qu|ibus*	to whom
Acc	*qu|ōs*	whom	*qu|ās*	whom	*qu|ae*	what (d.o.)
Abl	*qu|ibus*	by whom	*qu|ibus*	by whom	*qu|ibus*	by which

Emphatic Near Demonstrative Pronouns

Cases	M. S.	F. S.	N. S.	Example Translation
Nom	*hic*	*haec*	*hoc*	this (one)
Gen	*huius*	*huius*	*huius*	of this (one)
Dat	*huic*	*huic*	*huic*	to this (one)
Acc	*hunc*	*hanc*	*hoc*	this (one) (d.o.)
Abl	*hōc*	*hāc*	*hōc*	by that (one)

Cases	M. P.	F. P.	N. P.	Example Translation
Nom	*hī*	*hae*	*haec*	these (ones)
Gen	*hōrum*	*hārum*	*hōrum*	of these (ones)
Dat	*hīs*	*hīs*	*hīs*	to these (ones)
Acc	*hōs*	*hās*	*hōs*	these (ones)
Abl	*hīs*	*hīs*	*hīs*	by these (ones)

Emphatic Far Demonstrative ProNouns

Cases	M. S.	F. S.	N. S.	Example Translation
Nom	*ill\e*	*ill\a*	*ill\ud*	that (one)
Gen	*ill\ius*	*ill\ius*	*ill\ius*	of that (one)
Dat	*ill\ī*	*ill\ī*	*ill\ī*	to that (one)
Acc	*ill\um*	*ill\am*	*ill\ud*	that (one) (d.o.)
Abl	*ill\ō*	*ill\ā*	*ill\ō*	by that (one)

Cases	M. P.	F. P.	N. P.	Example Translation
Nom	*ill\ī*	*ill\ae*	*ill\ae*	those (ones)
Gen	*ill\ōrum*	*ill\ārum*	*ill\ōrum*	of those (ones)
Dat	*ill\īs*	*ill\īs*	*ill\īs*	to those (ones)
Acc	*ill\ōs*	*ill\am*	*ill\ae*	those (ones) (d.o.)
Abl	*ill\īs*	*ill\īs*	*ill\īs*	by those (ones)

Intensive Pronouns or Adjectives

Cases	M. S.	F. S.	N. S.	Example Translation
Nom	*ips\e*	*ips\a*	*ips\um*	himself
Gen	*ips\ius*	*ips\ius*	*ips\ius*	of himself
Dat	*ips\ī*	*ips\ī*	*ips\ī*	to himself
Acc	*ips\um*	*ips\am*	*ips\ud*	himself (d.o.)
Abl	*ips\ō*	*ips\ā*	*ips\ō*	by himself

Cases	M. P.	F. P.	N. P.	Example Translation
Nom	ips|ī	ips|ae	ips|ae	themselves
Gen	ips|ōrum	ips|ārum	ips|ōrum	of themselves
Dat	ips|īs	ips|īs	ips|īs	to themselves
Acc	ips|ōs	ips|as	ips|ae	themselves (d.o.)
Abl	ips|īs	ips|īs	ips|īs	by themselves

Adjectives

Quick Definition: adjectives provide more information about a noun. English adjectives often come before nouns and have only one form. Latin adjectives must agree with the nouns they modify in gender, number, and case (but not always declension).

Positive Adjectives "A/O" Adjectives

Cases	M. S.	F. S.	N. S.	M. P.	F. P.	N. P.
Nom	parv|us	parv|a	parv|um	parv|ī	parv|ae	parv|a
Gen	parv|ī	parv|ae	parv|ī	parv|ōrum	parv|ārum	parv|ōrum
Dat	parv|ō	parv|ae	parv|ō	parv|īs	parv|īs	parv|īs
Acc	parv|um	parv|am	parv|um	parv|ōs	parv|ās	parv|a
Abl	parv|ō	parv|ā	parv|ō	parv|īs	parv|īs	parv|īs

APPENDICES

Positive Adjectives "I/E" Adjectives

** Some third declension adjectives, like *fēlīx*, have the same nominative form for masculine, feminine, or nominative singular. Also, neuters always have the same nominative and accusative, so neuter accusative singular is *fēlīx*.

	M. S.	F. S.	N. S.	M. P.	F. P.	N. P.
Nom	ācer	ācr|is	ācr|e	ācr|ēs	ācr|ēs	ācr|ia
Gen	ācr|is	ācr|is	ācr|is	ācr|ium	ācr|ium	ācr|ium
Dat	ācr|ī	ācr|ī	ācr|ī	ācr|ibus	ācr|ibus	ācr|ibus
Acc	ācr|em	ācr|em	ācr|e	ācr|ēs	ācr|ēs	ācr|ia
Abl	ācr|ī	ācr|ī	ācr|ī	ācr|ibus	ācr|ibus	ācr|ibus

Comparative Adjectives

These are usually paired with a noun in the same case and are translated with "more" something or "-er"; for example, "more foolish," "higher."

	M. S.	F. S.	N. S.	M. P.	F. P.	N. P.
Nom	altior	altior	altius	altiōr|ēs	altiōr|ēs	altiōr|a
Gen	altiōr|is	altiōr|is	altiōr|is	altiōr|um	altiōr|um	altiōr|um
Dat	altiōr|ī	altiōr|ī	altiōr|ī	altiōr|ibus	altiōr|ibus	altiōr|ibus
Acc	altiōr|em	altiōr|em	altius	altiōr|ēs	altiōr|ēs	altiōr|a
Abl	altiōr|e	altiōr|e	altiōr|e	altiōr|ibus	altiōr|ibus	altiōr|ibus

Superlative Adjectives

These are usually paired with a noun in the same case and are translated with "most" something or "-est"; for example, "most foolish," "highest."

Case	M. S.	F. S.	N. S.	M. P.	F. P.	N. P.
Nom	altissim|us	altissim|a	altissim|um	altissim|ī	altissim|ae	altissim|a
Gen	altissim|ī	altissim|ae	altissim|ī	altissim|ōrum	altissim|ārum	altissim|ōrum
Dat	altissim|ō	altissim|ae	altissim|ō	altissim|īs	altissim|īs	altissim|īs
Acc	altissim|um	altissim|am	altissim|um	altissim|ōs	altissim|ās	altissim|a
Abl	altissim|ō	altissim|ā	altissim|ō	altissim|īs	altissim|īs	altissim|īs

Adverbs

Quick Definition: adverbs provide more information about verbs, as well as other adjectives and adverbs. These do not have gender in Latin, because they modify verbs. To make an adverb from an adjective, you can follow this chart below. Often, though not always, adverbs come from adjectives.

	A/O-Adjectives / 1st and 2nd declension adjective	Adverb
Positive	*foed|us, -a, -um* ugly	*foed|ē* in an ugly way
Comparative	*foed|ior, -ior, -e* uglier	*foed|ius* in an uglier way
Superlative	*foed|issim|us, -a, um* ugliest	*foed|issim|ē* in the ugliest way

	I/E-Adjectives / 3rd Declension	Adverb
Positive	*dulc|is, dulc|is, dulc|e* sweet	*dulc|iter* sweetly
Comparative	*dulc|ior, -ior, -e* sweeter	*dulc|ius* in a sweeter way
Superlative	*dulc|issim|us, -a, -um* sweetest	*dulc|issim|ē* in the sweetest way

Verb Morphology

Present Indicative

Quick Definition: The present tense verbs speak as if the action is happening and indicate that the action does happen.

Tense Formation: *stem + conjugation vowel + regular personal endings*
laud + a + t
Simple translation, active: [verb]
Simple translation, passive: "is being [verb]-ed"

Active

ā-verb	ē-verb	i/e-verb	i-verb	Example Translation
laud\ō	*monē\ō*	*dūc\ō*	*audi\ō*	I hear
laudā\s	*monē\s*	*dūci\s*	*audī\s*	You hear
lauda\t	*mone\t*	*dūci\t*	*audi\t*	He hears
laudā\mus	*monē\mus*	*dūci\mus*	*aud\mus*	We hear
laudā\tis	*monē\tis*	*dūci\tis*	*audī\tis*	You (pl.) hear
lauda\nt	*mone\nt*	*dūcu\nt*	*audiu\nt*	They hear

Passive

ā-verb	ē-verb	i/e-verb	i-verb	Example Translation
laudo\r	*moneo\r*	*dūco\r*	*audio\r*	I am being heard
laudā\rīs (*laudā\re*)	*monē\ris* (*monē\re*)	*dūce\ris* (*dūce\re*)	*audīe\ris* (*audī\re*)	You are being heard
laudā\tur	*monē\tur*	*dūci\tur*	*audī\tur*	He is being heard
laudā\mur	*monē\mur*	*dūci\mur*	*audī\mur*	We are being heard
laudā\minī	*monē\minī*	*dūci\minī*	*audī\minī*	You (pl.) are being heard
lauda\ntur	*mone\ntur*	*dūcu\ntur*	*audiu\ntur*	They are being heard

Irregular Verbs

We will include four representative irregular verbs in the charts that follow. The verbs *esse* and *posse* conjugate in essentially the same way, though the syllable *pot-* or *pos-* is added depending on whether the form of *esse* has an *s* or an *e* before it. The modal verbs *velle, nolle,* and *malle* all conjugate nearly the same way, though *nolle* is missing in some forms where *non* is put in front of the form of *velle*. The verb *ferre*, and all its forms with prepositional prefixes like *adferre, auferre,* etc., has one of the most difficult-to-remember changes. The perfect forms have a new stem, *tulisse*, and the perfect participle has a new stem, *latus*, which can be easily mistaken for a new verb. Finally, the verb *ire*, and all its forms with prepositional prefixes like *adire, abire,* etc., can be difficult because the stem is technically just the short vowel *i*. So the verb looks different in some forms when it begins with a different vowel, though grammatically it is the same stem.

Only *ferre* has passive forms.

ESSE	VELLE	IRE	FERRE	FERRI
sum	*volō*	*eō*	*ferō*	*feror*
es	*vis*	*īs*	*fers*	*ferris*
est	*vult*	*it*	*fert*	*fertur*
sumus	*volumus*	*īmus*	*ferimus*	*ferimur*
estis	*vultis*	*ītis*	*fertis*	*feriminī*
sunt	*volunt*	*eunt*	*ferunt*	*feruntur*

Imperfect Indicative

Definition: Uncompleted and often ongoing action in the past that did occur.
Tense formation: stem + conjugation vowel + tense formant + regular personal endings
vid-e-ba-t
Translation, active voice: "was/were [verb]-ing"
Translation, passive voice: "was/were being [verb]-ed"

Active

ā-verb	ē-verb	i/e-verb	i-verb	Example Translation
laudā\ba\m	*monē\ba\m*	*ducē\ba\m*	*audiē\ba\m*	I was hearing
laudā\bā\s	*monē\bā\s*	*ducē\bā\s*	*audiē\bā\s*	You were hearing
laudā\ba\t	*monē\ba\t*	*ducē\ba\t*	*audiē\ba\t*	He was hearing
laudā\bā\mus	*monē\bā\mus*	*ducē\bā\mus*	*audiē\bā\mus*	We were hearing
laudā\bā\tis	*monē\bā\tis*	*ducē\ba\tis*	*audiē\ba\tis*	You all were hearing
laudā\ba\nt	*monē\ba\nt*	*ducē\ba\nt*	*audiē\ba\nt*	They were hearing

Passive

ā-verb	ē-verb	i/e-verb	i-verb	Example Translation
laudā\ba\r	*monē\ba\r*	*ducē\ba\r*	*audiē\ba\r*	I was (being) heard
laudā\bā\ris (*laudābāre*)	*monē\bā\ris* (*monē\bā\re*)	*ducē\bā\ris* (*ducē\bā\re*)	*audiē\bā\ris* (*audiē\bā\re*)	You were (being) heard
laudā\bā\tur	*monē\ba\tur*	*ducē\ba\tur*	*audiē\ba\tur*	He / She / It was (being) heard
laudā\bā\mur	*monē\bā\mur*	*ducē\bā\mur*	*audiē\bā\mur*	We were (being) heard
laudā\bā\minī	*monē\bā\minī*	*ducē\bā\minī*	*audiē\bā\minī*	You all were (being) heard
laudā\ba\ntur	*monē\ba\ntur*	*ducē\ba\ntur*	*audiē\ba\ntur*	They were (being) heard

Irregular Verbs

ESSE	VELLE	IRE	FERRE	FERRI
eram	*volēbam*	*ībam*	*ferēbam*	*ferēbar*
erās	*volēbās*	*ībās*	*ferēbās*	*ferēbāris*
erat	*volēbat*	*ībat*	*ferēbat*	*ferēbatur*
erāmus	*volēbāmus*	*ībāmus*	*ferēbāmus*	*ferēbāmur*
erātis	*volēbātis*	*ībātis*	*ferēbātis*	*ferēbāminī*
erant	*volēbant*	*ībant*	*ferēbant*	*ferēbantur*

Future Indicative

Quick Definition: Action that will happen in the future.
Tense Formation: stem + *-bi-* (ā-verb, ē-verb) **or** stem + *-e-* (i/e-verb, i-verb) + personal endings
Representative Translation, Active Voice: will [verb]
Representative Translation, Passive Voice: will be [verb]-ed

Active

ā-verb	ē-verb	i/e-verb	i-verb	Example Translation
laudā|b|ō	*monē|b|ō*	*dūc|a|m*	*audi|a|m*	I will hear
laudā|b|is	*monē|b|is*	*dūc|ē|s*	*audi|ē|s*	You will hear
laudā|b|it	*monē|b|it*	*dūc|e|t*	*audi|e|t*	He will hear
laudā|b|imus	*monē|b|imus*	*dūc|ē|mus*	*audi|ē|mus*	We will hear
laudā|b|itis	*monē|b|itis*	*dūc|ē|itis*	*audi|ē|itis*	You all will hear
laudā|b|unt	*monē|b|unt*	*dūc|e|nt*	*audi|e|nt*	They will hear

Passive

ā-verb	ē-verb	i/e-verb	i-verb	Example Translation
laudā|b|or	*monē|b|or*	*dūc|a|r*	*audi|a|r*	I will be heard
laudā|b|eris	*monē|b|eris*	*dūc|ē|ris*	*audi|e|ris*	You will be heard
laudā|b|itur	*monē|b|itur*	*dūc|ē|tur*	*audi|e|tur*	He will be heard
laudā|b|imur	*monē|b|imur*	*dūc|ē|mur*	*audi|e|mur*	We will be heard
laudā|b|iminī	*monē|b|iminī*	*dūc|ē|minī*	*audi|e|minī*	You all will be heard
laudā|b|untur	*monē|b|unt*	*dūc|e|ntur*	*audi|e|ntur*	They will be heard

Irregular Verbs

ESSE	IRE	VELLE	FERRE	FERRI
erō	ībō	volam	feram	ferar
eris	ībis	volēs	ferēs	ferēris
erit	ībit	volet	feret	ferētur
erimus	ībimus	volēmus	ferēmus	ferēmur
eritis	ībitis	volētis	ferētis	ferēminī
erunt	ībunt	volent	ferēnt	ferentur

Perfect Indicative

Quick Definition: Completed action in the past.
Tense Formation: perfect stem + perfect personal endings
Translation, Active Voice: [verb]-ed or have [verb]-ed
Translation, Passive Voice: is [verb]-ed or have been [verb]-ed

Active

ā-verb	ē-verb	i/e-verb	i-verb	Example Translation
laudāvī	monuī	dūxī	audīvī	I have heard
laudāvistī	monuistī	dūxistī	audīvistī	You have heard
laudāvit	monuit	dūxit	audīvit	He has heard
laudāvimus	monuimus	dūximus	audīvimus	We have heard
laudāvistis	monuistis	dūxistis	audīvistis	You all have heard
laudāvērunt	monuērunt	dūxērunt	audīvērunt	They have heard

Passive

The perfect passive requires the perfect passive participle plus a present form of *esse*.

ā-verb	ē-verb	i/e-verb	i-verb	esse	Example Translation
laudātus (-a, -um)	*monitus* (-a, -um)	*ductus* (-a, -um)	*audītus* (-a, -um)	*sum*	I have been heard (I am heard)
laudātus (-a, -um)	*monitus* (-a, -um)	*ductus* (-a, -um)	*audītus* (-a, -um)	*es*	You have been heard (You are heard)
laudātus (-a, -um)	*monitus* (-a, -um)	*ductus* (-a, -um)	*audītus* (-a, -um)	*est*	He has been heard (He is heard)
laudātī (-ae, -a)	*monitī* (-ae, -a)	*ductī* (-ae, -a)	*audītī* (-ae, -a)	*sumus*	We have been heard (We are heard)
laudātī (-ae, -a)	*monitī* (-ae, -a)	*ductī* (-ae, -a)	*audītī* (-ae, -a)	*estis*	You (pl.) have been heard (You are heard)
laudātī (-ae, -a)	*monitī* (-ae, -a)	*ductī* (-ae, -a)	*audītī* (-ae, -a)	*sunt*	They have been heard (They are heard)

Irregular Verbs

ESSE	IRE	VELLE	FERRE	FERRI
fui	*īvī*	*voluī*	*tulī*	*lātus sum*
fuisti	*īvistī*	*voluistī*	*tulistī*	*lātus es*
fuit	*īvit*	*voluit*	*tulit*	*lātus est*
fuimus	*īvimus*	*voluimus*	*tulimus*	*lātī sumus*
fuistis	*īvistis*	*voluistis*	*tulistis*	*lātī estis*
fuerunt	*īvērunt*	*voluērunt*	*tulērunt*	*lātī sunt*

Pluperfect Indicative

Quick Definition: Action already completed in the past before something else.

Tense Formation, Active: perfect stem + imperfect of *esse*

Tense Formation, Passive: perfect passive participle + imperfect of *esse*

Translation, Active: had [verb]-ed

Translation, Passive: had been [verb]-ed

Active

ā-verb	ē-verb	i/e-verb	i-verb	Example Translation
laudāveram	*monueram*	*dūxeram*	*audīveram*	I had praised
laudāverās	*monuerās*	*dūxerās*	*audīverās*	You had praised
laudāverat	*monuerat*	*dūxerat*	*audīverat*	He had praised
laudāverāmus	*monuerāmus*	*dūxerāmus*	*audīverāmus*	We had praised
laudāverātis	*monuerātis*	*dūxerātis*	*audīverātis*	You all had praised
laudāverant	*monuerant*	*dūxerant*	*audīverant*	They had praised

Passive

The pluperfect passive requires the perfect passive participle plus an imperfect form of *esse*.

ā-verb	ē-verb	i/e-verb	i-verb	*esse*	
laudātus (-a, -um)	*monitus* (-a, -um)	*ductus* (-a, -um)	*audītus* (-a, -um)	*eram*	I had been heard
laudātus (-a, -um)	*monitus* (-a, -um)	*ductus* (-a, -um)	*audītus* (-a, -um)	*erās*	You had been heard
laudātus (-a, -um)	*monitus* (-a, -um)	*ductus* (-a, -um)	*audītus* (-a, -um)	*erat*	He / She / It had been heard
laudātī (-ae, -a)	*monitī* (-ae, -a)	*ductī* (-ae, -a)	*audītī* (-ae, -a)	*erāmus*	We had been heard
laudātī (-ae, -a)	*monitī* (-ae, -a)	*ductī* (-ae, -a)	*audītī* (-ae, -a)	*erātis*	You all had been heard
laudātī (-ae, -a)	*monitī* (-ae, -a)	*ductī* (-ae, -a)	*audītī* (-ae, -a)	*erant*	They had been heard

Irregular Verbs

ESSE	IRE	VELLE	FERRE	FERRI
fueram	*īveram*	*volueram*	*tuleram*	*lātus eram*
fuerās	*īverās*	*voluerās*	*tulerās*	*lātus erās*
fuerat	*īverat*	*voluerat*	*tulerat*	*lātus erat*
fuerāmus	*īverāmus*	*voluerāmus*	*tulerāmus*	*lātī erāmus*
fuerātis	*īverātis*	*voluerātis*	*tulerātis*	*lātī erātis*
fuerant	*īverant*	*voluerant*	*tulerant*	*lātī erant*

Future-Perfect Indicative

Quick Definition: Action that will have been completed in the future.
Tense Formation, Active: perfect stem + future of *esse*
Tense Formation, Passive: perfect passive participle + future of *esse*
Translation, Active Voice: will have [verb]-ed
Translation, Passive Voice: will have been [verb]-ed

Active

ā-verb	ē-verb	i/e-verb	i-verb	Example Translation
laudāverō	*monuerō*	*dūxerō*	*audīverō*	I will have heard
laudāveris	*monueris*	*dūxeris*	*audīveris*	You will have heard
laudāverit	*monuerit*	*dūxerit*	*audīverit*	He will have heard
laudāverimus	*monuerimus*	*dūxerimus*	*audīverimus*	We will have heard
laudāveritis	*monueritis*	*dūxeritis*	*audīveritis*	You (pl.) will have heard
laudāverint	*monuerint*	*dūxerint*	*audīverint*	They will have heard

Passive [perfect passive participle + a form of *esse*]

The pluperfect passive requires the perfect passive participle plus an imperfect form of *esse*.

ā-verb	ē-verb	i/e-verb	i-verb	esse	
laudātus (-a, -um)	*monitus* (-a, -um)	*ductus* (-a, -um)	*audītus* (-a, -um)	erō	I will have been heard
laudātus (-a, -um)	*monitus* (-a, -um)	*ductus* (-a, -um)	*audītus* (-a, -um)	eris	You will have been heard
laudātus (-a, -um)	*monitus* (-a, -um)	*ductus* (-a, -um)	*audītus* (-a, -um)	erit	He will have been heard
laudātī (-ae, -a)	*monitī* (-ae, -a)	*ductī* (-ae, -a)	*audītī* (-ae, -a)	erimus	We will have been heard
laudātī (-ae, -a)	*monitī* (-ae, -a)	*ductī* (-ae, -a)	*audītī* (-ae, -a)	eritis	You (pl.) will have been heard
laudātī (-ae, -a)	*monitī* (-ae, -a)	*ductī* (-ae, -a)	*audītī* (-ae, -a)	erunt	They will have been heard

Irregular Verbs

ESSE	IRE	VELLE	FERRE	FERRI
fuerō	*īverō*	*voluerō*	*tulerō*	*lātus erō*
fueris	*īveris*	*volueris*	*tuleris*	*lātus eris*
fuerit	*īverit*	*voluerit*	*tulerit*	*lātus erat*
fuerimus	*īverimus*	*voluerimus*	*tulerimus*	*lātī erimus*
fueritis	*īveritis*	*volueritis*	*tuleritis*	*lātī eritis*
fuerint	*īverint*	*voluerint*	*tulerint*	*lātī erunt*

Present Subjunctive

Quick Definition: Subjunctive indicates either action that might occur, action that did occur in the present, or action that the speaker desires to occur.

Tense Formation: stem + -e- + personal endings
Translation: depends entirely on context

Active

ā-verb	ē-verb	i/e-verb	i-verb
laud|e|m	mone|a|m	duc|a|m	audi|a|m
laud|ē|s	mone|ā|s	duc|ās	audi|ā|s
laud|e|t	mone|a|t	duc|a|t	audi|a|t
laud|ē|mus	mone|ā|mus	duc|ā|mus	audi|ā|mus
laud|ē|tis	mone|ā|tis	duc|ā|tis	audi|ā|tis
laud|e|nt	mone|a|nt	duc|a|nt	audi|a|nt

Passive

ā-verb	ē-verb	i/e-verb	i-verb
laud|e|r	mone|a|r	duc|a|r	audi|a|r
laud|ē|ris	mone|ā|ris	duc|ā|ris	audi|ā|ris
laud|ē|tur	mone|ā|tur	duc|ā|tur	audi|ā|tur
laud|ē|mur	mone|ā|mur	duc|ā|mur	audi|ā|mur
laud|ē|minī	mone|ā|minī	duc|ā|minī	audi|ā|minī
laud|e|ntur	mone|a|ntur	duc|a|ntur	audi|a|ntur

Irregular Verbs

ESSE	IRE	VELLE	CAPERE	CAPI	FERRE	FERRI
sim	eam	velim	capiam	capiar	feram	ferar
sīs	eās	velīs	capiās	capiāris (capiāre)	ferās	ferāris (ferāre)
sit	eat	velit	capiat	capiātur	ferat	ferātur
sīmus	eāmus	velīmus	capiāmus	capiāmur	ferāmus	ferāmur
sītis	eātis	velītis	capiātis	capiāminī	ferātis	ferāminī
sint	eant	velint	capiant	capiantur	ferant	ferantur

Imperfect Subjunctive

Quick Definition: Subjunctive indicates either action that might occur, action that occurred at the same time as a past tense verb, or action that the speaker desires to have occurred.

Tense Formation: stem + *-re-* + personal endings

Translation: depends on context

Active

ā-verb	ē-verb	i/e-verb	i-verb
laudā|re|m	monē|re|m	dūce|re|m	audī|re|m
laudā|rē|s	monē|rē|s	dūce|rē|s	audī|rē|s
laudā|re|t	monē|re|t	dūce|re|t	audī|re|t
laudā|rē|mus	monē|rē|mus	dūce|rē|mus	audī|rē|mus
laudā|rē|tis	monē|rē|tis	dūce|rē|tis	audī|rē|tis
laudā|re|nt	monē|re|nt	dūce|re|nt	audī|re|nt

Passive

ā-verb	ē-verb	i/e-verb	i-verb
laudā|re|r	*monē|re|r*	*dūce|re|r*	*audī|re|r*
laudā|rē|ris	*monē|rē|ris*	*dūce|rē|ris*	*audī|rē|ris*
laudā|rē|tur	*monē|rē|tur*	*dūce|rē|tur*	*audī|rē|tur*
laudā|rē|mur	*monē|rē|mur*	*dūce|rē|mur*	*audī|rē|mur*
laudā|rē|minī	*monē|rē|minī*	*dūce|rē|minī*	*audī|rē|minī*
laudā|re|ntur	*monē|re|ntur*	*dūce|re|ntur*	*audī|re|ntur*

Irregular Verbs

ESSE	IRE	VELLE	CAPERE	CAPI	FERRE	FERRI
esse|m	*īrem*	*vellem*	*cape|re|m*	*cape|re|r*	*ferrem*	*ferrer*
essē|s	*īrēs*	*velles*	*cape|rē|s*	*cape|rē|ris*	*ferrēs*	*ferrēris (ferrēre)*
esse|t	*īret*	*vellet*	*cape|re|t*	*cape|rē|tur*	*ferret*	*ferrētur*
essē|mus	*īrēmus*	*vellēmus*	*cape|rē|mus*	*cape|rē|mur*	*ferrēmus*	*ferrēmur*
essē|tis	*īrētis*	*vellētis*	*cape|rē|tis*	*cape|rē|minī*	*ferrētis*	*ferrēminī*
esse|nt	*īrent*	*vellent*	*cape|re|nt*	*cape|re|ntur*	*ferrent*	*ferrentur*

Perfect Subjunctive

Quick Definition: Perfect subjunctive indicates some event that occurred in the past tense, or action that the speaker desires to have occurred.

Tense Formation: perfect stem + future of *esse*
Translation: depends on context

Active

ā-verb	ē-verb	i/e-verb	i-verb
laudāv|eri|m	*monu|eri|m*	*dūx|eri|m*	*audīv|eri|m*
laudāv|eri|s	*monu|eri|s*	*dūx|eri|s*	*audīv|eri|s*
laudāv|eri|t	*monu|eri|t*	*dūx|eri|t*	*audīv|eri|t*
laudāv|eri|mus	*monu|eri|mus*	*dūx|eri|mus*	*audīv|eri|mus*
laudāv|eri|tis	*monu|eri|tis*	*dūx|eri|tis*	*audīv|eri|tis*
laudāv|eri|nt	*monu|eri|nt*	*dūx|eri|nt*	*audīv|eri|nt*

Passive [perfect passive participle + a form of *esse*]

ā-verb	ē-verb	i/e-verb	i-verb	*esse*
laudātus (-a, -um)	*monitus (-a, -um)*	*ductus (-a, -um)*	*audītus (-a, -um)*	*sim*
laudātus (-a, -um)	*monitus (-a, -um)*	*ductus (-a, -um)*	*audītus (-a, -um)*	*sīs*
laudātus (-a, -um)	*monitus (-a, -um)*	*ductus (-a, -um)*	*audītus (-a, -um)*	*sit*
laudātī (-ae, -a)	*monitī (-ae, -a)*	*ductī (-ae, -a)*	*audītī (-ae, -a)*	*sīmus*
laudātī (-ae, -a)	*monitī (-ae, -a)*	*ductī (-ae, -a)*	*audītī (-ae, -a)*	*sītis*
laudātī (-ae, -a)	*monitī (-ae, -a)*	*ductī (-ae, -a)*	*audītī (-ae, -a)*	*sint*

Irregular Verbs

ESSE	IRE	VELLE	CAPERE	CAPI	FERRE	FERRI
fu|eri|m	*īverim*	*voluerim*	*cēp|eri|m*	*captus sim*	*tulerim*	*lātus sim*
fu|eri|s	*īveris*	*volueris*	*cēp|eri|s*	*captus sīs*	*tulēris*	*lātus sīs*
fu|eri|t	*īverit*	*voluerit*	*cēp|eri|t*	*captus sit*	*tulērit*	*lātus sit*
fu|eri|mus	*īverimus*	*voluerimus*	*cēp|eri|mus*	*captī sīmus*	*tulērimus*	*lātī sīmus*
fu|eri|tis	*īveritis*	*volueritis*	*cēp|eri|tis*	*captī sītis*	*tulēritis*	*lātī sītis*
fu|eri|nt	*īverint*	*voluerint*	*cēp|eri|nt*	*captī sint*	*tulērint*	*lātī sint*

Pluperfect Subjunctive

Quick Definition: Pluperfect subjunctive indicates either action that occurred more in the past, or action that the speaker desires to have occurred.

Tense Formation, Active: Perfect infinitive + personal endings
Tense Formation, Passive: Perfect passive participle + present subjunctive of *esse*
Translation: Depends on context

Active

ā-verb	ē-verb	i/e-verb	i-verb
laudāv|isse|m	*monu|isse|m*	*dūx|isse|m*	*audīv|isse|m*
laudāv|issē|s	*monu|issē|s*	*dūx|i|ss|ēs*	*audīv|issē|s*
laudāv|isse|t	*monu|isse|t*	*dūx|isse|t*	*audīv|isse|t*
laudāv|issē|mus	*monu|issē|mus*	*dūx|issē|mus*	*audīv|issē|mus*
laudāv|issē|tis	*monu|issē|tis*	*dūx|issē|tis*	*audīv|issē|tis*
laudāv|isse|nt	*monu|isse|nt*	*dūx|isse|nt*	*audīv|isse|nt*

Passive [perfect passive participle + a form of *esse*]

ā-verb	ē-verb	i/e-verb	i-verb	*esse*
laudātus (-a, -um)	*monitus (-a, -um)*	*ductus (-a, -um)*	*audītus (-a, -um)*	*essem*
laudātus (-a, -um)	*monitus (-a, -um)*	*ductus (-a, -um)*	*audītus (-a, -um)*	*essēs*
laudātus (-a, -um)	*monitus (-a, -um)*	*ductus (-a, -um)*	*audītus (-a, -um)*	*esset*
laudātī (-ae, -a)	*monitī (-ae, -a)*	*ductī (-ae, -a)*	*audītī (-ae, -a)*	*essēmus*
laudātī (-ae, -a)	*monitī (-ae, -a)*	*ductī (-ae, -a)*	*audītī (-ae, -a)*	*essētis*
laudātī (-ae, -a)	*monitī (-ae, -a)*	*ductī (-ae, -a)*	*audītī (-ae, -a)*	*essent*

Irregular Verbs

ESSE	IRE	VELLE	CAPERE	CAPI	FERRE	FERRI
fu|isse|m	*īvissem*	*voluissem*	*cēp|isse|m*	*captus essem*	*tulissem*	*lātus essem*
fu|issē|s	*īvissēs*	*voluissēs*	*cēp|issē|s*	*captus essēs*	*tulissēs*	*lātus essēs*
fu|isse|t	*īvisset*	*voluisset*	*cēp|isse|t*	*captus esset*	*tulisset*	*lātus esset*
fu|issē|mus	*īvissēmus*	*voluissēmus*	*cēp|issē|mus*	*captī essēmus*	*tulissēmus*	*lātī essēmus*
fu|issē|tis	*īvissētis*	*voluissētis*	*cēp|issē|tis*	*captī essētis*	*tulissētis*	*lātī essētis*
fu|isse|nt	*īvissent*	*voluissent*	*cēp|isse|nt*	*captī essent*	*tulissent*	*lātī essent*

Nonfinite Verb Forms

Imperatives

Definition: command; verbs that express a desire for another to do something.

Active

Singular Addressee	Translation	Plural Addressee	Translation
laud|ā	praise!	*laudā|te*	[you all] praise!
mon|ē	warn!	*monē|te*	[you all] warn!
duc|	lead!	*duci|te*	[you all] lead!
aud|ī	hear!	*audī|te*	[you all] hear!
es	be!	*este*	[you all] be!
ferr|e	carry!	*fer|te*	[you all] carry!
cap|e	take!	*cap|ite*	[you all] take!

Passive

Singular Addressee	Translation	Plural Addressee	Translation
laud|āre	be praised!	*laudā|mini*	[you all] be praised!
mon|ēre	be warned!	*monē|mini*	[you all] be warned!
duc|ere	be led!	*duci|mini*	[you all] be led!
aud|īre	be heard!	*audī|mini*	[you all] be heard!
cap|e	be taken!	*capi|mini*	[you all] be taken!
ferr|e	be carried!	*feri|mini*	[you all] be carried!

Present Infinitives

Definition: verbal nouns; verbs that function as nouns in a sentence.

Active	Translation	Passive	Translation
laud\āre	to praise	laud\ārī	to be praised
vid\ēre	to see	vid\ērī	to be seen
duc\ere	to lead	duc\ī	to be led
aud\īre	to hear	aud\īrī	to be heard
esse	to be		
ire	to go		
velle	to want		
capere	to take	capi	to be taken
ferre	to carry	ferri	to be carried

Perfect Infinitives

Active	Example Translation	Passive	Example Translation
laudāv\isse	to have praised	laudātum esse	to have been praised
monu\isse	to have warned	visum esse	to have been warned
dux\isse	to have led	ductum esse	to have been led
audīv\isse	to have heard	audītum esse	to have been heard
fu\isse	to be		
iv\isse	to go		
volu\isse	to want		
cep\isse	to take	captum esse	to be taken
tul\isse	to carry	fertum esse	to be carried

Future Infinitives

Active	Example Translation	Passive	Example Translation
laudāt|ur|um esse	to be about to praise	*laudātum iri*	to be about to have been praised
monit|ur|um esse	to be about to warn	*visum iri*	to be about to have been warned
duct|ur|um esse	to be about to lead	*ductum iri*	to be about have been led
audīt|ur|um esse	to be about to hear	*audītum iri*	to be about to have been heard
futurum esse	to be about to be		
iturum esse	to be about to go		
capturum esse	to be about to take	*capturum iri*	to be about to be taken
laturum esse	to be about to carry	*laturum iri*	to be about to be carried

Present Active Participles

Definition: verbal adjectives; verbs that provide more information about a noun they modify. They follow the pattern of a third declension adjective. Only the singular are provided here. See the chart of third declension adjectives for a complete list. There are only present active participles and no present passive participles.

Masculine / Feminine Singular	Neuter Singular
laudā|ns (gen. *laudantis*)	*laudā|nte (laudantis)*
vidē|ns (videntis)	*vidē|nte (videntis)*
ducē|ns (ducentis)	*ducē|nte (ducentis)*
audiē|ns (audientis)	*audiē|nte (audientis)*
ie|ns (ientis)	*ie|nte (ientis)*
vole|ns (volentis)	*vole|nte (volentis)*
capie|ns (capientis)	*capie|nte (capientis)*
fere|ns (ferentis)	*fere|nte (ferente)*

Perfect Passive Participles

Perfect participles are always passive in form, though some deponent verbs can have perfect passive participles that are active in meaning. As an adjective, these perfect passive participles usually come with a noun or an implied noun and take an *-ed* form. These follow the patterns of first and second declension adjectives.

Present Forms (m./f./n.)	Example Translation
laudāt|us, -a, -um	praised
vis|us, -a, -um	seen
duct|us, -a, -um	led
audīt|us, -a, -um	heard
it|us, -a, -um	gone
capt|us, -a, -um	taken
lat|us, -a, -um	carried

Future Active Participles

Future participles in Latin have both active and passive forms. These follow the patterns of first and second declension adjectives.

M. F. and N. Present Forms	Example Translation
laudāt|ur|us, -a, -um	about to praise
monit|ur|us, -a, -um	about to warn
duct|ur|us, -a, -um	about to lead
audīt|ur|us, -a, -um	about to hear
fut|ur|us, -a, -um	about to be
it|ur|us, -a, -um	about to go
capt|ur|us, -a, -um	about to capture
lat|ur|us, -a, -um	about to carry

Future Passive Participles (Gerundives)

M. F. and N. Present Forms	Example Translation
lauda|nd|us, -a, -um	ought to be praised
mone|nd|us, -a, -um	ought to be warned
duce|nd|us, -a, -um	ought to be led
audie|nd|us, -a, -um	ought to be heard
eu|nd|us, -a, -um	ought to go
capta|nd|us, -a, -um	ought to be captured
fere|nd|us, -a, -um	ought to be carried

Gerunds

Definition: verbal nouns; verbs that function like nouns. Gerunds follow the pattern of a second declension neuter noun.

	ā-verb	ē-verb	i/e-verb	i-verb	Example Translation
Nom	*laudā|re*	*monē|re*	*duce|re*	*audī|re*	to hear
Gen	*laudand|ī*	*monend|ī*	*ducend|ī*	*audiend|ī*	of hearing
Dat	*laudand|ō*	*monend|ō*	*ducend|ō*	*audiend|ō*	to / for seeing
Acc	*laudand|um*	*monend|um*	*ducend|um*	*audiend|um*	seeing (d.o.)
Abl	*laudand|ō*	*monend|ō*	*ducend|ō*	*audiend|ō*	by seeing

ferre, ferendi, ferendo, ferendum

capere, capiendi, capiendo, capiendum

Supine

Supines are very uncommon in Ecclesiastical Latin. They are kinds of verbal nouns that are used either for purpose with a verb of movement or used in the ablative and often translated with just *to* and the verb. Most verbs do not have a supine form, but they are included here as examples.

M. F. and N. Present Forms	Example Translation
laudāt|um, -u	for the purpose of praising, to praise
monit|um, -u	for the purpose of warning, to warn
duct|um, -u	for the purpose of leading, to lead
audīt|um, -u	for the purpose of hearing, to hear

LATIN TO ENGLISH VOCABULARY

LATIN	ENGLISH
-que	and [added to the end of another word]
—, *memini*,—	[+gen or +acc] remember
—, *nōvī, nōtus*	know
—, *ōdī, ōsus*	hate
ā / ab [+abl]	by, from
abnegō [ab + negō], abnegāre, abnegāvī, abnegātus	deny
abscondō, abscondere, abscondī, absconditus	hide, conceal
absolvō [ab + solvō], absolvere, absolvī, absolūtus	absolve
abyssus, abyssī (f.)	abyss
ac	and
accēdō [ad + cēdō], accēdere, accessī, accessus	come near, approach
acceptō [ad + capiō], acceptāre, acceptāvī, acceptātus	accept [repeatedly]
accipiō [ad + capiō], accipere, accēpī, acceptus	accept
accūsō [ad + causā], accūsāre, accūsāvī, accūsātus	accuse, blame, charge
ad [+acc]	to, towards; for the purpose of
adhibeō [ad + habeō], adhibēre, adhibuī, adhibitus	employ, adhere to, summon
adhūc	still, yet
adjūnctus, -a, -um	added
adjuvō [ad + juvō], adjuvāre, adjūvī, adjūtus	help
admoneō [ad + moneō], admonēre, admonuī, admonitus	warn, admonish
adōrō, adōrāre, adōrāvī, adōrātus	worship, bow down
adquīrō [ad + quaerō], adquīrere, adquīsīvī, adquīsītus	acquire, obtain
adversārius, adversāriī (m.)	adversary
aedificō [aedes + faciō], aedificāre, aedificāvī, aedificātus	build up
aeger, -a, -um	sick
aequitās, aequitātis (f.)	equity

āetās, aetātis (f.)	age
aeternus, -a, -um	eternal
āger, agrī (m.)	field
aggredior [ad + gredior], aggredī,—, aggressus sum	go to
agnōscō [ag + nōscō], agnōscere, agnōvī, agnitus	acknowledge, recognize
āgnus, āgnī (m.)	lamb
agō, agere, ēgī, āctus	do, lead; with *gratias*: give thanks
agricola, agricolae (m.)	farmer
aiō,—,—,—	say [defective verb]
albus, -a, -um	white; ready for the harvest
aliēnus, -a, -um	foreign
aliquandō	sometime, finally, at last
aliqui, aliqua, aliquod	some person, some thing
aliquis, aliquis, aliquid	someone, something
aliunde	elsewhere, from elsewhere
alius, -a, -ud	another
alius, -a, -ud	another
altāre, altāris (n.)	altar
altus, alta, altum	high, tall
ambitiō, ambitiōnis (f.)	ambition, desire
ambulant	they walk
ambulat	he / she / it walks
ambulō, ambulāre, ambulāvī, ambulātus	walk
amīcus, amīcī (m.)	friend
āmittō [ab + mitto], āmittere, āmīsī, amīsus	lose, dismiss [in the passive voice, "missing"]
amō, amāre, amāvī, amātus	love

amplius	greater, furthermore
an	or [exclusive]
ancilla, ancillae (f.)	maidservant
anima, animae (f.)	soul
animal, animālis (n.)	animal
animus, animī (m.)	mind, intellect, soul, heart
annus, annī (m.)	year
ante [+acc]	in front of, before
aperiō, aperīre, aperuī, apertus	open
appāreō, appārēre, appāruī, appāritus	appear
appetō [ad + petere] appetere, appetīvi, appetītus	seek
appropinquō [ad + propinquo], appropinquāre, appropinquāvī, appropinquātus	approach, draw near towards
apud	[+abl] near, in the presence of
aqua, aquae (f.)	water
aquila, aquilae (f.)	eagle
ārdeō, ārdēre, ārsi, ārsus	burn, be on fire
arma, armōrum (n. pl.)	arms, weapons
ars, artīs (f.)	art
ascendit	he / she / it ascends
āscendō [ad-scando], ascendere, ascendī, ascēnsus	ascend
ascendunt	they ascend
ascēnsiō, ascēnsiōnis (f.)	ascent, progress
aspergō [ad + spergo], aspergere, aspersī, aspersus	sprinkle, wash
at	but, but yet
atque	and
audeō, audēre,—, ausus sum	dare
audiō, audīre, audīvī (audiī), audītus	hear, obey

audit	he / she / it hears / obeys
audiunt	they hear / obey
aurīs, aurīs (f.)	ear
aurum, aurī (n.)	gold
autem	but, however
auxilium, -ī (n.)	help
avis, avis (f.)	bird
baptīzō, baptīzāre, baptīzāvī, baptīzātus	baptize
beatus, -a, -um	happy, blessed
benedīcō [bene + dicere], benedīcere, benedīxi, benedictus	bless
benedictiō, benedictiōnis (f.)	blessing
bibō, bibere, bibī, bibitus	drink
bonus, -a, -um	good
cadō, cadere, cecidī, cāsus	fall
caelestis, caelestis, caeleste	heavenly, celestial
caelum, caelī (n.)	heaven
calix, calicīs (m.)	cup
canticum, cantici (n.)	hymn, canticle
cantō, cantāre, cantāvī, cantātus	sing
capiō, capere, cēpī, captus	take, seize
caput, capitis (n.)	head
careō, carēre, caruī, caritus	[+abl] lack, be without
cāritās, cāritātis (f.)	love, charity
carnis, carnis (f.)	flesh, meat
castellum, castellī (n.)	castle, town
castra, castrōrum (n. pl.)	camp
catholicus, -a, -um	universal

caveō, cavēre, cāvī, cautus	be aware [can be used as a verb of fearing]
cēdō, cēdere, cessī, cessus	go
cēnō, cēnāre, cēnāvī, cēnātus	dine
Christus, -ī (m.)	Anointed One [often translated simply as Christ]
cibus, cibī (m.)	food
circus, circī (m.)	circus
cito, citius, citissimē	quickly, more quickly, most quickly
cīvitās, cīvitātis (f.)	city, commonwealth
clāmō, clāmāre, clāmāvī, clāmātus	shout
claudō, claudere, clausī, clausus	close
cognāta, cognātae (f.)	kinsman, someone related by birth
cognōscō [con + gnosco], cognōscere, cognōvī, cognitus	know, recognize
colligō [con + ligare], colligere, collēgī, collēctus	collect [*lit.* bind together]
colō, colere, coluī, cultus	worship, cultivate
colonus, colonī (m.)	settler, farmer
com-patior [con + patior], compatī,—, compassus sum	suffer, suffer with
comedō, comedere, comēdī, comestus	eat
comminō [cōn + minō], commināre, commināvī, cominatus	threaten
compleō, complēre, complēvī, complētus	fill, fulfill
complexō [con + plecto], complexāre, complexāvī, complexātus	hug
concipiō [con + capio], concipere, concēpī, conceptus	to conceive
concupiscentia, concupiscentiae (f.)	desire [negative since Augustine]
condō [cōn + dō], condere, condidī, conditus	put, build, found
cōnfīdō [cōn + fīdō], cōnfīdere,—, cōnfīsus	trust
cōnfiteor [con + fari], cōnfitērī,—, cōnfessus sum	confess
conjūnx, conjugis (m. / f.)	spouse

cōnor, cōnārī,—, cōnātus sum	try
cōnscientia, cōnscientiae (f.)	knowledge, conscience
cōnsīdō, cōnsīderāre, cōnsīderāvī, cōnsīderātus	examine, reflect one
cōnspectus, cōnspectus (m.)	sight
cōnsuētūdō, cōnsuētūdinis (f.)	custom
cōnsūmō [con + sumo], cōnsūmere, cōnsūmpsī, cōnsūmptus	burn up, use up, expend
continuō	immediately
conveniō [cōn + veniō], convenīre, convēnī, conventūs	come together
convenit, convenīre, convenit,—	it is fitting [impersonal]
convertō [con + verto], convertere, convertī, convertus	turn around, convert
convīvium, convīvī(ī) (n.)	party
cor, cordis (n.)	heart
coram	in front of, before
cornū, cornus (n.)	horn
corpus, corporis (n.)	body
corrumpō [cōn-rumpō], corrumpere, corrūpī, corruptus	corrupt
cotīdiē; quotīdiē	daily
creātor, creātōris (m.)	creator
crēdō, crēdere, crēdidī, crēditus	believe
creō, creāre, creāvī, creātus	create
cuī	to whom
cujus	whose
culpō, culpāre, culpāvī, culpātus	blame
cum [+abl]	with [paired with noun in ablatives]
cum	when [without a noun in the ablative]
cūnctus, -a, -um	all
cupiō, cupere, cupīvī, cupītus	desire
cūr	why?

cūra, cūrae (f.)	care
cūrō, cūrāre, cūrāvī, cūrātus	cure, care for
cūstōdiō, cūstōdīre, cūstōdīvī, cūstōdītus	keep
cūstōdit	he / she / it keeps
cūstōdiunt	they keep
de [+abl]	from
dēbeō, dēbēre, dēbuī, dēbitus	ought; must; owe
dēficiō [dē-faciō], dēficere, dēfēcī, dēfectus	die, become defunct
dein, deinde	then
dēleō, dēlēre, dēlēvī, dēlētus	destroy, delete
dēnique	finally, in the end
dēprecor [de + precor], dēprecārī,—, dēprecātus	entreat, pray
dērelinquō [dē + relinquō], dērelinquere, dēreliquī, dērelictus	leave behind, discard
dēsīderō [de + sidus], dēsīderāre, dēsīderāvī, dēsīderātus	desire
dēsinō [de + sino], dēsinere, dēsīvī, dēsitus	stop
dēstruō, dēstruere, dēstrūxī, dēstrūctus	destroy, demolish
Deus, Deī (m.)	God
devovō [de + vovo], dēvovēre, dēvōvī, dēvōtus	devote
dicit	he / she / it says
dīcō, dīcere, dīxī, dictus	say
dicunt	they say
diēs, diēī (m./f.)	day
difficilis, difficilis, difficile	difficult
dignor, dignārī,—, dignus	deign, condescend
dignus, digna, dignum	worthy [+abl]
dīlēctus, -a, -um	beloved
dīligit	he / she / it loves
dīligō, dīligere, dīlēxī, dīlēctus	love

dīligunt	they love
dīluvium, dīluviī (n.)	flood
dīmittō [dī + mittō], dīmittere, dīmīsī, dīmissus	send away, forgive
discipulus, discipulī (m.)	student, disciple
discō, discere, didicī, discitus	learn
displicet [dis + placere], displicēre, displicuit,—	[impersonal] it is displeasing
dīves, dīvitis [gen. sing.]	wealthy
dō, dare, dedī, datus	give
doceō, docēre, docuī, doctus	teach
dolōrōsus, -a, -um	full of pain or sadness
dolus, -a, -um	fraud, deceit
domina, dominae (f.)	lady
dominicus, -a, -um	dominical, relating to the Lord
dominus, dominī (m.)	lord, Lord
domus, domūs (f.)	home
dōnec	[+subj] until
dormio, dormire, dormivi, dormitus	sleep
dūco, dūcere, dūxisse, ductus	lead
dulcis, dulcis, dulce	sweet
duo, duae, duo	2
dux, dūcis (m.)	leader
ecce	behold
ecclēsia, ecclēsiae (f.)	church
ēdictum, ēdictī (n.)	decree, edict
efficiō [ex + facio], efficere, effectī, effectūs	bring about, make, effect
ego	I
ēgredior [ex + gredior], ēgredī,—, ēgressus sum	go out
ējiciō [ē + jaciō], ējicere, ējēcī, ējectus	throw out

emō, emere, ēmī, ēmptus	buy
enim	for
eō, īre, īvī (iī), itus	go
ēripiō [ex + rapiō], ēripere, ēripuī, ēreptus	snatch away
ērrō, errāre, errāvi, errātus	wander, err
ēsca, ēscae (f.)	food
est	he / she / it is
et	and
etenim	indeed, because, as a matter of fact
etiam	also
etsi	even though
ēvītō [ex + vito], ēvītāre, ēvītāvī, ēvītātus	avoid
ex [+abl]	out of
excitō [ex + cieo], excitāre, excitāvī, excitātus	be awakened
excūsātiō, excūsātiōnis (f.)	excuse
excūsō [ex + causa], excūsāre, excūsāvī, excūsātus	excuse, acquit
exercitus, exercitūs (m.)	army, host
exoptō [ex + optō], exoptāre, exoptāvī, exoptātus	desire, choose
expono [ex + pono], exponere, exposui, expositus	lay out, explain
expugnō [ex + pugno], expugnāre, expugnāvī, expugnātus	conquer
ēxspectō [ex + specto], exspectāre, exspectāvī, expectātus	wait, await
exterius	outside
facies, faciei (f.)	face
facile, facilius, facillimē	easily, easier
facilis, facilis, facile	easy
faciō, facere, fēcī, factus	do, make
fama, famae (f.)	word, fame
familia, familiae (f.)	family

fēlīcitās, fēlīcitātis (f.)	happiness
fēmina, fēminae (f.)	woman
fenestra, fenestrae (f.)	window
fessus, -a, -um	tired
fēstus, -a, -um	festal day, joyous day
fidēlis, fidēlis, fidēle	faithful
fidēs, fideī (f.)	faith
fidūcia, fidūciae (f.)	faith
fīlia, fīliae (f.)	daughter
fīlius, fīliī (m.)	son
fīō, fierī,—, factus sum	become, happen
firmāmentum, firmāmentī (n.)	support, prop, firmament
fleō, flēre, flēvī, flētus	cry, weep
fluctus, fluctūs (m.)	wave
flūvius, flūviī (m.)	river
foedus, -a, -um	ugly
foedus, foederis (n.)	treaty, covenant
forās	outside
forsitan	[+subj] perhaps; [fors-sit-an, "it would be a chance whether")
fortasse	[+ind] maybe
fortis, fortis, forte	strong
frangō, frangere, frēgī, frāctus	break
frāter, frātris (m.)	brother
fructus, fructūs (m.)	fruit
fruor, fruī,—, frūctūs	[+abl] enjoy
fugiō, fugere, fūgī, fugitus	flee
fundāmentum, fundāmentī (n.)	foundation

gallus, gallī (m.)	rooster, Gaul
gaudeō, gaudēre,—, gāvīsus sum	rejoice
generātiō, generātiōnis (f.)	generation
gēns, gentīs (f.)	nation
gerō, gerere, gessī, gestus	bear, carry
gignō, gignere, genuī, genitus	give birth to
glaciēs, glaciēī (f.)	ice
gladius, gladiī (m.)	sword
glōrificō [gloria-facio], glōrificāre, glōrificāvī, glōrificātus	glorify
grabātus, grabātī (m.)	mat, cot
gradus, gradūs (m.)	step
gratia, gratiae (f.)	grace
gravis, gravis, grave	heavy
grex, gregis (m.)	flock
gustō, gustāre, gustāvī, gustātus	taste
habent	they have
habeō, habēre, habuī, habitus	have
habēt	he / she / it has
habitō, habitāre, habitāvī, habitātus	live, dwell
heri	yesterday
hic, haec, hoc	this
hīc	here
hiems, hiemis (f.)	winter
hilarius, -a, -um	merry, drunk
hinc	from here
hodiē	today
holocaustum, holocaustī (n.)	sacrifice
homo, hominis (m.)	person, human

honōrō, honōrāre, honōrāvī, honōrātus	honor
hora, horae (f.)	hour
horreō, horrēre, horruī,—	be horrified by, despise
hostia, hostiae (f.)	victim, sacrifice
hūc	here
humilitās, humilitātis (f.)	humility
hymnus, hymnī (m.)	hymn
iānuā, iānuae (f.)	door
ibi	there
īdōlum, īdōlī (n.)	idol
ille, illa, illud	that
illicitus, -a, -um	forbidden, illicit
illūc	over there
illūminātiō, illūminātiōnis (f.)	illumination
illūminō, illūmināre, illūmināvī, illūminātus	illuminate
imāgō, imāginis (f.)	image
imitor, imitārī,—, imitātus sum	imitate
immolō, immolāre, immolāvī, immolātus	sacrifice
impleō [in + pleo], implēre, implēvī, implētus	fill in, fulfill
in [+abl]	in
in [+acc]	into
incēdō [in + cēdō], incedere, incessī, incessus	advance, march
incipiō [in + capio], incipere, incēpī, inceptus	begin
indigena, indigenae (m./f.)	native
indigeō, indigēre, indiguī,—	need, lack [with gen. or abl.]
indignus, indigna, indignum	unworthy [+abl]
induō, induere, induī, indūtus	put on
ingenium, ingeniī (n.)	disposition, ability, talent

ingēns, ingēntis [gen. sing.]	not natural, huge
ingredior, [in + gredior], ingredī,—, ingressus sum	go in
inimīcus, inimīcī (m.)	enemy
inīquitās, inīquitātis (f.)	iniquity, sin
inquam,—,—,—	say [postpositive and defective verb]
īnsidiā, īnsidiae (f.)	trap, snare, plot
īnsonō [in + sono], īnsonāre, īnsonuī, īnsonitus	resound
intellectus, intellectūs (m.)	understanding
intellegit	he / she / it understands
intellegō, intellegere, intellēxī, intellexus	to understand
intellegunt	they understand
inter [+acc]	between
interficiō [inter + facio], interficere, interfēcisse, interfectus:	kill
interius	inside
interrogō [inter + rogo], interrogāre, interrogāvī, interrogātus	ask
intueor, intuērī,—, intuitus sum	look at, consider
inveniō [in + veniō], invenīre, invēnī, inventus	find [*lit.* to come into]
invicem	one another
invocō [in + vocō], invocāre, invocāvī, invocātus	invoke, pray
iste, ista, istud	this one, that one [of yours]
iter, itineris (n.)	journey
Iūdaeus, Iūdaea	Jewish person
jaceō, jacere, jacuī, jacitus	lie down
jaciō, jacēre, jēcī, jactus	throw
Jēsus, Jēsū [gen], Jēsū [dat], Jēsum [acc], Jēsū [abl]	Jesus
jubeō, jubēre, jussī, jussus	order, tell, command
jūbilō, jūbilāre, jūbilāvī, jūbilātum	rejoice

jūcunditās, jūcunditātis (f.)	charm, pleasantness
jūdex, jūdicis (m.)	judge
judicium, judiciī (n.)	judgment
jūdico, jūdicāre, jūdicāvi, jūdicātus	judge
jūrāmentum, jūrāmentī (n.)	oath
jūro, jurāre, juravī, juratus	swear
justus, -a, -um	just
juvō, juvāre, jūvī, jūtus	help
labium, labiī (n.)	lip
labor, labōris (m.)	labor, pain
labōrō, labōrāre, labōrāvi, labōrātus	labor, work
lacrima, lacrimae (f.)	tears
lacrimōsus, -a, -um	full of tears
laetor, laetārī,—laetātus sum	rejoice, be happy
lapis, lapidis (m.)	stone
laudo, laudare, laudavi, laudatus	praise
laus, laudis (f.)	praise, merit
lavō, lavāre, lavāvī, lāvātus	clean
lēgō, legere, lēgī, lēctus	read
leō, leōnis (m.)	lion
leprōsus, -a, -um	full of leprosy
levis, levis, leve	light
levō, levāre, levāvī, levātus	lift up
lex, legis (f.)	law
liber, libri (m.)	book
līberī, līberōrum (m.)	children
līberō, līberāre, līberāvī, līberātus	set free, to liberate
licet, licēre, licuit,—	(impersonal) it is allowed / permitted

lignum, lignī (n.)	tree, wood
ligō, ligāre, ligāvī, ligātus	bind
lingua, linguae (f.)	tongue
loquor, loquī,—, locūtus sum	say, speak
lucerna, lucernae (f.)	lamp
lūmen, lūminis (n.)	light
lūx, lūcis (f.)	light, daylight
magnificō [mangus-facio], magnificāre, magnificāvī, magnificātus	magnify
magnus, -a, -um	great, large
magus, magī (m.)	astrologer, magician, "wise man"
maledico [male + dico], maledīcere, maledīxi, maledictus	curse
malum, mali (n.)	apple, fruit
malus, -a, -um	evil, bad
mandatum, mandati (n.)	commandment
mandūcant	they eat
mandūcat	he / she / it eats
mandūcō, mandūcāre, mandūcāvī, mandūcātus	eat
mane (n.)	morning [indeclinable]
maneo, manēre, mānsi, mānsus	remain
manūs, manūs (f.)	hand
mare, maris (n.)	sea
massa, massae (f.)	mass
me	myself
medium, mediī (n.)	middle
medius, media, medium	middle, means
membrum, membrī (n.)	member, part of the body
memetipsum	myself

memoria, memoriae (f.)	memory
memoror, memorārī,—, memorātus sum	[+gen or +acc] be mindful of, remember
mendācium, mendāciī (n.)	lie
mēns, mentis (f.)	mind
mēnsis, mēnsis (m.)	month
mentior, mentīrī,—, mentītus	lie
mercēs, mercēdis (f.)	reward, wage, pay
messis, messis (n.)	harvest
metō, metere, messui, messus	harvest
meus, tuus, suus	my, your, his / her
migrō, migrāre, migrāvi, migrātus	transport, move
mīles, mīlitis (m.)	soldier
ministrō, ministrāre, ministrāvī, ministrātus	serve
mīrābilis, mīrābilis, mīrābile	wonderful, marvelous
mīror, mīrārī,—, mīrātus sum	marvel [at]
mīsceō, miscēre, miscuī, mixtus	mix
misereor, miserērī,—, miseritus sum	have mercy on
misericordia, -ae (f.)	mercy
missa, missae (f.)	mass
mittō, mittere, mīsī, missum	send
modicum, modicī (n.)	short / small time; little, small amount
moneō, monēre monuī monitus	warn; teach
mōns, montīs (m.)	mountain
monumentum, monumentī (n.)	tomb
morbus, morbī (m.)	sickness, illness
morior, mori,—, mortuus sum	die
mors, mortis (f.)	death
mōtiō, mōtiōnis (f.)	motion, movement

mox	soon
multitūdō, multitūdinis (f.)	multitude
multus, -a, -um	many
mundō, mundāre, mundāvī, mundātus	make clean
mundus, -a, -um	clean
mundus, mundī (m.)	world
mūnus, mūneris (n.)	gift, office
murmurō, murmurāre, murmurāvī, murmurātus	grumble, complain
mūtō, mūtāre, mūtāvī, mūtātus	change, move, shift
mūtus, mūta, mūtum	mute
mystērium, mystēriī (n.)	mystery
nam	for
nāscor, nāscī,—, nātus sum	be born
nātūra, nātūrae (f.)	nature
nātus, -a, -um	born
nāvicula, nāviculae (f.)	small boat
nāvis, nāvis (f.)	boat
nē [in a fear clause]	that
necessārius, -a, -um	necessary
necessis, necessis, necesse	necessary
necō, necāre, necavī, necatus	kill
nēmō, nēminis (m.)	no one
neque [nec]	not, neither
nescio [ne + scio], nescire, nescivi, nescitus	not know
nihil (n.)	nothing
nimis	too [much]
nisi	unless, except
nōlī	don't [in negative singular commands]

nōlīte	don't [in negative plural commands]
nōlō, nōlle, nōluī,—	not want to; be unwilling to
nōmen, nōminis (n.)	name, noun
nōn	not
nōs	we
noster, vester	our, your [plural]
novus, -a, -um	new
nūllus, -a, -um	no, nothing
num	surely not … [introduces a question expecting a negative answer
nunc	now
nūntiō, nūntiāre, nūntiāvī, nūntiātus	announce
nūptiae, nūptiārum (f. pl.)	wedding, marriage
oblātiō, oblātiōnis (f.)	offering
oblīvīscor, oblīvīscī, oblītus sum	to forget
oboediō, oboedīre, oboedīvī, oboedītus	obey
obsecrō, obsecrāre, obsecrāvī, obsectrātus	beg
occīdō [ob + caedo], occīdere, occīdī, occāsus	go down; kill
oculus, oculī (m.)	eye
offēnsiō, offēnsiōnis (f.)	displeasure; accident
omnipotēns, [gen. sing.: omnipotentis]	almighty
operātiō, operātiōnis (f.)	work
operor, operārī,—, operātus	work
oppidum, oppidī (n.)	town
opus, operis (n.)	work
ōrant	they pray
ōrat	he / she / it prays
orbis, orbis (m.)	sphere

ōrdinō, ōrdināre, ōrdināvī, ōrdinātus	order, arrange
orior, orīrī,—, ortus sum	arise
ōrō, ōrāre, ōrāvī, ōrātus	pray
os, oris (n.)	mouth
ōsculum, osculī (n.)	kiss
ostendō [obs + tendo], ostendere, ostendī, ostēnsus	show
ōstium, ōstiī (n.)	door
ovis, ovis, ovium [gen. pl.] (m.)	sheep
pactum, pactī (n.)	covenant
paene	almost
paenitet, paenitēre, paenituit,—	[impersonal] it is displeasing
pānis, pānis (m.)	bread
papa, -ae (m.)	pope
parcō, parcere, pepercī, parsus	spare
parēns, parentis (m.)	parent
pareo, parēre, paruī, paritus	appear; obey
pariō, parere, peperī, partus	give birth
pars, partis (f.)	part
pasco, pāscere, pāvi, pāstus	pasture, graze
pāstor, pāstōris (m.)	shepherd
pater, patris (m.)	father
pauper, pauperis [gen. sing.]	poor
pavor, pavōris (m.)	panic
pāx, pācis (f.)	peace
peccātum, peccātī (n.)	sin
peccō, peccāre, peccāvī, peccātus	sin
pecūnia, pecūniae (f.)	money
pendō, pendere, pependī, pēnsus	hang

per [+acc]	through
percūtiō [per + quatiō], percutere, percussi, percussus	strike, beat
perdō [per + do], perdere, perdidī, perditus	ruin, destroy
peregrīnātiō, peregrīnātiōnis (f.)	pilgrimage
peregrinor, peregrinari,—, peregrinatus sum	sojourn
perficiō [per + facio], perficere, perfēcī, perfectus	complete
pergō pergere, perrēxī, perrēctus	go on, proceed
perhibeō [per + habeo], perhibēre, perhibuī, perhibitus	present, give
perīculum, perīculī (n.)	danger, peril
persequor [per + sequor], persequī,—, persecutus sum	persecute
pēs, pedis (m.)	foot
petō, petere, petivī, petitus	seek
petra, petrae (f.)	rock
phantasma, phantasmae (f.)	ghost, phantasm
pirum, pira (n.)	pear
piscātor, piscātōris (m.)	fisherman
piscis, piscis (m.)	fish
placet, placēre,—, placitus est	[impersonal] it is pleasing
plēbs, plēbis (f.)	people
plenus, -a, -um	full
poculum, poculī (n.)	cup
poena, poenae (f.)	penalty
pōnō, pōnere, posuī, positus	put
pontifex, pontificis (m.)	bishop, pope [*lit.* "bridge"]
populus, populī, (m.)	people
portō, portāre, portāvī, portātus	carry
possum, posse, potuī,—	be able to
post [+acc]	after

postulō, postulāre, postulāvī, postulātus	ask, request
potens, potentis (f.)	power, ability
praebeō, praebēre, praebui, praebitus	supply, provide, present
praedēstinō, praedēstināre, praedēstināvī, praedēstinātus	determine beforehand, provide beforehand
praeferō [prae + ferō], praeferre, praetulī, praelātus	carry in front, give preference to
praeeo, praeire, praeivi(ii), praeitus	go before
praeparō [prae + parō], praeparāre, praeparāvī, praeparātus	prepare
praesentia, praesentiae (f.)	presence
precor, precārī,—, precātus sum	pray
prīnceps, prīncipis (m.)	prince
pro	[+abl] on behalf, before, about
proelium, proeliī (n.)	battle
prōficiō [pro + facio], prōficere, prōfēcī, profectus	make, accomplish
prōgeniēs, prōgeniēī (f.)	progeny
prōnūntiō [pro + nuntio], prōnūntiāre, prōnūntiāvī, pronunciātus	pronounce, declare
prope [+acc]	near
propheta, prophetae (m.)	prophet
prōpōnō [pro + pono], prōpōnere, prōposuī, prōpositus	propose, decide
proprius, -a, -um	one's own, own
propter [+acc]	on account of
prōspiciō [prō + specto], prōspicere, prōspexī, prōspectus	foresee, look for
prōsum [pro + sum], prōdesse, prōfui, prōfutūrus	profit, benefit
proximus, proximī (m.)	neighbor
pūblicānus, pūblicānī (m.)	publican, tax collector
puella, puellae (f.)	girl
puer, puerī (m.)	boy
pugnō, pugnāre, pugnāvī, pugnātus	fight

pulcher, pulchra, pulchrum	beautiful, handsome
pullus, pullī (m.)	young animal, colt, young chicken
pūniō, pūnīre, pūnīvī, pūnītus	punish
pusillum	a little bit
pusillus, pusilla, pusillum	little
puteus, puteī (m.)	well
putō, putāre, putāvī, putātus	think
quadraginta	40
quaerō, quaerere, quaesīvī, quaesītus	seek
quamquam	although
quandō	when
quantus, -a, -um	as great, how great
quarē	why
quattuor	4
quem, quam, quod	whom, which
quem	whom [direct object]
quemadmodum	how, in what way
quī, quae, quod	who, which
quia	because [or to a begin a quotation]
quibus	to whom [plural]
quīcumque, quaecumque, quidcumque	whoever, whatever
quilibet, quaelibet, quidlibet	whomever you please, what you please, anyone / anything whatever
quin	that, indeed
quinque	5
quis	who?
quō	by whom
quōcumque	to wherever
quomodō	how, in what way

quoniam	since [or to begin a quotation]
quoque	also
rapiō, rapere, rapui, raptus	drag off, snatch, seize
ratiō, ratiōnis (f.)	reason, rationality
re-probo [re + probo], reprobāre, reprobāvī, reprobātus	condemn
recēdō [rē + cēdō], recēdere, recessi, recessus	recede, withdraw
recipiō [re + capio], recipere, recēpī, receptus	receive
recordor [re + cor + do], recordārī,—, recordātus	call to mind, remember [often comes with a noun in the genitive]
recumbō [re + cumbo], recumbere, recubi,—	recline
redēmō [rē-d-emō], redemere, redēmī, redēmptus	buy back
reflōreō [rē + flōreō], reflōrēre, reflōruī,—	flourish
rēgīna, rēgīnae (f.)	queen
rēgiō, regiōnis (f.)	region, area
rēgnum, rēgnī (n.)	kingdom
relinquō, relinquere, relīquī, relictus	leave behind, abandon
reperiō, reperīre, repperī, repertus	find
reprehendō [re + prehendo], reprehendere, reprehēnsī, reprehēnsus	blame, seize
requiēs, requiēī (f.)	rest
requīrō [rē + quaerō], requīrere, requīsīvī, requīsītus	require, seek, need
rēs, reī (f.)	thing
reservō [re + servo], reservāre, reservāvi, reservātus	save
resignō [re + signo], resignāre, resignāvī, resignātus	resign
respondeō, respondēre, respondī, respōnsus	respond
restituō [re + statuo], restituere, restituisse, restitūtus	restore, revive
resurgo [re + surgo], resurgere, resurrēxī, resurrectus	arise, rise
resurrēctiō, resurrēctiōnis (f.)	resurrection
revereor [re + vereor], revereri,—, reveritus sum	fear

revolvō [re + volvo], revolvere, revolvi, revolūtus	turn, move
rēx, rēgis (m.)	king
rīdeō, rīdēre, rīsī, rīsus	laugh
rogō, rogāre, rogāvī, rogātus	ask
sacerdōs, sacerdōtis (m.)	priest
saeculum, saeculī (n.)	age
saepe	often
salūs, salūtis (f.)	salvation, health
salvātor, salvātōris (m.)	savior
salvō, salvāre, salvāvī, salvātus	save
Samaritānus, Samaritāna	Samaritan
sānātus, -a, -um	healed
sānctificō [sanctus + facere], sānctificāre, sānctificāvī, sānctificātus	make holy
sanguis, sanguinis (m.)	blood
sānō, sānāre, sānāvī, sānātus	heal
sapiens, sapientis [gen. sing.]	wise
scandalizō, scandalizāre, scandalizāvī, scandalizātus	tempt to evil, cause to stumble
scelus, sceleris (n.)	crime, wicked deed
scientia, scientiae (f.)	knowledge
scindō, scindere, scidī, scīsum	rend, tear
sciō, scīre, scīvī (sciī), scītus	know
scrībō, scrībere, scrīpsī, scrīptus	write
scūtum, scūtī (n.)	shield
se	himself, herself, itself
sed	but
sedent	they sit
sedeō, sedēre, sēdī, sessus	sit
sedet	he / she / it sits

sēdūcō [se + duco], sēdūcere, sēdūxī, sēductus	seduce
semetipsum	himself
sēminō, sēmināre, sēmināvī, sēminātus	sow
sentiō, sentīre, sēnsī, sēnsus	sense, think
sequor, sequī,—, secūtus sum	follow
sermō, sermōnis (m.)	word, sermon
serpēns, serpentis (n.)	snake
servō, servāre, servāvī, servātus	keep, preserve
servus, -ī (m.)	servant
sex	6
si	if
sīcut[i]	just as, like
sīdus, sīderis (n.)	star, constellation
signum, signī (n.)	sign
similiter	similarly
similitūdō, similitūdinis (f.)	likeness, resemblance
simplex, simplicis [gen. sing.]	simple
simulō, simulāre, simulāvī, simulātus	imitate
sine [+abl]	without
singulus, -a, -um	each, every
sive	whether, or [inclusive]
sōl, sōlis (m.)	sun
soleo, solere,—, solitus	be in the habit of, be accustomed to
sollicitus, -a, -um	worry
solum	only
solus -a, -um	only, alone
somnium, somniī (n.)	sleep
soror, sorōris (f.)	sister

speciōsus, -a, -um	beautiful, marvelous
spectō, spectāre, spectāvī, spectātus	see, regard
spērō, spērāre, spērāvī, spērātus	hope
spēs, speī (f.)	hope
spīritus, spīritus (m.)	spirit
spīrō, spīrāre, spīrāvī, spīrātus	breathe
splēndidus, -a, -um	splendid
statim	immediately
statuō, statuere, statuī, statūtus	establish, set up, decide
stella, stellae (f.)	star
stō, stāre, stetī, status	stand
strepitus, strepitūs (m.)	racket, noise
stultus, -a, -um	foolish, stupid
suāvis, suāvis, suāve	agreeable, pleasant
sub [+abl]	under
subeo [sub + eo], subire, subivi, subitus	go under
subitō	suddenly
sum, esse, fuī, futūrus	be
sunt	they are
super [+acc or +abl]	over
superbia, superbiae (f.)	pride
superveniō [super + venio], supervenīre, supervēnī, superventus	to come over
supplicium, supplic[i]ī (n.)	punishment
suscipiō [sub + capio], suscipere, suscēpī, susceptus	undertake, take on
synagōga, synagōgae (f.)	gathering, synagogue
tacent	they are quiet
taceō, tacēre, tacuī, tacitus	be quiet

tacēt	he / she / it is quiet
taedet, taedēre, taeduit,—	[impersonal] it is tiring
tandem	finally, at last
tangō, tangere, tetigī, tāctus	touch
tantum	only
tantus, -a, -um	so great
tardus, -a, -um	slow
te	yourself
temetipsum	yourself
templum, templī (n.)	temple
temptō, temptāre, temptāvī, temptātus	test, try
tenebra, tenebrae (f.)	darkness [often found in the plural]
teneō, tenēre, tenuī, tentus	hold
terra, terrae (f.)	earth, land
terrenus, -a, -um	earthly
testāmentum, testāmentī (n.)	covenant
timent	they fear
timeō, timēre, timuī,—	fear
timet	he / she / it fears
tollō, tollere, sustulī, sublātus	pick up, take up
tōtus, -a, -um	whole
tractō, tractāre, tractāvī, tractātus	draw, pull, discuss, preach
trado [trans + do], tradere, tradidi, traditus	betray, hand over, pass down
trahō, trahere, trāxī, tractus	draw, drag
trānsferō [trāns + ferō], trānsferre, trānstuli, trānslātum	carry across
transitus, transitūs (m.)	passage
tremor, tremōris (m.)	shuddering
tres, tres, tria	3

trībulātiō, tribulationis (f.)	tribulation
trīstis, -is, -e	sad
tu	you
turba, turbae (f.)	crowd
turbō, turbāre, turbāvī, turbātus	throw into confusion
turpis, turpis, turpe	ugly
typus, typī (m.)	figure, plan, type
ubicumque	wherever
ubique	everywhere
ulcīscor, ulcīscī,—, ultus sum	avenge, punish
ūllus, -a, -um	any
umquam	ever
unde	from where
unus, una, unum	1
urbs, urbis (f.)	city
usque ad [+acc]	up to, to
ūtilis, ūtilis, ūtile	useful
utinam	if only, would that [+subj]
utique	certainly
ūtor, utī,—, ūsus	[+abl] use
uxor, uxōris (f.)	wife
vadō, vādere, vāsī,—	go
valdē	really, very
valeō, valēre, valuī, valitus	be able; be strong
vānitās, vānitātis (f.)	vanity
vel	either, or [inclusive]
vēlōcis, vēlōcis, vēlōce	with haste / speed
vēlōciter, vēlōcius, vēlōcissimē	quickly, more quickly, most quickly, very quickly

vēnerō, venerāre, venerāvī, venerātus	venerate, worship
veniō, venīre, vēnī, ventus	come
ventus, ventī (m.)	wind
verbum, verbī (n.)	word
vereor, verērī, —, veritus	fear
vērō	but, however
verumtamen	although
verus, -a, -um	true
vesper, vesperis (m.)	evening
vestīgium, vestīgiī (n.)	footprint
vestīmentum, vestīmentī (n.)	clothes
vexō, vexāre, vexāvī, vexātus	vex, trouble
via, -ae (f.)	way
vident	they see
videō, vidēre, vīdī, vīsus	see
videor, vidērī, —, vīsus	seem, think
videt	he / she / it sees
vigilia, vigiliae (f.)	watch, lookout
vigilō, vigilāre, vigilāvī, vigilātus	stay awake
vinculum, vinculī (n.)	chain
vīnum, vīnī (n.)	wine
vir, virī (m.)	man
virga, virgae (f.)	scepter, rod
virgō, virginis (f.)	virgin
virtūs, virtūtis (f.)	power, virtue
vīs, vīs (f.)	strength, force, power
vita, -ae (f.)	life
vitium, vitiī (n.)	fault, vice, crime

vīvō, vīvere, vīxī, victus	live
vīvus, -a, -um - alive, living	alive, living
voco, vocare, vocavi, vocatus	call
volant	they fly, flee
volat	he / she / it flies, flees
volō, velle, voluī,—	want to; be willing to
volō, volāre, volāvī, volātus	fly, flee
volucer, volucris (f.)	flying thing, bird
vos	you all
vōx, vōcis (f.)	voice, word, sound

ENGLISH TO LATIN VOCABULARY

ENGLISH	LATIN
1	*unus, una, unum*
2	*duo, duae, duo*
3	*tres, tres, tria*
4	*quattuor*
5	*quinque*
6	*sex*
40	*quadraginta*
a little bit	*pusillum*
absolve	*absolvō [ab + solvō], absolvere, absolvī, absolūtus*
abyss	*abyssus, abyssī (f.)*
accept	*accipiō [ad + capio], accipere, accēpī, acceptus*
accept [repeatedly]	*acceptō [ad + capio], acceptāre, acceptāvi, acceptātus*
accuse, blame, charge	*accūsō [ad + causa], accūsāre, accūsāvī, accūsātus*
acknowledge, recognize	*agnōscō [ag + nōscō], agnōscere, agnōvī, agnitus*
acquire, obtain	*adquīrō [ad + quaerō], adquīrere, adquīsīvī, adquīsītus*
added	*adjūnctus, -a, -um*
added	*adjūnctus, -a, -um*
advance, march	*incēdō [in + cēdō], incedere, incessī, incessus*
adversary	*adversārius, adversāriī (m.)*
after	*post [+acc]*
age	*āetās, aetātis (f.)*
age	*saeculum, saeculī (n.)*
agreeable, pleasant	*suāvis, suāvis, suāve*
alive, living	*vīvus, -a, -um - alive, living*
all	*cūnctus, -a, -um*
almighty	*omnipotēns, [gen. sing.: omnipotentis]*

almost	*paene*
also	*etiam*
also	*quoque*
altar	*altāre, altāris (n.)*
although	*quamquam*
although	*verumtamen*
ambition, desire	*ambitiō, ambitiōnis (f.)*
and	*ac*
and	*atque*
and	*et*
and [added to the end of another word]	*-que*
animal	*animal, animālis (n.)*
announce	*nūntiō, nūntiāre, nūntiāvī, nūntiātus*
Anointed One [often translated simply as Christ]	*Christus, -ī (m.)*
another	*alius, -a, -ud*
another	*alius, -a, -ud*
any	*ūllus, -a, -um*
appear	*appāreō, appārēre, appāruī, appāritus*
appear; obey	*pareo, parēre, paruī, paritus*
apple, fruit	*malum, mali (n.)*
approach, draw near towards	*appropinquō [ad + propinquo], appropinquāre, appropinquāvī, appropinquātus*
arise	*orior, orīrī,——, ortus sum*
arise, rise	*resurgo [re + surgo], resurgere, resurrēxī, resurrectus*
arms, weapons	*arma, armōrum (n. pl.)*
army, host	*exercitus, exercitūs (m.)*
art	*ars, artīs (f.)*

as great, how great	*quantus, -a, -um*
ascend	*āscendō [ad-scando], ascendere, ascendī, ascēnsus*
ascent, progress	*ascēnsiō, ascēnsiōnis (f.)*
ask	*interrogō [inter + rogo], interrogāre, interrogāvī, interrogātus*
ask	*rogō, rogāre, rogāvī, rogātus*
ask, request	*postulō, postulāre, postulāvī, postulātus*
astrologer, magician, "wise man"	*magus, magī (m.)*
avenge, punish	*ulcīscor, ulcīscī, —, ultus sum*
avoid	*ēvītō [ex + vito], ēvītāre, ēvītāvī, ēvītātus*
baptize	*baptīzō, baptīzāre, baptīzāvī, baptīzātus*
battle	*proelium, proeliī (n.)*
be	*sum, esse, fuī, futūrus*
be able to	*possum, posse, potuī, —*
be able; be strong	*valeō, valēre, valuī, valitus*
be awakened	*excitō [ex + cieo], excitāre, excitāvī, excitātus*
be aware [can be used as a verb of fearing]	*caveō, cavēre, cāvī, cautus*
be born	*nāscor, nāscī, —, nātus sum*
be horrified by, despise	*horreō, horrēre, horruī, —*
be in the habit of, be accustomed to	*soleo, solere, —, solitus*
be mindful of, remember	*memoror, memorārī, —, memorātus sum*
be quiet	*taceō, tacēre, tacuī, tacitus*
bear, carry	*gerō, gerere, gessī, gestus*
beautiful, handsome	*pulcher, pulchra, pulchrum*
beautiful, marvelous	*speciōsus, -a, -um*
because [or to a begin a quotation]	*quia*
become, happen	*fiō, fierī, —, factus sum*
beg	*obsecrō, obsecrāre, obsecrāvī, obsectrātus*

begin	*incipiō [in + capio], incipere, incēpi, inceptus*
behold	*ecce*
believe	*crēdō, crēdere, crēdidī, crēditus*
beloved	*dīlēctus, -a, -um*
betray, hand over, pass down	*trado [trans + do], tradere, tradidi, traditus*
between	*inter [+acc]*
bind	*ligō, ligāre, ligāvī, ligātus*
bird	*avis, avis (f.)*
bishop, pope [*lit.* "bridge"]	*pontifex, pontificis (m.)*
blame	*culpō, culpāre, culpāvī, culpātus*
blame, seize	*reprehendō [re + prehendo], reprehendere, reprehēnsī, reprehēnsus*
bless	*benedīcō [bene + dicere], benedīcere, benedīxi, benedictus*
blessing	*benedictiō, benedictiōnis (f.)*
blood	*sanguis, sanguinis (m.)*
boat	*nāvis, nāvis (f.)*
body	*corpus, corporis (n.)*
book	*liber, libri (m.)*
born	*nātus, -a, -um*
boy	*puer, puerī (m.)*
bread	*pānis, pānis (m.)*
break	*frangō, frangere, frēgī, frāctus*
breathe	*spīrō, spīrāre, spīrāvī, spīrātus*
bring about, make, effect	*efficiō [ex + facio], efficere, effectī, effectūs*
brother	*frāter, frātris (m.)*
build [*lit.* make a building]	*aedificō [aedis-facere], aedificāre, aedificāvī, aedificātus*
build up	*aedificō [aedes + facio], aedificāre, aedificāvī, aedificātus*
burn up, use up, expend	*cōnsūmō [con + sumo], cōnsūmere, cōnsūmpsī, cōnsūmptus*

burn, be on fire	*ārdeō, ārdēre, ārsi, ārsus*
but	*at*
but	*sed*
but, but yet	*at*
but, however	*autem*
but, however	*verō*
buy	*emō, emere, ēmī, ēmptus*
buy back	*redēmō [rē-d-emō], redemere, redēmī, redēmptus*
by whom	*quō*
by, from	*ā / ab [+abl]*
call	*voco, vocare, vocavi, vocatus*
call to mind, remember [often comes with a noun in the genitive]	*recordor [re + cor + do], recordārī,—, recordātus*
camp	*castra, castrōrum (n. pl.)*
care	*cūra, cūrae (f.)*
carry	*portō, portāre, portāvī, portātus*
carry across	*trānsferō [trāns + ferō], trānsferre, trānstuli, trānslātum*
carry in front, give preference to	*praeferō [prae + ferō], praeferre, praetulī, praelātus*
castle, town	*castellum, castellī (n.)*
certainly	*utique*
chain	*vinculum, vinculī (n.)*
change, move, shift	*mūtō, mūtāre, mūtāvī, mūtātus*
charm, pleasantness	*jūcunditās, jūcunditātis (f.)*
children	*līberī, līberōrum (m.)*
church	*ecclēsia, ecclēsiae (f.)*
circus	*circus, circī (m.)*
city	*urbs, urbis (f.)*
city, commonwealth	*cīvitās, cīvitātis (f.)*
clean	*lavō, lavāre, lavāvī, lāvātus*

clean	*mundus, -a, -um*
close	*claudō, claudere, clausī, clausus*
clothes	*vestīmentum, vestīmentī (n.)*
collect [*lit.* bind together]	*colligō [con + ligare], colligere, collēgī, collēctus*
come	*veniō, venīre, vēnī, ventus*
come near, approach	*accēdō [ad + cēdō], accēdere, accessī, accessus*
come over	*superveniō [super + venio], supervenīre, supervēnī, superventus*
come together	*conveniō [cōn + veniō], convenīre, convēnī, conventūs*
commandment	*mandatum, mandati (n.)*
complete	*perficiō [per + facio], perficere, perfēcī, perfectus*
conceive	*concipiō [con + capio], concipere, concēpī, conceptus*
condemn	*re-probo [re + probo], reprobāre, reprobāvī, reprobātus*
confess	*cōnfiteor [con + fari], cōnfitērī,—, cōnfessus sum*
convert	*convertō [con + verto], convertere, convertī, conversus*
corrupt	*corrumpō [cōn-rumpō], corrumpere, corrūpī, corruptus*
covenant	*pactum, pactī (n.)*
covenant	*testāmentum, testāmentī (n.)*
create	*creō, creāre, creāvī, creātus*
creator	*creātor, creātōris (m.)*
crime, wicked deed	*scelus, sceleris (n.)*
crowd	*turba, turbae (f.)*
cry, weep	*fleō, flēre, flēvī, flētus*
cup, chalice	*calix, calicīs (m.)*
cup	*poculum, poculī (n.)*
cure, care for	*cūrō, cūrāre, cūrāvī, cūrātus*
curse	*maledico [male + dico], maledīcere, maledīxi, maledīctus*
custom	*cōnsuētūdō, cōnsuētūdinis (f.)*
daily	*cotīdiē; quotīdiē*

daily	*cotīdiē; quotīdiē*
danger, peril	*perīculum, perīculī (n.)*
dare	*audeō, audēre,—, ausus sum*
darkness [often found in the plural]	*tenebra, tenebrae (f.)*
daughter	*fīlia, fīliae (f.)*
day	*diēs, diēī (m./f.)*
death	*mors, mortis (f.)*
decree, edict	*ēdictum, ēdictī (n.)*
deign, condescend	*dignor, dignārī,—, dignus*
deny	*abnegō [ab + negō], abnegāre, abnegāvī, abnegātus*
desire	*cupiō, cupere, cupīvī, cupītus*
desire	*dēsīderō [de + sidus], dēsīderāre, dēsīderāvī, dēsīderātus*
desire [negative since Augustine]	*concupiscentia, concupiscentiae (f.)*
desire, choose	*exoptō [ex + optō], exoptāre, exoptāvī, exoptātus*
destroy, delete	*dēleō, dēlēre, dēlēvī, dēlētus*
destroy, demolish	*dēstruō, dēstruere, dēstrūxī, dēstrūctus*
determine beforehand, provide beforehand	*praedēstinō, praedēstināre, praedēstināvī, praedēstinātus*
devote	*devovō [de + vovo], dēvovēre, dēvōvī, dēvōtus*
die	*morior, morī,—, mortuus sum*
die, become defunct	*dēficiō [dē-faciō], dēficere, dēfēcī, dēfectus*
difficult	*difficilis, difficilis, difficile*
dine	*cēnō, cēnāre, cēnāvī, cēnātus*
displeasure; accident	*offēnsiō, offēnsiōnis (f.)*
disposition, ability, talent	*ingenium, ingeniī (n.)*
do, lead; with *gratias*: give thanks	*agō, agere, ēgī, āctus*
do, make	*faciō, facere, fēcī, factus*
dominical, relating to the Lord	*dominicus, -a, -um*
don't [in negative plural commands]	*nōlīte*

don't [in negative singular commands]	nōlī
door	iānuā, iānuae (f.)
door	ōstium, ōstiī (n.)
drag off, snatch, seize	rapiō, rapere, rapuī, raptus
draw, drag	trahō, trahere, trāxī, tractus
draw, pull, discuss, preach	tractō, tractāre, tractāvī, tractātus
drink	bibō, bibere, bibī, bibitus
drink	bibō, bibere, bibī, bibitus
each, every	singulus, -a, -um
eagle	aquila, aquilae (f.)
ear	aurīs, aurīs (f.)
earth, land	terra, terrae (f.)
earthly	terrenus, -a, -um
easily, easier	facile, facilius, facillimē
easy	facilis, facilis, facile
eat	comedō, comedere, comēdī, comestus
eat, chew	mandūcō, mandūcāre, mandūcāvī, mandūcātus
either, or [inclusive]	vel
elsewhere, from elsewhere	aliunde
employ, adhere to, summon	adhibeō [ad + habeō], adhibēre, adhibuī, adhibitus
enemy	inimīcus, inimīcī (m.)
enjoy	fruor, fruī, —, frūctūs
entreat, pray	dēprecor [de + precor], dēprecārī, —, dēprecātus
equity	aequitās, aequitātis (f.)
establish, set up, decide	statuō, statuere, statuī, statūtus
eternal	aeternus, -a, -um
even though	etsi
evening	vesper, vesperis (m.)

ever	*umquam*
everywhere	*ubique*
evil, bad	*malus, -a, -um*
examine, reflect one	*cōnsīdō, cōnsīderāre, cōnsīderāvī, cōnsīderātus*
excuse	*excūsātiō, excūsātiōnis (f.)*
excuse, acquit	*excūsō [ex + causa], excūsāre, excūsāvī, excūsātus*
eye	*oculus, oculī (m.)*
face	*facies, faciei (f.)*
faith	*fidēs, fideī (f.)*
faith	*fidūcia, fidūciae (f.)*
faithful	*fidēlis, fidēlis, fidēle*
fall	*cadō, cadere, cecidī, cāsus*
family	*familia, familiae (f.)*
family	*familia, familiae (f.)*
farmer	*agricola, agricolae (m.)*
father	*pater, patris (m.)*
fault, vice, crime	*vitium, vitiī (n.)*
fear	*revereor [re + vereor], reverērī,—, reveritus sum*
fear	*timeō, timēre, timuī,—*
fear	*vereor, verērī,—, veritus*
festal day, joyous day	*fēstus, -a, -um*
field	*āger, agrī (m.)*
fight	*pugnō, pugnāre, pugnāvī, pugnātus*
figure, plan, type	*typus, typī (m.)*
fill in, fulfill	*impleō [in + pleo], implēre, implēvī, implētus*
fill, fulfill	*compleō, complēre, complēvī, complētus*
finally, at last	*tandem*
finally, in the end	*dēnique*

find	*reperiō, reperīre, repperī, repertus*
find [*lit.* to come into]	*inveniō [in + veniō], invenīre, invēnī, inventus*
fish	*piscis, piscis (m.)*
fisherman	*piscātor, piscātōris (m.)*
flee	*fugiō, fugere, fūgī, fugitus*
flesh, meat	*carnis, carnis (f.)*
flock	*grex, gregis (m.)*
flood	*dīluvium, dīluviī (n.)*
flourish	*reflōreō [rē + flōreō], reflōrēre, reflōruī,—*
fly, flee	*volō, volāre, volāvī, volātus*
flying thing, bird	*volucer, volucris (f.)*
follow	*sequor, sequī,—, secūtus sum*
food	*cibus, cibī (m.)*
food	*ēsca, ēscae (f.)*
foolish, stupid	*stultus, -a, -um*
foot	*pēs, pedis (m.)*
footprint	*vestīgium, vestīgiī (n.)*
for	*enim*
for	*nam*
forbidden, illicit	*illicitus, -a, -um*
foreign	*aliēnus, -a, -um*
foresee, look for	*prōspiciō [prō + specto], prōspicere, prōspexī, prōspectus*
forget	*oblīvīscor, oblīvīscī, oblītus sum*
foundation	*fundāmentum, fundāmentī (n.)*
fraud, deceit	*dolus, -a, -um*
friend	*amīcus, amīcī (m.)*
from	*de [+abl]*
from here	*hinc*

from where	*unde*
fruit	*fructus, fructūs (m.)*
full	*plenus, -a, -um*
full of leprosy	*leprōsus, -a, -um*
full of pain or sadness	*dolōrōsus, -a, -um*
full of tears	*lacrimōsus, -a, -um*
gathering, synagogue	*synagōga, synagōgae (f.)*
generation	*generātiō, generātiōnis (f.)*
ghost, phantasm	*phantasma, phantasmae (f.)*
gift, office	*mūnus, mūneris (n.)*
girl	*puella, puellae (f.)*
give	*dō, dare, dedī, datus*
give birth	*pariō, parere, peperī, partus*
give birth to	*gignō, gignere, genuī, genitus*
glorify	*glōrificō [gloria-facio], glōrificāre, glōrificāvī, glōrificātus*
go	*cēdō, cēdere, cessī, cessus*
go	*eō, īre, īvī (iī), itus*
go	*vadō, vādere, vāsī, —*
go down; kill	*occīdo [ob + caedo], occīdere, occīdī, occāsus*
go in	*ingredior, [in + gredior], ingredī, —, ingressus sum*
go on, proceed	*pergō pergere, perrēxī, perrēctus*
go out	*ēgredior [ex + gredior], ēgredī, —, ēgressus sum*
go to	*aggredior [ad + gredior], aggredī, —, aggressus sum*
go under	*subeo [sub + eo], subire, subivi, subitus*
God	*Deus, Deī (m.)*
gold	*aurum, aurī (n.)*
good	*bonus, -a, -um*
grace	*gratia, gratiae (f.)*

great, large	*magnus, -a, -um*
greater, furthermore	*amplius*
grumble, complain	*murmurō, murmurāre, murmurāvī, murmurātus*
hand	*manūs, manūs (f.)*
hang	*pendō, pendere, pependī, pēnsus*
happiness	*fēlīcitās, fēlīcitātis (f.)*
happy, blessed	*beatus, -a, -um*
harvest	*messis, messis (n.)*
harvest (verb)	*metō, metere, messui, messus*
hate	*—, ōdī, ōsus*
have	*habeō, habēre, habuī, habitus*
have mercy on	*misereor, miserērī, —, miseritus sum*
he / she / it ascends	*ascendit*
he / she / it eats	*mandūcat*
he / she / it fears	*timet*
he / she / it flies, flees	*volat*
he / she / it has	*habēt*
he / she / it hears / obeys	*audit*
he / she / it is	*est*
he / she / it is quiet	*tacēt*
he / she / it keeps	*cūstōdit*
he / she / it loves	*dīligit*
he / she / it prays	*ōrat*
he / she / it says	*dicit*
he / she / it sees	*videt*
he / she / it sits	*sedet*
he / she / it understands	*intellegit*
he / she / it walks	*ambulat*

head	*caput, capitis (n.)*
heal	*sānō, sānāre, sānāvī, sānātus*
healed	*sānātus, -a, -um*
hear, obey	*audiō, audīre, audīvī (audiī), audītus*
heart	*cor, cordis (n.)*
heaven	*caelum, caelī (n.)*
heavenly, celestial	*caelestis, caelestis, caeleste*
heavy	*gravis, gravis, grave*
help (verb)	*adjuvō [ad + juvō], adjuvāre, adjūvī, adjūtus*
help	*auxilium, -ī (n.)*
help (verb)	*juvō, juvāre, jūvī, jūtus*
here	*hīc*
here	*hūc*
hide, conceal	*abscondō, abscondere, abscondī, absconditus*
high, tall	*altus, alta, altum*
himself	*semetipsum*
himself, herself, itself	*se*
hold	*teneō, tenēre, tenuī, tentus*
home	*domus, domūs (f.)*
honor	*honōrō, honōrāre, honōrāvī, honōrātus*
hope (verb)	*spērō, spērāre, spērāvī, spērātus*
hope	*spēs, speī (f.)*
horn	*cornū, cornus (n.)*
hour	*hora, horae (f.)*
how, in what way	*quemadmodum*
how, in what way	*quomodō*
hug	*complexō [con + plecto], complexāre, complexāvī complexātus*
humility	*humilitās, humilitātis (f.)*

hymn	*hymnus, hymni (m.)*
hymn, canticle	*canticum, cantici (n.)*
I	*ego*
ice	*glaciēs, glaciēī (f.)*
idol	*īdōlum, īdōlī (n.)*
if	*si*
if only, would that [+subj]	*utinam*
illuminate	*illūminō, illūmināre, illūmināvī, illūminātus*
illumination	*illūminātiō, illūminātiōnis (f.)*
image	*imāgō, imāginis (f.)*
imitate	*imitor, imitārī,—, imitātus sum*
imitate	*simulō, simulāre, simulāvī, simulātus*
immediately	*continuō*
immediately	*statim*
in	*in [+abl]*
in front of, before	*ante [+acc]*
in front of, before	*coram*
indeed, because, as a matter of fact	*etenim*
iniquity, sin	*inīquitās, inīquitātis (f.)*
inside	*interius*
instead of, or in the place of	*pro [+abl]*
into	*in [+acc]*
invoke, pray	*invocō [in-vocō], invocāre, invocāvī, invocātus*
it is allowed / permitted	*licet, licēre, licuit,—*
it is displeasing	*displicet [dis + placere], displicēre, displicuit,—*
it is displeasing	*paenitet, paenitēre, paenituit,—*
it is fitting	*convenit, convenīre, convenit,—*
it is pleasing	*placet, placēre,—, placitus est*

it is tiring	taedet, taedēre, taeduit,—
Jesus	Jēsus, Jēsū [gen], Jēsū [dat], Jēsum [acc], Jēsū [abl]
Jewish person	Iūdaeus, Iūdaea
journey	iter, itineris (n.)
judge	jūdex, jūdicis (m.)
judge (verb)	jūdico, jūdicāre, jūdicāvi, jūdicātus
judgment	judicium, judiciī (n.)
just	justus, -a, -um
just as, like	sīcut[i]
keep	cūstōdiō, cūstōdīre, cūstōdīvī, cūstōdītus
keep, preserve	servō, servāre, servāvī, servātus
kill	interficiō [inter + facio], interficere, interfēcisse, interfectus
kill, murder	necō, necāre, necavī, necatus
king	rēx, rēgis (m)
kingdom	rēgnum, rēgnī (n.)
kinsman, someone related by birth	cognāta, cognātae (f.)
kiss	ōsculum, osculī (n.)
know	—, nōvi, nōtus
know	sciō, scīre, scīvī (sciī), scītus
know, recognize	cognōscō [con + gnosco], cognōscere, cognōvī, cognitus
knowledge	scientia, scientiae (f.)
knowledge, conscience	cōnscientia, cōnscientiae (f.)
labor, pain	labor, labōris (m.)
labor, work	labōrō, labōrāre, labōrāvi, labōrātus
lack, be without	careō, carēre, caruī, caritus
lady	domina, dominae (f.)
lamb	āgnus, āgnī (m.)
lamp	lucerna, lucernae (f.)

laugh	*rīdeō, rīdēre, rīsī, rīsus*
law	*lex, legis (f.)*
lay out, explain	*expono [ex + pono], exponere, exposui, expositus*
lead	*dūco, dūcere, dūxisse, ductus*
leader	*dux, dūcis (m.)*
learn	*discō, discere, didicī, discitus*
leave behind, abandon	*relinquō, relinquere, relīquī, relictus*
leave behind, discard	*dērelinquō [dē + relinquō], dērelinquere, dērelīquī, dērelictus*
lie	*mendācium, mendāciī (n.)*
lie (verb)	*mentior, mentīrī,—, mentītus*
lie down	*jaceō, jacere, jacuī, jacitus*
life	*vita, -ae (f.)*
lift up	*levō, levāre, levāvī, levātus*
light	*levis, levis, leve*
light	*lūmen, lūminis (n.)*
light, daylight	*lūx, lūcīs (f.)*
likeness, resemblance	*similitūdō, similitūdinis (f.)*
lion	*leō, leōnis (m.)*
lip	*labium, labiī (n.)*
little	*pusillus, pusilla, pusillum*
live	*vīvō, vīvere, vīxī, victus*
live in, well	*habito, habitare, habitavi, habitatus*
live, dwell	*habitō, habitāre, habitāvī, habitātus*
look at, consider	*intueor, intuērī,—, intuitus sum*
look at, regard	*spectō, spectāre, spectāvī, spectātus*
lord, Lord	*dominus, dominī (m.)*
lose, dismiss [in the passive voice, "missing"]	*āmittō [ab + mitto], āmittere, āmīsī, amīsus*

love	*amō, amāre, amāvī, amātus*
love, cherish	*dīligō, dīligere, dīlēxī, dīlēctus*
love, charity	*cāritās, cāritātis (f.)*
magnify	*magnificō [mangus-facio], magnificāre, magnificāvī, magnificātus*
maidservant	*ancilla, ancillae (f.)*
make clean	*mundō, mundāre, mundāvī, mundātus*
make holy	*sānctificō [sanctus + facere], sānctificāre, sānctificāvī, sānctificātus*
make, accomplish	*prōficiō [pro + facio], prōficere, prōfēcī, profectus*
man	*vir, virī (m.)*
many	*multus, -a, -um*
marvel [at]	*mīror, mīrārī, —, mīrātus sum*
mass	*massa, massae (f.)*
mass	*missa, missae (f.)*
mat, cot	*grabātus, grabātī (m.)*
maybe	*fortasse*
member, part of the body	*membrum, membrī (n.)*
memory	*memoria, memoriae (f.)*
mercy	*misericordia, -ae (f.)*
merry, drunk	*hilarius, -a, -um*
middle	*medium, mediī (n.)*
middle (adjective)	*medius, media, medium*
mind	*mēns, mentis (f.)*
mind, intellect, soul, heart	*animus, animī (m.)*
mix	*mīsceō, miscēre, miscuī, mixtus*
money	*pecūnia, pecūniae (f.)*
month	*mēnsis, mēnsis (m.)*
morning [indeclinable]	*mane (n.)*

motion, movement	*mōtiō, mōtiōnis (f.)*
mountain	*mōns, montīs (m.)*
mouth	*os, oris (n.)*
multitude	*multitūdō, multitūdinis (f.)*
mute	*mūtus, mūta, mūtum*
my, your, his / her	*meus, tuus, suus*
myself	*me*
myself	*memetipsum*
mystery	*mystērium, mystēriī (n.)*
name, noun	*nōmen, nōminis (n.)*
nation	*gēns, gentīs (f.)*
native	*indigena, indigenae (m./f.)*
nature	*nātūra, nātūrae (f.)*
near	*prope [+acc]*
near, in the presence of	*apud*
necessary	*necessārius, -a, -um*
necessary	*necessis, necessis, necesse*
need, lack [with gen. or abl.]	*indigeō, indigēre, indiguī,—*
neighbor	*proximus, proximī (m.)*
new	*novus, -a, -um*
no one	*nēmō, nēminis (m.)*
no, nothing	*nūllus, -a, -um*
not	*non*
not know	*nescio [ne + scio], nescire, nescivi, nescitus*
not natural, huge	*ingēns, ingēntis [gen. sing.]*
not want to; be unwilling to	*nolō, nōlle, nōluī,—*
not, neither	*neque [nec]*
nothing	*nihil (n.)*

now	*nunc*
oath	*jūrāmentum, jūrāmentī (n.)*
obey	*oboediō, oboedīre, oboedīvī, oboedītus*
offering	*oblātiō, oblātiōnis (f.)*
often	*saepe*
on account of	*propter [+acc]*
on behalf, before, about	*pro*
one another	*invicem*
one's own, own	*proprius, -a, -um*
only	*solum*
only	*tantum*
only, alone	*solus -a, -um*
open	*aperiō, aperīre, aperuī, apertus*
or [exclusive]	*an*
order, arrange	*ōrdinō, ōrdināre, ōrdināvī, ōrdinātus*
order, tell, command	*jubeō, jubēre, jussī, jussus*
ought; must; owe	*dēbeō, dēbēre, dēbuī, dēbitus*
our, your [plural]	*noster, vester*
out of	*ex [+abl]*
outside	*exterius*
outside	*forās*
over	*super [+acc or +abl]*
over there	*illūc*
panic	*pavor, pavōris (m.)*
parent	*parēns, parentis (m.)*
part	*pars, partis (f.)*
party	*convīvium, convīvi(ī) (n.)*
passage	*transitus, transitūs (m.)*

pasture, graze	*pasco, pāscere, pāvi, pāstus*
peace	*pāx, pācis (f.)*
pear	*pirum, pira (n.)*
penalty	*poena, poenae (f.)*
people	*plēbs, plēbis (f.)*
people	*populus, populī, (m.)*
perhaps [+subj]	*forsitan*
persecute	*persequor [per + sequor], persequī,—, persecutus sum*
person, human	*homo, hominis (m.)*
pick up, take up	*tollō, tollere, sustulī, sublātus*
pilgrimage	*peregrīnātiō, peregrīnātiōnis (f.)*
poor	*pauper, pauperis [gen. sing.]*
pope	*papa, -ae (m.)*
power, ability	*potens, potentīs (f.)*
power, virtue	*virtūs, virtūtis (f.)*
praise	*laudo, laudare, laudavi, laudatus*
praise, merit	*laus, laudis (f.)*
pray	*ōrō, ōrāre, ōrāvī, ōrātus*
pray	*precor, precārī,—, precātus sum*
prepare	*praeparō [prae-parō], praeparāre, praeparāvī, praeparātus*
presence	*praesentia, praesentiae (f.)*
present, give	*perhibeō [per + habeo], perhibēre, perhibuī, perhibitus*
pride	*superbia, superbiae (f.)*
priest	*sacerdōs, sacerdōtīs (m.)*
prince	*prīnceps, prīncipis (m.)*
profit, benefit	*prōsum [pro + sum], prōdesse, prōfuī, prōfutūrus*
progeny	*prōgeniēs, prōgeniēī (f.)*

pronounce, declare	*prōnūntiō [pro + nuntio], prōnūntiāre, prōnūntiāvi, pronunciātus*
prophet	*propheta, prophetae (m.)*
propose, decide	*prōpōnō [pro + pono], prōpōnere, prōposuī, prōpositus*
publican, tax collector	*pūblicānus, pūblicānī (m.)*
punish	*pūniō, pūnīre, pūnīvī, pūnītus*
punishment	*supplicium, supplic[i]ī (n.)*
put	*pōnō, pōnere, posuī, positus*
put on	*induō, induere, induī, indūtus*
put, build, found	*condō [cōn + dō], condere, condidī, conditus*
queen	*rēgīna, rēgīnae (f.)*
quickly, more quickly, most quickly	*cito, citius, citissimē*
quickly, more quickly, most quickly, very quickly	*vēlōciter, vēlōcius, vēlōcissimē*
racket, noise	*strepitus, strepitūs (m.)*
read	*lēgō, legere, lēgī, lēctus*
really, very	*valdē*
reason, rationality	*ratiō, ratiōnis (f.)*
recede, withdraw	*recēdō [rē + cēdō], recēdere, recessi, recessus*
receive	*recipiō [re + capio], recipere, recēpī, receptus*
recline	*recumbō [re + cumbo], recumbere, recubi,—*
region, area	*rēgiō, regiōnis (f.)*
rejoice	*gaudeō, gaudēre,—, gāvīsus sum*
rejoice, be jubilant	*jūbilō, jūbilāre, jūbilāvī, jūbilātum*
rejoice, be happy	*laetor, laetārī,—laetātus sum*
remain	*maneo, manēre, mānsi, mānsus*
remember	*—, memini,—*
remember	*memorō, memorāre, memorāvi, memorātus*
rend, tear	*scindō, scindere, scidī, scīsum*

require, seek, need	*requīrō [rē + quaerō], requīrere, requīsīvī, requīsītus*
resign	*resignō [re + signo], resignāre, resignāvī, resignātus*
resound	*īnsonō [in + sono], īnsonāre, īnsonuī, īnsonitus*
respond	*respondeō, respondēre, respondī, respōnsus*
rest	*requiēs, requiēī (f.)*
restore, revive	*restituō [re + statuo], restituere, restituisse, restitūtus*
resurrection	*resurrēctiō, resurrēctiōnis (f.)*
reward, wage, pay	*mercēs, mercēdis (f.)*
river	*flūvius, flūviī (m.)*
rock	*petra, petrae (f.)*
rooster, Gaul	*gallus, gallī (m.)*
ruin, destroy	*perdō [per + do], perdere, perdidī, perditus*
sacrifice	*holocaustum, holocaustī (n.)*
sacrifice	*immolō, immolāre, immolāvī, immolātus*
sad	*trīstis, -is, -e*
salvation, health	*salūs, salūtis (f.)*
Samaritan	*Samaritānus, Samaritāna*
save	*reservō [re + servo], reservāre, reservāvī, reservātus*
save	*salvō, salvāre, salvāvī, salvātus*
savior	*salvātor, salvātōris (m.)*
say	*dīcō, dīcere, dīxī, dictus*
say [defective verb that typically only appears in the third person: *ait* and *aiunt*]	*aiō,—,—,—*
say [postpositive and defective verb, usually in the third person singular: *inquit*]	*inquam,—,—,—*
say, speak	*loquor, loquī,—, locūtus sum*
scepter, rod	*virga, virgae (f.)*
sea	*mare, maris (n.)*

seduce	sēdūcō [se + duco], sēdūcere, sēdūxī, sēductus
see	videō, vidēre, vīdī, vīsus
seek, go towards	appetō [ad + petere] appetere, appetīvī, appetītus
seek, aim at	petō, petere, petīvī, petitus
seek, question	quaerō, quaerere, quaesīvī, quaesītus
seem, think	videor, vidērī,—, vīsus
send	mittō, mittere, mīsī, missum
send away, forgive	dīmittō [dī + mittō], dīmittere, dīmīsī, dīmissus
sense, think	sentiō, sentīre, sēnsī, sēnsus
servant	servus, -ī (m.)
serve	ministrō, ministrāre, ministrāvī, ministrātus
set free, to liberate	līberō, līberāre, līberāvī, līberātus
settler, farmer	colonus, colonī (m.)
sheep	ovis, ovis, ovium [gen. pl.] (m.)
shepherd	pāstor, pāstōris (m.)
shield	scūtum, scūtī (n.)
short / small time; little, small amount	modicum, modicī (n.)
shout	clāmō, clāmāre, clāmāvī, clāmātus
show	ostendō [obs + tendo], ostendere, ostendī, ostēnsus
shuddering	tremor, tremōris (m.)
sick	aeger, -a, -um
sickness, illness	morbus, morbī (m.)
sight	cōnspectus, cōnspectus (m.)
sign	signum, signī (n.)
similarly	similiter
simple	simplex, simplicis [gen. sing.]
sin	peccātum, peccātī (n.)
sin	peccō, peccāre, peccāvī, peccātus

since [or to begin a quotation]	*quoniam*
sing	*cantō, cantāre, cantāvī, cantātus*
sister	*soror, sorōris (f.)*
sit	*sedeō, sedēre, sēdī, sessus*
sleep (verb)	*dormio, dormire, dormivi, dormitus*
sleep	*somnium, somniī (n.)*
slow	*tardus, -a, -um*
small boat	*nāvicula, nāviculae (f.)*
snake	*serpēns, serpentis (n.)*
snatch away	*ēripiō [ex + rapiō], ēripere, ēripuī, ēreptus*
so great	*tantus, -a, -um*
sojourn	*peregrinor, peregrinari,—, peregrinatus sum*
soldier	*mīles, mīlitis (m.)*
some person, some thing	*aliqui, aliqua, aliquod*
someone, something	*aliquis, aliquis, aliquid*
sometime, finally, at last	*aliquandō*
son	*filius, filiī (m.)*
soon	*mox*
soul	*anima, animae (f.)*
sow	*sēminō, sēmināre, sēmināvī, sēminātus*
spare	*parcō, parcere, pepercī, parsus*
sphere	*orbis, orbis (m.)*
spirit	*spīritus, spīritus (m.)*
splendid	*splēndidus, -a, -um*
spouse	*conjūnx, conjugis (m./f.)*
sprinkle, wash	*aspergō [ad + spergo], aspergere, aspersī, aspersus*
stand	*stō, stāre, stetī, status*
star	*stella, stellae (f.)*

star, constellation	*sīdus, sīderis (n.)*
stay awake	*vigilō, vigilāre, vigilāvī, vigilātus*
step	*gradus, gradūs (m.)*
still, yet	*adhūc*
stone	*lapis, lapidis (m.)*
stop	*dēsinō [de + sino], dēsinere, dēsīvī, dēsitus*
strength, force, power	*vīs, vīs (f.)*
strike, beat	*percūtiō [per + quatiō], percutere, percussi, percussus*
strong	*fortis, fortis, forte*
student, disciple	*discipulus, discipulī (m.)*
suddenly	*subitō*
suffer, suffer with	*com-patior [con + patior], compatī,—, compassus sum*
sun	*sōl, sōlis (m.)*
supply, provide, present	*praebeō, praebēre, praebui, praebitus*
support, prop, firmament	*firmāmentum, firmāmentī (n.)*
surely not ... [introduces a question expecting a negative answer]	*num*
swear	*jūro, jurāre, juravī, juratus*
sweet	*dulcis, dulcis, dulce*
sword	*gladius, gladiī (m.)*
take, seize	*capiō, capere, cēpī, captus*
taste	*gustō, gustāre, gustāvī, gustātus*
teach	*doceō, docēre, docuī, doctus*
tears	*lacrima, lacrimae (f.)*
temple	*templum, templī (n.)*
tempt to evil, cause to stumble	*scandalizō, scandalizāre, scandalizāvī, scandalizātus*
test, try	*temptō, temptāre, temptāvī, temptātus*
that	*ille, illa, illud*
that	*nē [in a fear clause]*

APPENDICES

that, indeed	*quin*
then	*dein, deinde*
there	*ibi*
they are	*sunt*
they are quiet	*tacent*
they ascend	*ascendunt*
they eat	*mandūcant*
they fear	*timent*
they fly, flee	*volant*
they have	*habent*
they hear / obey	*audiunt*
they keep	*cūstōdiunt*
they love	*dīligun*
they pray	*ōrant*
they say	*dicunt*
they see	*vident*
they sit	*sedent*
they understand	*intellegunt*
they walk	*ambulant*
thing	*rēs, reī (f.)*
think	*putō, putāre, putāvī, putātus*
this	*hic, haec, hoc*
this one, that one [of yours]	*iste, ista, istud*
threaten	*comminō [cōn + minō], commināre, commināvī, cominātus*
through	*per [+acc]*
throw	*jaciō, jacēre, jēcī, jactus*
throw into confusion	*turbō, turbāre, turbāvī, turbātus*
throw out	*ējiciō [ē + jaciō], ējicere, ējēcī, ējectus*

tired	*fessus, -a, -um*
to wherever	*quōcumque*
to whom	*cuī*
to whom [plural]	*quibus*
to, towards; for the purpose of	*ad [+acc]*
today	*hodiē*
tomb	*monumentum, monumentī (n.)*
tongue	*lingua, linguae (f.)*
too [much]	*nimis*
touch	*tangō, tangere, tetigī, tāctus*
town	*oppidum, oppidī (n.)*
transport, move	*migrō, migrāre, migrāvī, migrātus*
trap, snare, plot	*īnsidiā, īnsidiae (f.)*
treaty, covenant	*foedus, foederis (n.)*
tree, wood	*lignum, lignī (n.)*
tribulation	*trībulātiō, tribulationis (f.)*
true	*verus, -a, -um*
trust	*cōnfīdō [cōn + fīdō], cōnfīdere,—, cōnfīsus*
try	*cōnor, cōnārī,—, cōnātus sum*
turn around, convert	*convertō [con + verto], convertere, convertī, convertus*
turn, move	*revolvō [re + volvo], revolvere, revolvī, revolūtus*
ugly	*foedus, -a, -um*
ugly	*turpis, turpis, turpe*
under	*sub [+abl]*
understand	*intellegō, intellegere, intellēxī, intellexus*
understanding	*intellectus, intellectūs (m.)*
undertake, take on	*suscipiō [sub + capio], suscipere, suscēpī, susceptus*
universal	*catholicus, -a, -um*

unless, except	*nisi*
until	*donec*
unworthy [+abl]	*indignus, indigna, indignum*
up to, to	*usque ad [+acc]*
use	*ūtor, utī, —, ūsus*
useful	*ūtilis, ūtilis, ūtile*
vanity	*vānitās, vānitātis (f.)*
venerate, worship	*vēnerō, venerāre, venerāvī, venerātus*
vex, trouble	*vexō, vexāre, vexāvī, vexātus*
victim, sacrifice	*hostia, hostiae (f.)*
virgin	*virgō, virginis (f.)*
voice, word, sound	*vōx, vōcis (f.)*
wait, await	*exspectō [ex + specto], exspectāre, exspectāvī, expectātus*
walk	*ambulō, ambulāre, ambulāvī, ambulātus*
wander, err	*errō, errāre, errāvī, errātus*
want to; be willing to	*volō, velle, voluī, —*
warn, admonish	*admoneō [ad + moneo], admonēre, admonuī, admonitus*
warn; teach	*moneō, monēre monuī monitus*
watch, lookout	*vigilia, vigiliae (f.)*
water	*aqua, aqua (f.)*
wave	*fluctus, fluctūs (m.)*
way	*via, -ae (f.)*
we	*nos*
wealthy	*dīves, dīvitis [gen. sing.]*
wedding, marriage	*nūptiae, nūptiārum (f. pl.)*
well	*puteus, puteī (m.)*
when	*quandō*
when [without a noun in the ablative]	*cum*

wherever	*ubicumque*
whether, or [inclusive]	*sive*
white, ready for the harvest	*albus, -a, -um*
who [plural]?	*quī*
who, which	*quī, quae, quod*
who?	*quis*
whoever, whatever	*quīcumque, quaecumque, quidcumque*
whole	*tōtus, -a, -um*
whom [direct object]	*quem*
whom, which	*quem, quam, quod*
whomever you please, what you please, anyone / anything whatever	*quilibet, quaelibet, quidlibet*
whose	*cujus*
why	*quarē*
why?	*cūr*
wife	*uxor, uxōris (f.)*
wind	*ventus, ventī (m.)*
window	*fenestra, fenestrae (f.)*
wine	*vīnum, vīnī (n.)*
winter	*hiems, hiemis (f.)*
wise	*sapiens, sapientis [gen. sing.]*
with [paired with noun in ablatives]	*cum [+abl]*
with haste / speed	*vēlōcis, vēlōcis, vēlōce*
without	*sine [+abl]*
woman	*fēmina, fēminae (f.)*
wonderful, marvelous	*mīrābilis, mīrābilis, mīrābile*
word	*verbum, verbī (n.)*
word, fame	*fama, famae (f.)*
word, sermon	*sermō, sermōnis (m.)*

work, operation, activity	*operātiō, operātiōnis (f.)*
work (verb)	*operor, operārī,—, operātus*
work	*opus, operis (n.)*
world	*mundus, mundī (m.)*
worry	*sollicitus, -a, -um*
worship, bow down	*adōrō, adōrāre, adōrāvī, adōrātus*
worship, cultivate	*colō, colere, coluī, cultus*
worthy [+abl]	*dignus, digna, dignum*
write	*scrībō, scrībere, scrīpsī, scrīptus*
you all	*vos*
year	*annus, annī (m.)*
yesterday	*heri*
you	*tu*
young animal; colt; young chicken	*pullus, pullī (m.)*
yourself	*te*
yourself	*temetipsum*

INDEX

a-nouns, 1–6, 319
ablative absolute, 122, 192–93, 210
ablative case, 22–23, 52–54, 122–23
ablatives with certain verbs, 223–24
accusative case, 4–5, 24, 91–93, 122–23
adjectives: comparative forms, 103–5, 136–37; irregular, 136–37; superlative forms, 103–5, 136–37; third declension, 101–3
adverbs: formation, 129–31; irregular, 137
Agnus Dei (prayer), 299
alphabet, xxv–xxvi
Anima Christi (prayer), 298
Angelus Domini (prayer), 315–16
Annunciation, 292–93
article (lack of in Latin), xxii, 8, 24–25
Ave Maria (prayer), 309, 315

Benedictus (prayer), 314–15

cases: ablative, 22–23, 52–54, 122–23; accusative, 4–5, 24, 91–93, 122–23; dative, 41–45; genitive, 13–14; locative, 184; nominative, 1–3; vocative, 33
commands. *See* imperative
comparative adverbs, 129–31, 137
concessive clauses, 161
conditionals, 229–30, 282–84; contrary to fact, 282; future more vivid, 229–30
Confiteor (prayer), 302–3
conjunctions, 27–28, 65–66, 114, 148

consonants, xxv–xxvi
Crucifixion, 294

Daniel and Bel (story), 232–33
dative case, 41–45
declensions: first (a-nouns), 5–6, 13–14, 23, 42; second (o-nouns), 6, 14, 23, 43; third (i/e-nouns), 72–74, 101–3; fourth (u-nouns), 100–101; fifth (e-nouns), 113–14
demonstrative pronouns, 24–27, 44–47
deponent verbs, 145–47, 193, 215, 223; imperatives, 215; semi-deponent, 223
Dies Irae (prayer), 310–12
diphthongs, xxv

Ecclesiastical pronunciation, xxiv–xxvi
e-nouns (fifth declension), 113–14
Esther and Ahasuerus (story), 251–52

factum (syntax), 217–18
Familia Romana connections, 289–91
fear clauses, 271–72
Foot Washing, 286, 295–96
future active participles, 200–201
future infinitives, 202
future passive participles, 348
future perfect tense, 228–30, 336–37

gender, 1, 24–25, 102–3
genitive case, 13–14, 318–21
gerunds, 222–23, 348

411

INDEX

Gloria in Excelsis (prayer), 299
Gloria Patri (prayer), 298

Holy Family (Labor of), 293–94
hortatory subjunctive, 263

i/e-nouns (third declension), 72–74
imperative, 33–35, 167, 215, 230, 344; deponent, 215; irregular, 230, 344
imperfect subjunctive, 254–55, 339–40
imperfect tense, 154–57, 165–67, 330–31
independent subjunctives, 263
indirect questions, 272; speech, 92–94
infinitives, 81–82; future active, 202; with modals, 82–84; passive, 84, 193–94; perfect, 183–84interrogative pronouns, 26–27, 35, 55

jussive subjunctive, 263

Lazarus (story), 243–44
locative case, 184

Magnificat (prayer), 301
Mary at the Tomb, 295
Memorare (prayer), 313
modal verbs, 82–84, 262, 330–47
mood, 33–34, 60–61

narrative subjunctive, 280–81
negative commands, 167
nominative case, 1–3, 318–21
nouns, 318–21; a-nouns (first declension), 5–6, 13–14, 23, 42; o-nouns (second declension), 6, 14, 23, 43; i/e-nouns (third declension), 72–74; u-nouns (fourth declension), 100–101; e-nouns (fifth declension), 113–14
numbers: cardinal, 159–60; ordinal, 160–61
Nunc Dimittis (prayer), 299

o-nouns (second declension), 6, 14, 23, 43
optative subjunctive, 264, 282
Orationes Hebdomadae (Weekly Prayers), 297–317

participles: future active, 200–201; introduction to, 111–13; perfect passive, 190–93; present, 111–13
passive voice, 53–54, 180–82, 190–93
perfect passive participle, 190–93; subjunctive, 270–71, 341–42; tense, 154–57, 180–82, 190–93, 333–34
personal endings (verbs), 60–63, 127–28
Peter's Denial (story), 220
pluperfect subjunctive, 279–80, 342–43; tense, 155–56, 207–9, 335–36
possessive adjectives, 75; nouns, 13–14
prayers, 297–317
prepositions, 22–24, 139–40, 318
present participle, 111–13; subjunctive, 247–48, 338–39; tense, 1–7, 60–63, 329–30
pronouns 15–16; demonstrative, 24–27, 44–47; indefinite, 174–76; intensive, 94–95; interrogative, 26–27, 35; personal, 64–65; reflexive, 65; relative, 15–16, 26–27, 35, 323–24
purpose clauses, 255–56

realis vs. irrealis, 280–82
Regina Caeli (prayer), 315
reflexive pronouns, 65
relative clauses of characteristic, 256
result clauses, 255–56

Salve Regina (prayer), 301–2
Sanctus (prayer), 297
sequence of tenses, 156–57, 256–57, 273–74
Signum Crucis (prayer), 297
Stabat Mater (prayer), 305–8

subject. *See* nominative case
subjunctive, 247–57, 263–64, 270–74, 279–82, 338–43; deliberative, 264; doubting, 264; fear clauses, 271–72; hortatory, 263; imperfect, 254–55, 339–40; independent, 263; indirect questions, 272; jussive, 263; narrative, 280–81; optative, 264, 282; perfect, 270–71, 341–42; pluperfect, 279–80, 342–43; present, 247–48, 338–39; purpose clauses, 255–56; result clauses, 255–56; relative clauses of characteristic, 256
superlative adjectives, 103–5, 136–37; adverbs, 130–31, 137
supine, 217, 349
syllabication, xxvii

Tantum Ergo (prayer), 316
tantus. . .quantus and tam. . .quam, 210
teaching resources, 289–317
Te Deum (prayer), 303–4, 305
Temptation (story), 295
tenses, 154–57, 207–30, 329–37; future, 332–33; future perfect, 228–30, 336–37; imperfect, 330–31; perfect, 333–34; pluperfect, 207–9, 335–36; present, 329–30
translation (tips for), 149

Ubi Caritas (prayer), 317
u-nouns (fourth declension), 100–101

verbs, 207–30, 262, 329–49; active voice, 60–63; defective, 216; deponent, 145–47; esse ("to be"), 7–8, 157–59, 180–82; ferre ("to carry"), 138; future, 158–59, 173–74; future perfect, 155–56; imperfect, 154–57, 165–67; impersonal, 120–22; infinitives, 81–84, 183–84, 193–94, 202; ire ("to go"), 128–29; irregular, 330–47; morphology, 329–49; of memory, 217; passive voice, 53–54, 190–93; perfect, 154–57, 180–82, 190–93; pluperfect, 155–56; present, 1–7, 60–63; tense, 154–57, 165–67, 173–74, 180–82
vocative case, 33
vowels, xxv–xxvi